BUNNY**DROP**
yumi unita

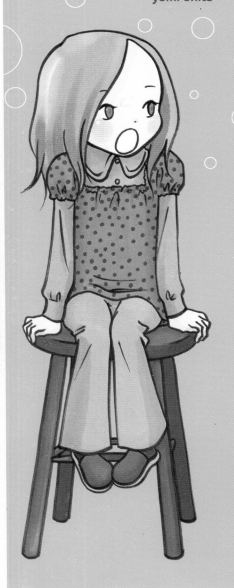

BUNNY**DROP** ³

yumi unita

STORY

After taking in his grandfather's love child, Rin, Daikichi finds himself doing a pretty good job raising her. He also discovers the identity of Rin's biological mother, Masako, who had been completely missing from the picture till now. But after meeting her in person, Daikichi doubly resolves to raise Rin himself.

MAIN CHARACTERS

MASAKO YOSHII
Rin's biological mother.
Works as a manga artist.

KOUKI & KOUKI'S MOM
Rin's friend from nursery
school and his mother.

DAIKICHI KAWACHI
Thirty-year-old bachelor.
Like a fish out of water
around women and
children.

RIN KAGA
A smart, responsible
six-year-old. Technically,
Daikichi's aunt.

contents

BUNNY**DROP**

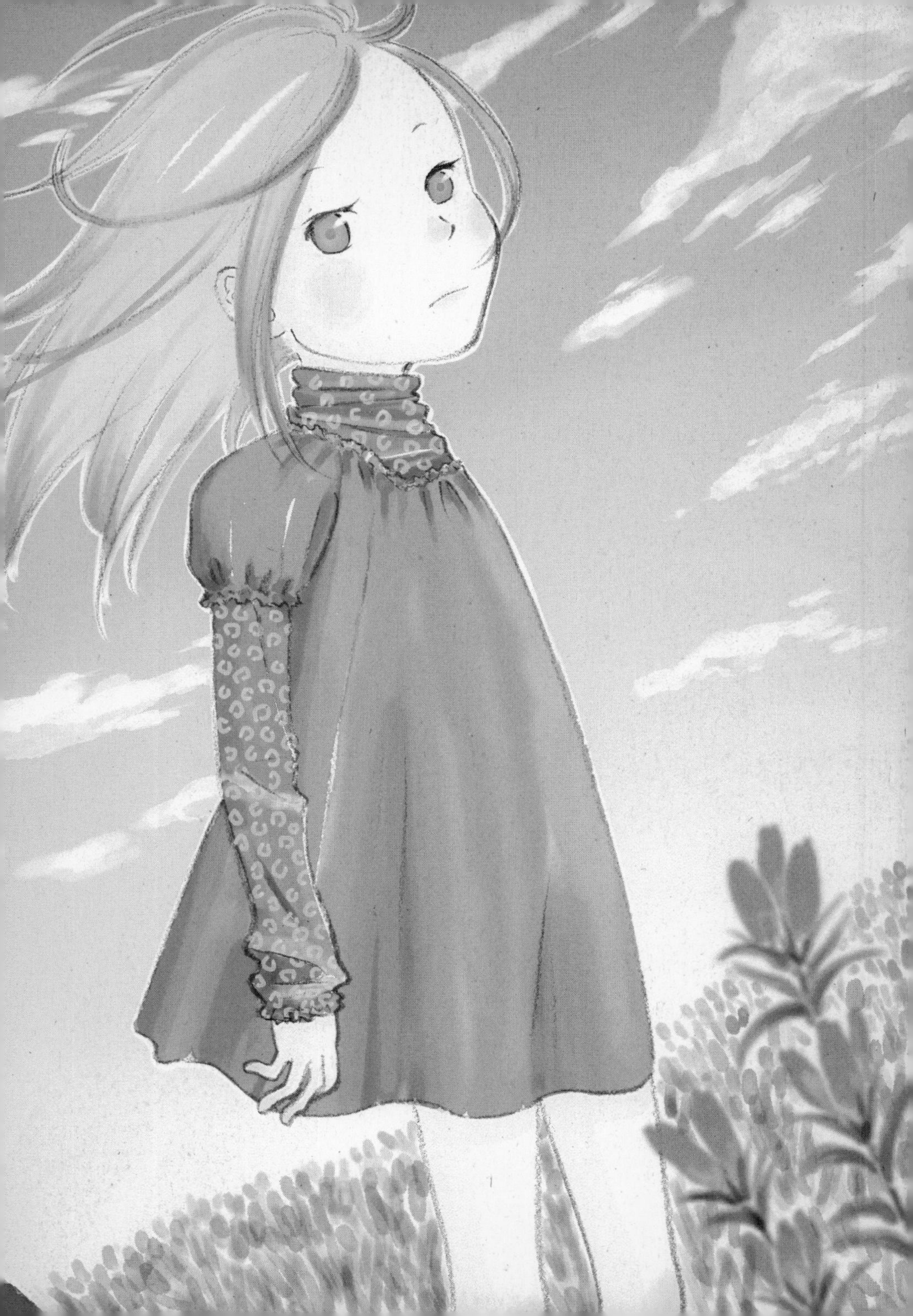

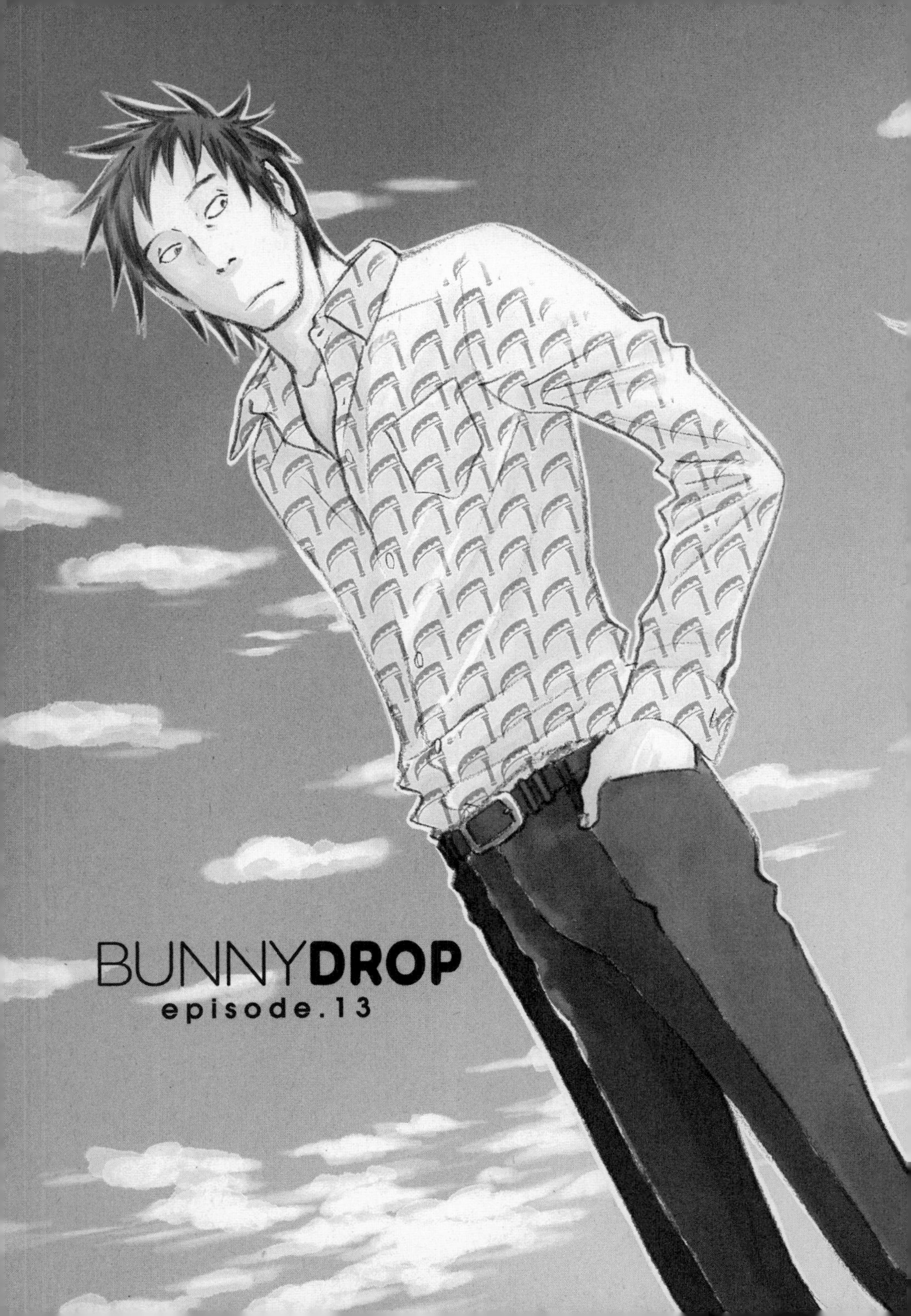
BUNNYDROP
episode.13

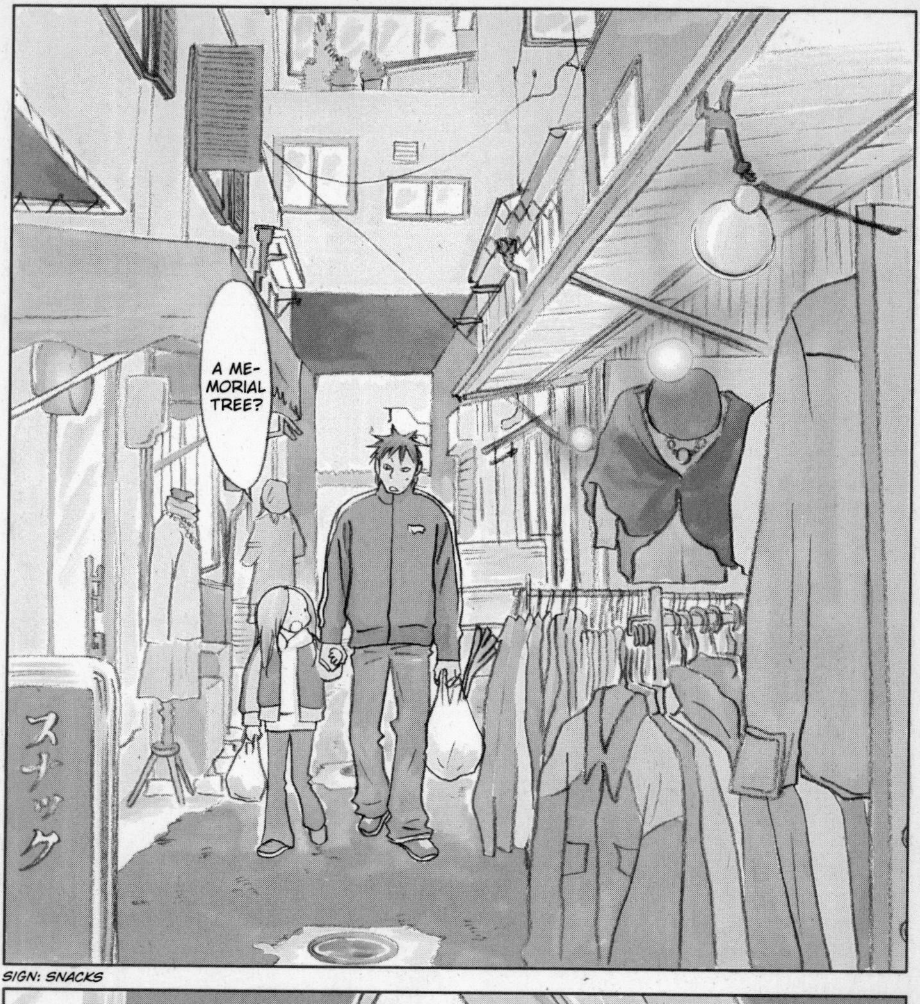
A MEMORIAL TREE?
スナック

SIGN: SNACKS

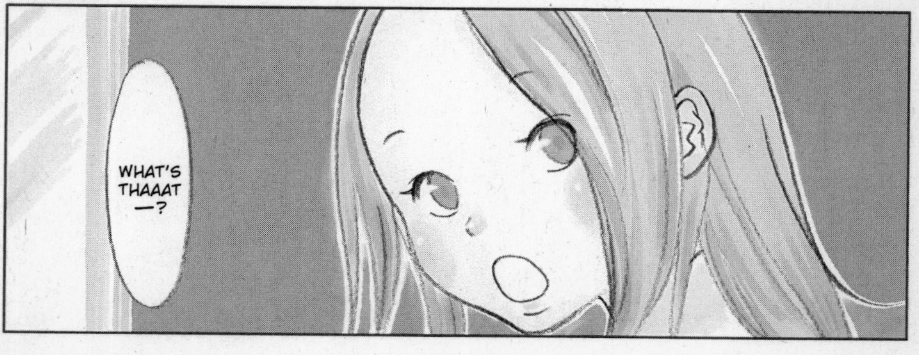
...
WHAT'S THAAAT—?

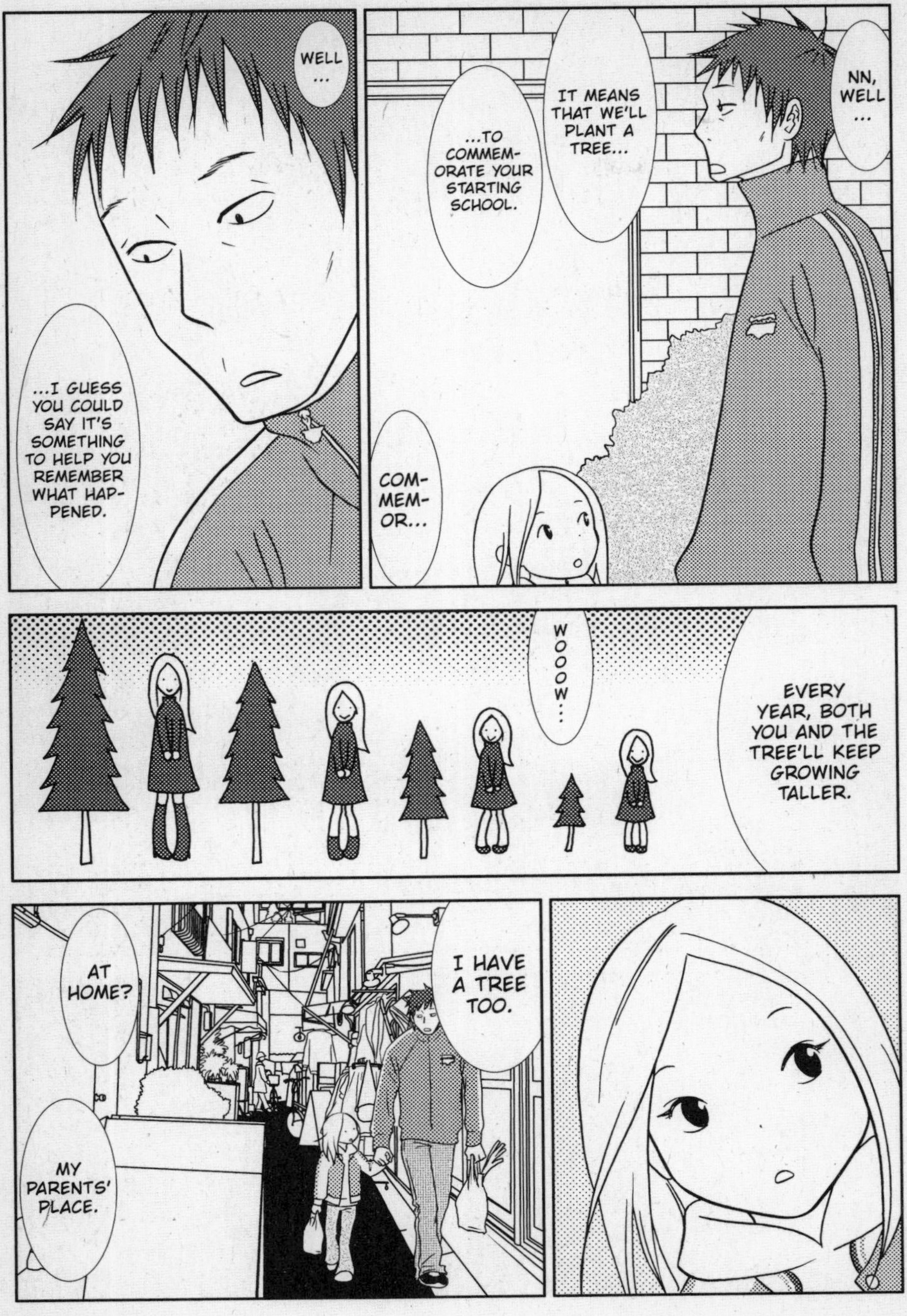
NN, WELL ...
IT MEANS THAT WE'LL PLANT A TREE...
...TO COMMEMORATE YOUR STARTING SCHOOL.
COMMEMOR...
WELL ...
...I GUESS YOU COULD SAY IT'S SOMETHING TO HELP YOU REMEMBER WHAT HAPPENED.
EVERY YEAR, BOTH YOU AND THE TREE'LL KEEP GROWING TALLER.
WOOOW...
I HAVE A TREE TOO.
AT HOME?
MY PARENTS' PLACE.

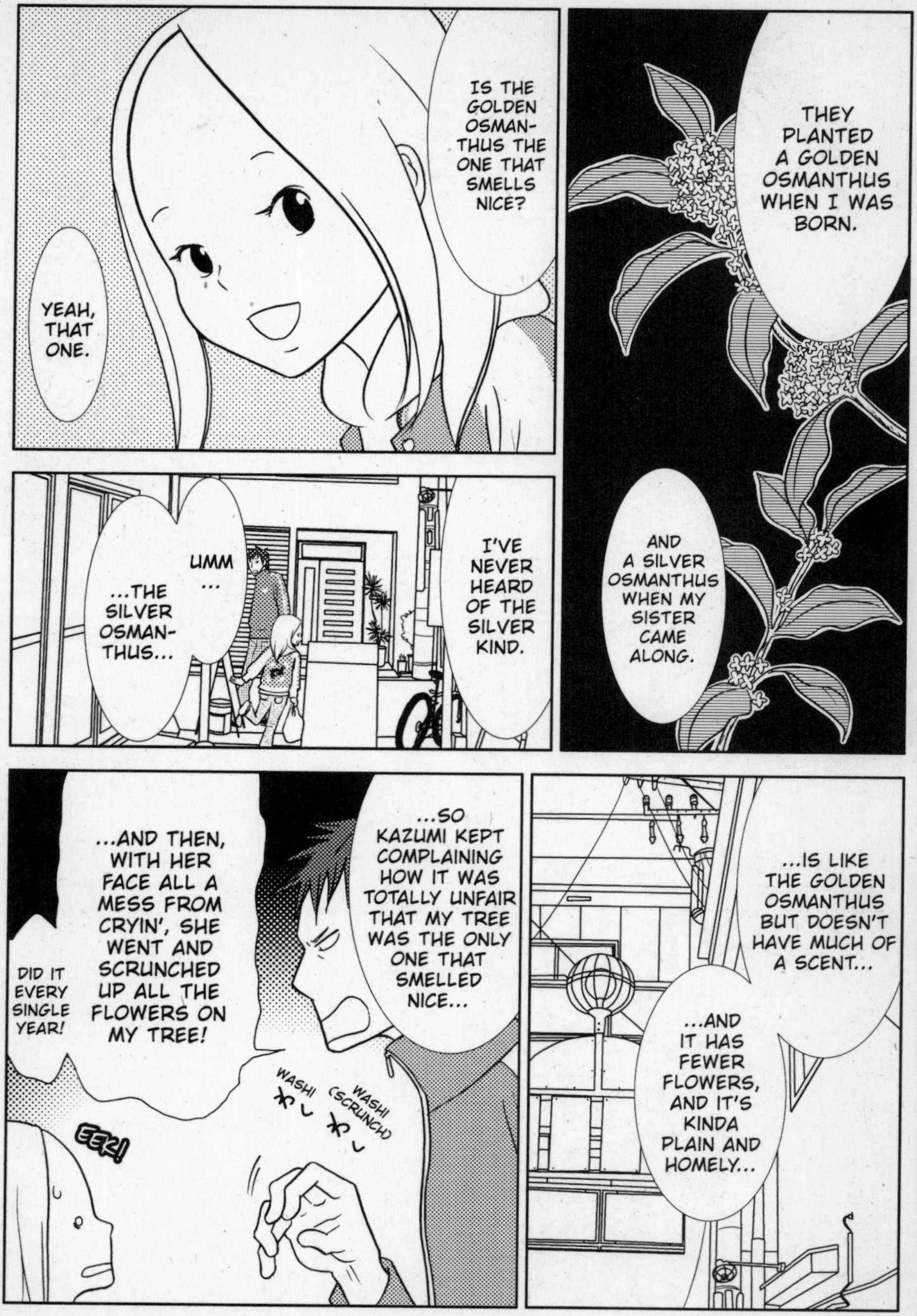
THEY PLANTED A GOLDEN OSMANTHUS WHEN I WAS BORN.
AND A SILVER OSMANTHUS WHEN MY SISTER CAME ALONG.
IS THE GOLDEN OSMAN-THUS THE ONE THAT SMELLS NICE?
YEAH, THAT ONE.
I'VE NEVER HEARD OF THE SILVER KIND.
UMM ...
...THE SILVER OSMAN-THUS...
...IS LIKE THE GOLDEN OSMANTHUS BUT DOESN'T HAVE MUCH OF A SCENT...
...AND IT HAS FEWER FLOWERS, AND IT'S KINDA PLAIN AND HOMELY...
...SO KAZUMI KEPT COMPLAINING HOW IT WAS TOTALLY UNFAIR THAT MY TREE WAS THE ONLY ONE THAT SMELLED NICE...
...AND THEN, WITH HER FACE ALL A MESS FROM CRYIN', SHE WENT AND SCRUNCHED UP ALL THE FLOWERS ON MY TREE!
DID IT EVERY SINGLE YEAR!
WASHI
WASHI (SCRUNCH)
EEK!

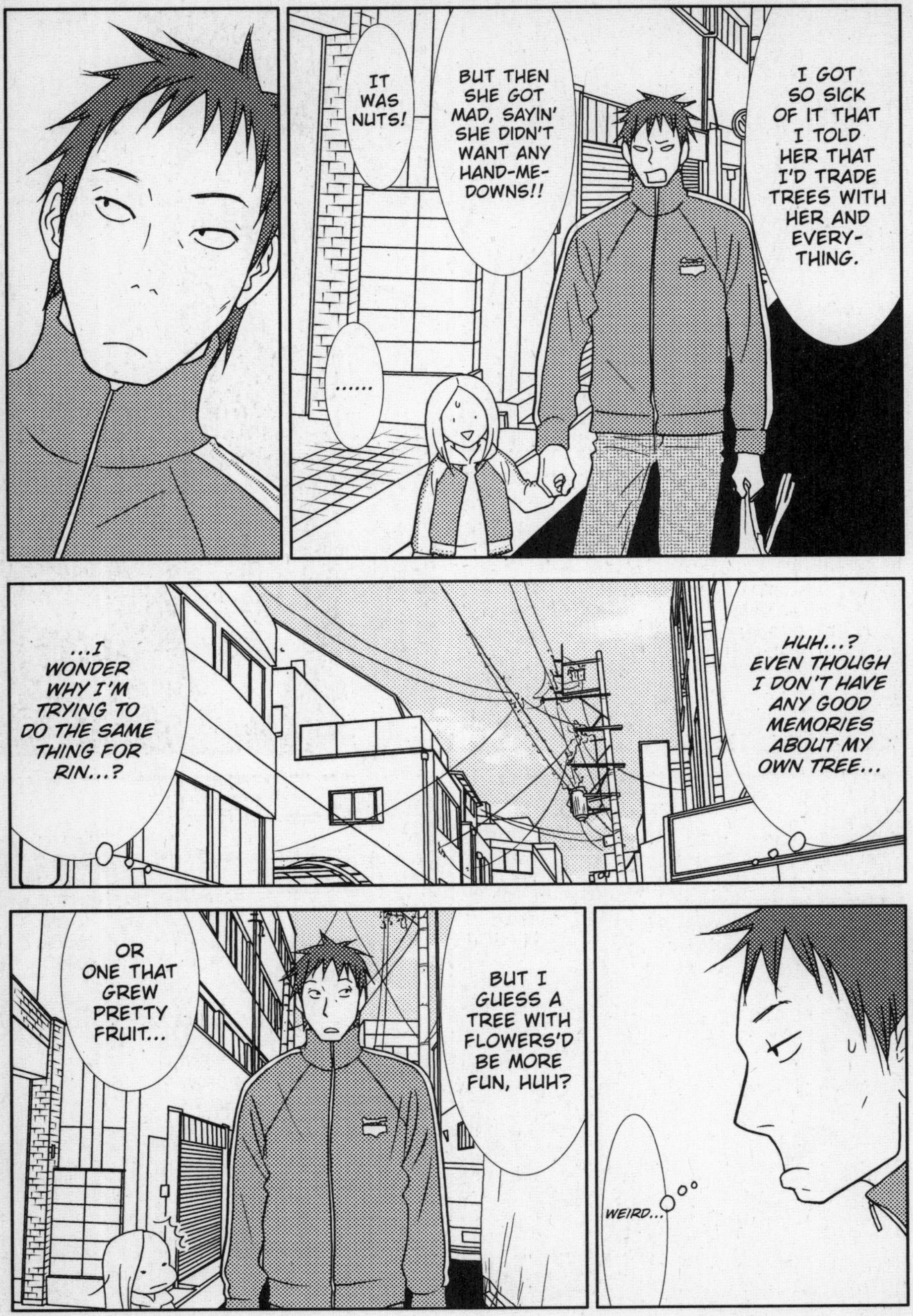
I GOT SO SICK OF IT THAT I TOLD HER THAT I'D TRADE TREES WITH HER AND EVERY-THING.
BUT THEN SHE GOT MAD, SAYIN' SHE DIDN'T WANT ANY HAND-ME-DOWNS!!
IT WAS NUTS!
......
HUH...? EVEN THOUGH I DON'T HAVE ANY GOOD MEMORIES ABOUT MY OWN TREE...
...I WONDER WHY I'M TRYING TO DO THE SAME THING FOR RIN...?
WEIRD...
BUT I GUESS A TREE WITH FLOWERS'D BE MORE FUN, HUH?
OR ONE THAT GREW PRETTY FRUIT...

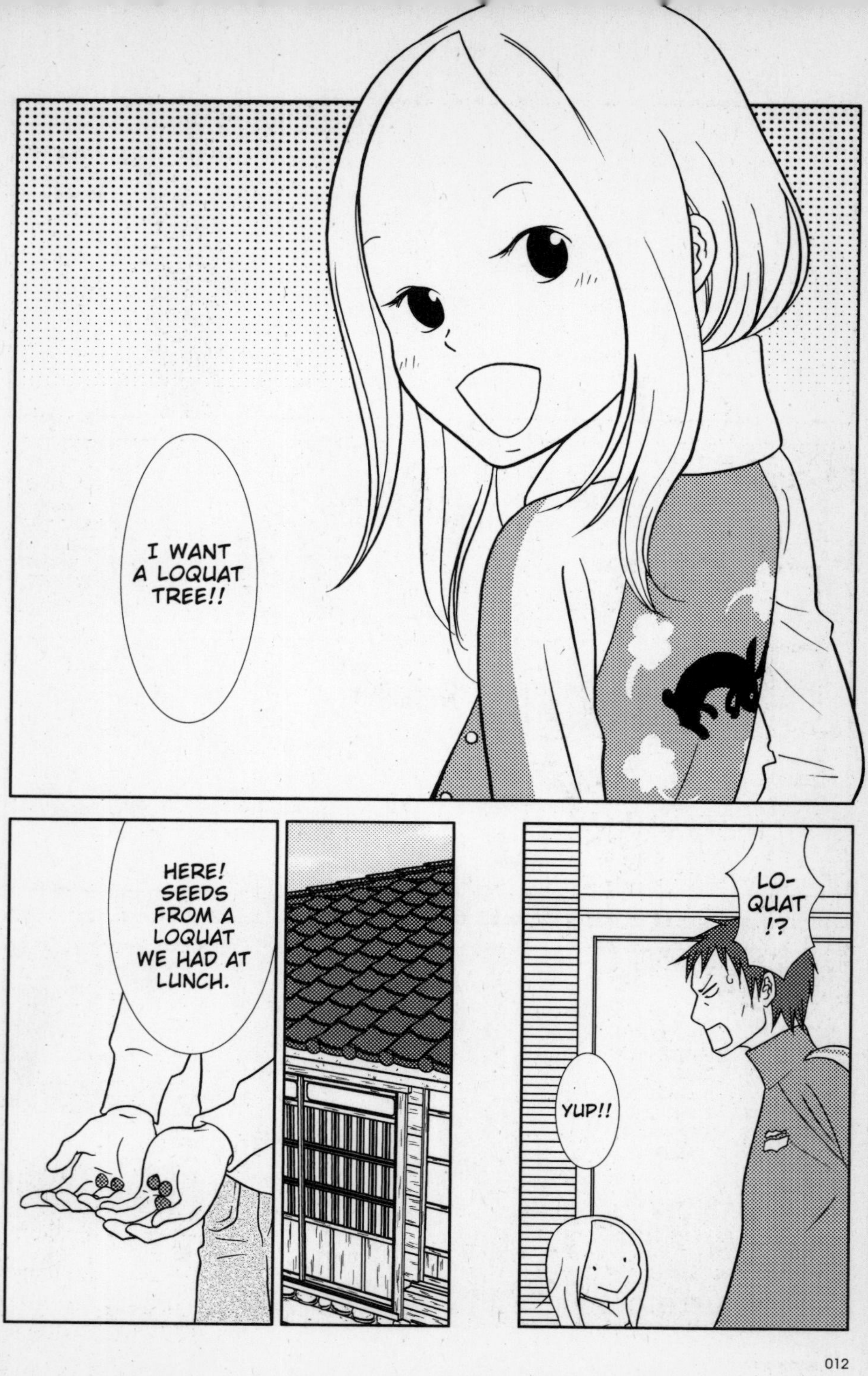
I WANT A LOQUAT TREE!!
LO-QUAT!?
YUP!!
HERE! SEEDS FROM A LOQUAT WE HAD AT LUNCH.

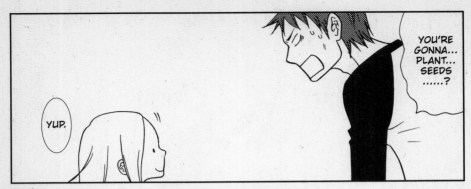

YOU'RE GONNA... PLANT... SEEDS ......?
YUP.
I CAN HAVE ALL THE LOQUATS I WANT TO EAT!
HEE!
THAT IS, IF AND WHEN THEY BEAR FRUIT...
......
SEE, I...WAS ACTUALLY THINKING ABOUT GOING OUT TO BUY A TREE...
ONE ABOUT THIS HIGH...
SO I CAN'T PLANT THE SEEDS?
HRNNN... IT'S NOT THAT YOU CAN'T, BUT...
...YA KNOW, TREES DON'T GROW FAST LIKE MORNING GLORIES OR SUN-FLOWERS...
THEY TAKE A LONG TIME.
IT'LL BE DAYS BEFORE YOU EVEN SEE A SHOOT... AND AS FOR FRUIT, HECK...
Y'KNOW THE OLD SAYING? "PEACHES AND CHESTNUTS THREE YEARS ..."

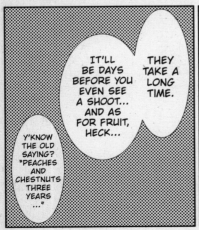

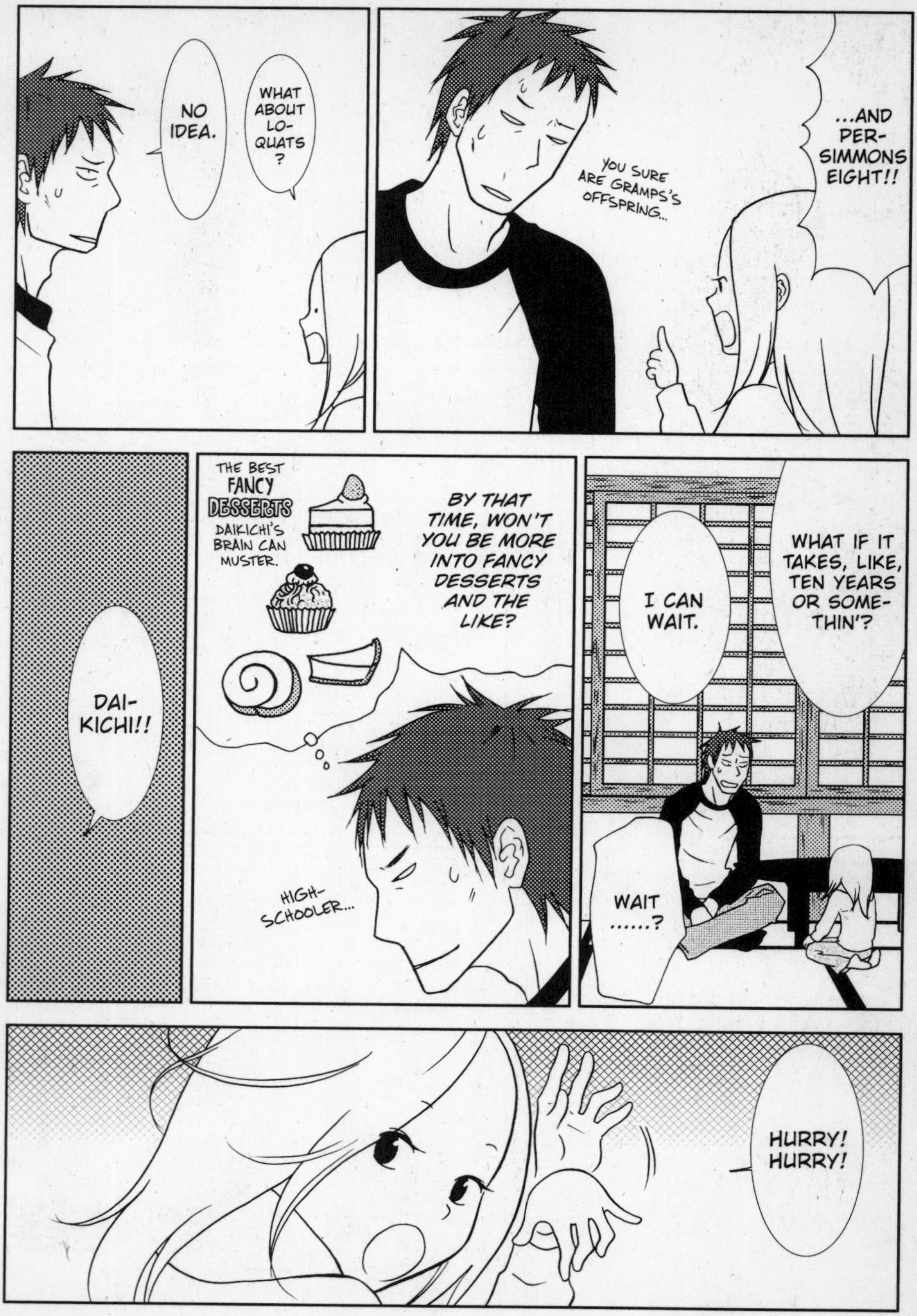
...AND PER-SIMMONS EIGHT!!
YOU SURE ARE GRAMPS'S OFFSPRING...
WHAT ABOUT LO-QUATS?
NO IDEA.
WHAT IF IT TAKES, LIKE, TEN YEARS OR SOME-THIN'?
I CAN WAIT.
WAIT ......?
BY THAT TIME, WON'T YOU BE MORE INTO FANCY DESSERTS AND THE LIKE?
THE BEST FANCY DESSERTS DAIKICHI'S BRAIN CAN MUSTER.
HIGH-SCHOOLER...
DAI-KICHI!!
HURRY! HURRY!

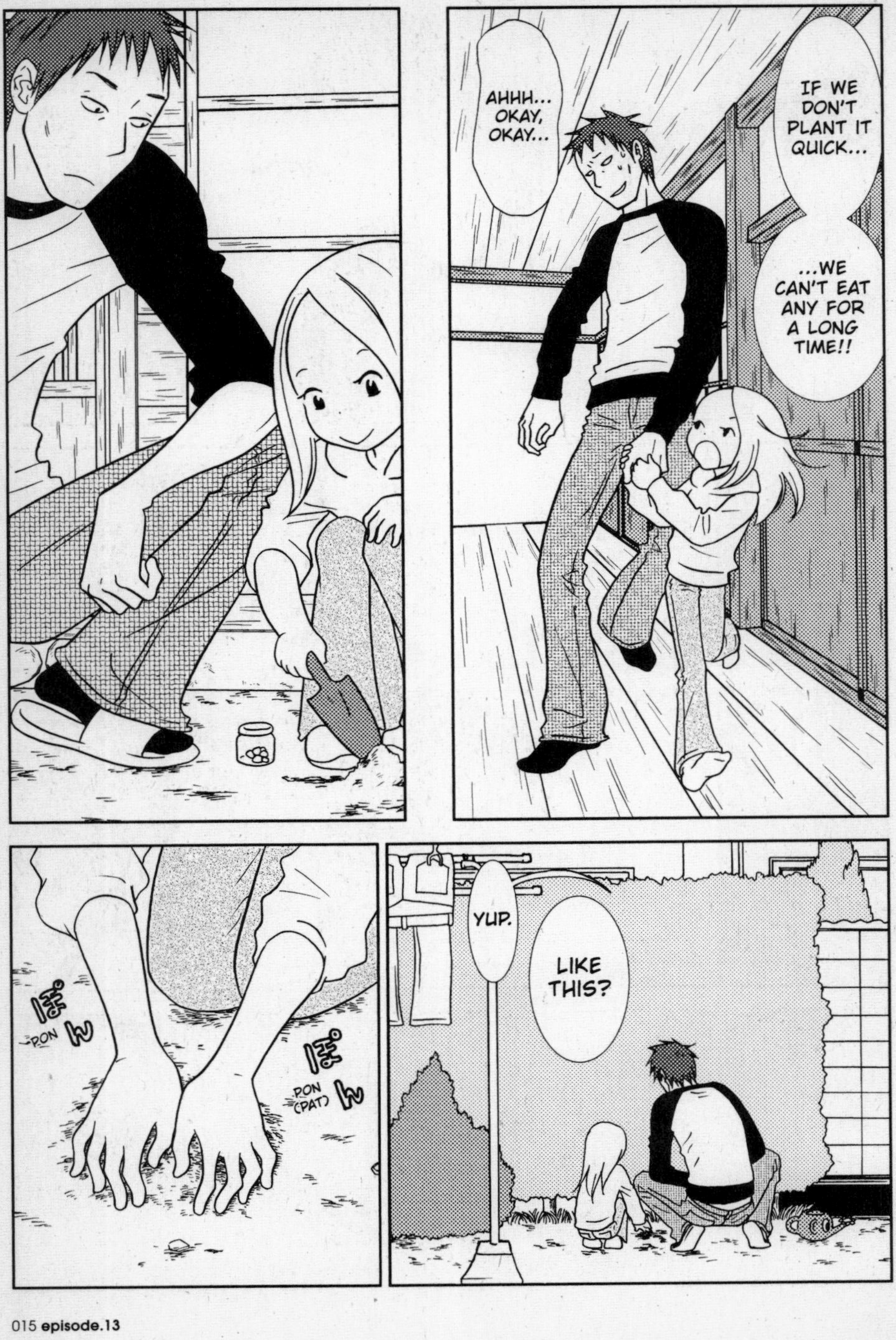
IF WE DON'T PLANT IT QUICK...
...WE CAN'T EAT ANY FOR A LONG TIME!!
AHHH... OKAY, OKAY...
LIKE THIS?
YUP.
ぽん
PON
ぽん
PON (PAT)

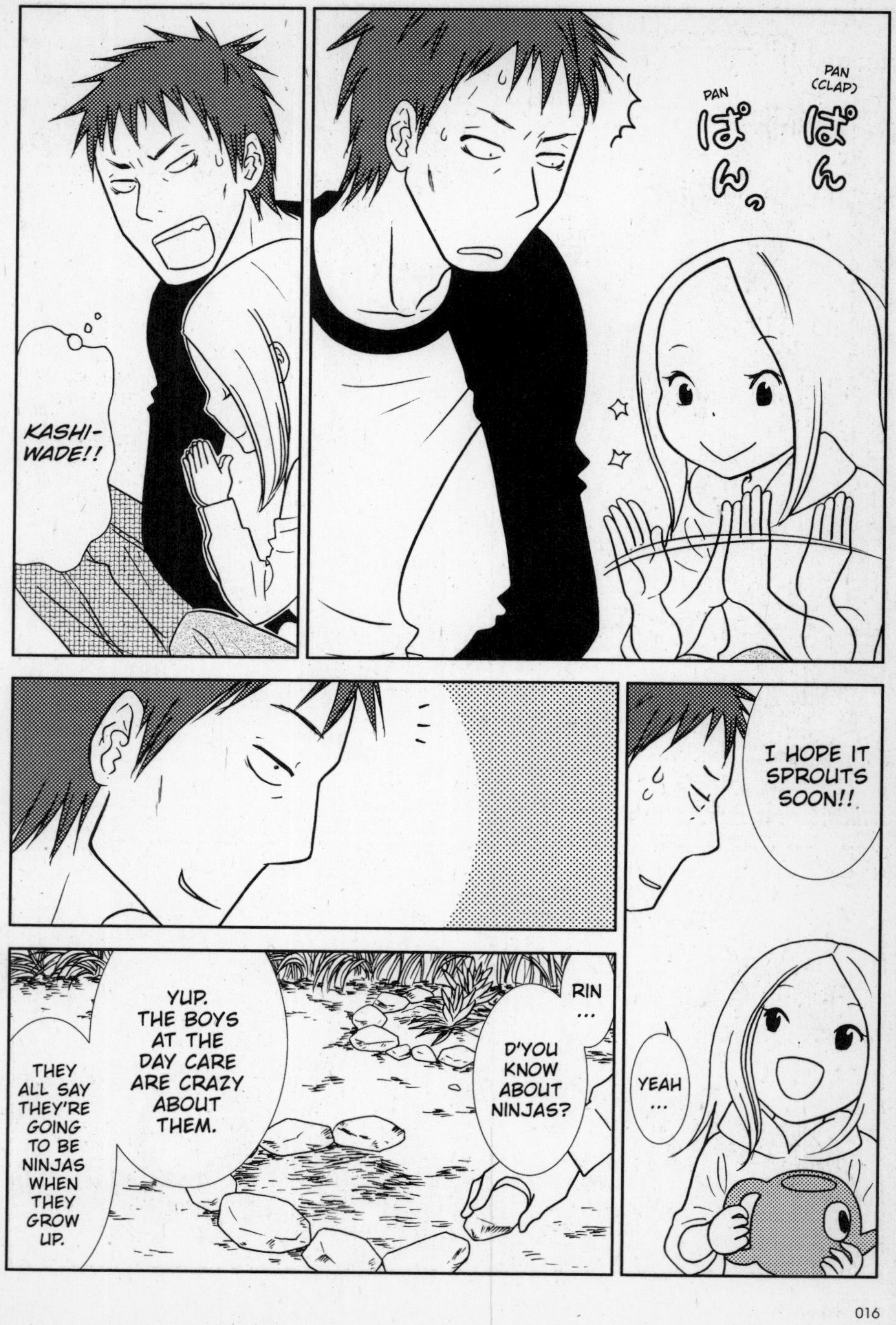
PAN (CLAP)
ぱん
PAN
ぱんっ
KASHI-WADE!!
I HOPE IT SPROUTS SOON!!
YEAH ...
RIN ...
D'YOU KNOW ABOUT NINJAS?
YUP. THE BOYS AT THE DAY CARE ARE CRAZY ABOUT THEM.
THEY ALL SAY THEY'RE GOING TO BE NINJAS WHEN THEY GROW UP.

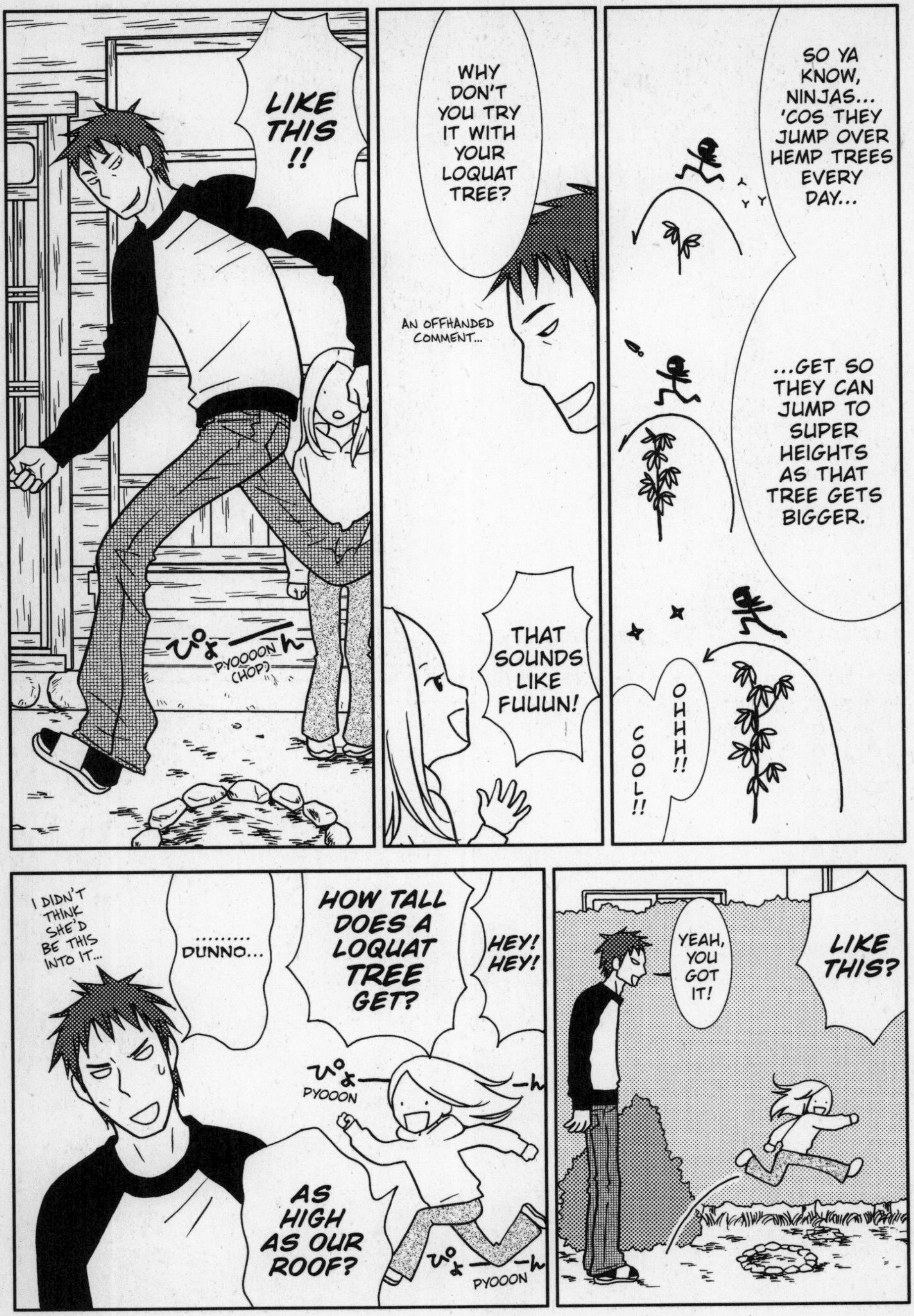
SO YA KNOW, NINJAS... 'COS THEY JUMP OVER HEMP TREES EVERY DAY...
...GET SO THEY CAN JUMP TO SUPER HEIGHTS AS THAT TREE GETS BIGGER.
OHHH!!
COOL!!
WHY DON'T YOU TRY IT WITH YOUR LOQUAT TREE?
AN OFFHANDED COMMENT...
THAT SOUNDS LIKE FUUUN!
LIKE THIS!!
ぴょ——ん
PYOOOON (HOP)
LIKE THIS?
YEAH, YOU GOT IT!
HEY! HEY!
HOW TALL DOES A LOQUAT TREE GET?
.... DUNNO...
I DIDN'T THINK SHE'D BE THIS INTO IT...
ぴょ——ん
PYOOON
AS HIGH AS OUR ROOF?
ぴょ——ん
PYOOON

I WONDER WHEN IT'LL *SPROUT?*
WHO KNOWS ...?
I HOPE THAT WAS OKAY FOR HER COMMEM-ORATIVE-TREE...?
?
SO...

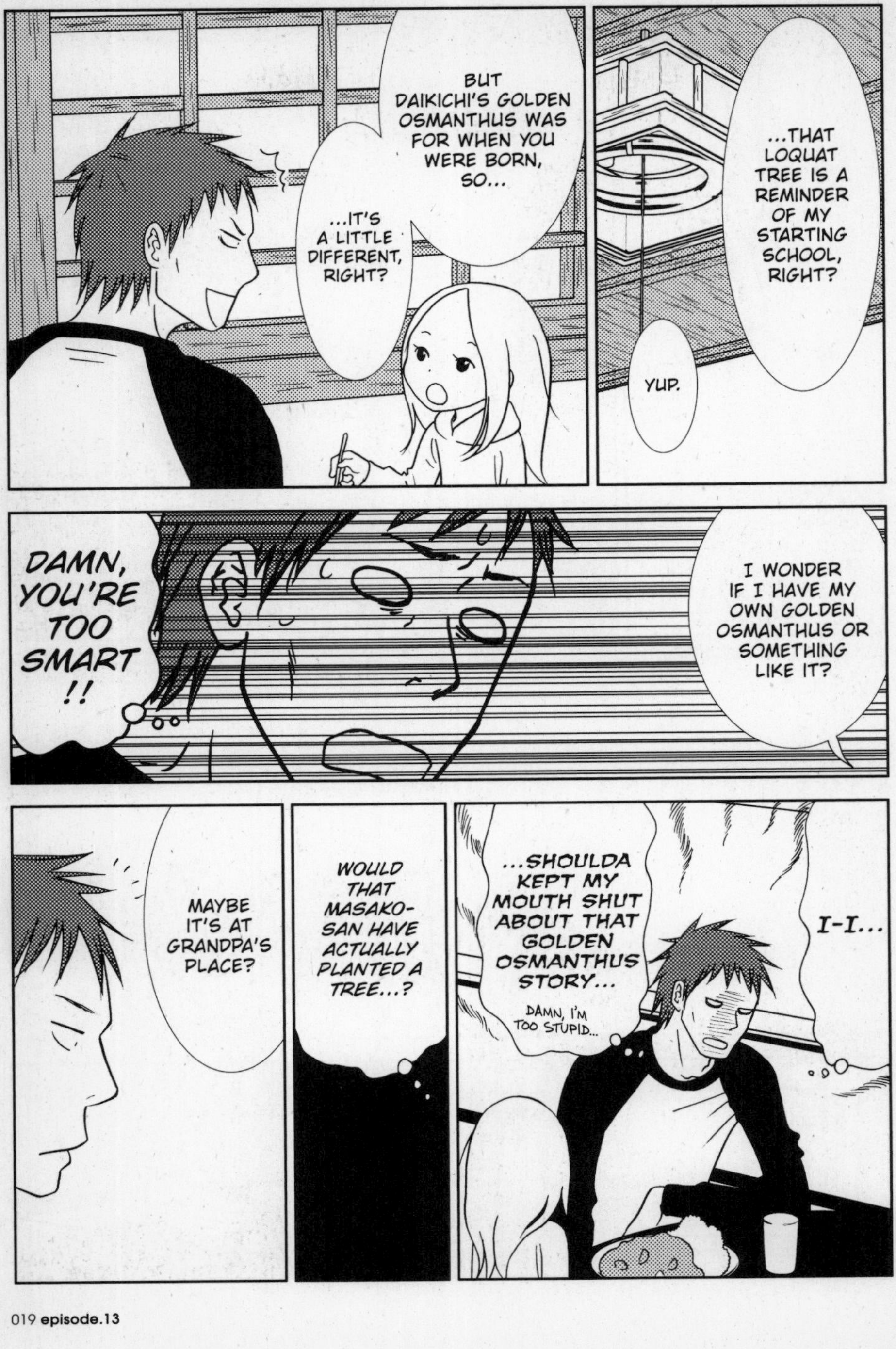
...THAT LOQUAT TREE IS A REMINDER OF MY STARTING SCHOOL, RIGHT?
YUP.
BUT DAIKICHI'S GOLDEN OSMANTHUS WAS FOR WHEN YOU WERE BORN, SO...
...IT'S A LITTLE DIFFERENT, RIGHT?
I WONDER IF I HAVE MY OWN GOLDEN OSMANTHUS OR SOMETHING LIKE IT?
DAMN, YOU'RE TOO SMART !!
I-I...
...SHOULDA KEPT MY MOUTH SHUT ABOUT THAT GOLDEN OSMANTHUS STORY...
DAMN, I'M TOO STUPID...
WOULD THAT MASAKO-SAN HAVE ACTUALLY PLANTED A TREE...?
MAYBE IT'S AT GRANDPA'S PLACE?

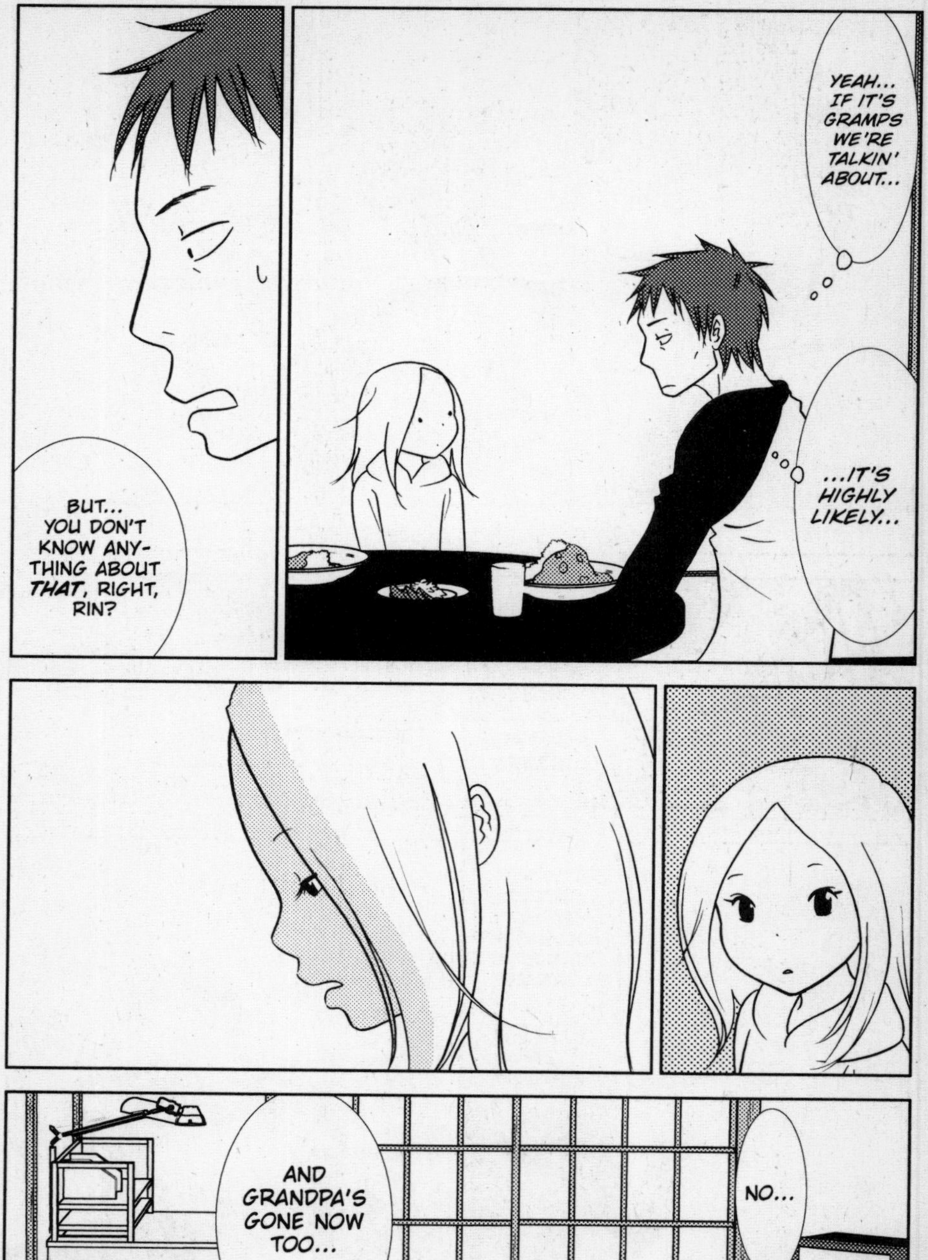
YEAH... IF IT'S GRAMPS WE'RE TALKIN' ABOUT...
...IT'S HIGHLY LIKELY...
BUT... YOU DON'T KNOW ANY-THING ABOUT *THAT*, RIGHT, RIN?
NO...
AND GRANDPA'S GONE NOW TOO...

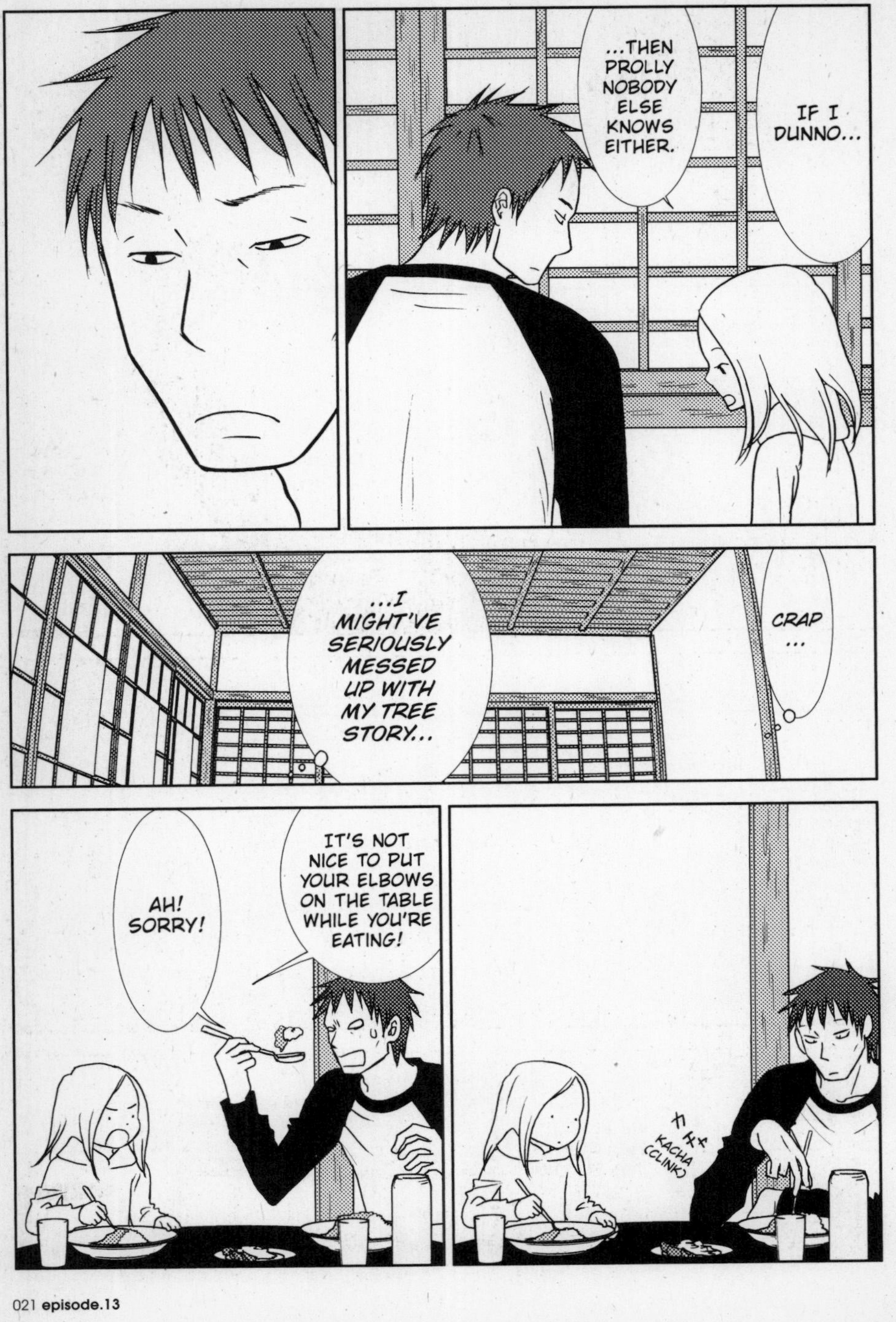
IF I DUNNO...
...THEN PROLLY NOBODY ELSE KNOWS EITHER.
CRAP...
...I MIGHT'VE SERIOUSLY MESSED UP WITH MY TREE STORY...
カチャ KACHA (CLINK)
IT'S NOT NICE TO PUT YOUR ELBOWS ON THE TABLE WHILE YOU'RE EATING!
AH! SORRY!

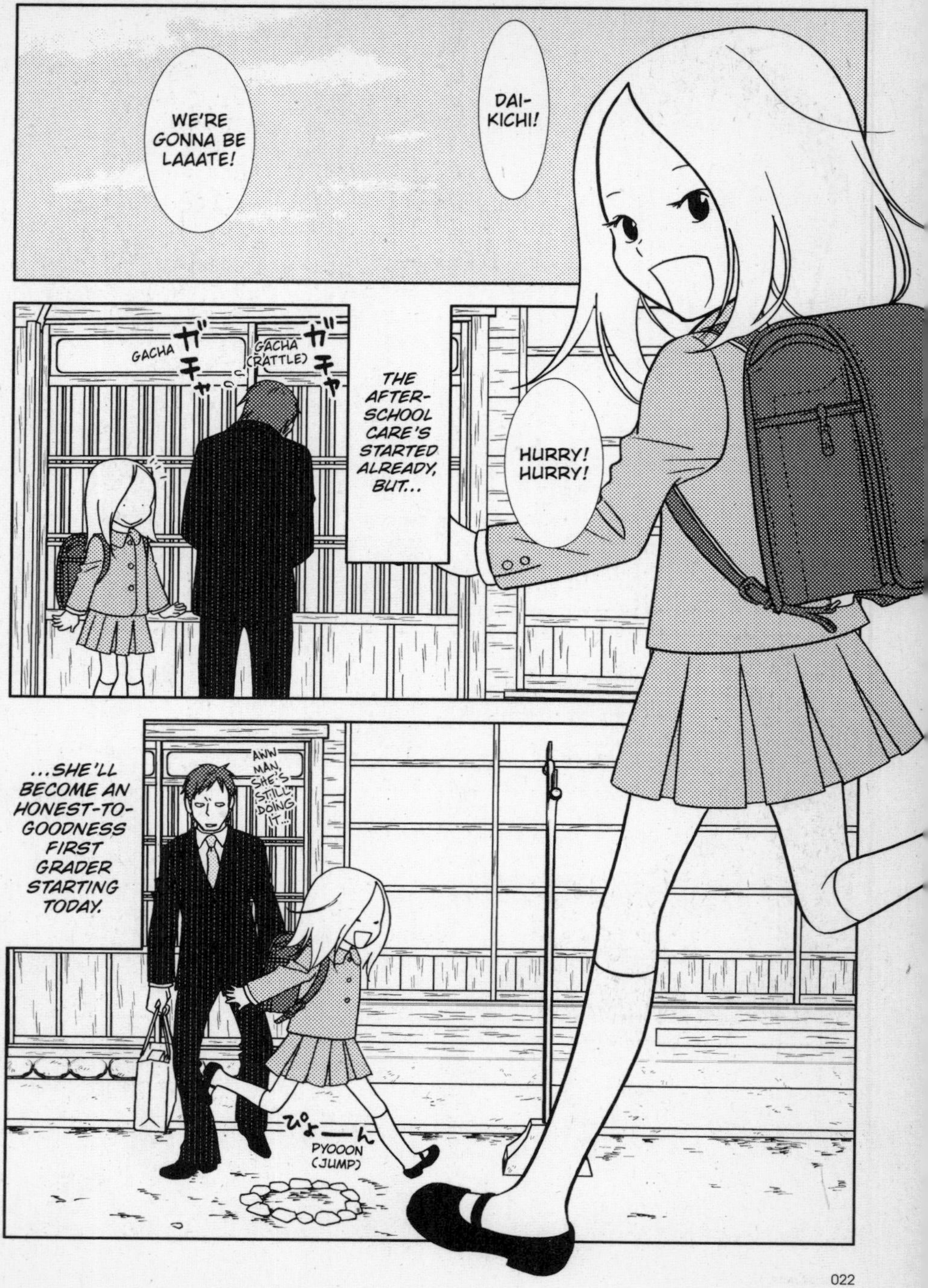
DAI-KICHI!
WE'RE GONNA BE LAAATE!
HURRY! HURRY!
ガチャ
GACHA (RATTLE)
ガチャ
GACHA
THE AFTER-SCHOOL CARE'S STARTED ALREADY, BUT...
AWW MAN, SHE'S STILL DOING IT...!
...SHE'LL BECOME AN HONEST-TO-GOODNESS FIRST GRADER STARTING TODAY.
ぴょーん
PYOOON (JUMP)

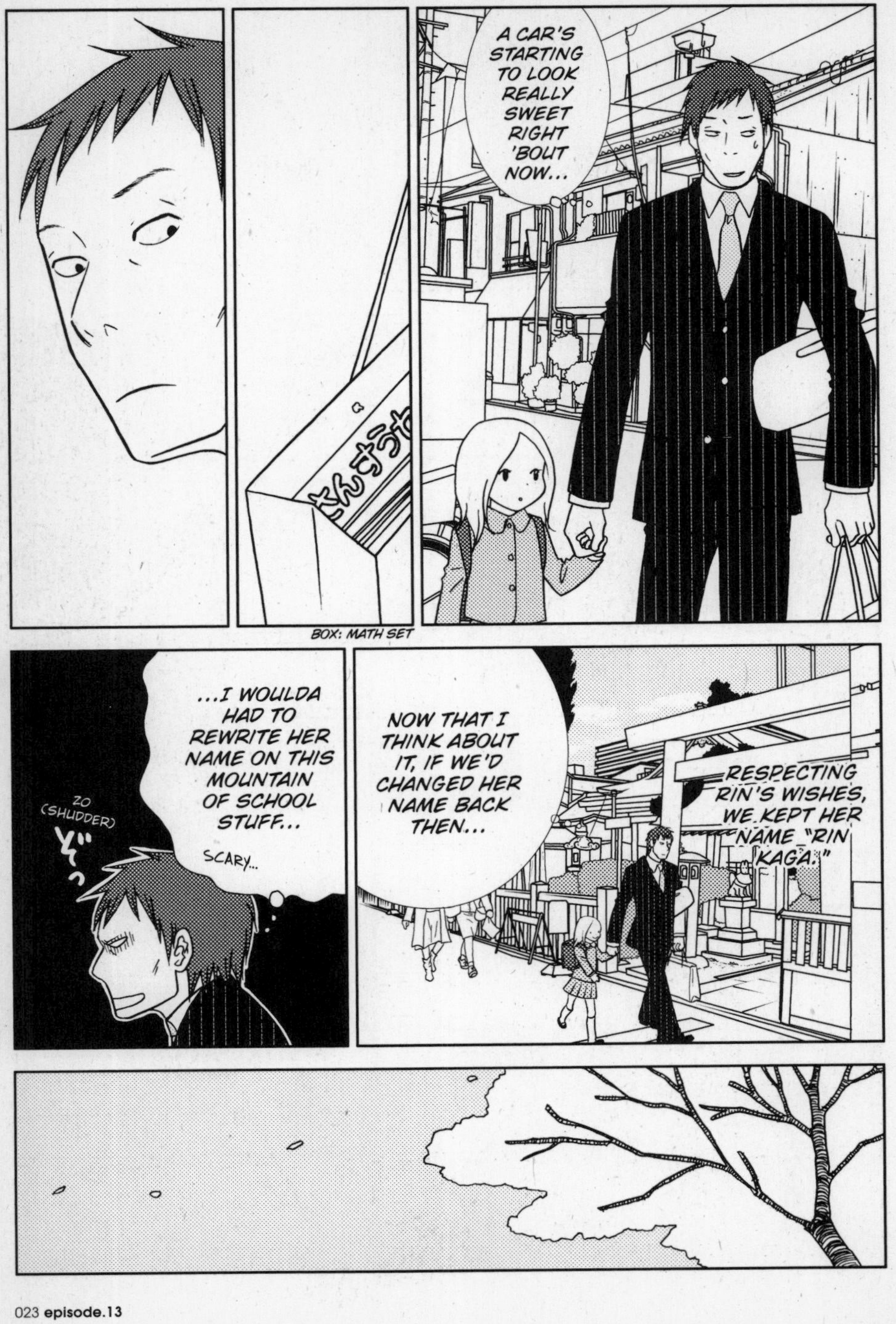
A CAR'S STARTING TO LOOK REALLY SWEET RIGHT 'BOUT NOW...
BOX: MATH SET
RESPECTING RIN'S WISHES, WE KEPT HER NAME "RIN KAGA."
NOW THAT I THINK ABOUT IT, IF WE'D CHANGED HER NAME BACK THEN...
...I WOULDA HAD TO REWRITE HER NAME ON THIS MOUNTAIN OF SCHOOL STUFF...
ZO (SHUDDER)
ぞっ
SCARY...

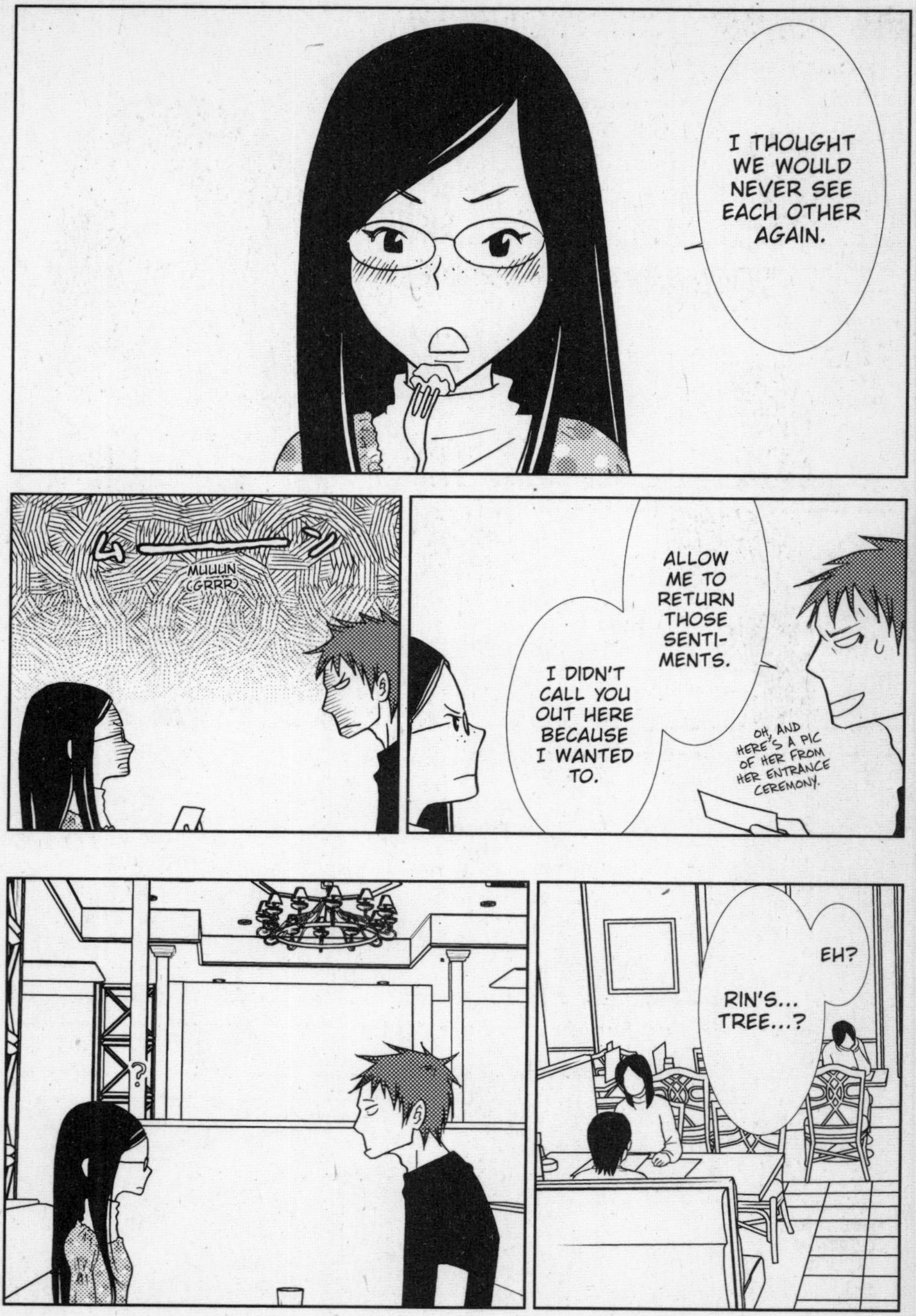
I THOUGHT WE WOULD NEVER SEE EACH OTHER AGAIN.
ALLOW ME TO RETURN THOSE SENTIMENTS.
I DIDN'T CALL YOU OUT HERE BECAUSE I WANTED TO.
OH, AND HERE'S A PIC OF HER FROM HER ENTRANCE CEREMONY.
MUUUN (GRRR)
EH?
RIN'S... TREE...?
?

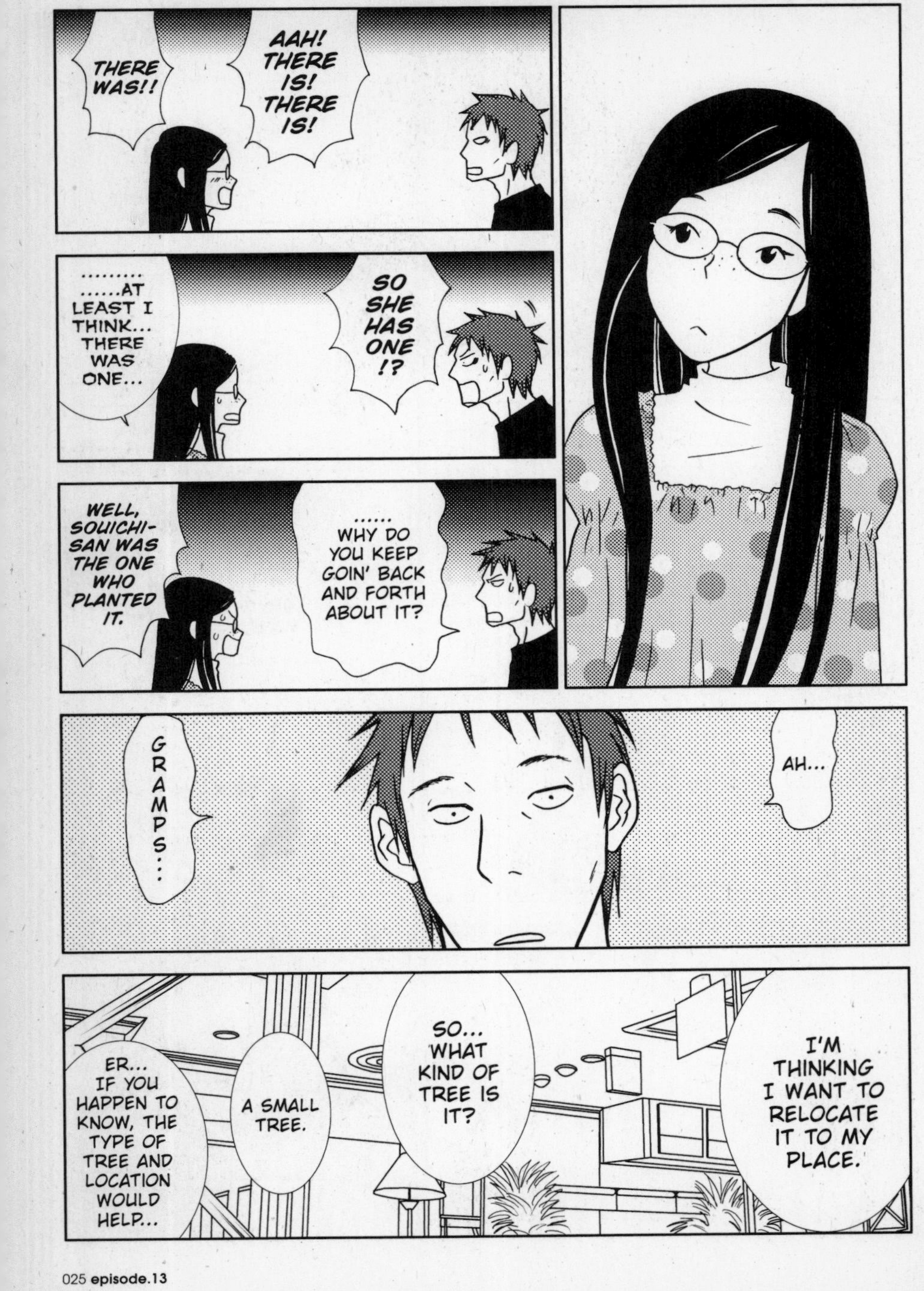
AAH! THERE IS! THERE IS!
THERE WAS!!
SO SHE HAS ONE !?
....
......AT LEAST I THINK... THERE WAS ONE...
......
WHY DO YOU KEEP GOIN' BACK AND FORTH ABOUT IT?
WELL, SOUICHI-SAN WAS THE ONE WHO PLANTED IT.
AH...
GRAMPS...
I'M THINKING I WANT TO RELOCATE IT TO MY PLACE.
SO... WHAT KIND OF TREE IS IT?
A SMALL TREE.
ER... IF YOU HAPPEN TO KNOW, THE TYPE OF TREE AND LOCATION WOULD HELP...

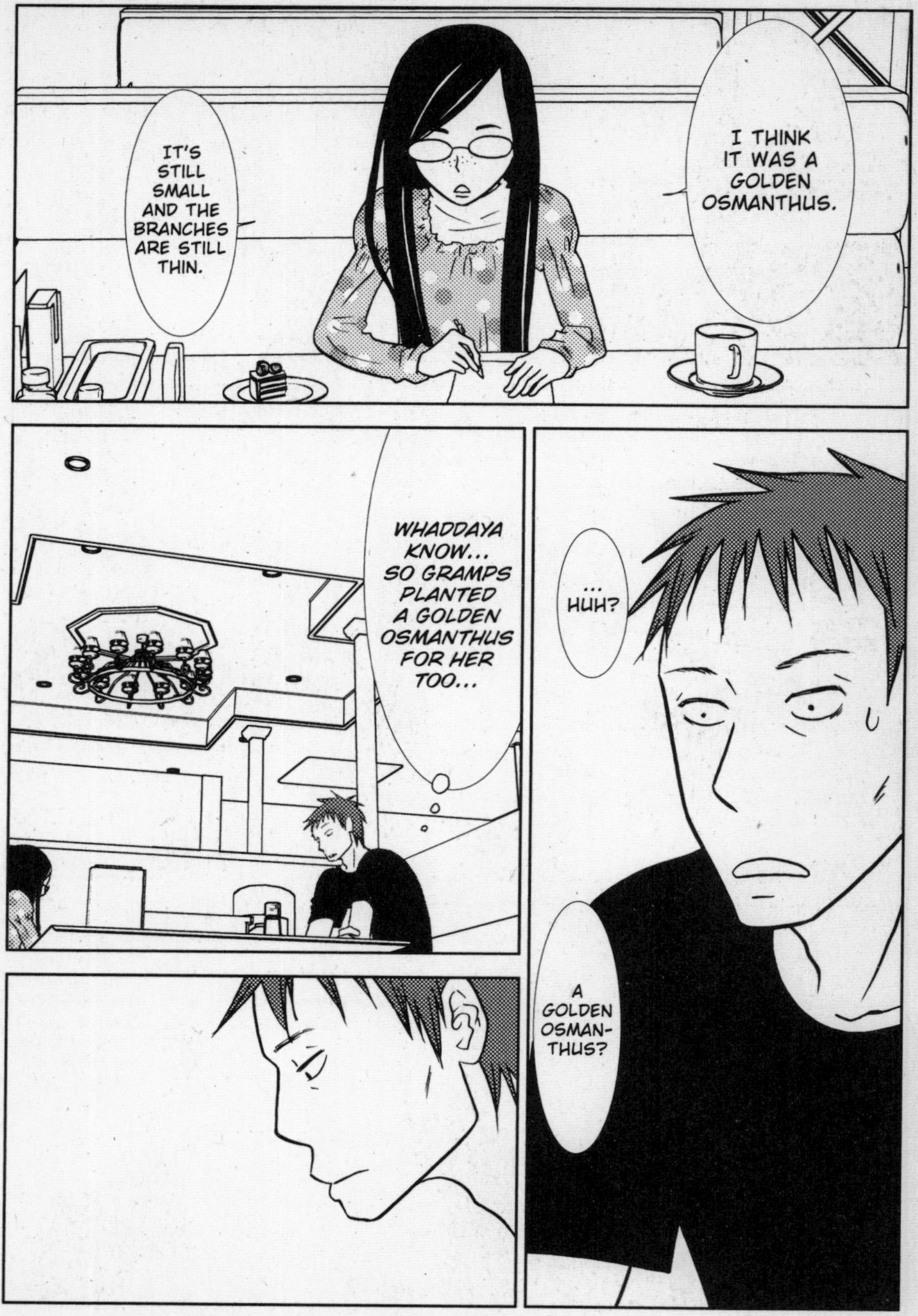
I THINK IT WAS A GOLDEN OSMANTHUS.
IT'S STILL SMALL AND THE BRANCHES ARE STILL THIN.
... HUH?
A GOLDEN OSMAN-THUS?
WHADDAYA KNOW... SO GRAMPS PLANTED A GOLDEN OSMANTHUS FOR HER TOO...

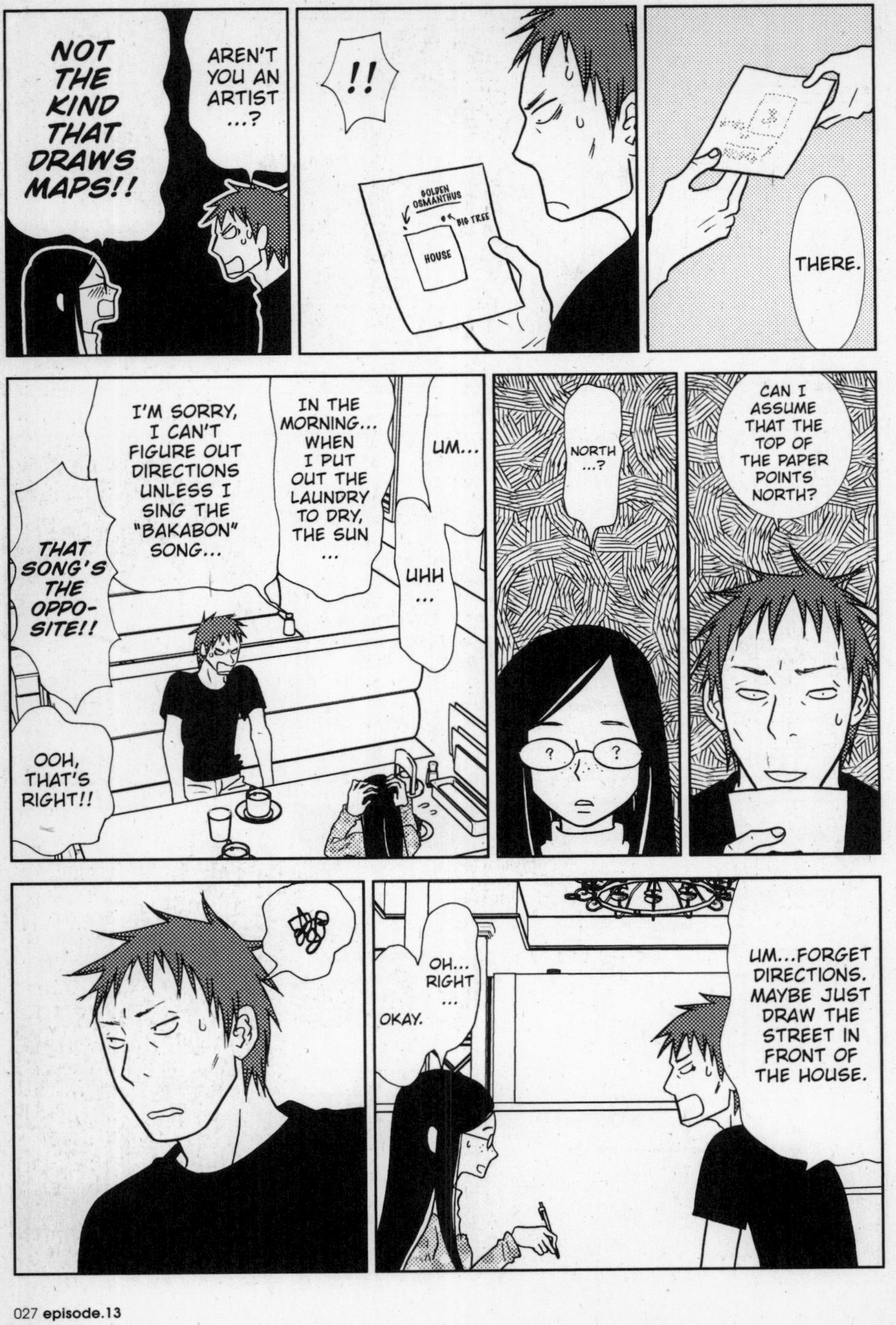
THERE.
!!
GOLDEN OSMANTHUS
BIG TREE
HOUSE
AREN'T YOU AN ARTIST ...?
NOT THE KIND THAT DRAWS MAPS!!
CAN I ASSUME THAT THE TOP OF THE PAPER POINTS NORTH?
NORTH ...?
UM...
IN THE MORNING... WHEN I PUT OUT THE LAUNDRY TO DRY, THE SUN ...
UHH ...
I'M SORRY, I CAN'T FIGURE OUT DIRECTIONS UNLESS I SING THE "BAKABON" SONG...
THAT SONG'S THE OPPO-SITE!!
OOH, THAT'S RIGHT!!
UM...FORGET DIRECTIONS. MAYBE JUST DRAW THE STREET IN FRONT OF THE HOUSE.
OH... RIGHT ...
OKAY.

WELL, I NEED TO GET BACK TO WORK SO IF YOU'LL EXCUSE ME.
GOLDEN OSMANTHUS
BIG TREE
HOUSE
STREET
THANK YOU FOR COMING.
USUALLY, WHEN PEOPLE WITH NO SENSE OF DIRECTION LOOK AT OR DRAW MAPS...
THEY DON'T THINK IN TERMS OF NORTH OR SOUTH. A LOT OF 'EM JUST MOVE THE MAP AROUND TO THE DIRECTION THEY'RE HEADED.
ROAD AT THE TOP.
SO WOULDN'T SOMEONE LIKE THAT DRAW A MAP OF THEIR OWN HOUSE LIKE THIS...?
HOUSE
KINDA LIKE THEY'RE IN THE HOUSE...?
BUT WHAT MASAKO-SAN DREW...
...SEEMS LIKE SHE'S "ON THE OUTSIDE GOING IN."
GOLDEN OSMANTHUS
BIG TREE
HOUSE
STREET

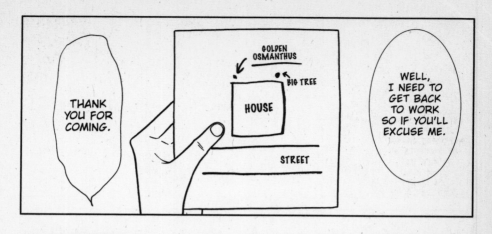

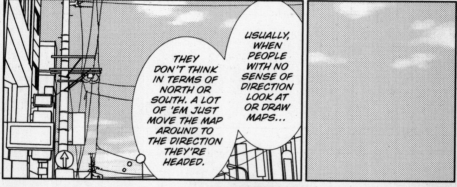

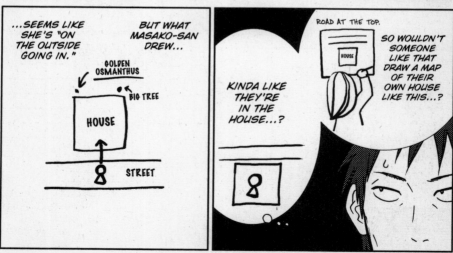

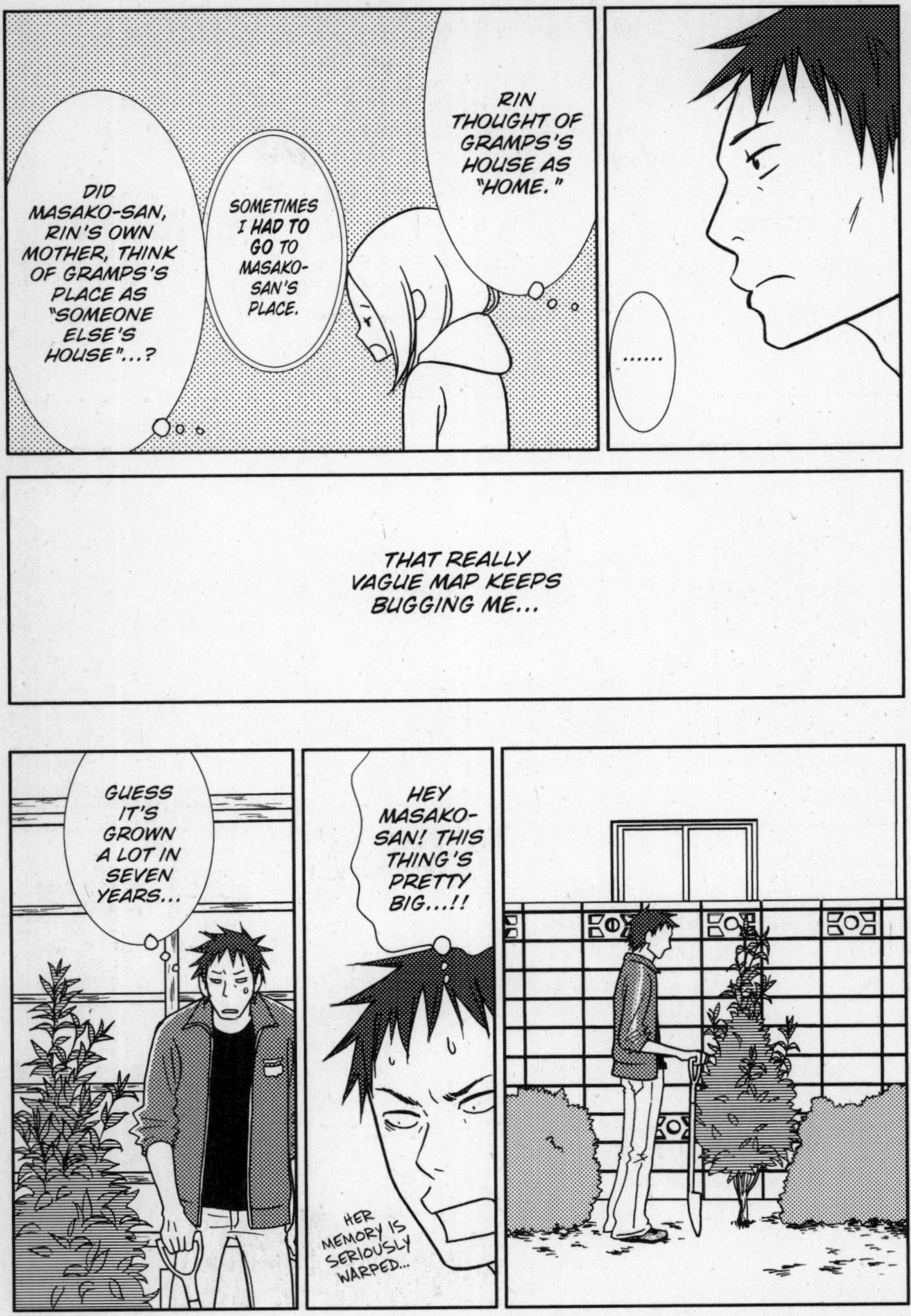
......
RIN THOUGHT OF GRAMPS'S HOUSE AS "HOME."
SOMETIMES I HAD TO GO TO MASAKO-SAN'S PLACE.
DID MASAKO-SAN, RIN'S OWN MOTHER, THINK OF GRAMPS'S PLACE AS "SOMEONE ELSE'S HOUSE"...?
THAT REALLY VAGUE MAP KEEPS BUGGING ME...
HEY MASAKO-SAN! THIS THING'S PRETTY BIG...!!
HER MEMORY IS SERIOUSLY WARPED...
GUESS IT'S GROWN A LOT IN SEVEN YEARS...

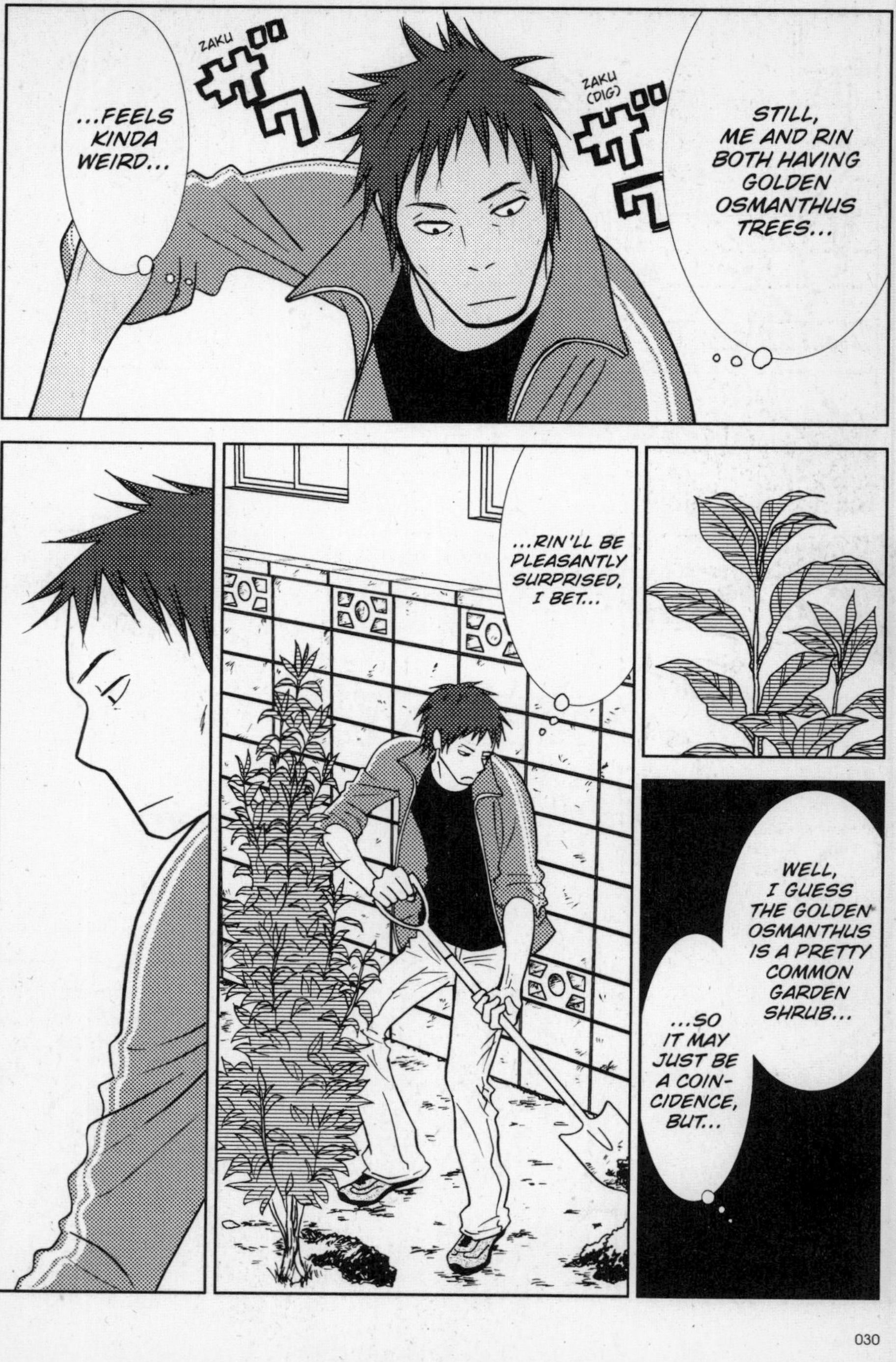
STILL, ME AND RIN BOTH HAVING GOLDEN OSMANTHUS TREES...
ZAKU (DIG)
ZAKU
...FEELS KINDA WEIRD...
WELL, I GUESS THE GOLDEN OSMANTHUS IS A PRETTY COMMON GARDEN SHRUB...
...SO IT MAY JUST BE A COINCIDENCE, BUT...
...RIN'LL BE PLEASANTLY SURPRISED, I BET...

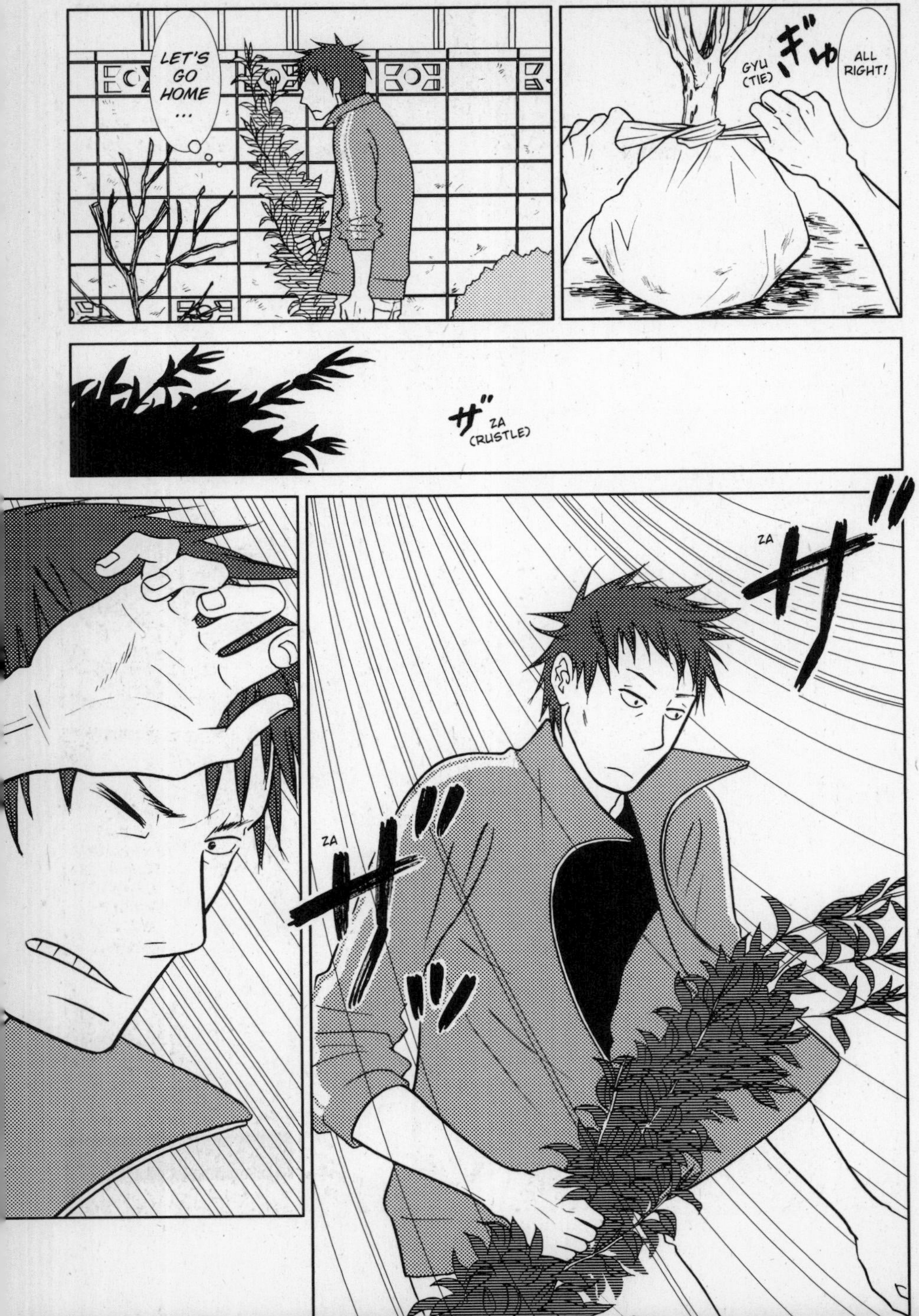
ALL RIGHT!
ぎゅ
GYU (TIE)
LET'S GO HOME ...
ザ
ZA (RUSTLE)
ザ
ZA
ザ
ZA

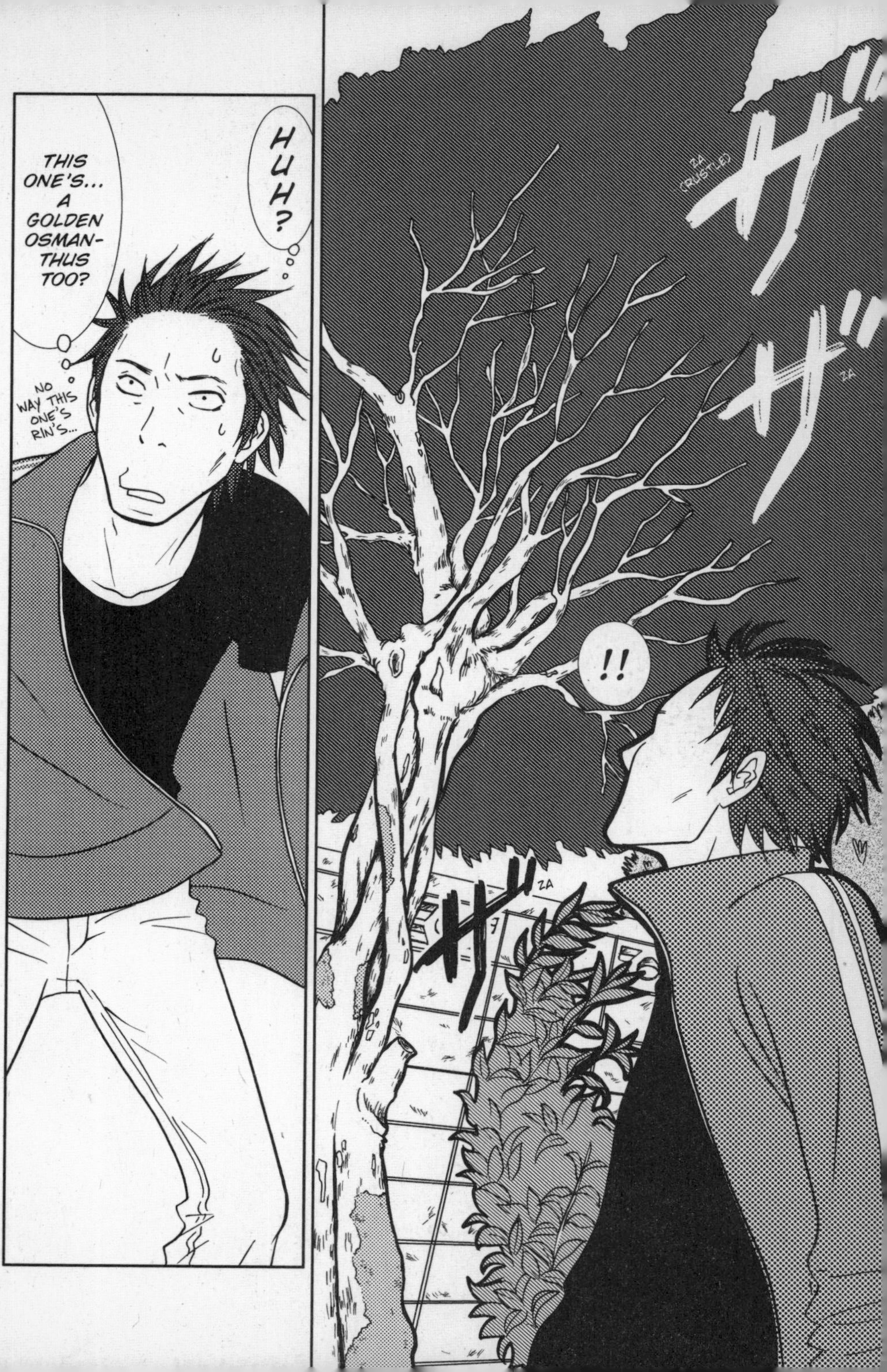
ザ
ZA (RUSTLE)
ザ
ZA
!!
ザ
ZA
HUH?
THIS ONE'S... A GOLDEN OSMANTHUS TOO?
NO WAY THIS ONE'S RIN'S...

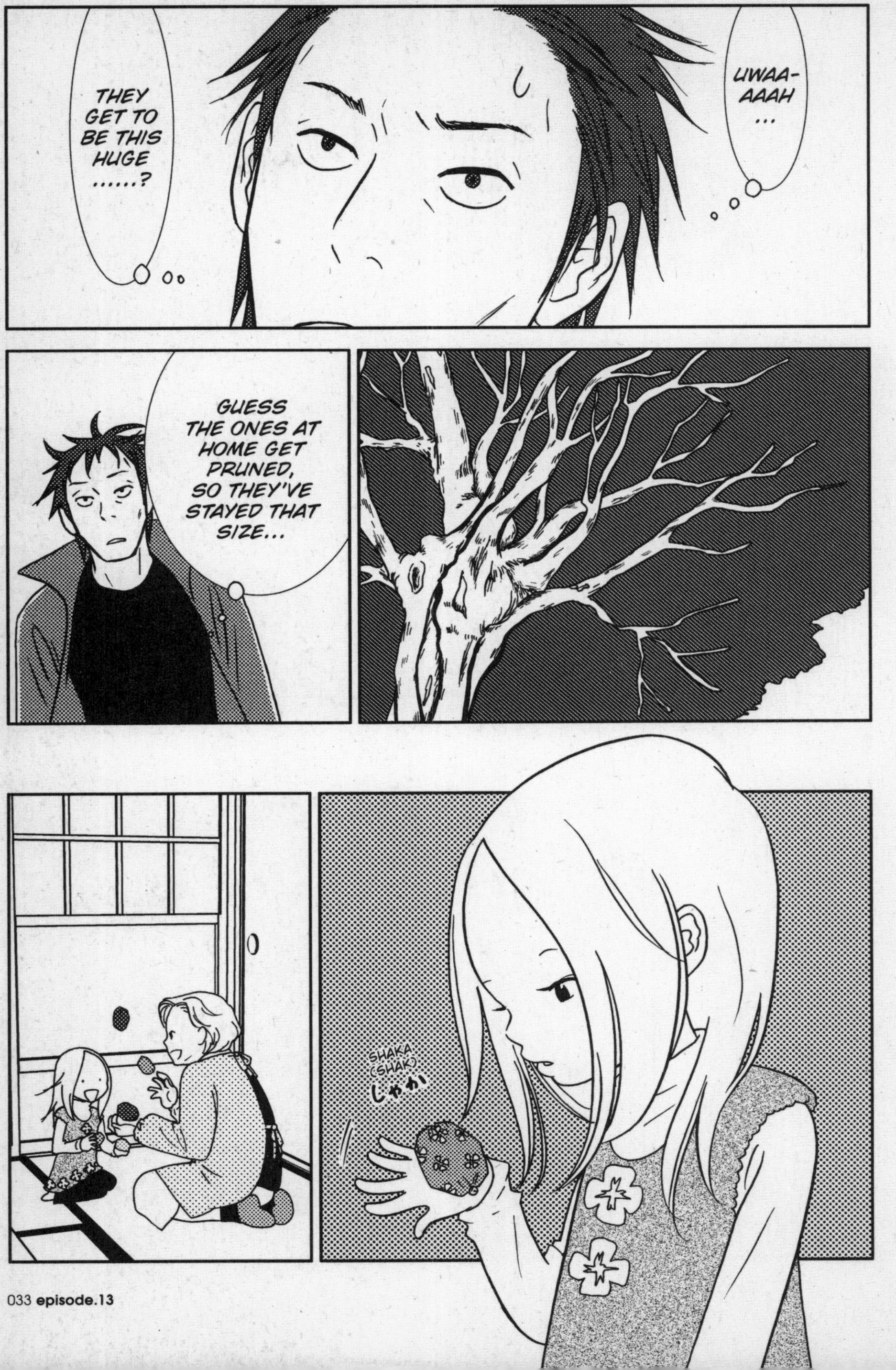
UWAA-AAAH ...
THEY GET TO BE THIS HUGE ......?
GUESS THE ONES AT HOME GET PRUNED, SO THEY'VE STAYED THAT SIZE...
SHAKA (SHAK)
しゃか

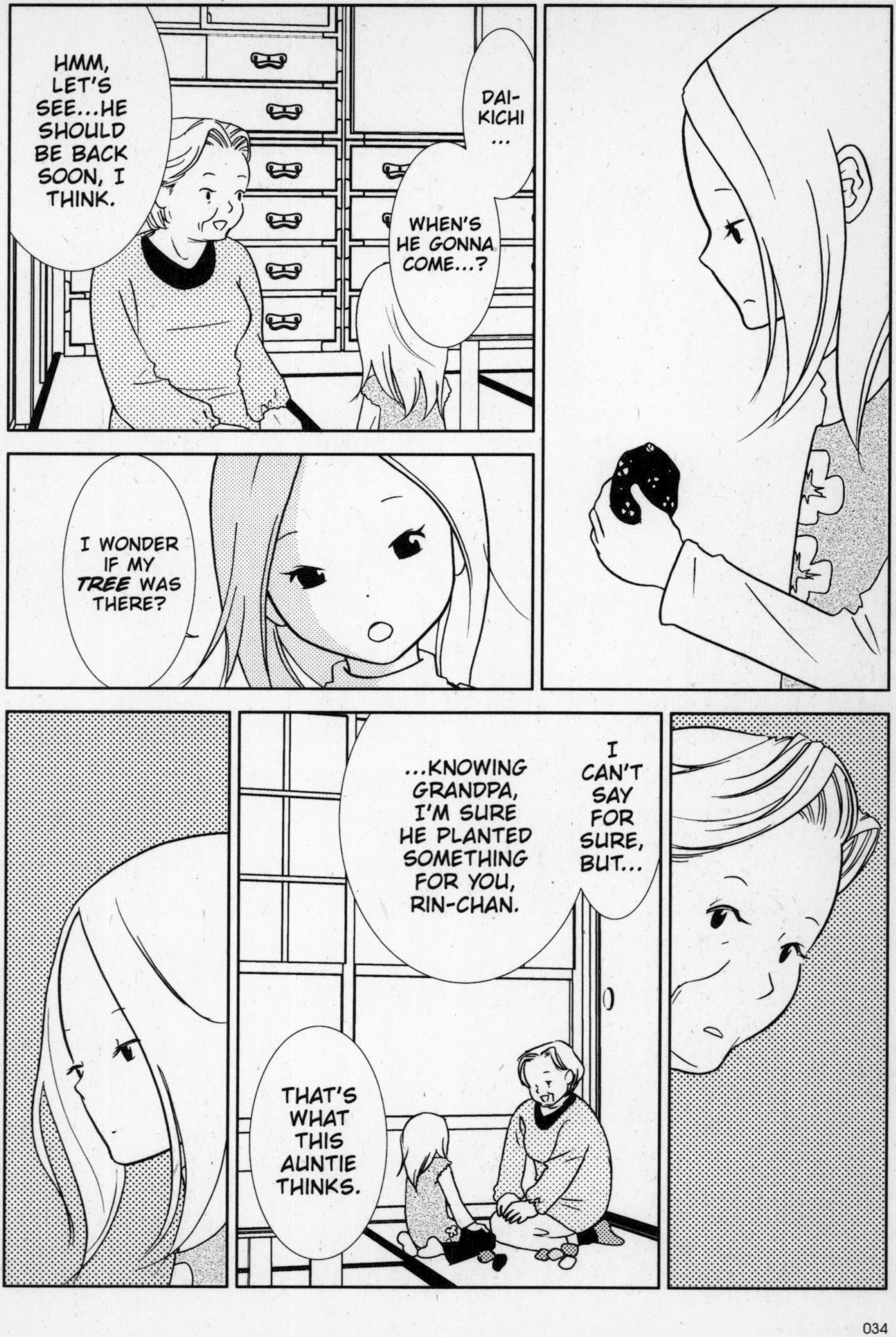
DAI-KICHI...
WHEN'S HE GONNA COME...?
HMM, LET'S SEE...HE SHOULD BE BACK SOON, I THINK.
I WONDER IF MY *TREE* WAS THERE?
I CAN'T SAY FOR SURE, BUT...
...KNOWING GRANDPA, I'M SURE HE PLANTED SOMETHING FOR YOU, RIN-CHAN.
THAT'S WHAT THIS AUNTIE THINKS.

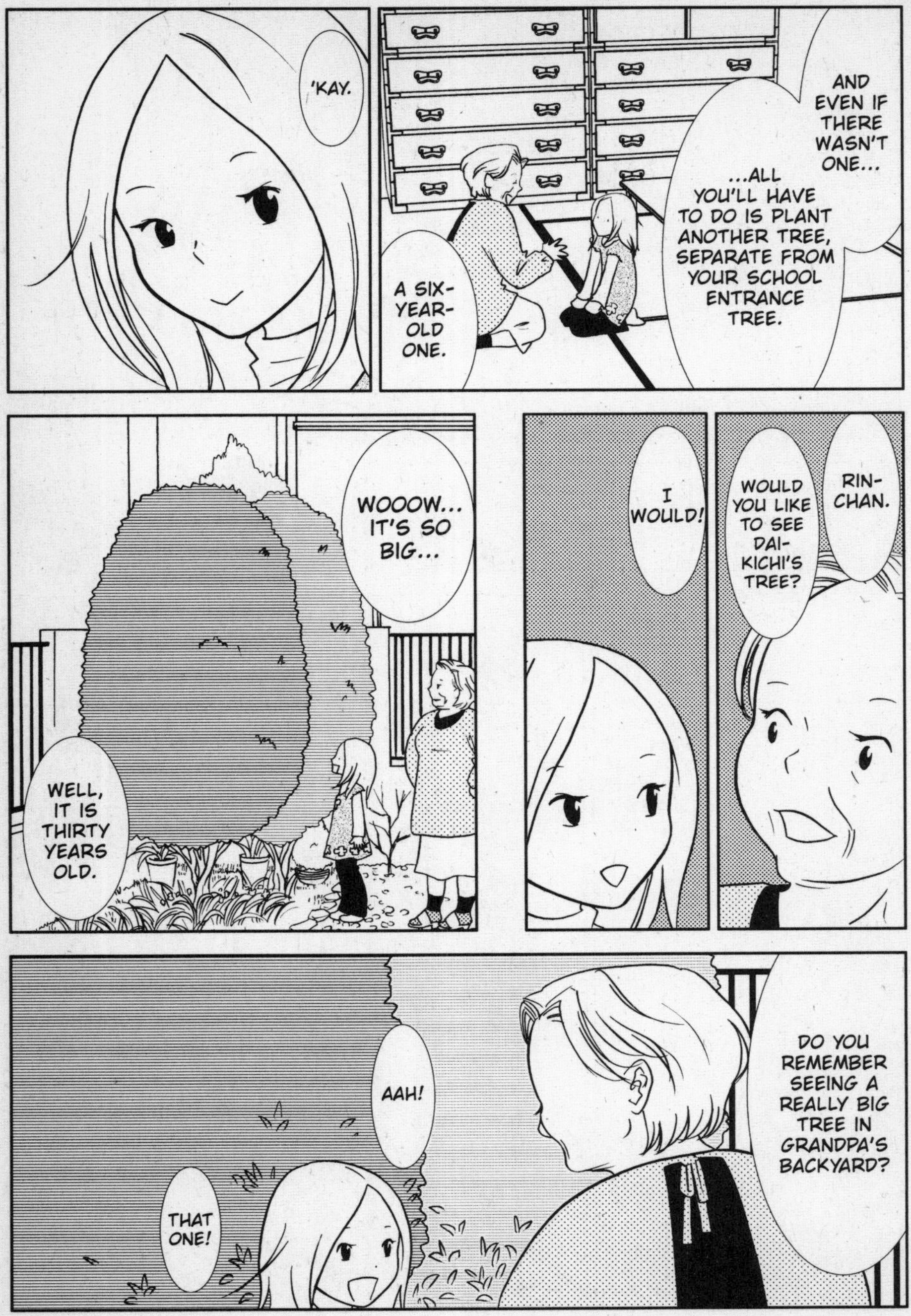
AND EVEN IF THERE WASN'T ONE...
...ALL YOU'LL HAVE TO DO IS PLANT ANOTHER TREE, SEPARATE FROM YOUR SCHOOL ENTRANCE TREE.
A SIX-YEAR-OLD ONE.
'KAY.
RIN-CHAN.
WOULD YOU LIKE TO SEE DAI-KICHI'S TREE?
I WOULD!
WOOOW... IT'S SO BIG...
WELL, IT IS THIRTY YEARS OLD.
DO YOU REMEMBER SEEING A REALLY BIG TREE IN GRANDPA'S BACKYARD?
AAH!
THAT ONE!

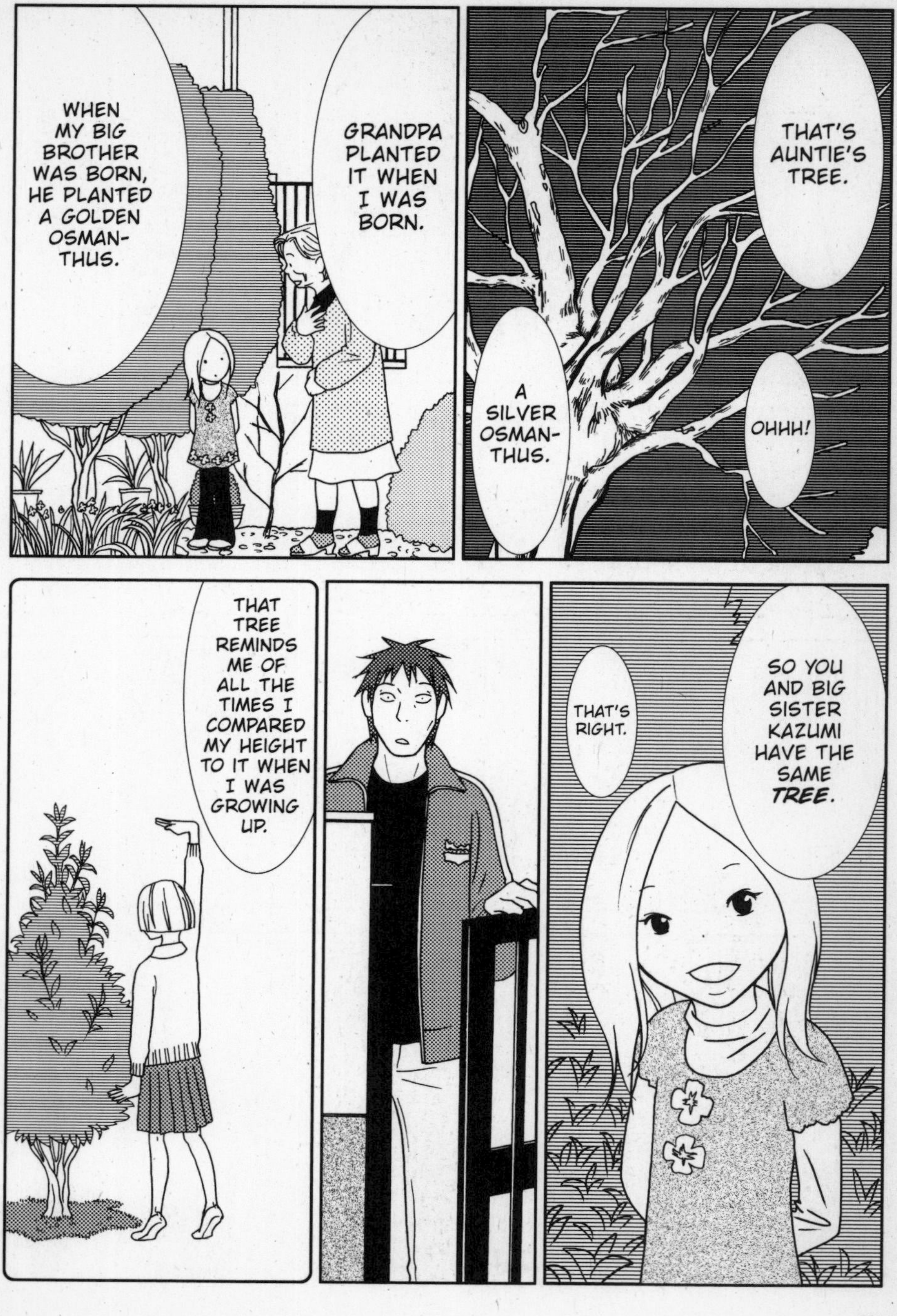
THAT'S AUNTIE'S TREE.
A SILVER OSMANTHUS.
OHHH!
GRANDPA PLANTED IT WHEN I WAS BORN.
WHEN MY BIG BROTHER WAS BORN, HE PLANTED A GOLDEN OSMANTHUS.
SO YOU AND BIG SISTER KAZUMI HAVE THE SAME ***TREE***.
THAT'S RIGHT.
THAT TREE REMINDS ME OF ALL THE TIMES I COMPARED MY HEIGHT TO IT WHEN I WAS GROWING UP.

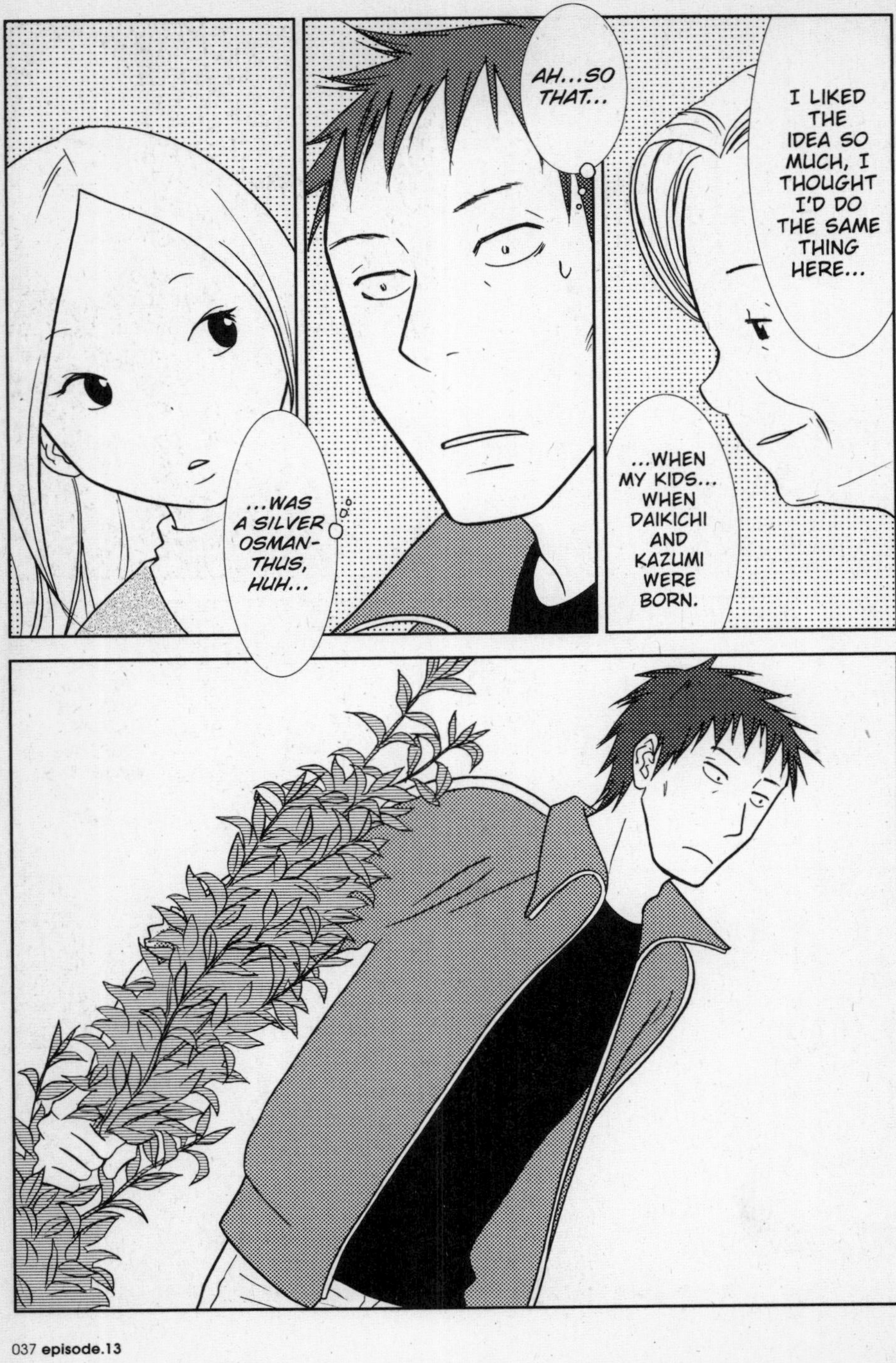
I LIKED THE IDEA SO MUCH, I THOUGHT I'D DO THE SAME THING HERE...
...WHEN MY KIDS... WHEN DAIKICHI AND KAZUMI WERE BORN.
AH...SO THAT...
...WAS A SILVER OSMAN-THUS, HUH...

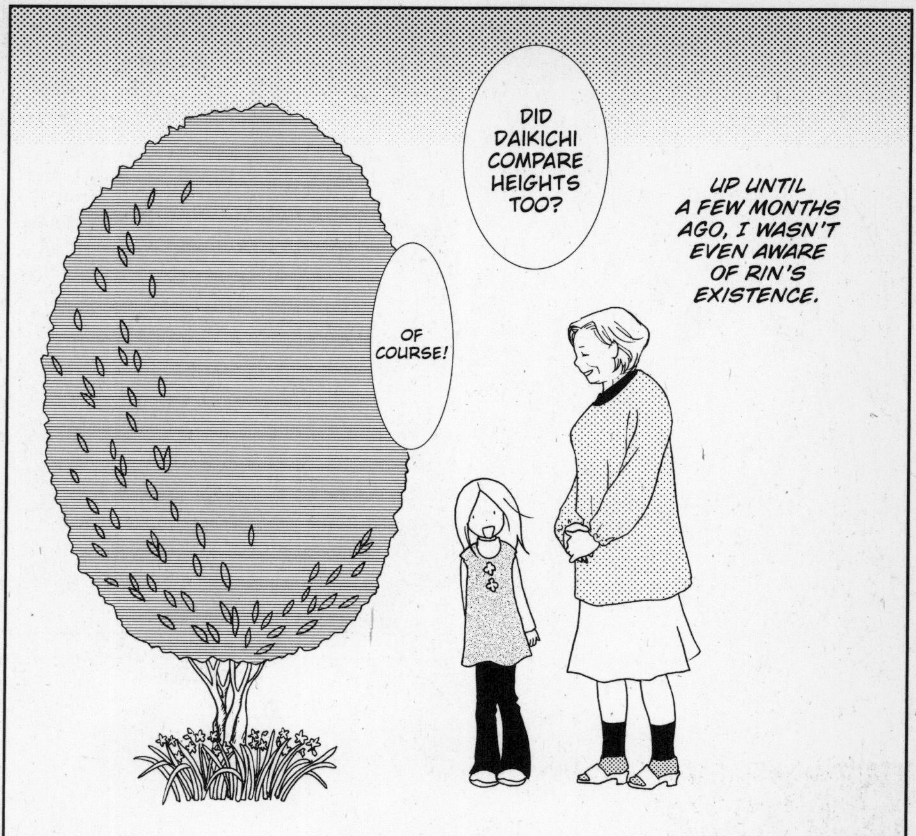
UP UNTIL A FEW MONTHS AGO, I WASN'T EVEN AWARE OF RIN'S EXISTENCE.
DID DAIKICHI COMPARE HEIGHTS TOO?
OF COURSE!

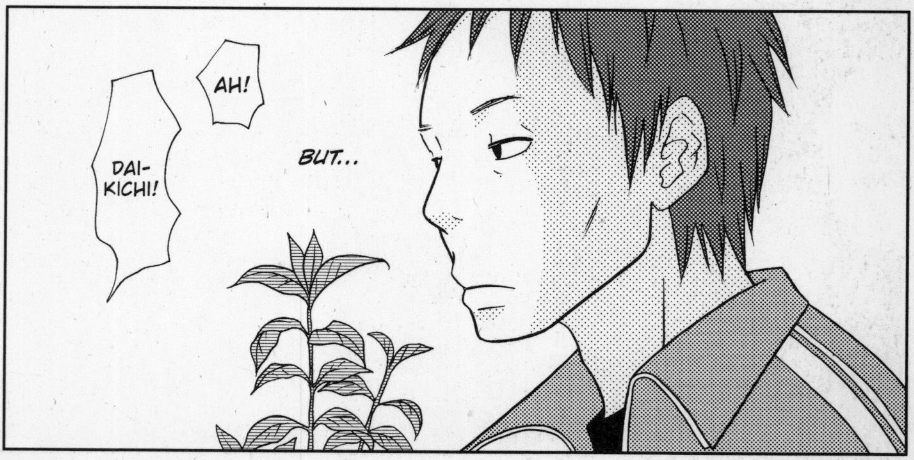
BUT...
AH!
DAI-KICHI!

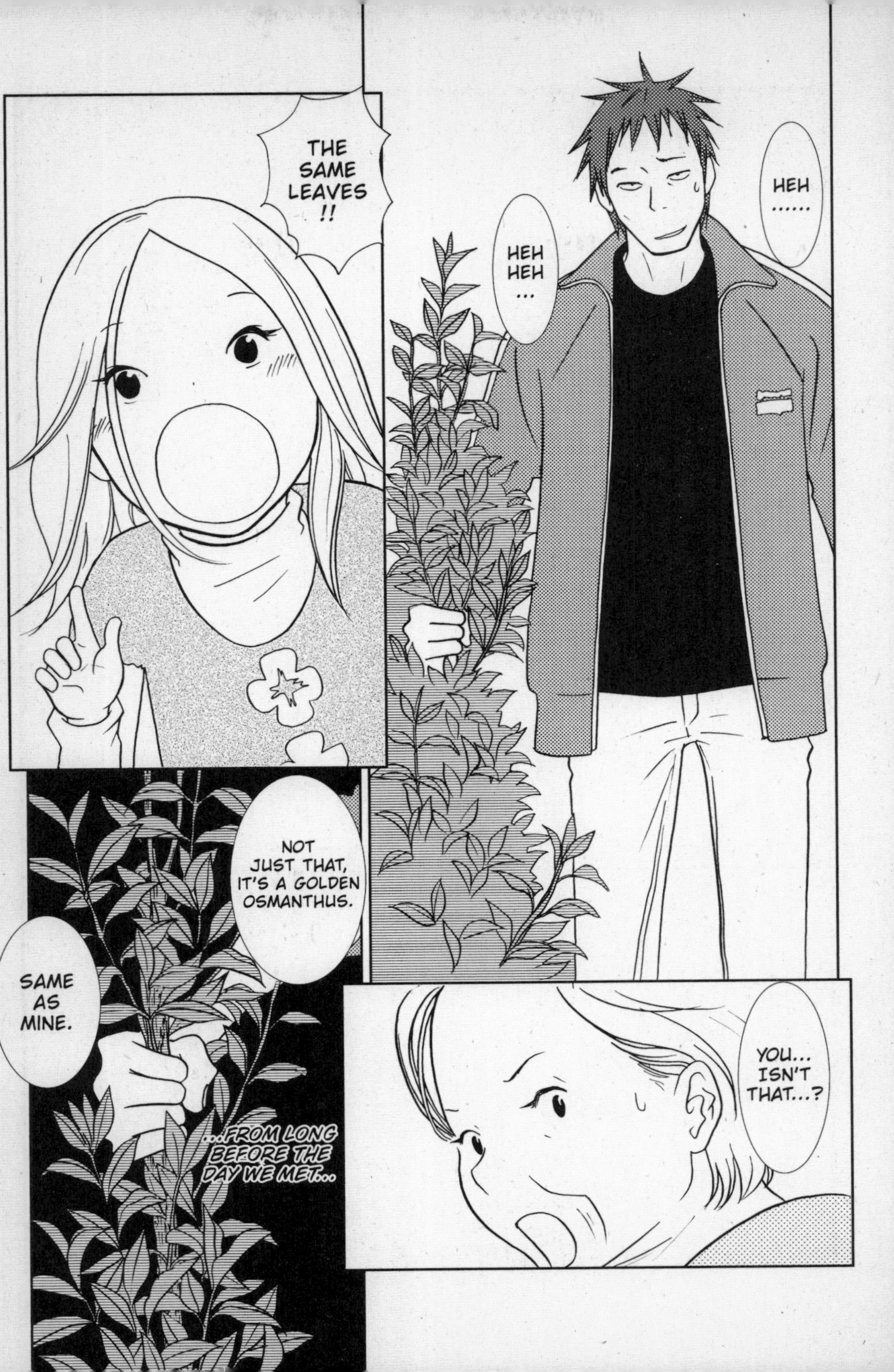
HEH ......
HEH HEH ...
THE SAME LEAVES !!
NOT JUST THAT, IT'S A GOLDEN OSMANTHUS.
SAME AS MINE.
...FROM LONG BEFORE THE DAY WE MET...
YOU... ISN'T THAT...?

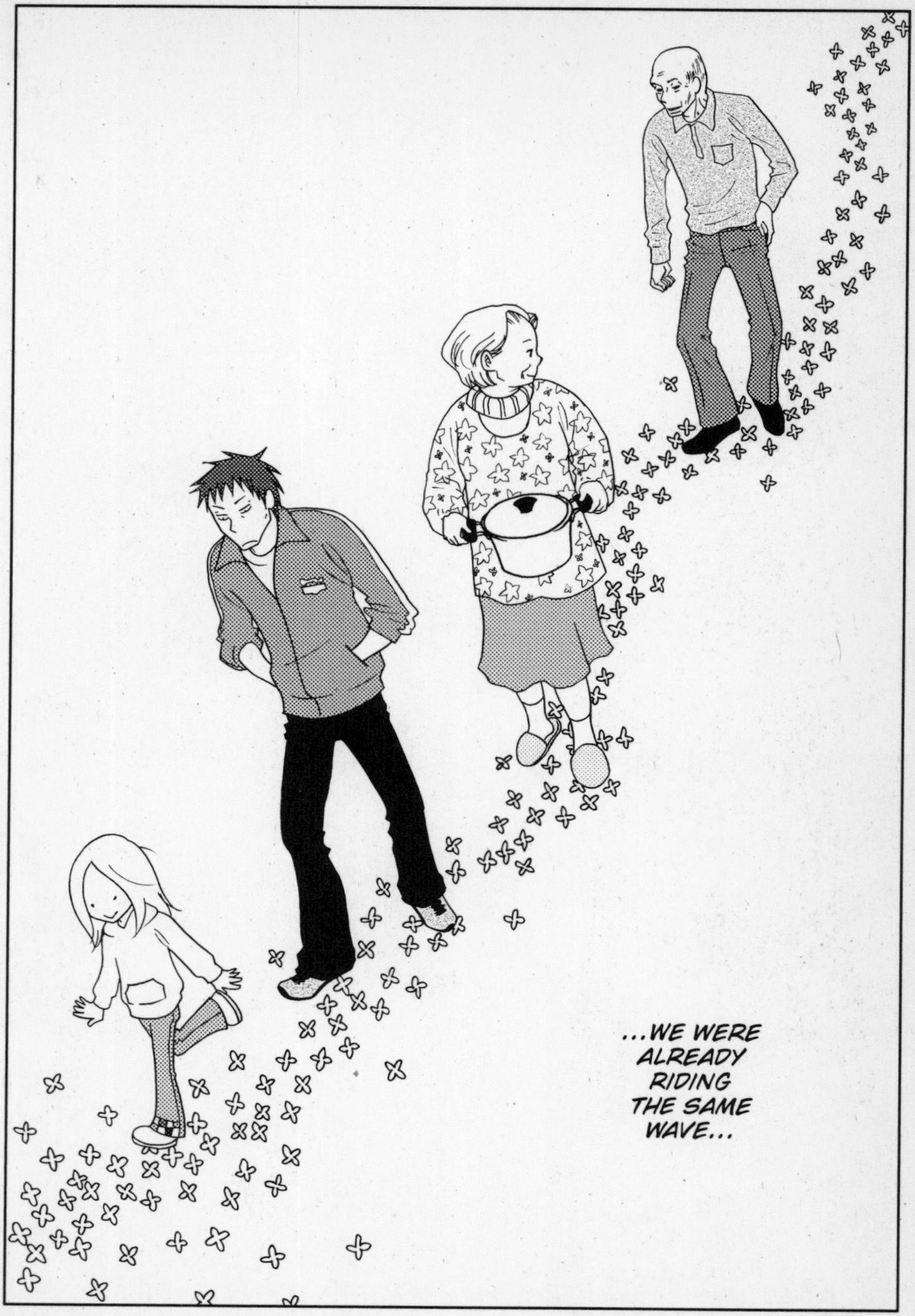
...WE WERE ALREADY RIDING THE SAME WAVE...

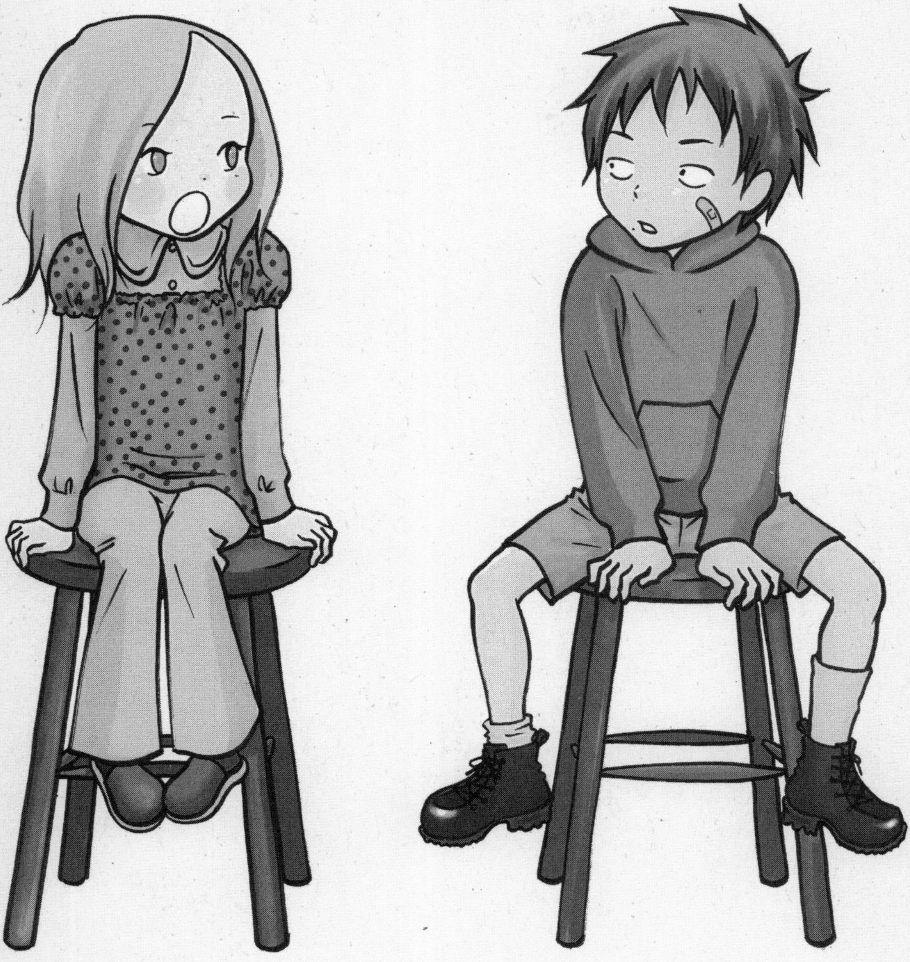

BUNNY**DROP**

episode.14

BUNNY**DROP**

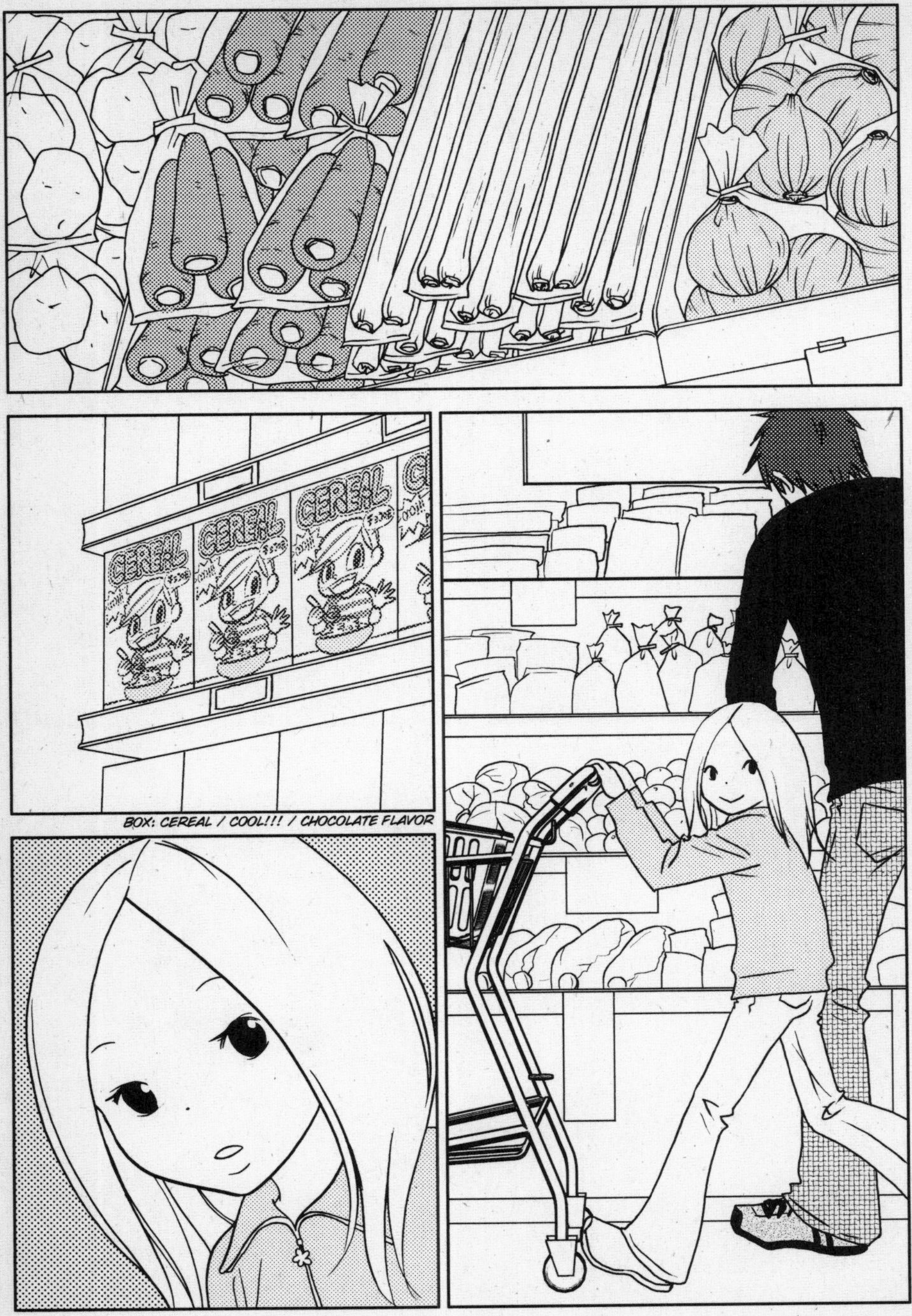
CEREAL
CEREAL
CEREAL
BOX: CEREAL / COOL!!! / CHOCOLATE FLAVOR

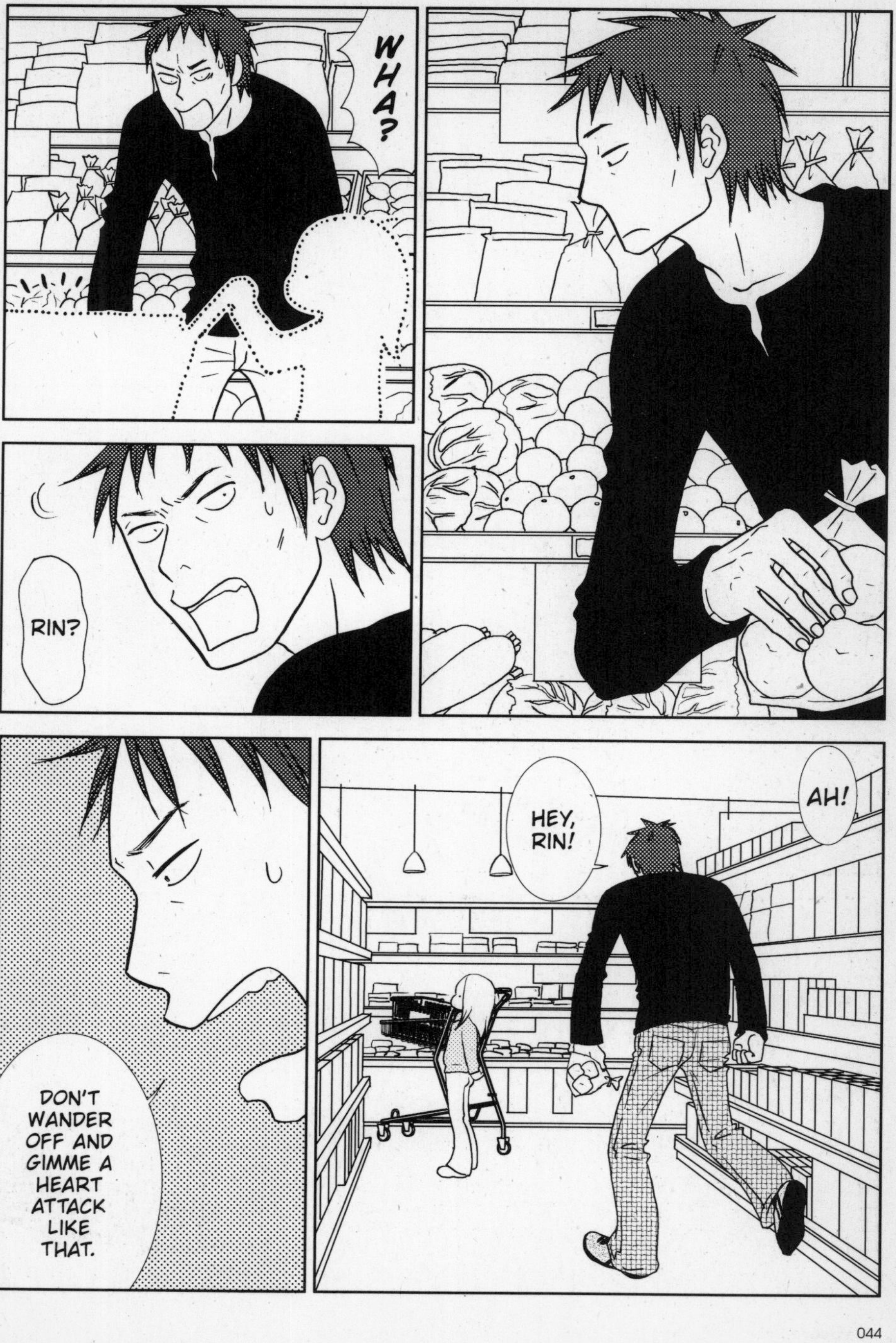
WHA?
RIN?
AH!
HEY, RIN!
DON'T WANDER OFF AND GIMME A HEART ATTACK LIKE THAT.

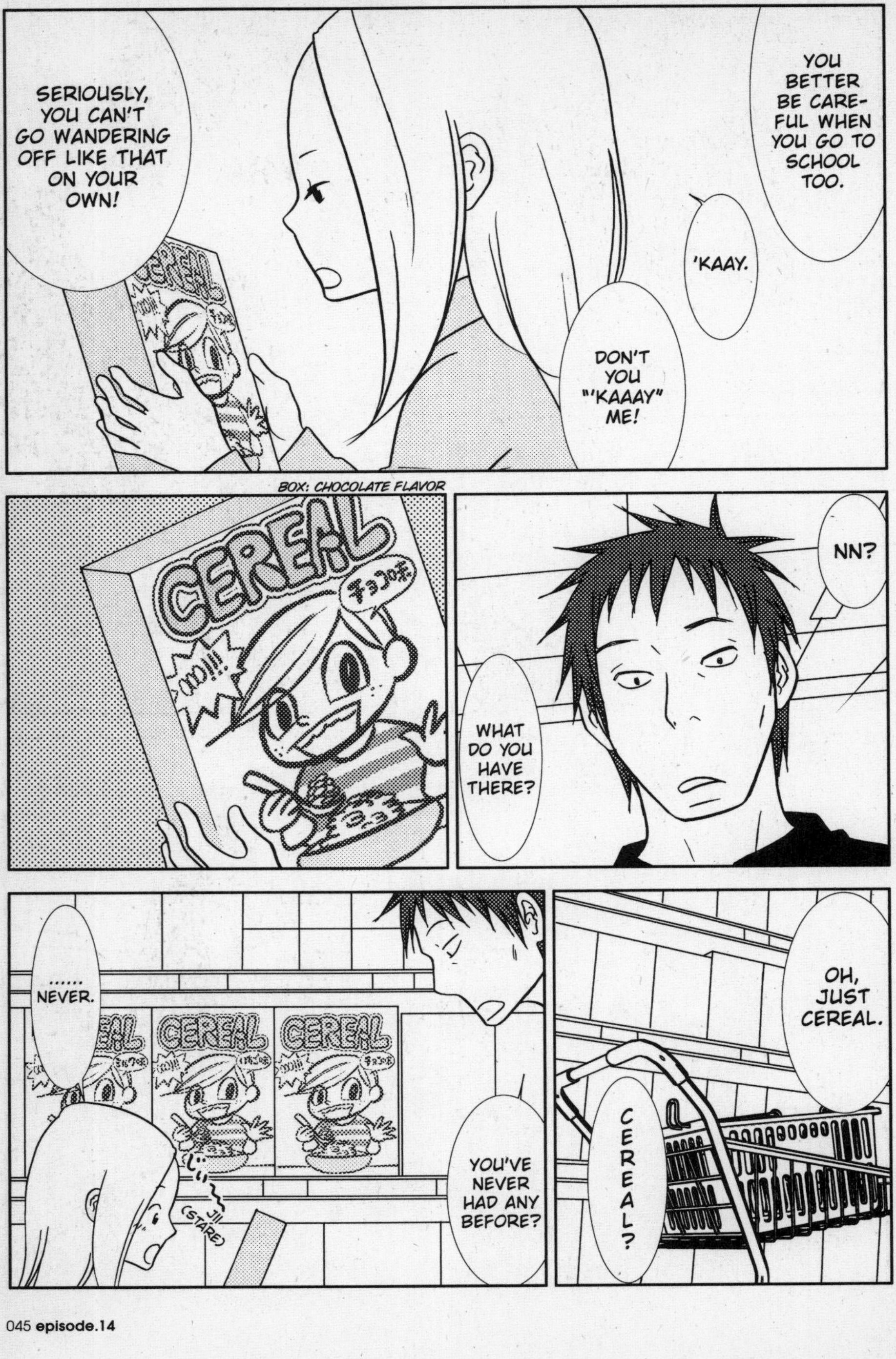
YOU BETTER BE CAREFUL WHEN YOU GO TO SCHOOL TOO.
'KAAY.
DON'T YOU "'KAAAY" ME!
SERIOUSLY, YOU CAN'T GO WANDERING OFF LIKE THAT ON YOUR OWN!
NN?
WHAT DO YOU HAVE THERE?
CEREAL
チョコ味
BOX: CHOCOLATE FLAVOR
OH, JUST CEREAL.
CEREAL?
YOU'VE NEVER HAD ANY BEFORE?
...... NEVER.
CEREAL
CEREAL
JI! (STARE)

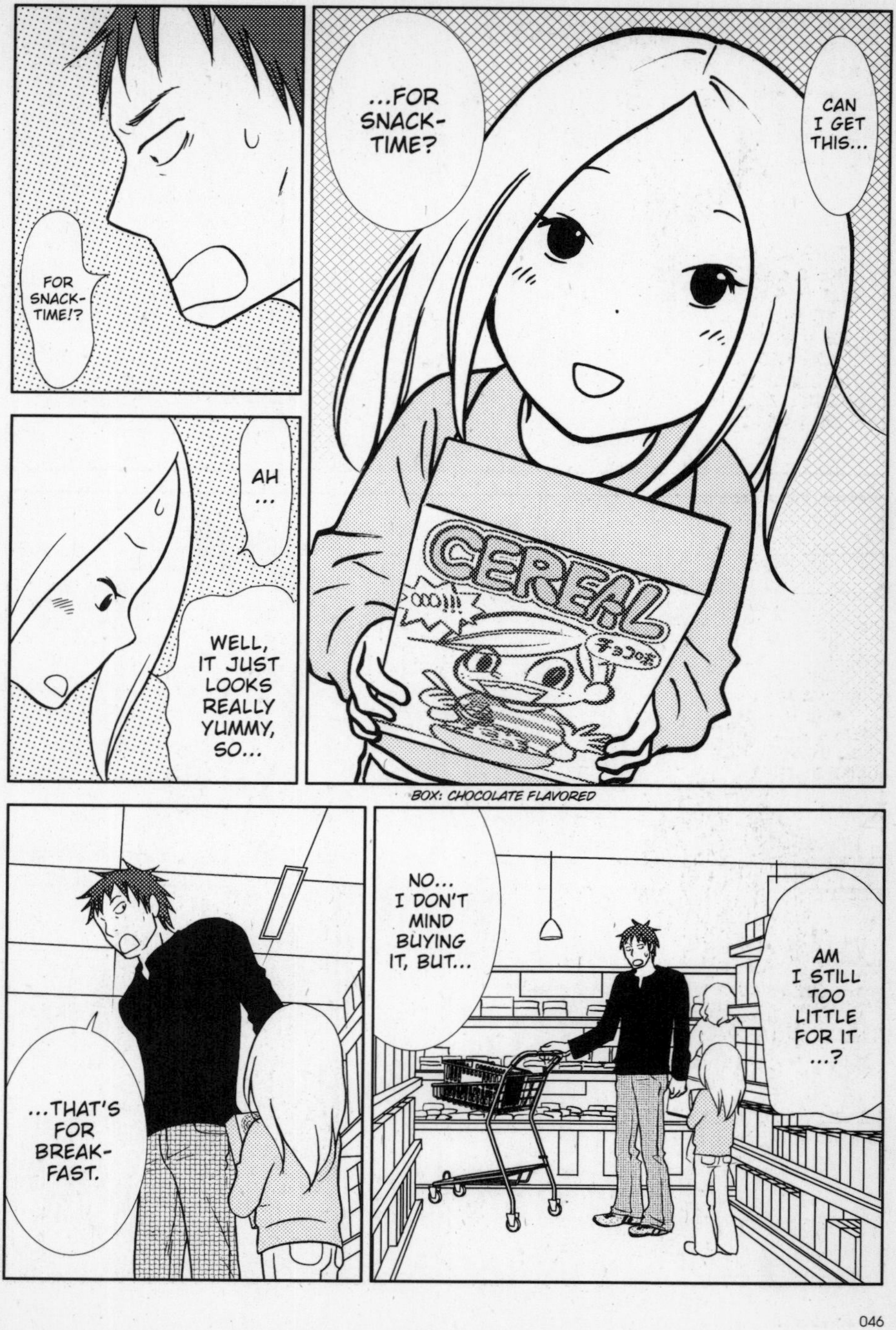
CAN I GET THIS...
...FOR SNACK-TIME?
FOR SNACK-TIME!?
AH ...
WELL, IT JUST LOOKS REALLY YUMMY, SO...
CEREAL
BOX: CHOCOLATE FLAVORED
AM I STILL TOO LITTLE FOR IT ...?
NO... I DON'T MIND BUYING IT, BUT...
...THAT'S FOR BREAKFAST.

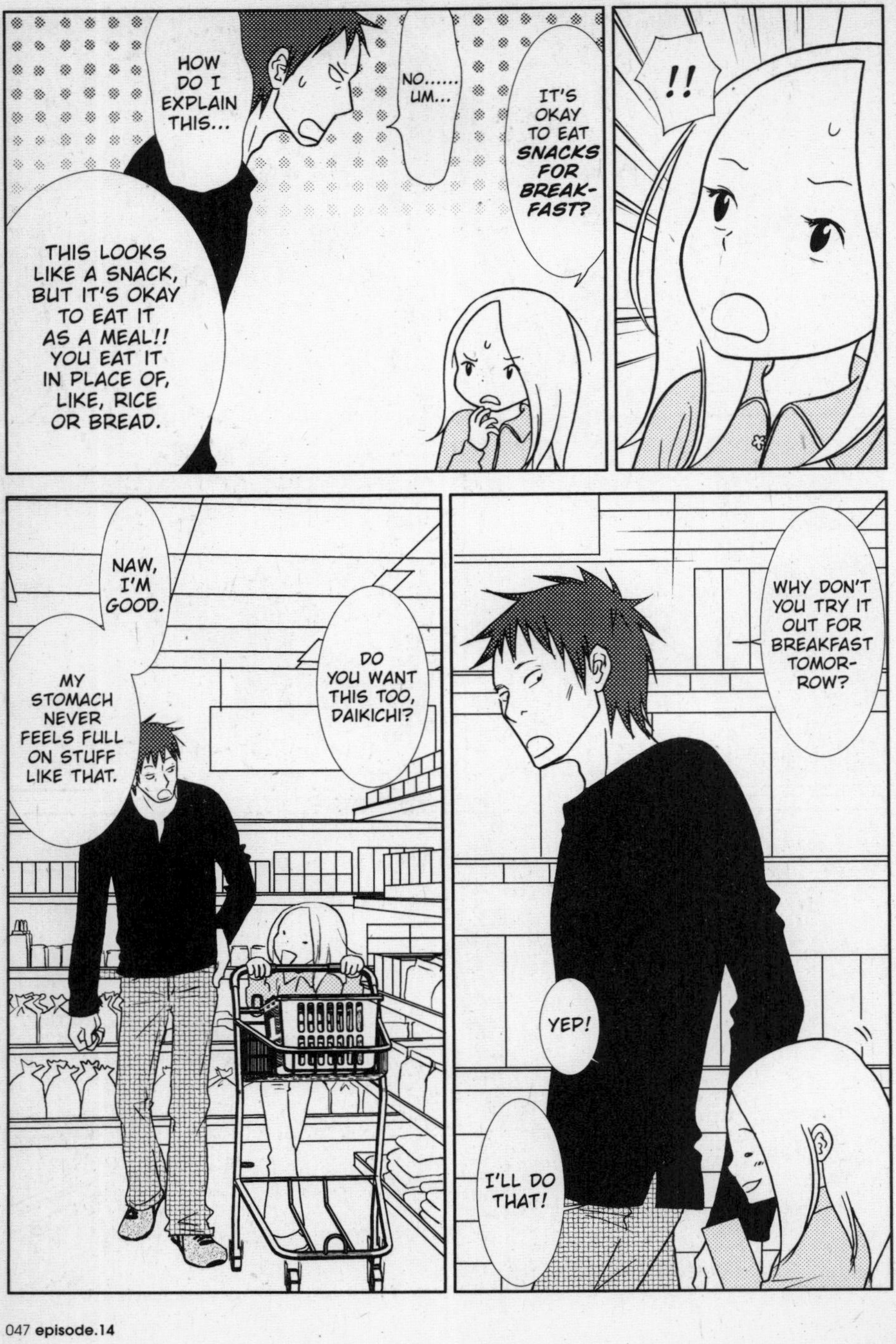
!!
IT'S OKAY TO EAT SNACKS FOR BREAKFAST?
NO...... UM...
HOW DO I EXPLAIN THIS...
THIS LOOKS LIKE A SNACK, BUT IT'S OKAY TO EAT IT AS A MEAL!! YOU EAT IT IN PLACE OF, LIKE, RICE OR BREAD.
WHY DON'T YOU TRY IT OUT FOR BREAKFAST TOMORROW?
YEP!
I'LL DO THAT!
DO YOU WANT THIS TOO, DAIKICHI?
NAW, I'M GOOD.
MY STOMACH NEVER FEELS FULL ON STUFF LIKE THAT.

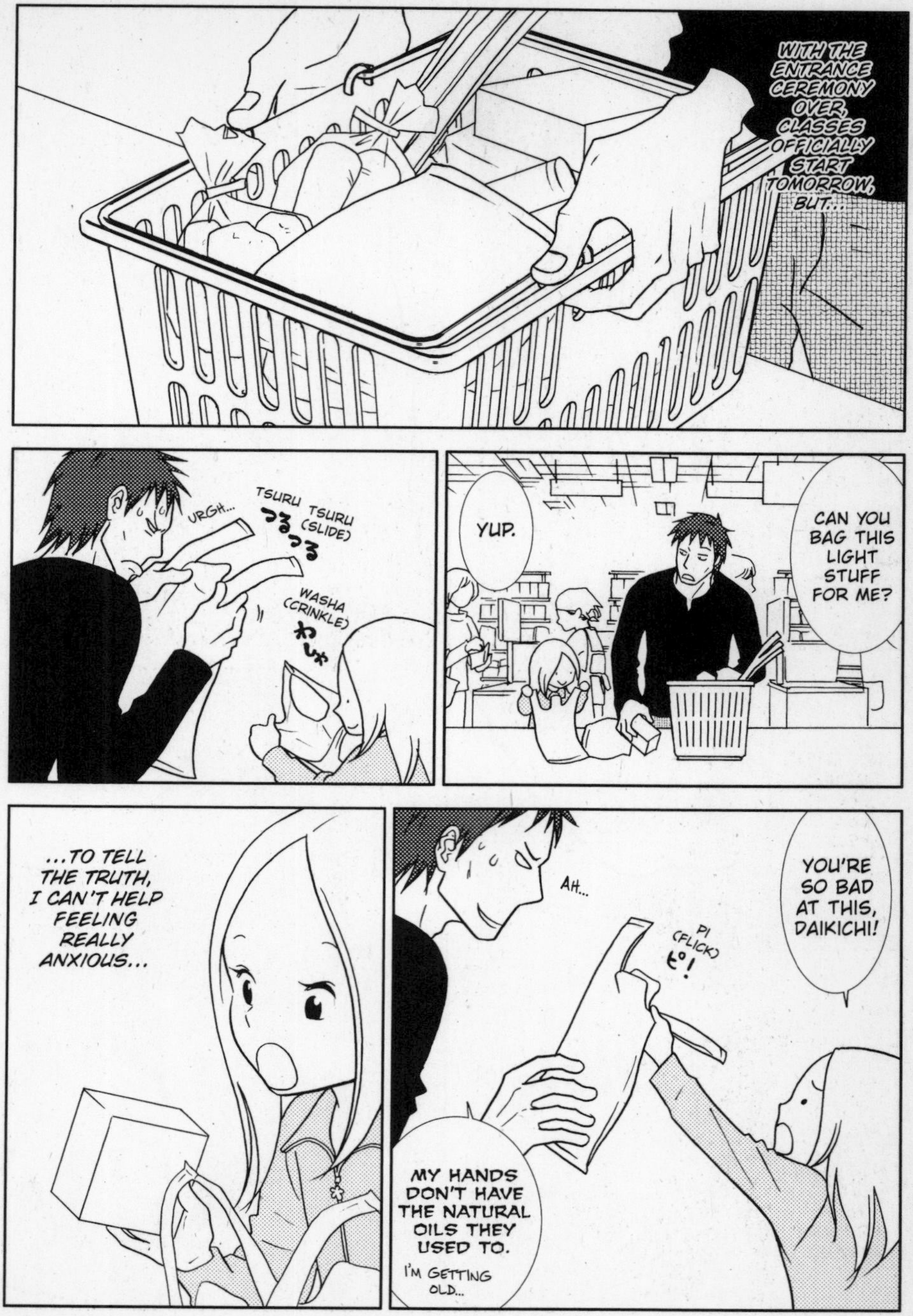
WITH THE ENTRANCE CEREMONY OVER, CLASSES OFFICIALLY START TOMORROW, BUT...
CAN YOU BAG THIS LIGHT STUFF FOR ME?
YUP.
TSURU TSURU (SLIDE) つるつる
URGH...
WASHA (CRINKLE) わしゃ
YOU'RE SO BAD AT THIS, DAIKICHI!
PI (FLICK) ピ!
AH...
MY HANDS DON'T HAVE THE NATURAL OILS THEY USED TO.
I'M GETTING OLD...
...TO TELL THE TRUTH, I CAN'T HELP FEELING REALLY ANXIOUS...

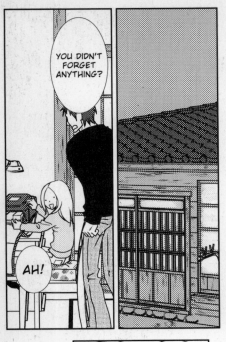

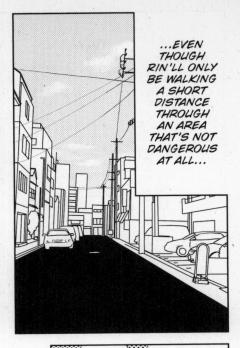

...EVEN THOUGH RIN'LL ONLY BE WALKING A SHORT DISTANCE THROUGH AN AREA THAT'S NOT DANGEROUS AT ALL...
YOU DIDN'T FORGET ANYTHING?
AH!
I'M SUPPOSED TO GET SOMEONE AT HOME TO **VERIFY MY SCHEDULE.**
EHHH? WHAT A PAIN...
保護者の皆様へお願い
WHEN I WAS SIX, I WALKED TO SCHOOL BY MYSELF.
YOU'RE RIGHT. IT SAYS I HAVE TO LOOK IT OVER...
I DON'T THINK I EVER HAD TO GET THIS DONE.
NOT ONLY THAT, I HAD TO WALK FARTHER THAN RIN.
AND BY THAT TIME, I WAS ALREADY BIKING TO MY FRIENDS' HOUSES.
PAPER: A REQUEST FOR THOSE AT HOME.

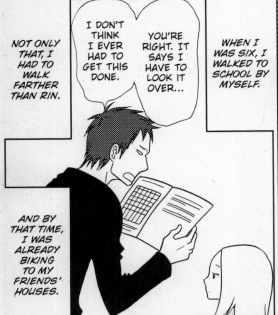

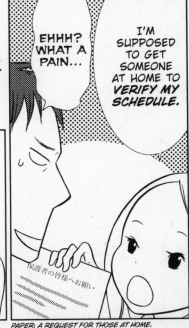

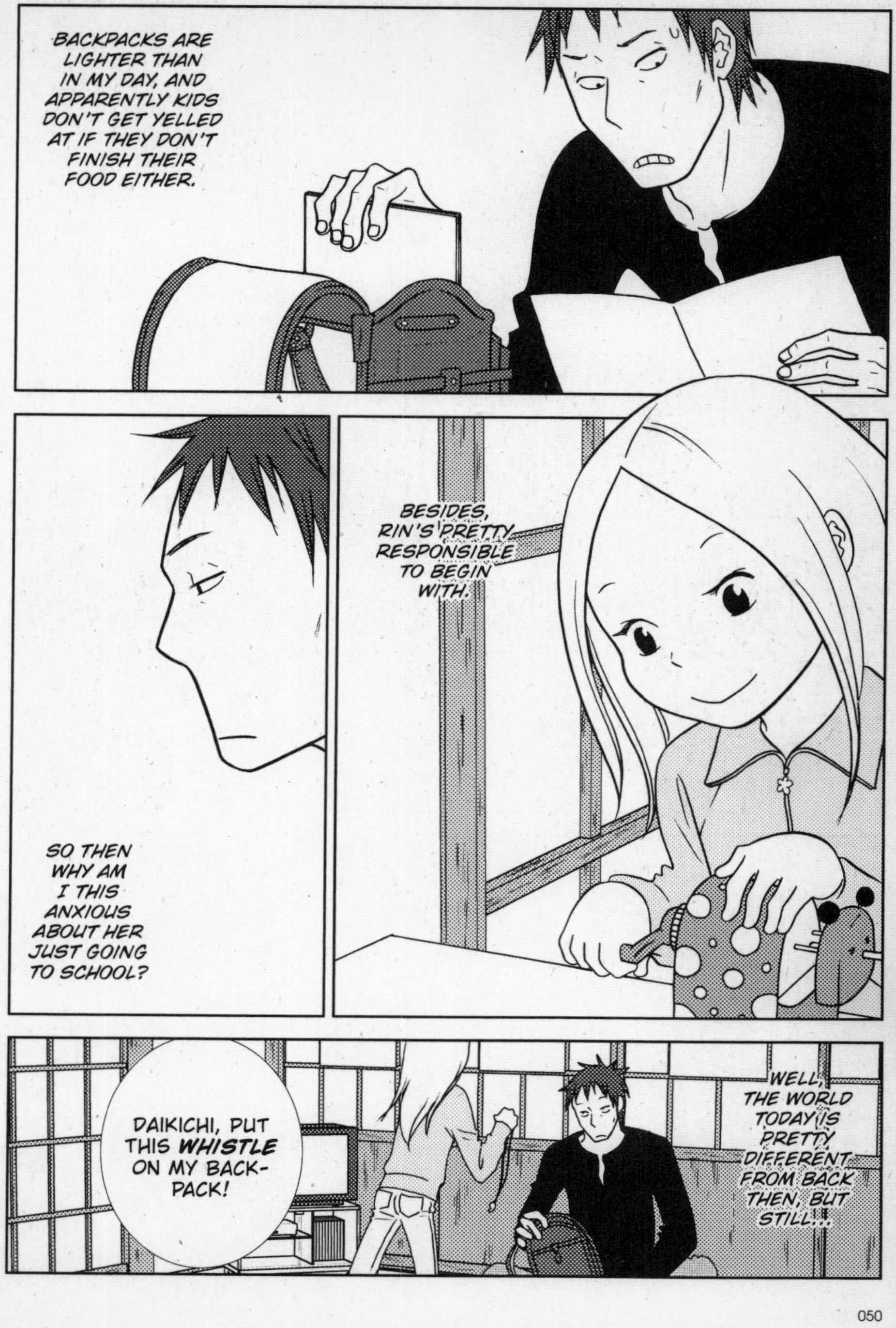
BACKPACKS ARE LIGHTER THAN IN MY DAY, AND APPARENTLY KIDS DON'T GET YELLED AT IF THEY DON'T FINISH THEIR FOOD EITHER.
BESIDES, RIN'S PRETTY RESPONSIBLE TO BEGIN WITH.
SO THEN WHY AM I THIS ANXIOUS ABOUT HER JUST GOING TO SCHOOL?
WELL, THE WORLD TODAY IS PRETTY DIFFERENT FROM BACK THEN, BUT STILL...
DAIKICHI, PUT THIS WHISTLE ON MY BACK-PACK!

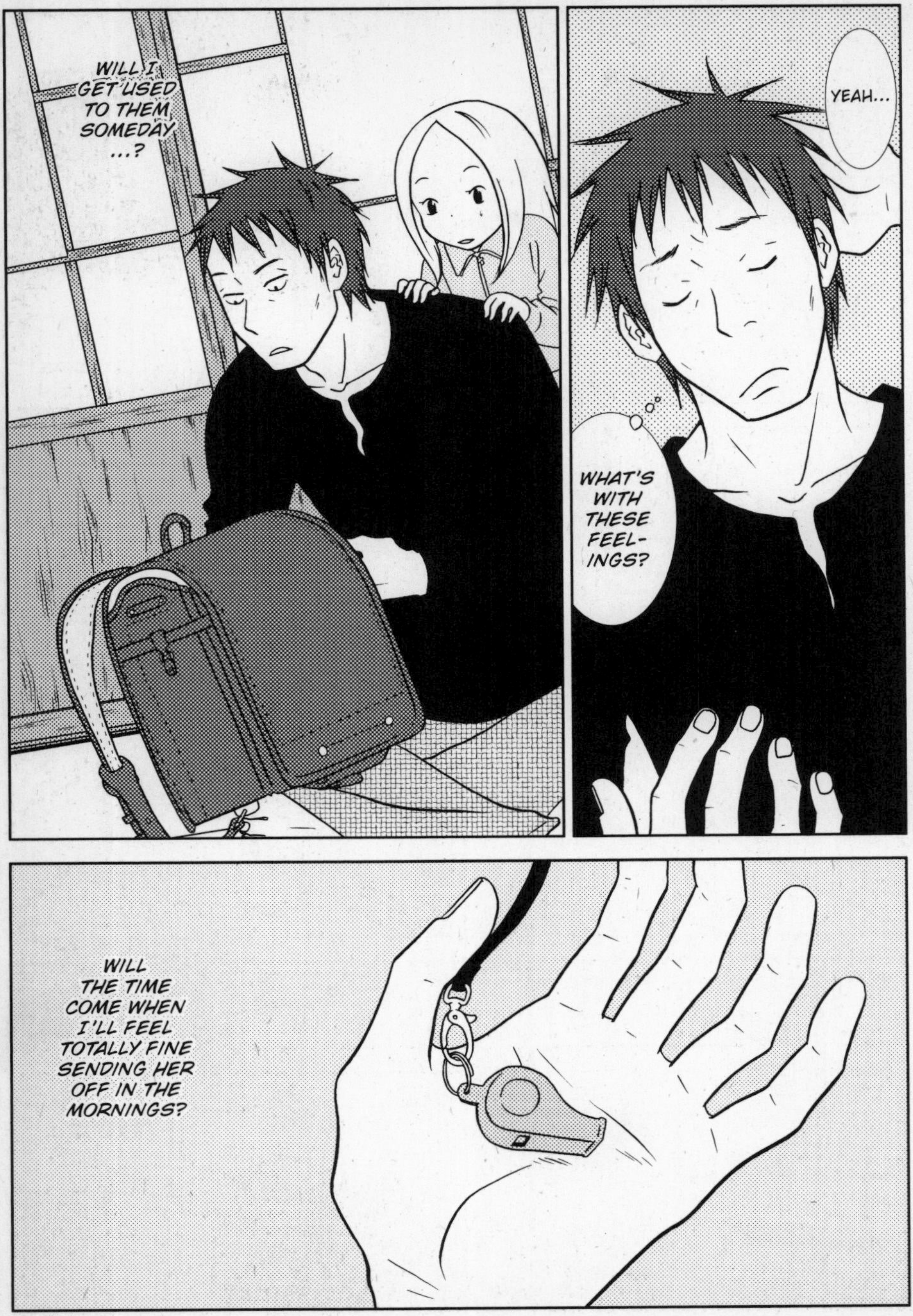
YEAH...
WHAT'S WITH THESE FEELINGS?
WILL I GET USED TO THEM SOMEDAY ...?
WILL THE TIME COME WHEN I'LL FEEL TOTALLY FINE SENDING HER OFF IN THE MORNINGS?

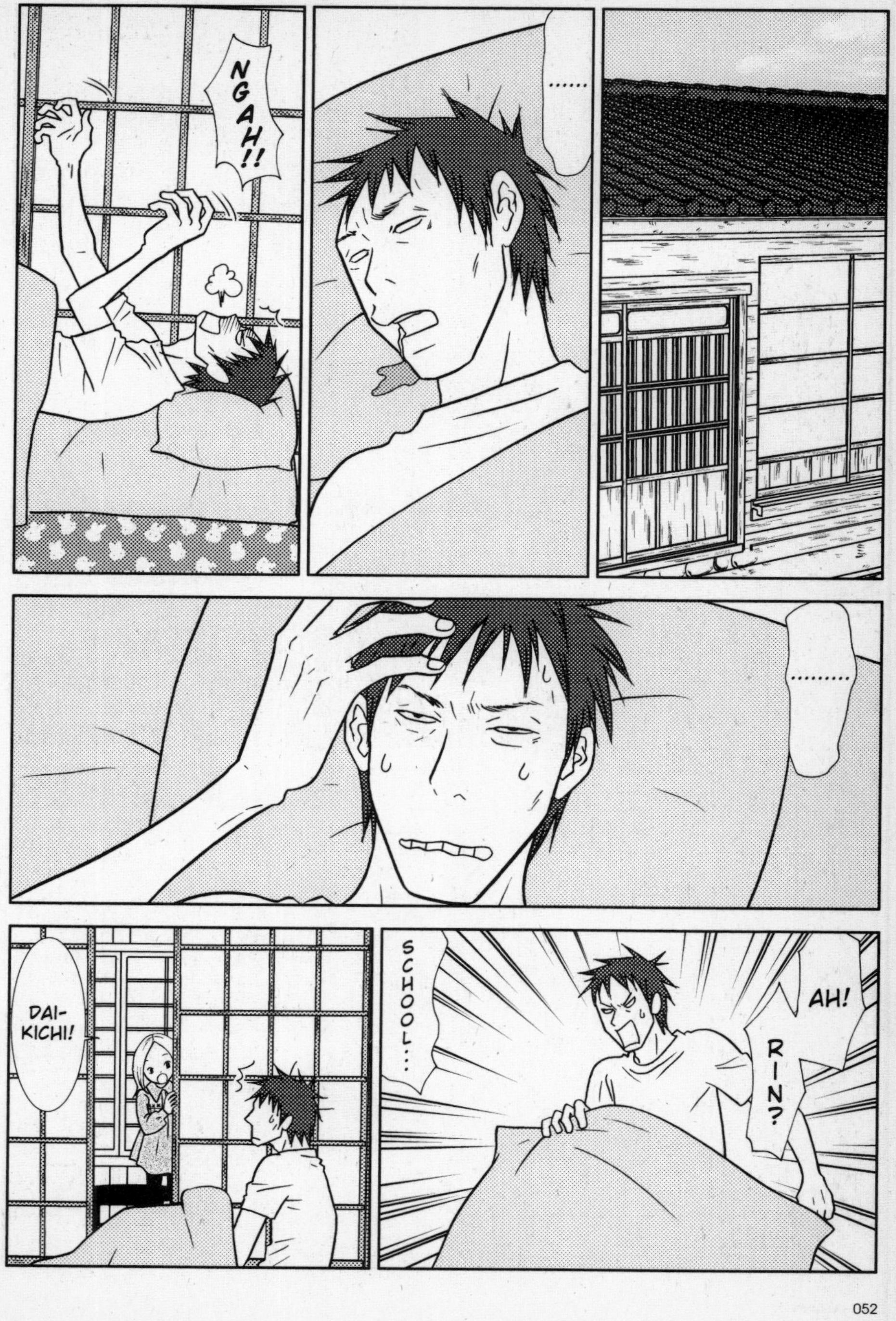
……
NGAH!!
………
AH!
RIN?
SCHOOL…
DAI-KICHI!

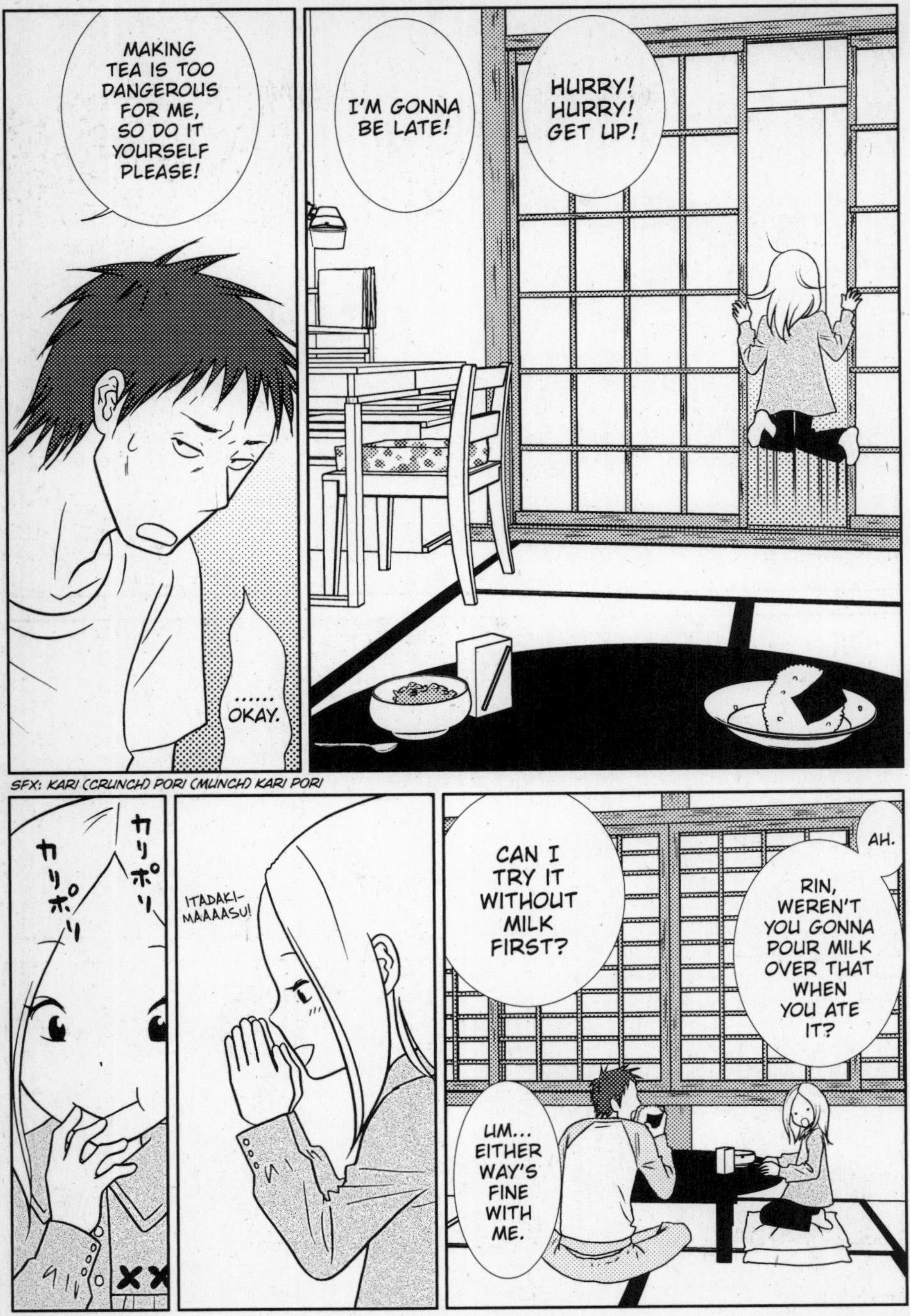
HURRY! HURRY! GET UP!
I'M GONNA BE LATE!
MAKING TEA IS TOO DANGEROUS FOR ME, SO DO IT YOURSELF PLEASE!
......OKAY.
SFX: KARI (CRUNCH) PORI (MUNCH) KARI PORI
AH.
RIN, WEREN'T YOU GONNA POUR MILK OVER THAT WHEN YOU ATE IT?
CAN I TRY IT WITHOUT MILK FIRST?
UM... EITHER WAY'S FINE WITH ME.
ITADAKI-MAAAASU!
カリポリ
カリポリ

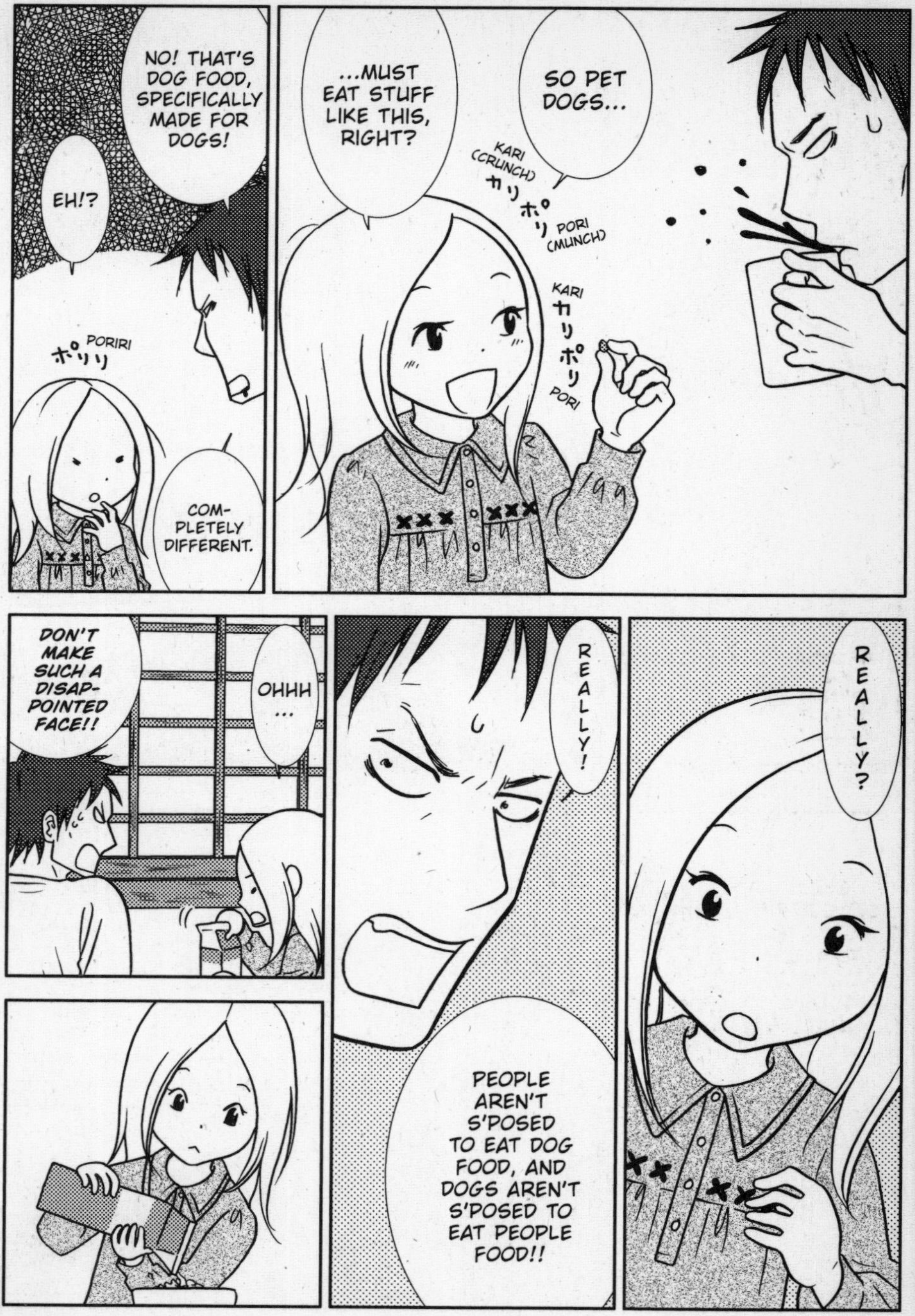
SO PET DOGS...
...MUST EAT STUFF LIKE THIS, RIGHT?
KARI (CRUNCH) カリ
ポリ PORI (MUNCH)
KARI カリポリ PORI
NO! THAT'S DOG FOOD, SPECIFICALLY MADE FOR DOGS!
EH!?
PORIRI ポリリ
COM-PLETELY DIFFERENT.
REALLY?
REALLY!
PEOPLE AREN'T S'POSED TO EAT DOG FOOD, AND DOGS AREN'T S'POSED TO EAT PEOPLE FOOD!!
OHHH...
DON'T MAKE SUCH A DISAP-POINTED FACE!!

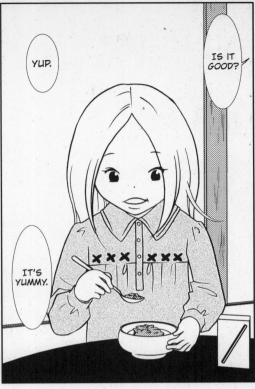

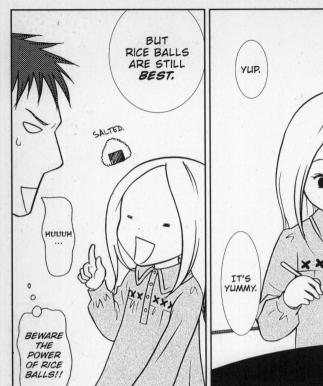

IS IT GOOD?
YUP.
IT'S YUMMY.
BUT RICE BALLS ARE STILL BEST.
SALTED.
HUUUH ...
BEWARE THE POWER OF RICE BALLS!!
DAIKICHI, YOUR CELL PHONE'S RINGING.
EH? WHAT DO THEY WANT AT THIS HOUR...
AH?
I-I'M SO SORRY. KOUKI'S REALLY EXCITED TODAY, AND...

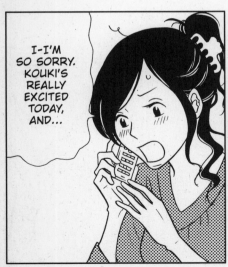

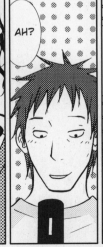

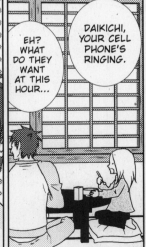

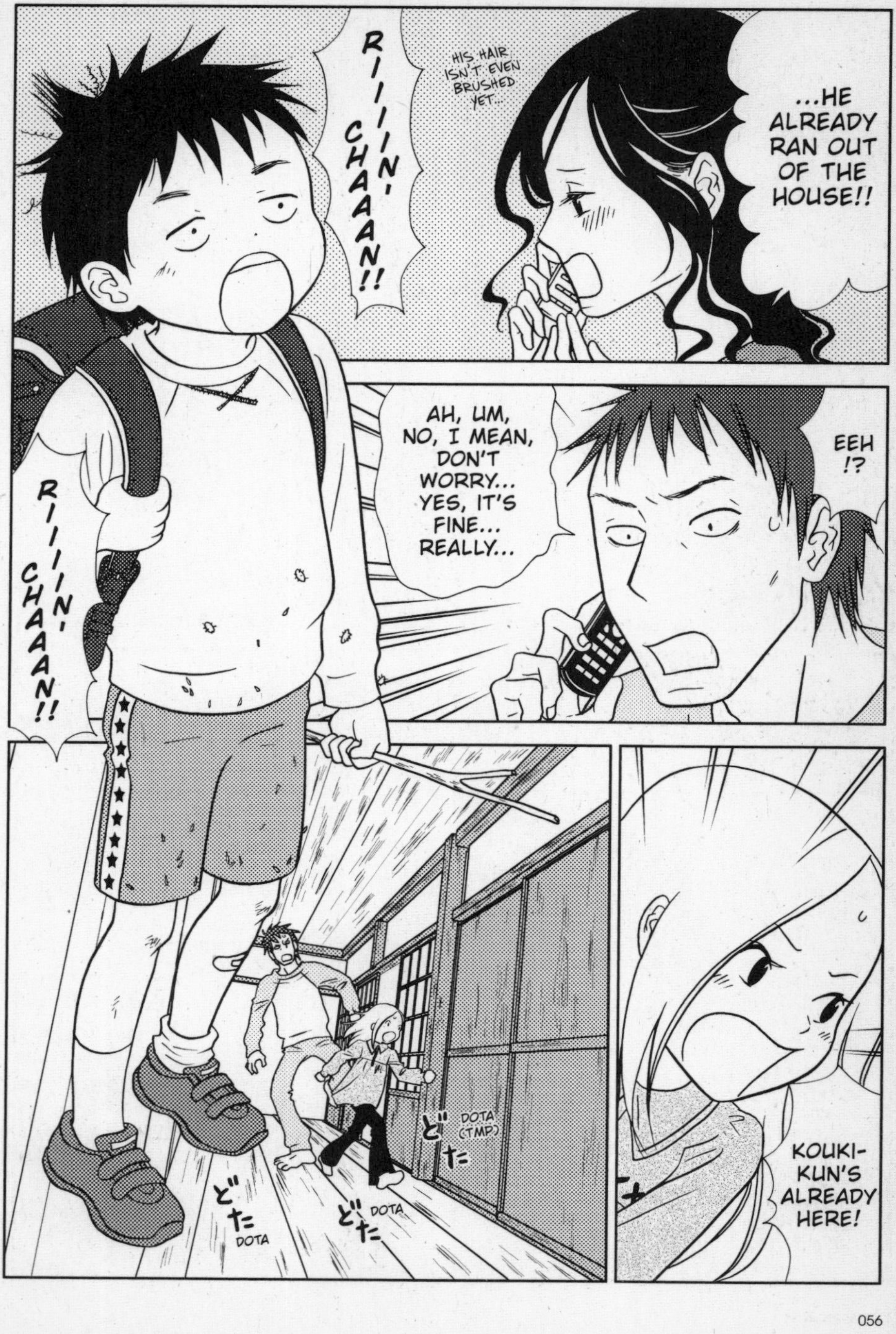
...HE ALREADY RAN OUT OF THE HOUSE!!
HIS HAIR ISN'T EVEN BRUSHED YET...
RIIIIIN CHAAAAN!!
EEH!?
AH, UM, NO, I MEAN, DON'T WORRY... YES, IT'S FINE... REALLY...
RIIIIIN CHAAAAN!!
KOUKI-KUN'S ALREADY HERE!
どた DOTA (TMP)
どた DOTA
どた DOTA

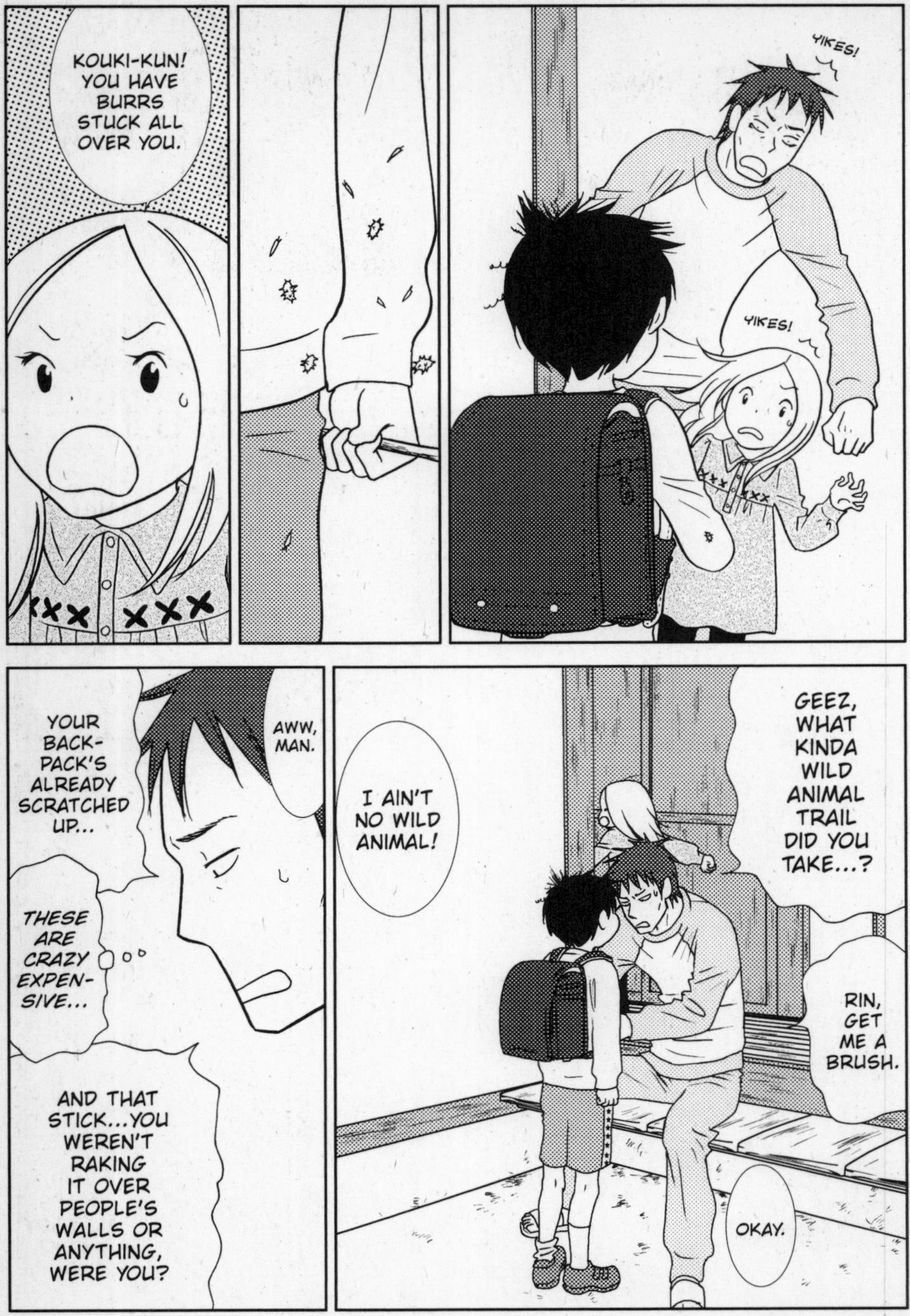
YIKES!
YIKES!
KOUKI-KUN! YOU HAVE BURRS STUCK ALL OVER YOU.
GEEZ, WHAT KINDA WILD ANIMAL TRAIL DID YOU TAKE...?
I AIN'T NO WILD ANIMAL!
RIN, GET ME A BRUSH.
OKAY.
AWW, MAN.
YOUR BACKPACK'S ALREADY SCRATCHED UP...
THESE ARE CRAZY EXPENSIVE...
AND THAT STICK...YOU WEREN'T RAKING IT OVER PEOPLE'S WALLS OR ANYTHING, WERE YOU?

SFX: GARI (RATTLE) GARI

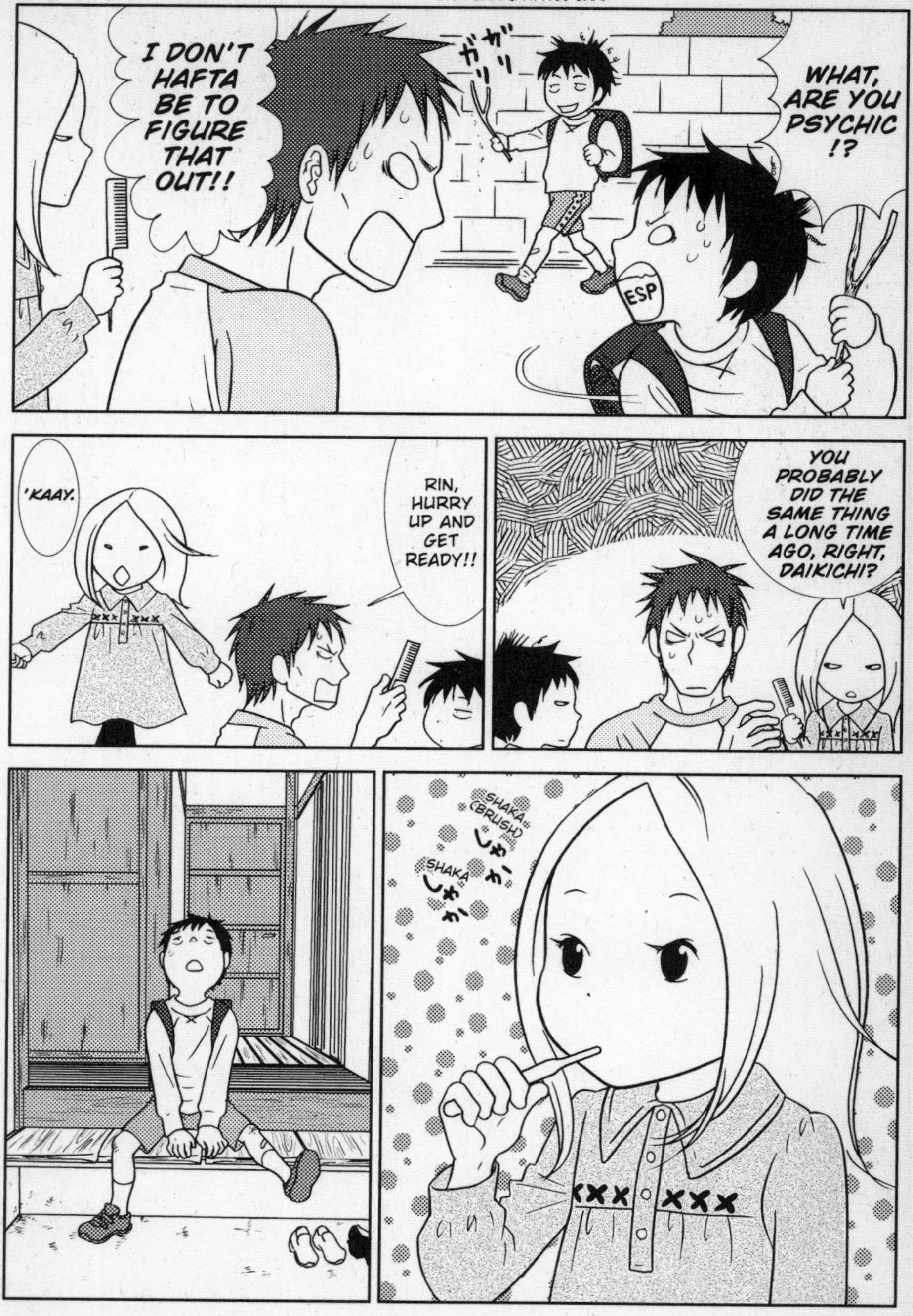
WHAT, ARE YOU PSYCHIC !?
ESP
I DON'T HAFTA BE TO FIGURE THAT OUT!!
YOU PROBABLY DID THE SAME THING A LONG TIME AGO, RIGHT, DAIKICHI?
RIN, HURRY UP AND GET READY!!
'KAAY.
SHAKA (BRUSH)
SHAKA

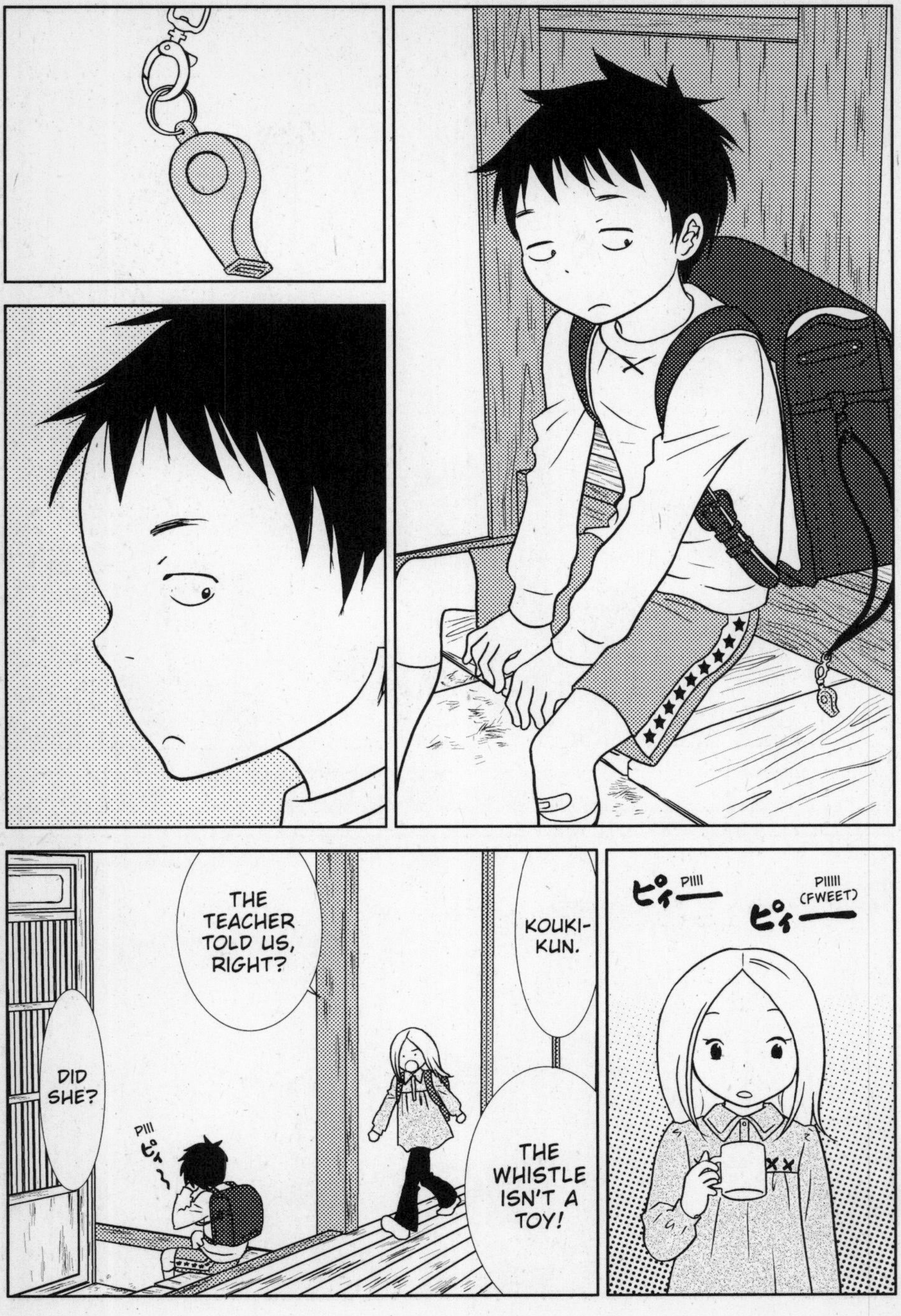
ピィー PIIIII (FWEET)
ピィー PIIII
KOUKI-KUN.
THE WHISTLE ISN'T A TOY!
THE TEACHER TOLD US, RIGHT?
DID SHE?
ピィ～ PIII

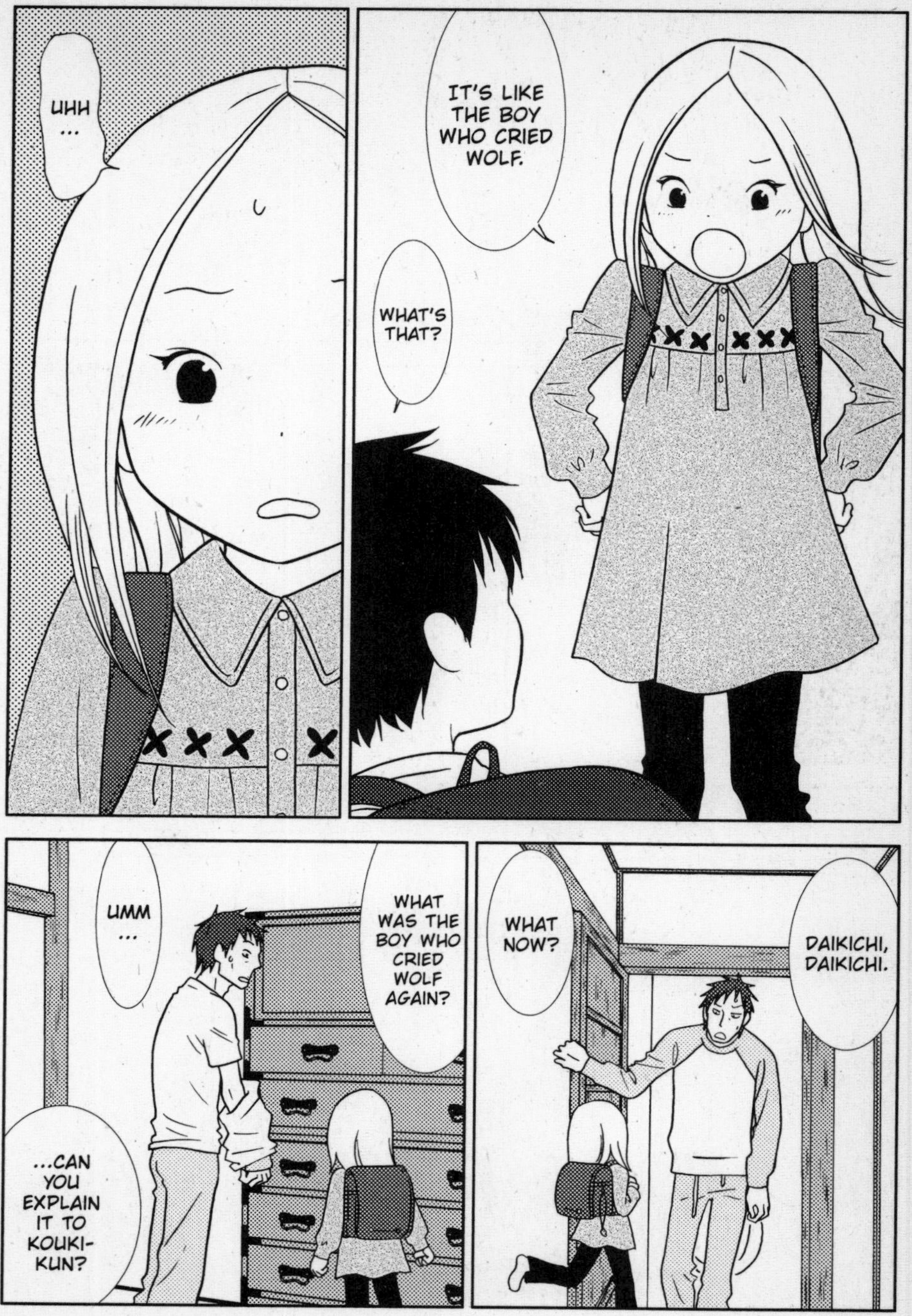
IT'S LIKE THE BOY WHO CRIED WOLF.
WHAT'S THAT?
UHH ...
DAIKICHI, DAIKICHI.
WHAT NOW?
WHAT WAS THE BOY WHO CRIED WOLF AGAIN?
UMM ...
...CAN YOU EXPLAIN IT TO KOUKI-KUN?

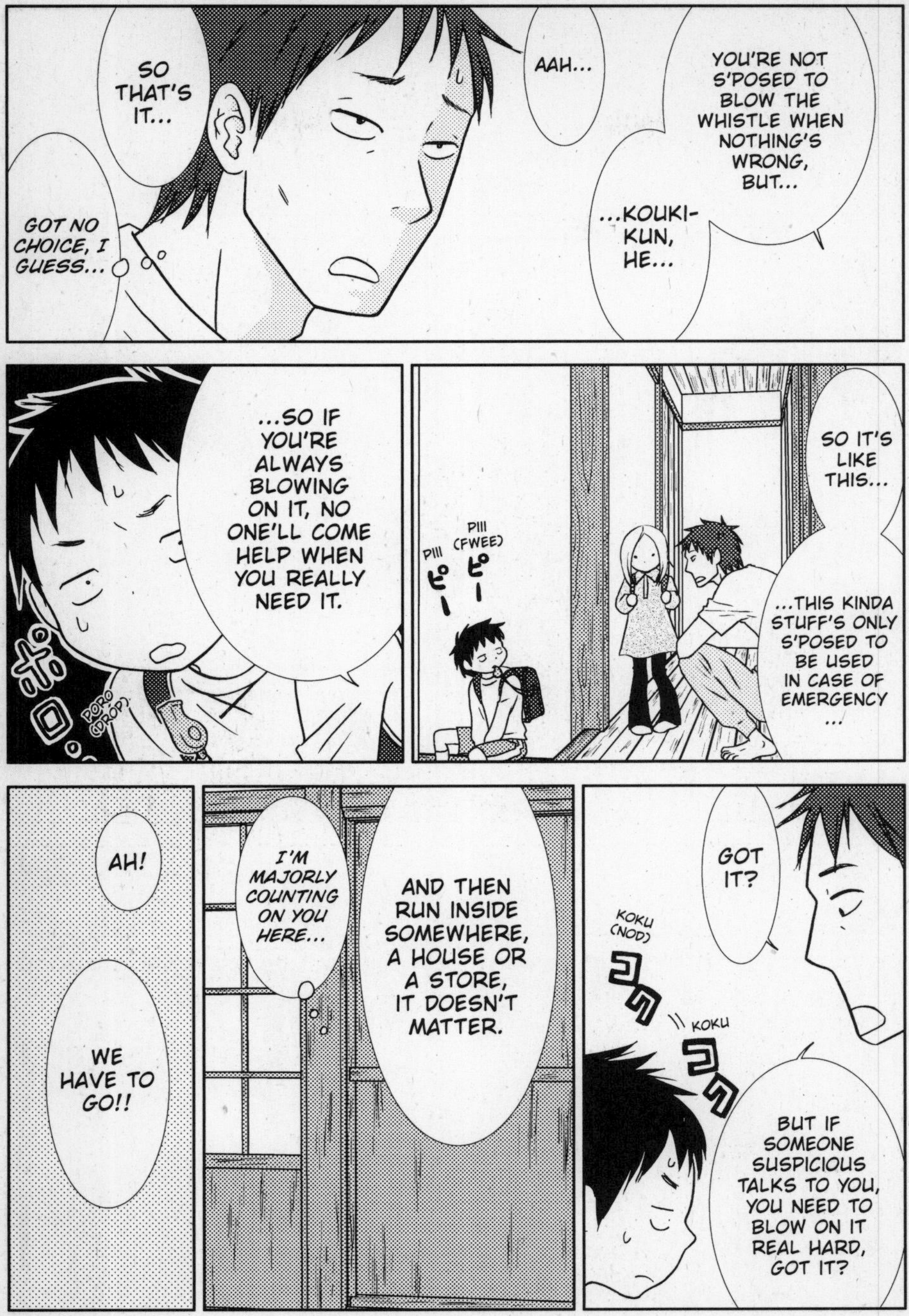
YOU'RE NOT S'POSED TO BLOW THE WHISTLE WHEN NOTHING'S WRONG, BUT...
AAH...
SO THAT'S IT...
...KOUKI-KUN, HE...
GOT NO CHOICE, I GUESS...
SO IT'S LIKE THIS...
...THIS KINDA STUFF'S ONLY S'POSED TO BE USED IN CASE OF EMERGENCY...
PIII (FWEE)
ピー
PIII
ピー
...SO IF YOU'RE ALWAYS BLOWING ON IT, NO ONE'LL COME HELP WHEN YOU REALLY NEED IT.
ポロ
PORO (DROP)
GOT IT?
KOKU (NOD)
コク
KOKU
コク
BUT IF SOMEONE SUSPICIOUS TALKS TO YOU, YOU NEED TO BLOW ON IT REAL HARD, GOT IT?
AND THEN RUN INSIDE SOMEWHERE, A HOUSE OR A STORE, IT DOESN'T MATTER.
I'M MAJORLY COUNTING ON YOU HERE...
AH!
WE HAVE TO GO!!

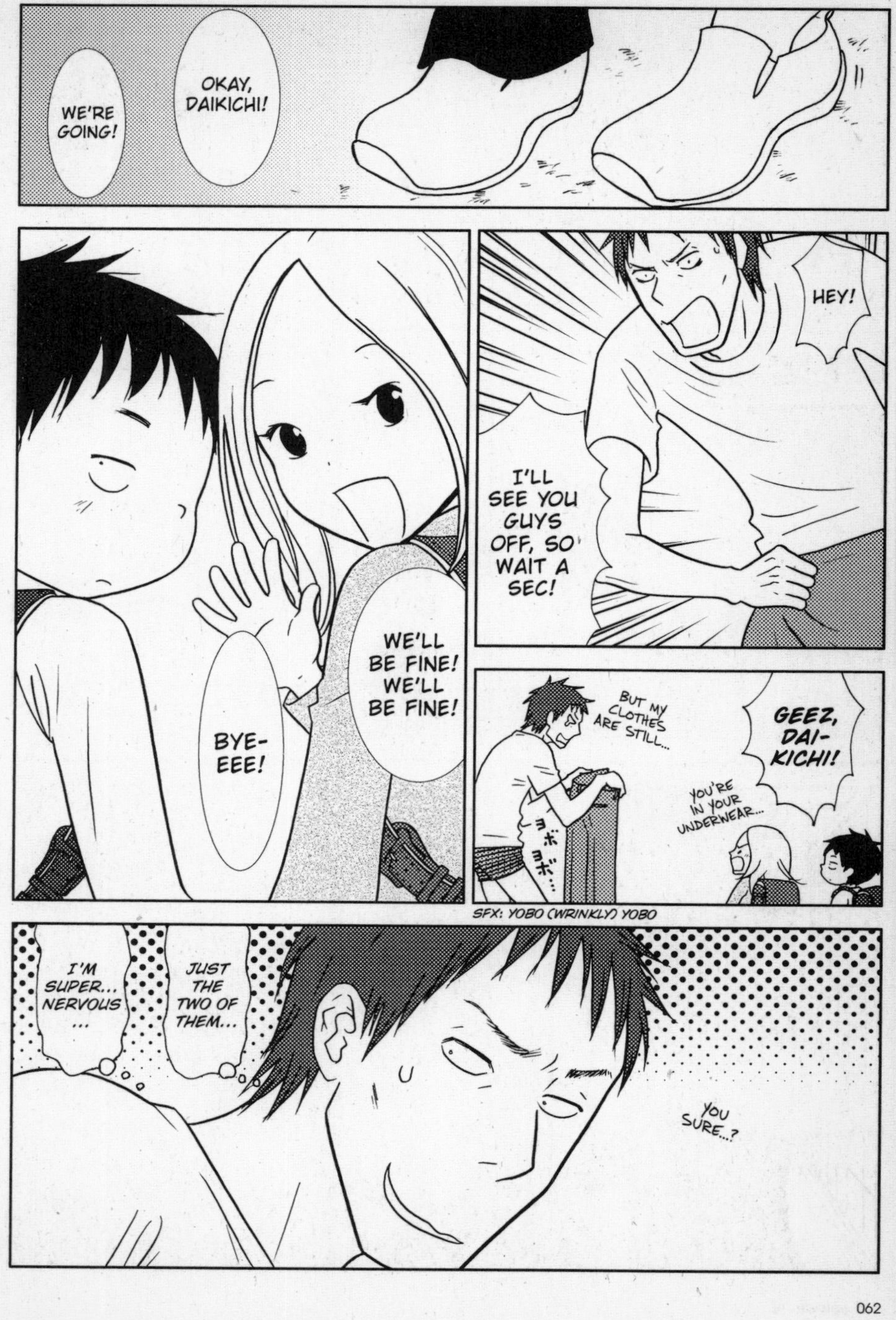
OKAY, DAIKICHI!
WE'RE GOING!
HEY!
I'LL SEE YOU GUYS OFF, SO WAIT A SEC!
GEEZ, DAI-KICHI!
BUT MY CLOTHES ARE STILL...
YOU'RE IN YOUR UNDERWEAR...
ヨボヨボ...
WE'LL BE FINE! WE'LL BE FINE!
BYE-EEE!
SFX: YOBO (WRINKLY) YOBO
JUST THE TWO OF THEM...
I'M SUPER... NERVOUS...
YOU SURE...?

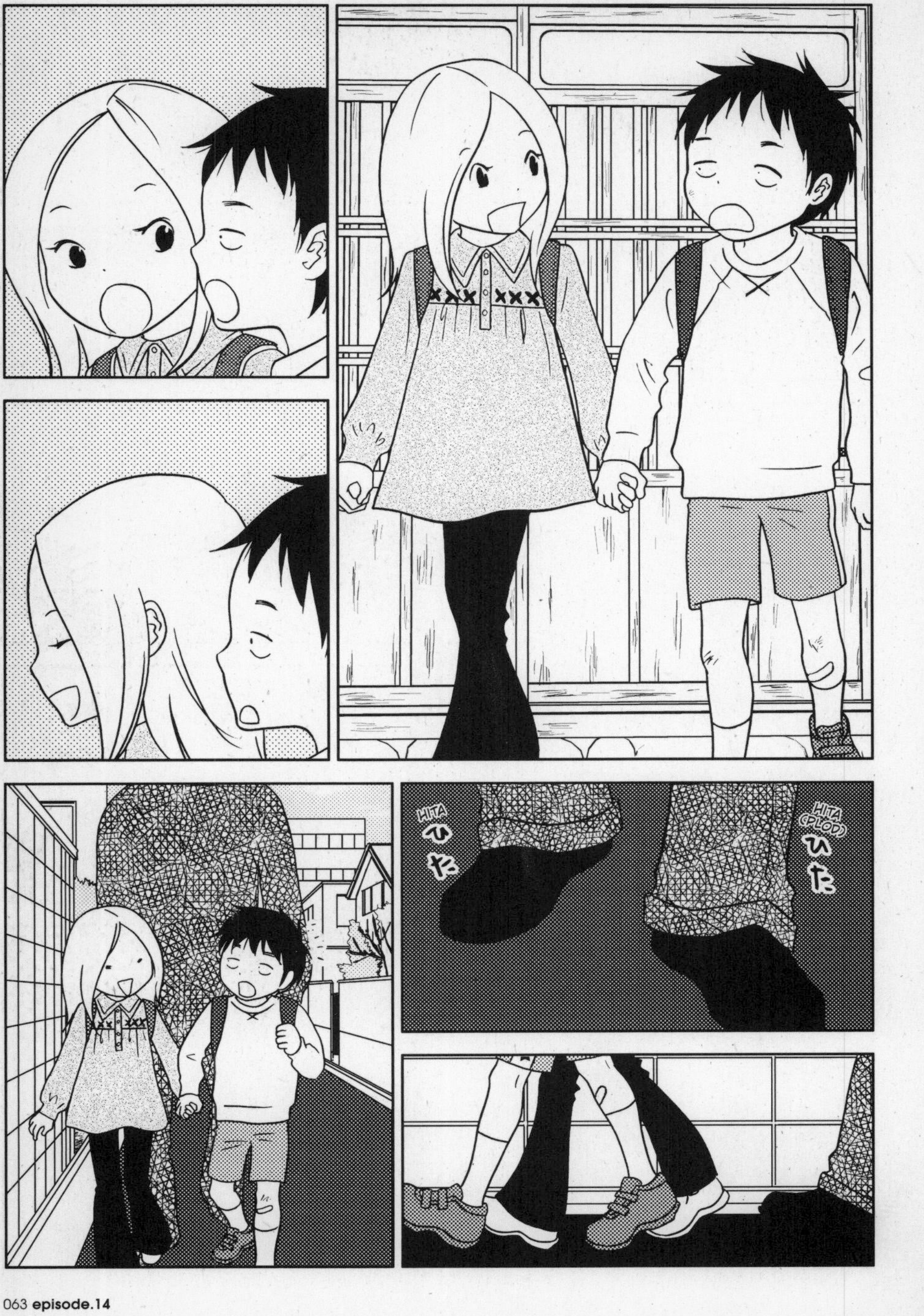
HITA (PLOD)
ひた
HITA
ひた

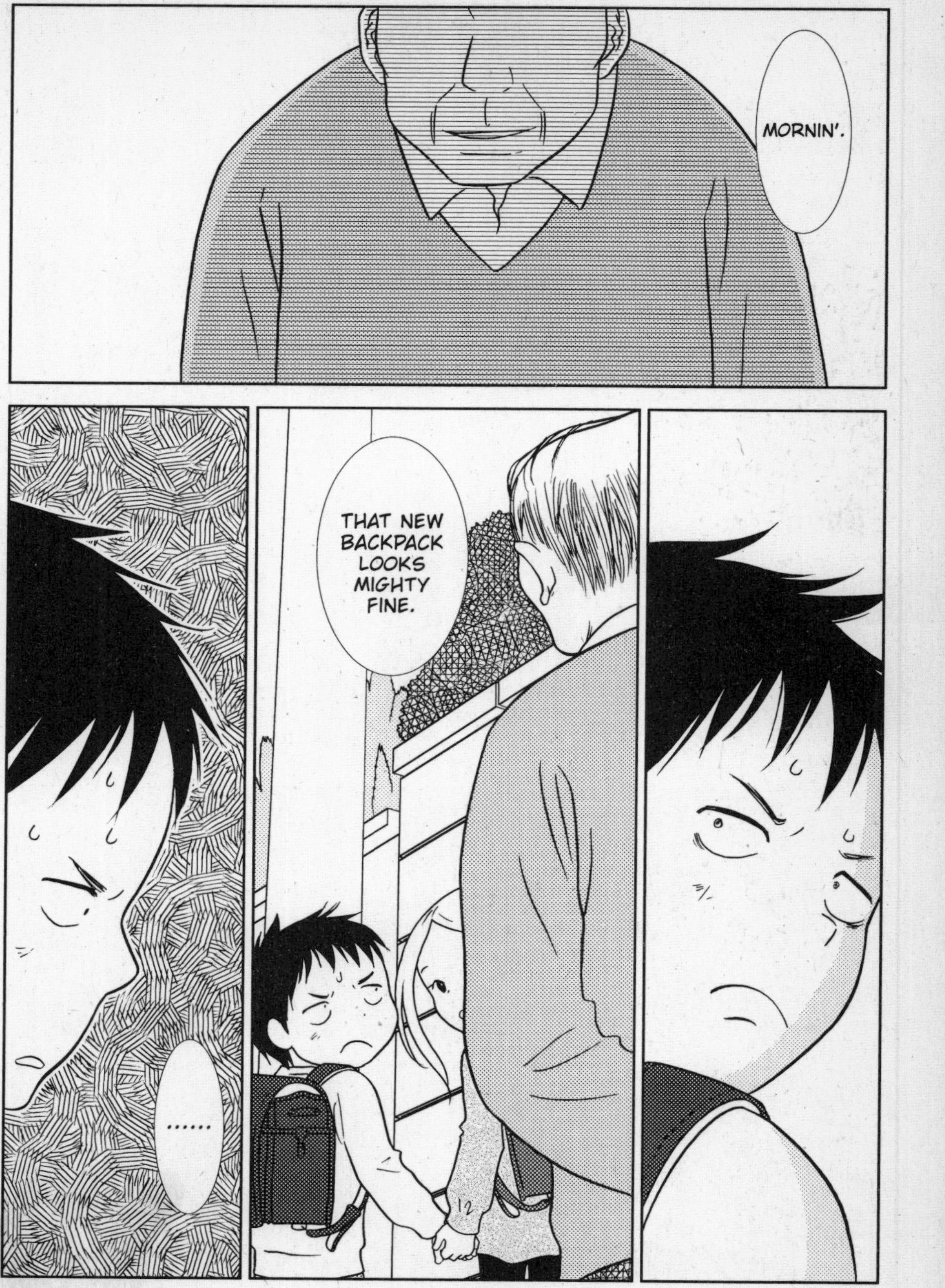
MORNIN'.
THAT NEW BACKPACK LOOKS MIGHTY FINE.
......

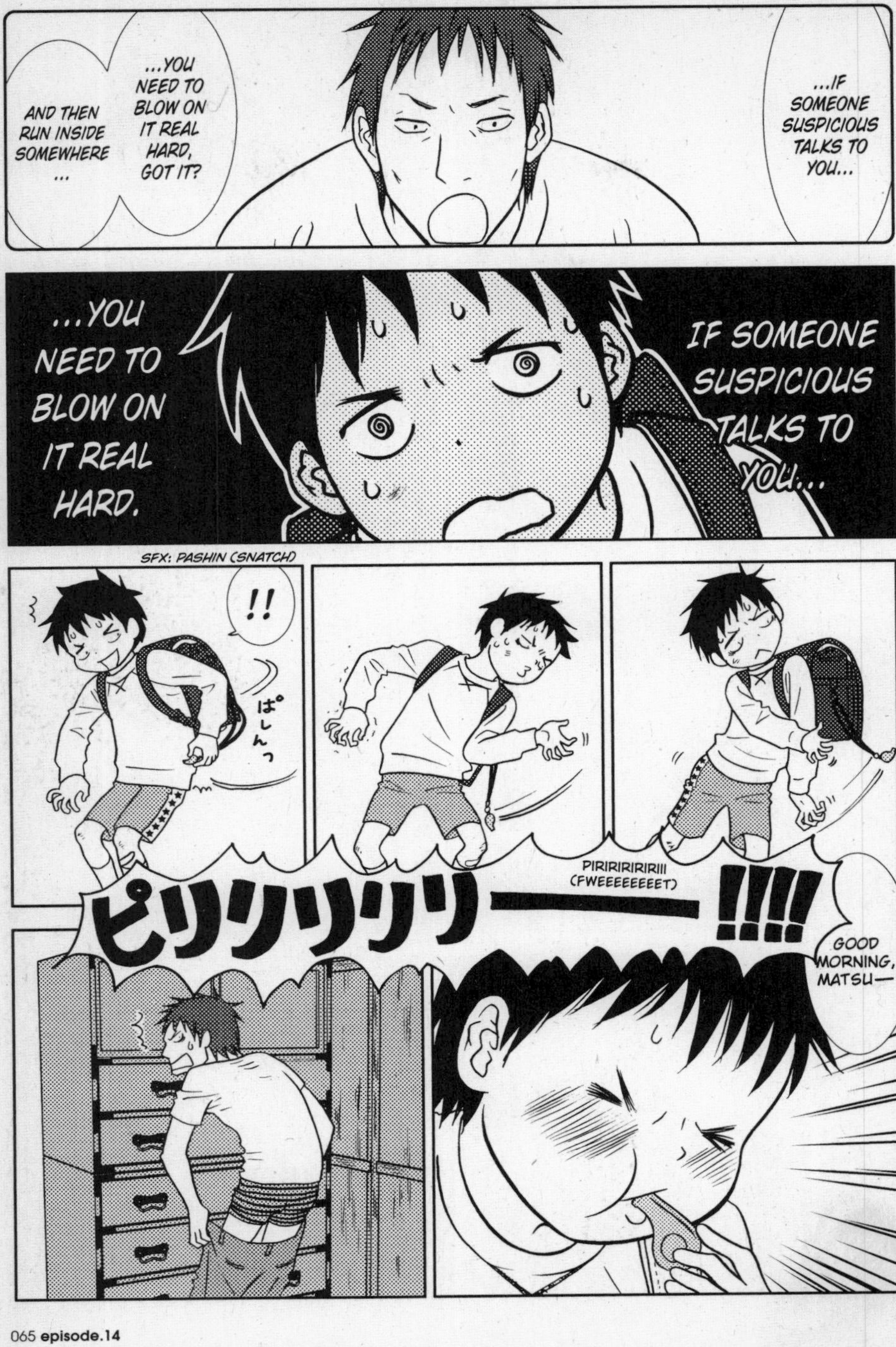
...IF SOMEONE SUSPICIOUS TALKS TO YOU...
...YOU NEED TO BLOW ON IT REAL HARD, GOT IT?
AND THEN RUN INSIDE SOMEWHERE ...
IF SOMEONE SUSPICIOUS TALKS TO YOU...
...YOU NEED TO BLOW ON IT REAL HARD.
!!
ぱしんっ
SFX: PASHIN (SNATCH)
ピリリリリリー!!!!
PIRIRIRIRIRIII (FWEEEEEEEET)
GOOD MORNING, MATSU—

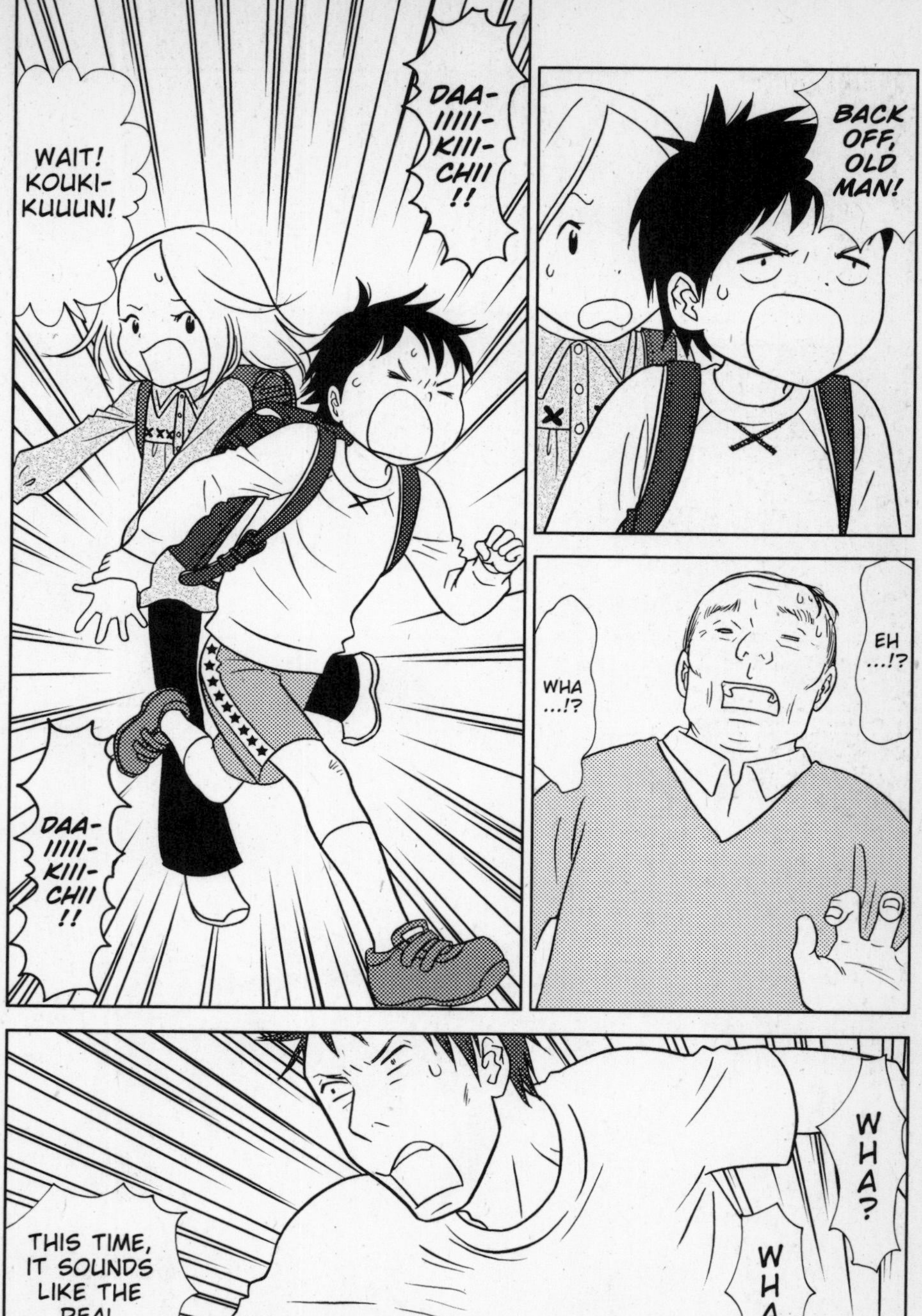
BACK OFF, OLD MAN!
EH ...!?
WHA ...!?
DAA-IIIII-KIII-CHII!!
WAIT! KOUKI-KUUUN!
DAA-IIIII-KIII-CHII!!
WHA?
WHA?
THIS TIME, IT SOUNDS LIKE THE REAL THING!

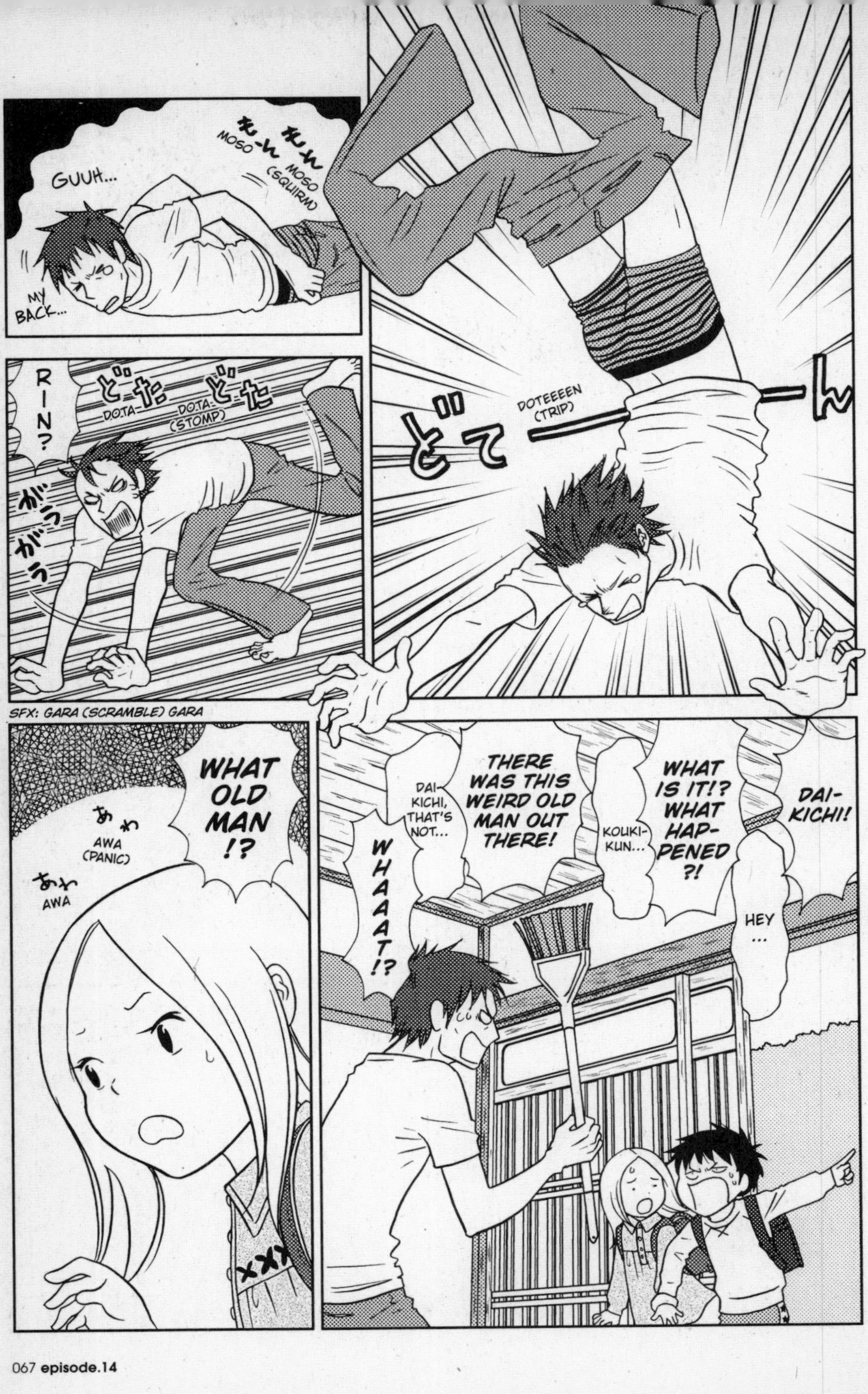
どて――――ん
DOTEEEEN (TRIP)
GUUH...
MY BACK...
もそ もそ
MOSO MOSO (SQUIRM)
RIN?
どた どた
DOTA DOTA (STOMP)
がら がら
SFX: GARA (SCRAMBLE) GARA
DAI-KICHI!
HEY ...
WHAT IS IT!? WHAT HAP-PENED?!
KOUKI-KUN...
THERE WAS THIS WEIRD OLD MAN OUT THERE!
DAI-KICHI, THAT'S NOT...
WHAAAAT!?
WHAT OLD MAN!?
あわ
AWA (PANIC)
あわ
AWA

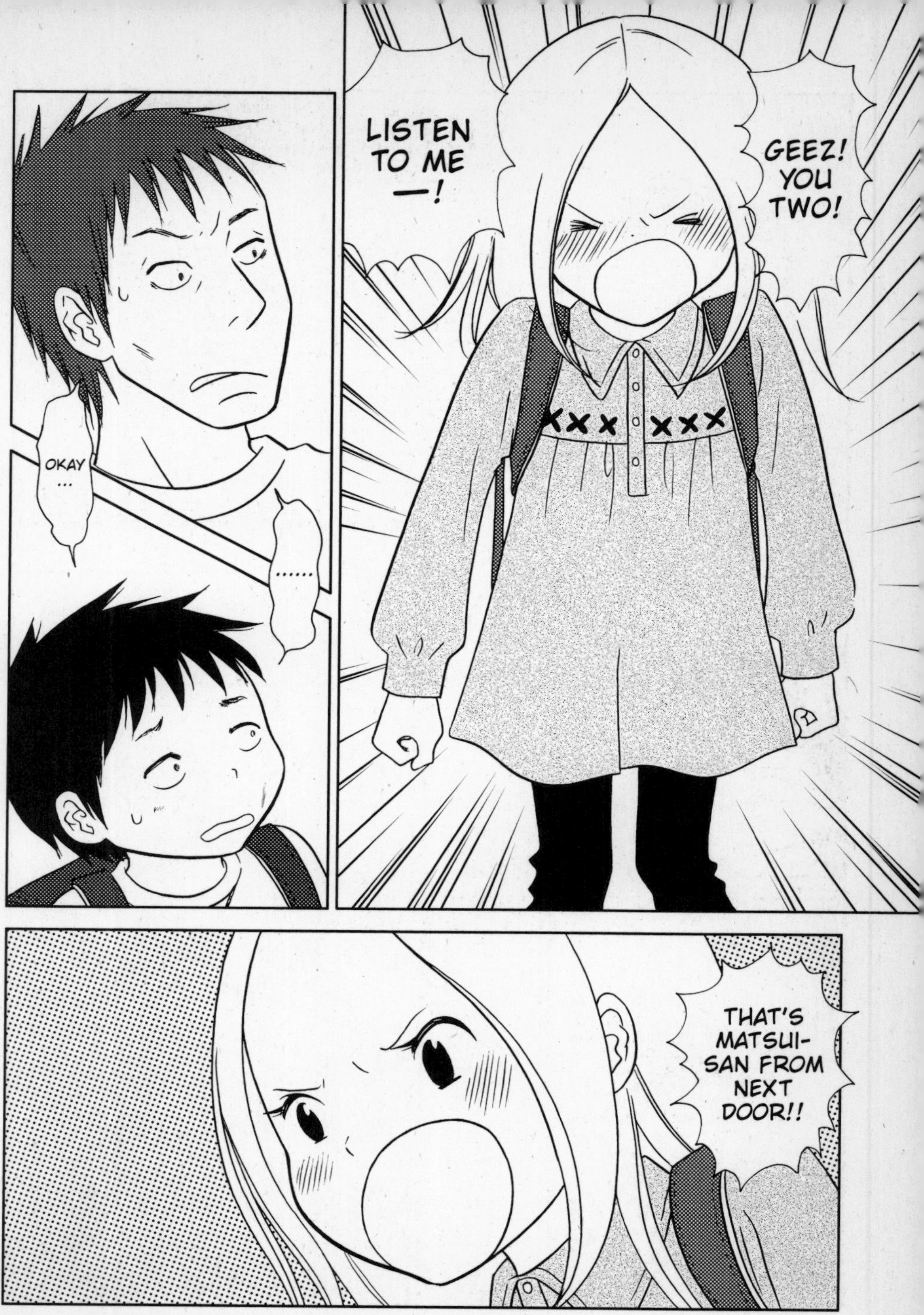
GEEZ! YOU TWO!
LISTEN TO ME —!
OKAY ...
......
THAT'S MATSUI-SAN FROM NEXT DOOR!!

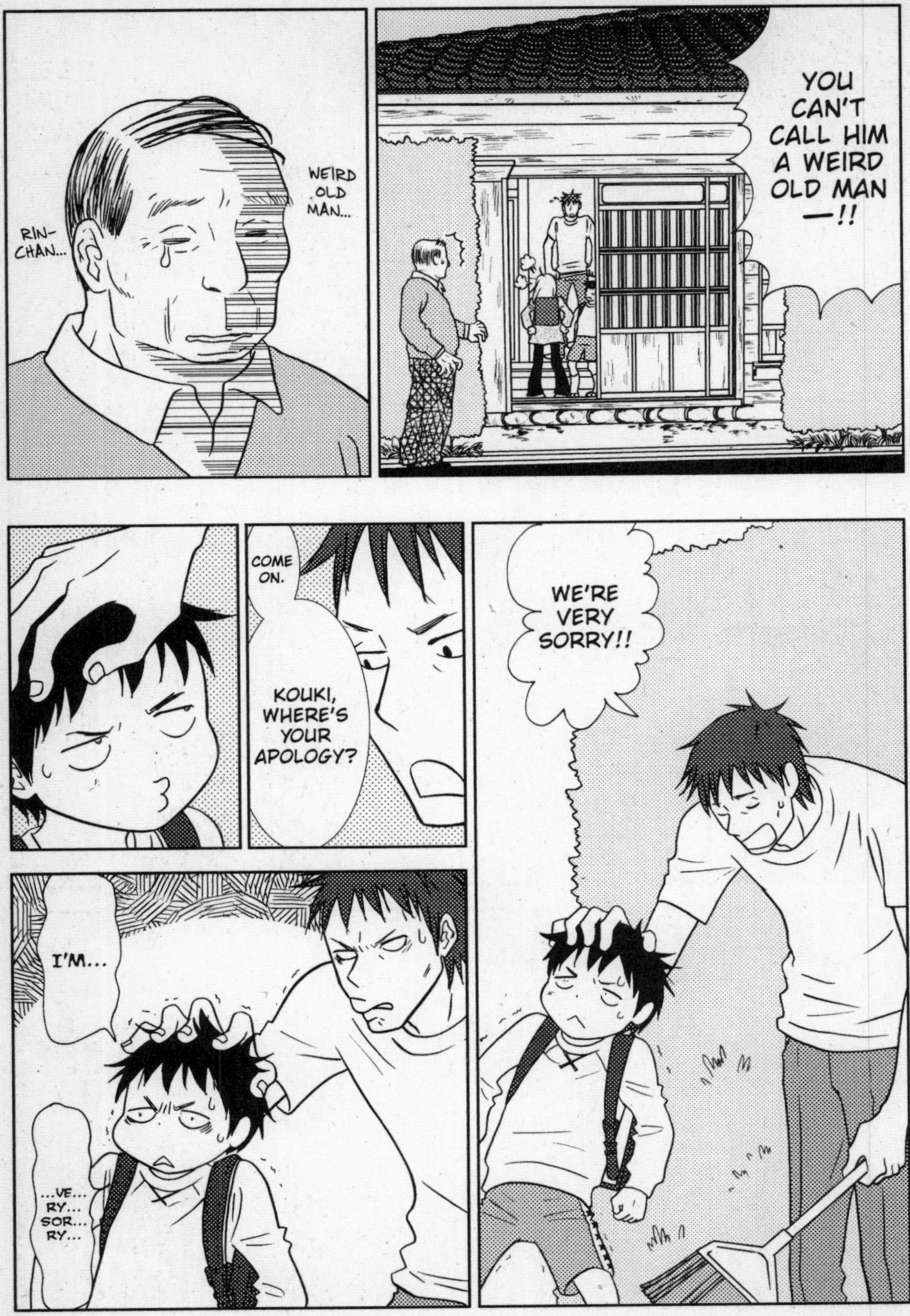
YOU CAN'T CALL HIM A WEIRD OLD MAN—!!
WEIRD OLD MAN...
RIN-CHAN...
WE'RE VERY SORRY!!
COME ON.
KOUKI, WHERE'S YOUR APOLOGY?
I'M...
...VE... RY... SOR... RY...

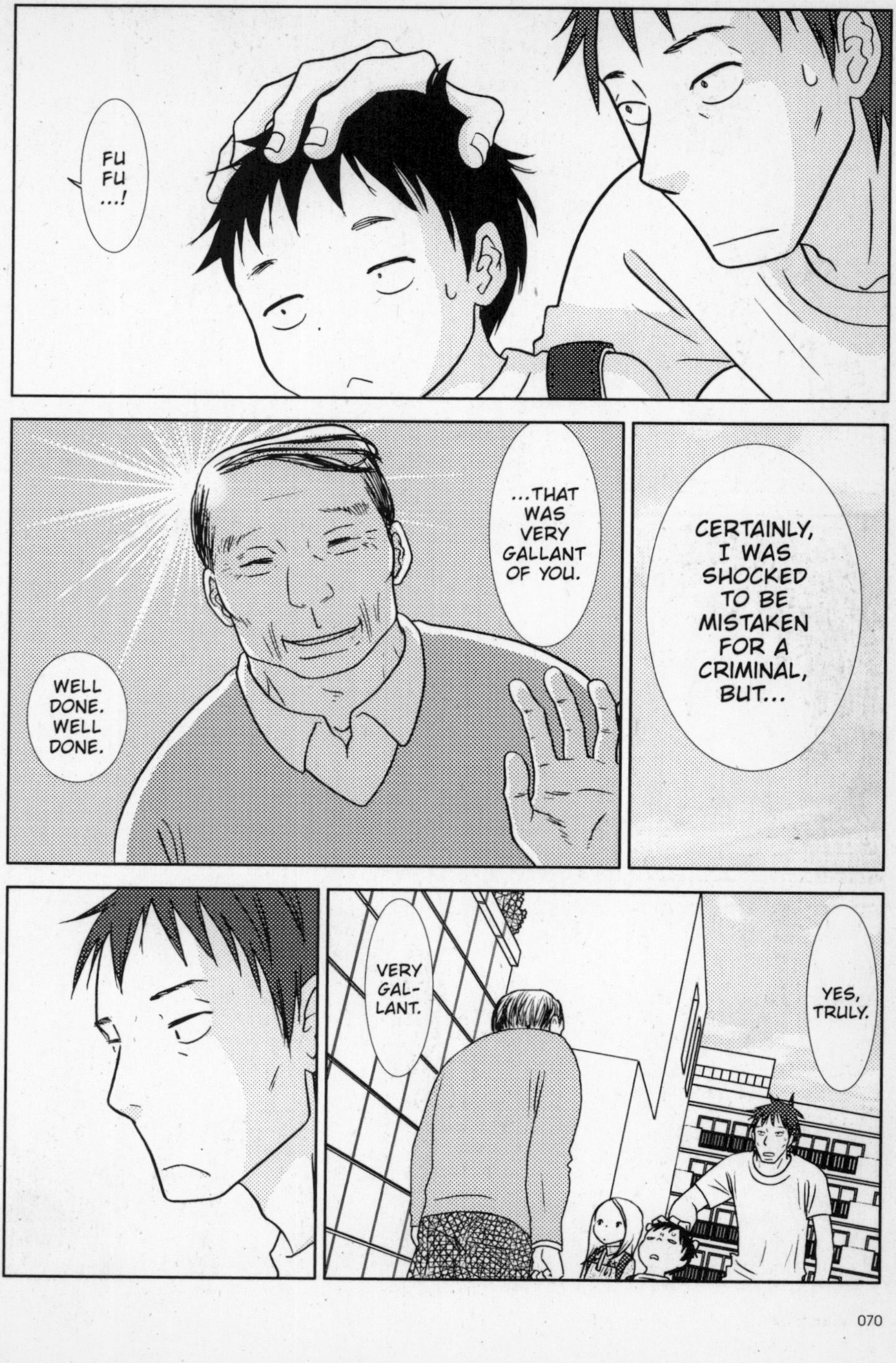
FU FU ...!
CERTAINLY, I WAS SHOCKED TO BE MISTAKEN FOR A CRIMINAL, BUT...
...THAT WAS VERY GALLANT OF YOU.
WELL DONE. WELL DONE.
YES, TRULY.
VERY GAL-LANT.

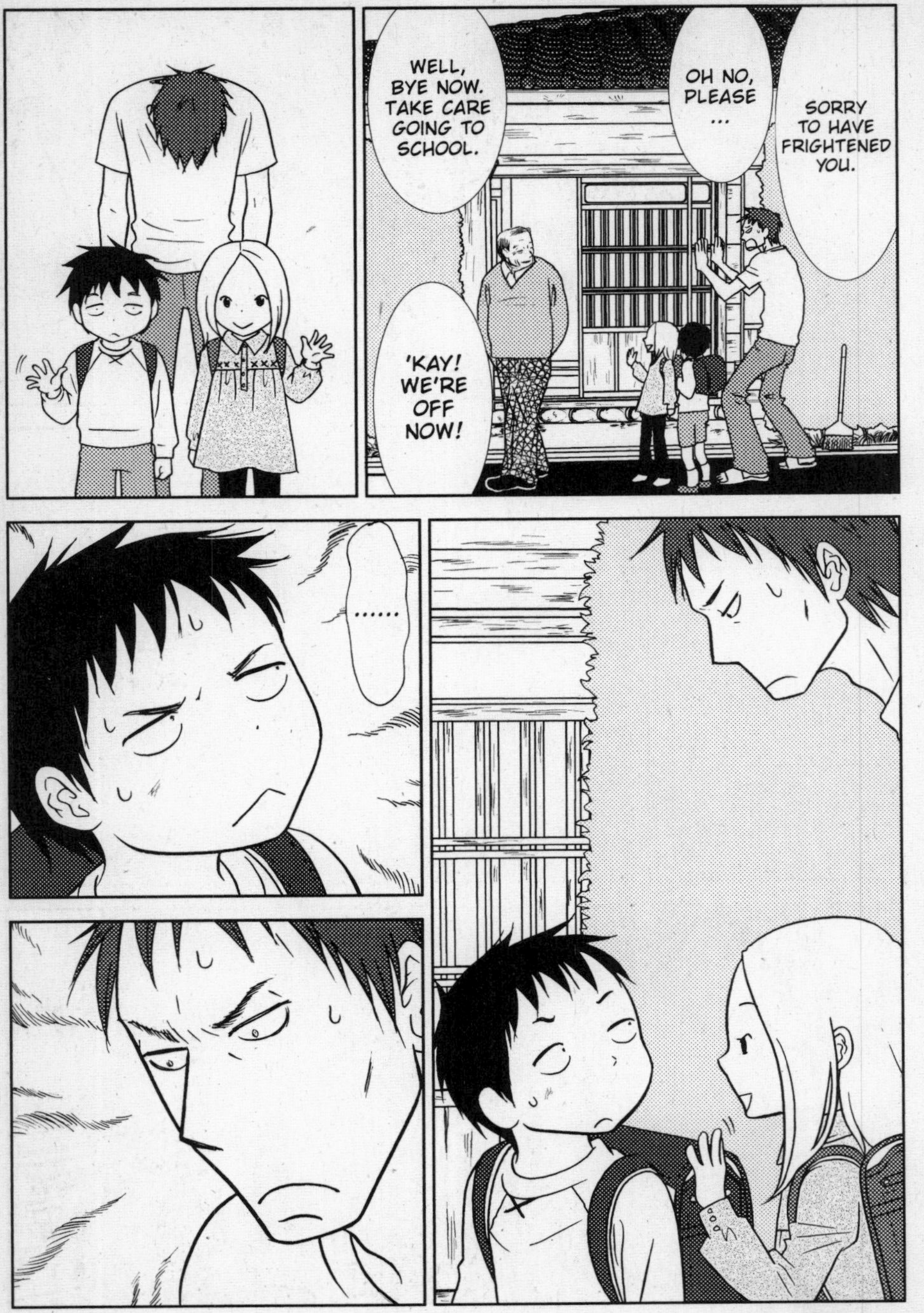
SORRY TO HAVE FRIGHTENED YOU.
OH NO, PLEASE ...
WELL, BYE NOW. TAKE CARE GOING TO SCHOOL.
'KAY! WE'RE OFF NOW!
......

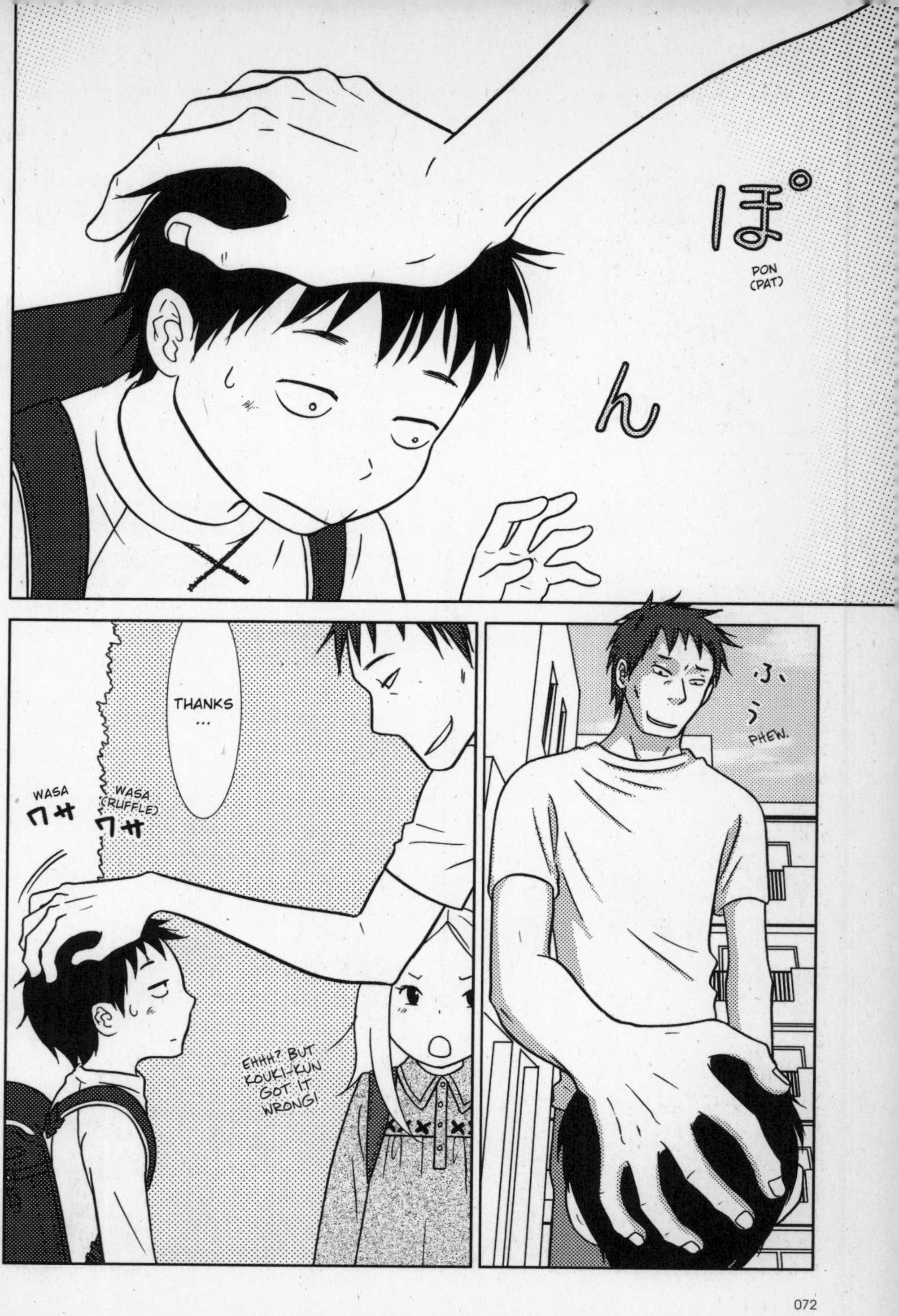
ぽん
PON (PAT)
ふぅ
PHEW.
THANKS ...
ワサ
WASA (RUFFLE)
ワサ
WASA
EHHH? BUT KOUKI-KUN GOT IT WRONG!

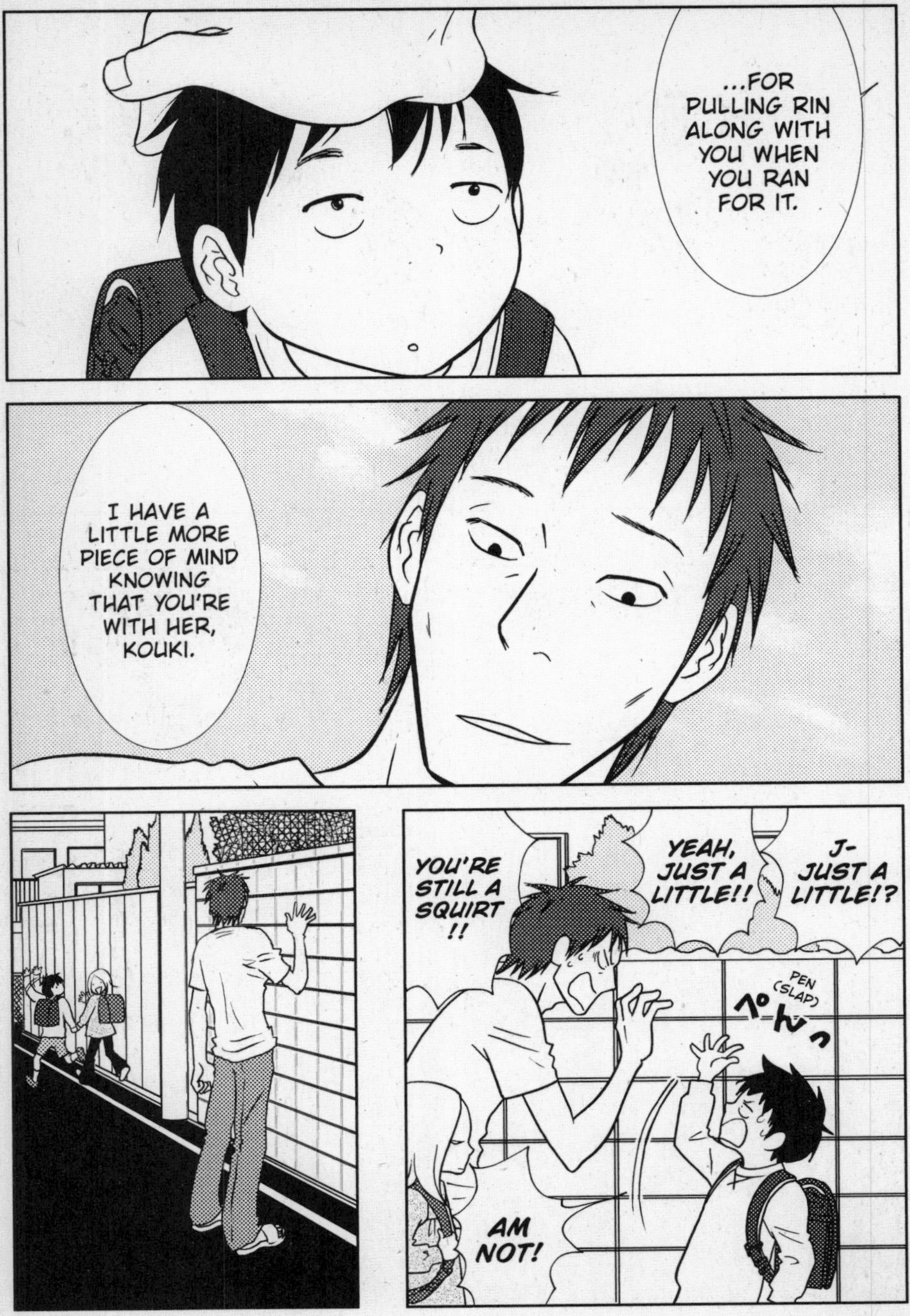
...FOR PULLING RIN ALONG WITH YOU WHEN YOU RAN FOR IT.
I HAVE A LITTLE MORE PIECE OF MIND KNOWING THAT YOU'RE WITH HER, KOUKI.
J- JUST A LITTLE!?
YEAH, JUST A LITTLE!!
YOU'RE STILL A SQUIRT !!
ぺんっ
PEN (SLAP)
AM NOT!

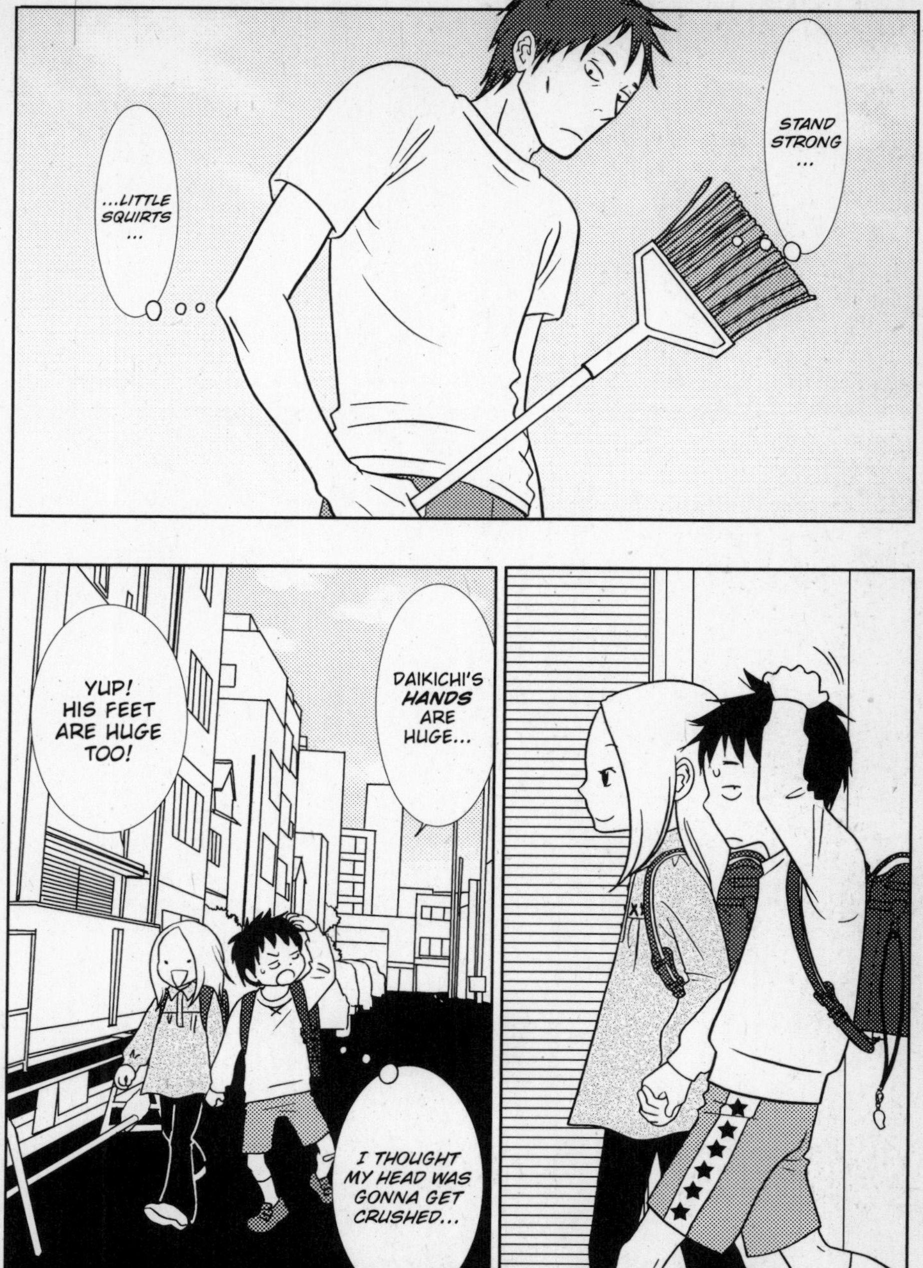
STAND STRONG ...
...LITTLE SQUIRTS ...
DAIKICHI'S *HANDS* ARE HUGE...
YUP! HIS FEET ARE HUGE TOO!
I THOUGHT MY HEAD WAS GONNA GET CRUSHED...

episode.15
BUNNY**DROP**

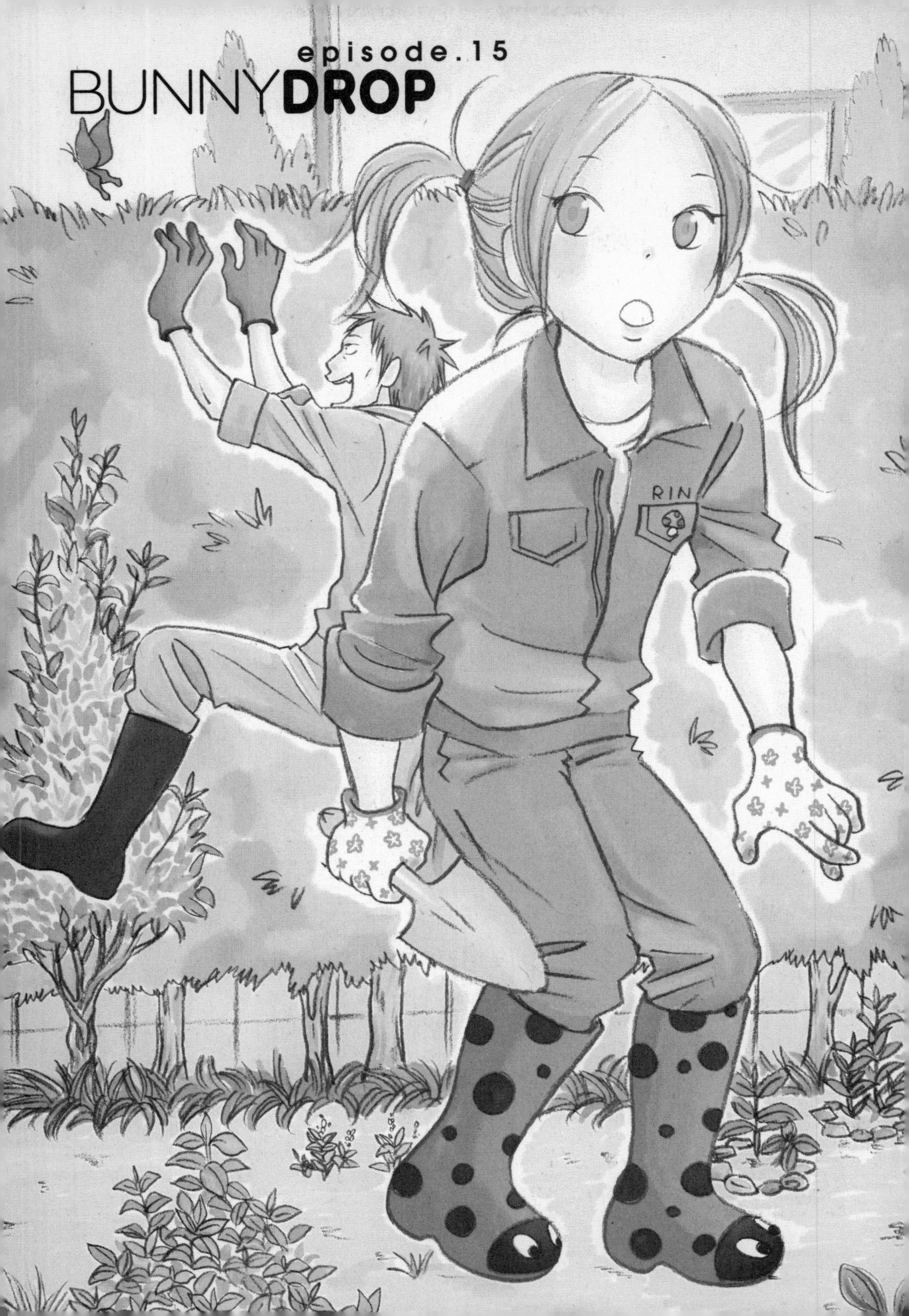
RIN

BUNNY**DROP**

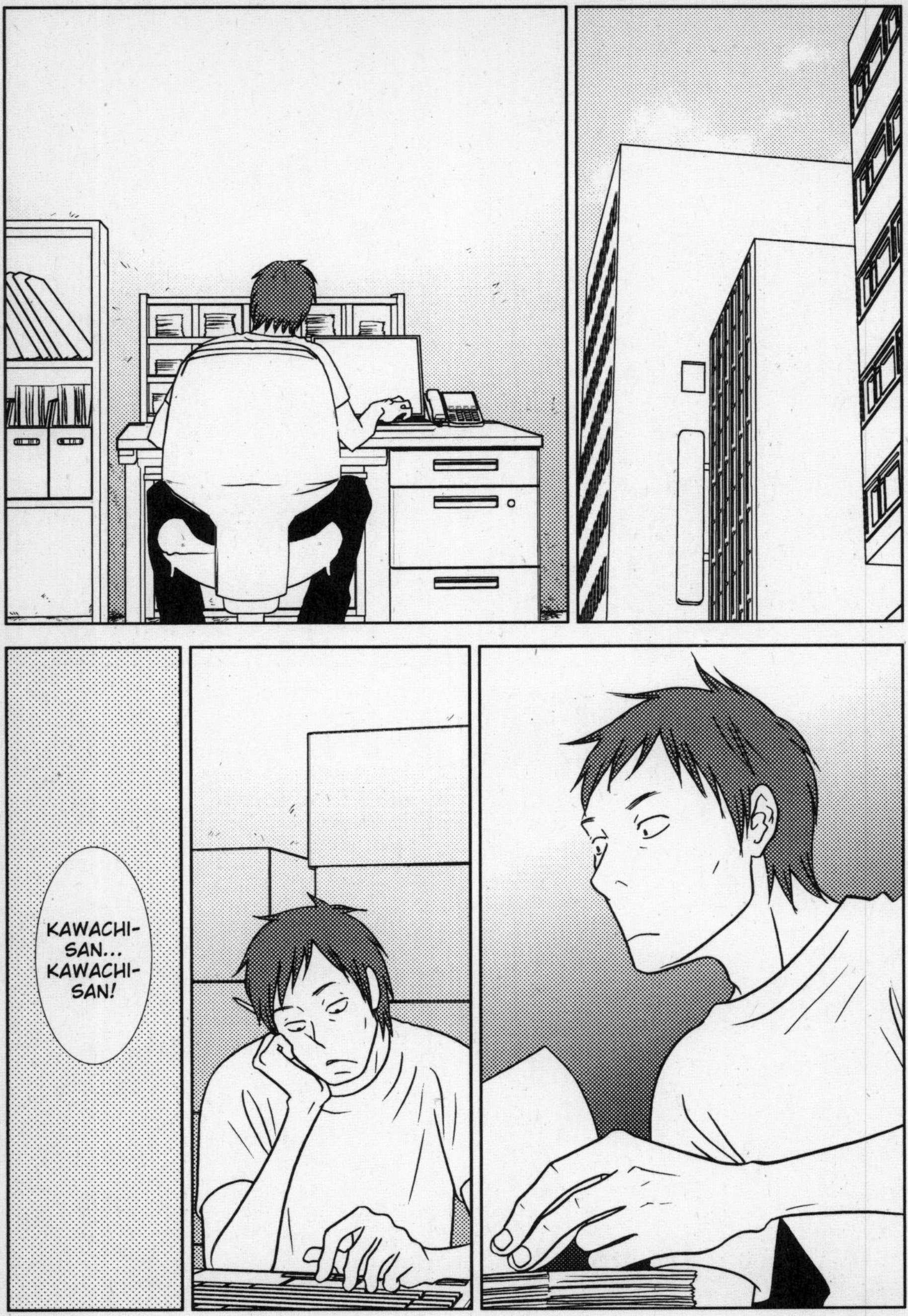
KAWACHI-SAN... KAWACHI-SAN!

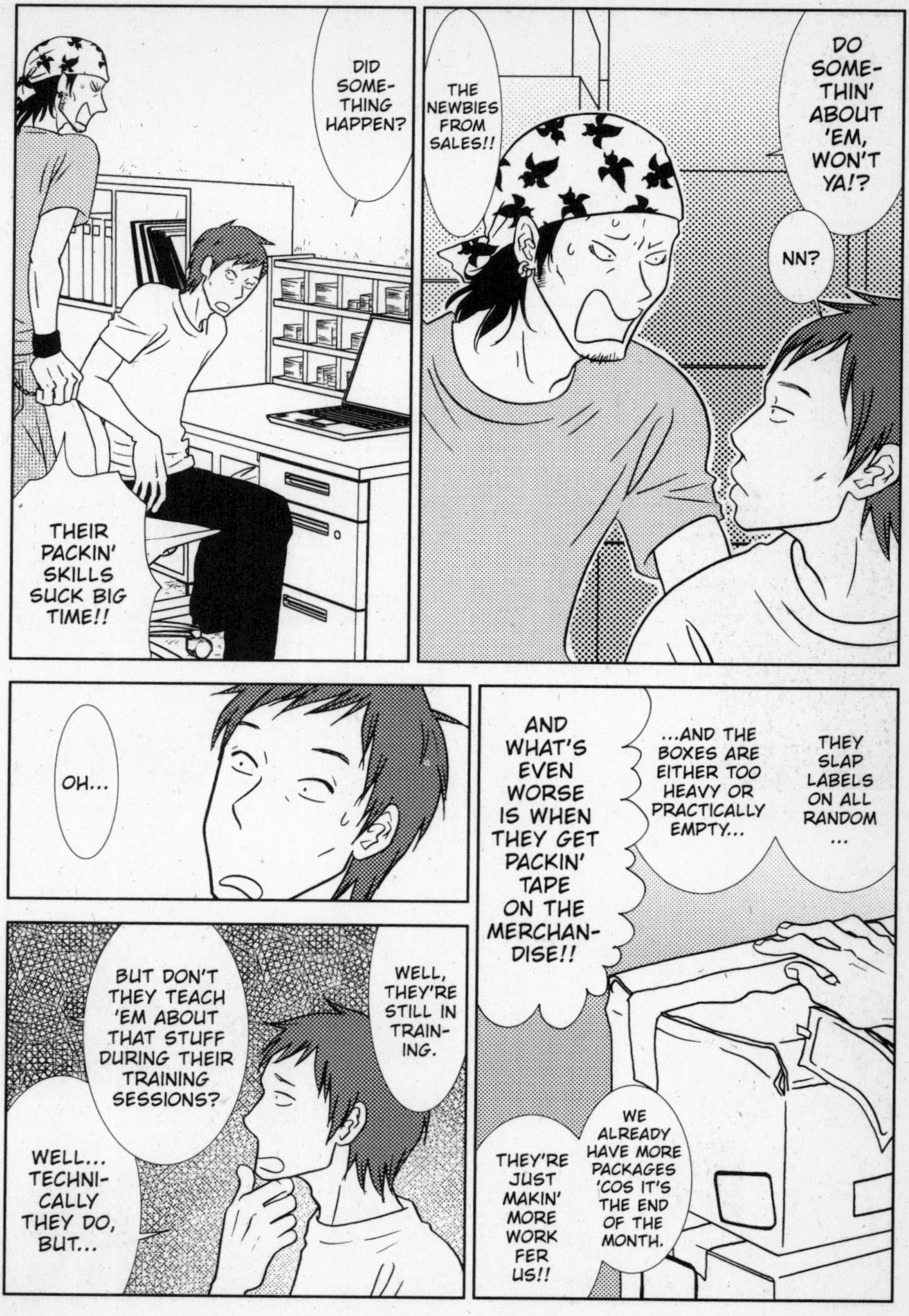
DO SOME-THIN' ABOUT 'EM, WON'T YA!?
NN?
THE NEWBIES FROM SALES!!
DID SOME-THING HAPPEN?
THEIR PACKIN' SKILLS SUCK BIG TIME!!
THEY SLAP LABELS ON ALL RANDOM ...
...AND THE BOXES ARE EITHER TOO HEAVY OR PRACTICALLY EMPTY...
AND WHAT'S EVEN WORSE IS WHEN THEY GET PACKIN' TAPE ON THE MERCHAN-DISE!!
WE ALREADY HAVE MORE PACKAGES 'COS IT'S THE END OF THE MONTH.
THEY'RE JUST MAKIN' MORE WORK FER US!!
OH...
WELL, THEY'RE STILL IN TRAIN-ING.
BUT DON'T THEY TEACH 'EM ABOUT THAT STUFF DURING THEIR TRAINING SESSIONS?
WELL... TECHNI-CALLY THEY DO, BUT...

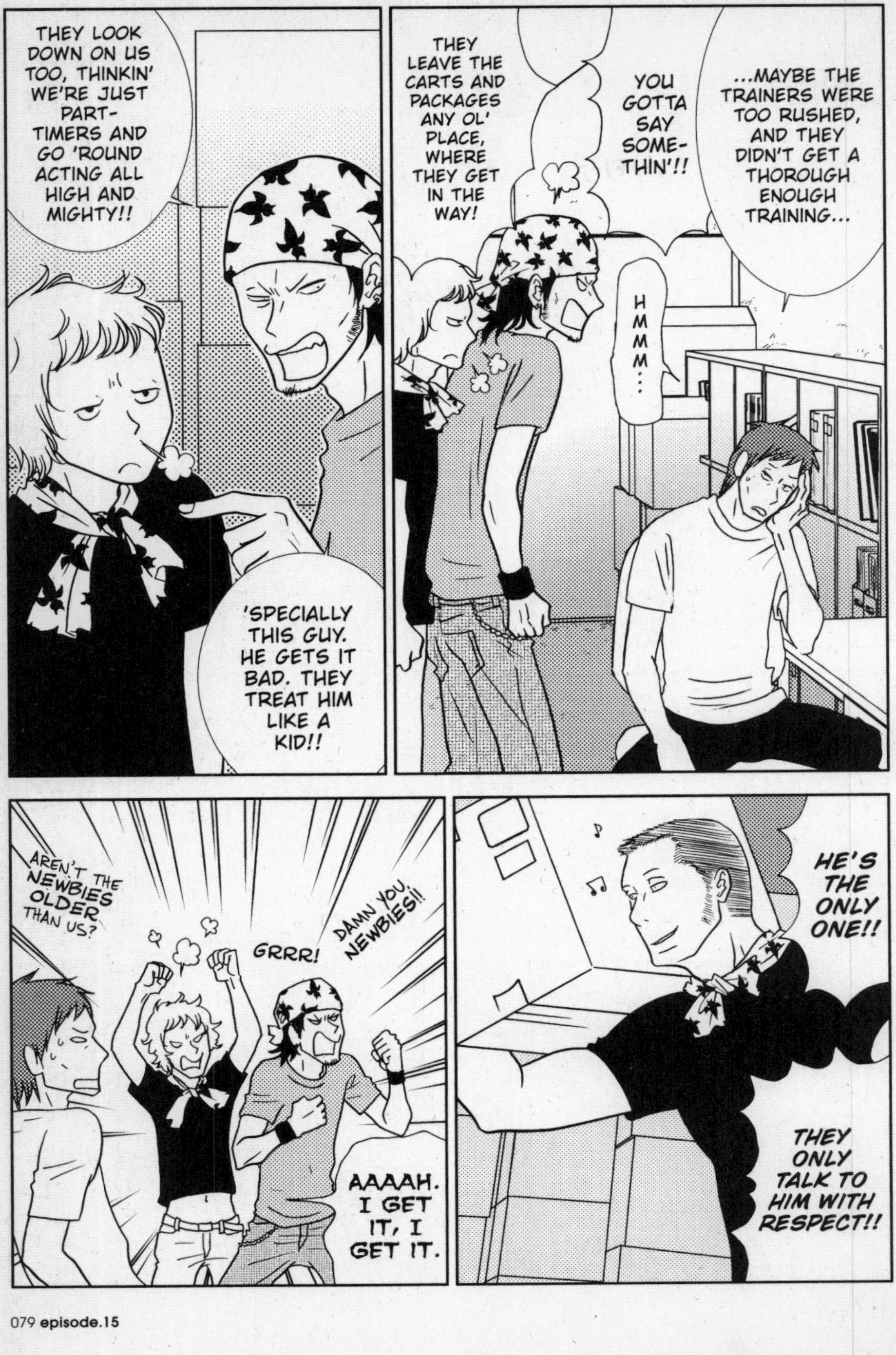
...MAYBE THE TRAINERS WERE TOO RUSHED, AND THEY DIDN'T GET A THOROUGH ENOUGH TRAINING...
YOU GOTTA SAY SOME-THIN'!!
THEY LEAVE THE CARTS AND PACKAGES ANY OL' PLACE, WHERE THEY GET IN THE WAY!
HMMM...
THEY LOOK DOWN ON US TOO, THINKIN' WE'RE JUST PART-TIMERS AND GO 'ROUND ACTING ALL HIGH AND MIGHTY!!
'SPECIALLY THIS GUY. HE GETS IT BAD. THEY TREAT HIM LIKE A KID!!
HE'S THE ONLY ONE!!
THEY ONLY TALK TO HIM WITH RESPECT!!
DAMN YOU, NEWBIES!!
GRRR!
AREN'T THE NEWBIES OLDER THAN US?
AAAAH. I GET IT, I GET IT.

SIGN: SECTION ONE / DEPARTMENT HEAD OFFICE

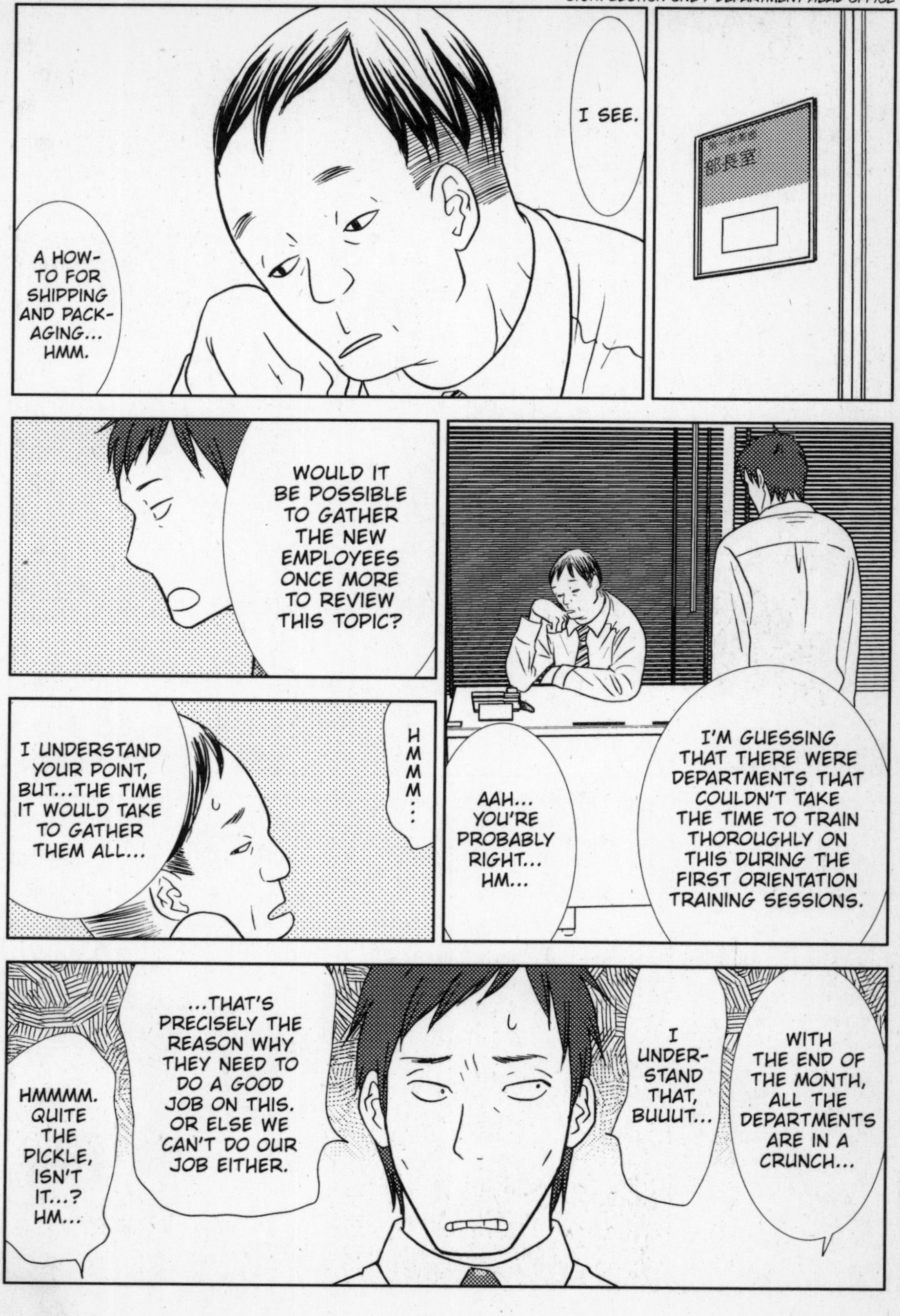

I SEE.
A HOW-TO FOR SHIPPING AND PACKAGING... HMM.
I'M GUESSING THAT THERE WERE DEPARTMENTS THAT COULDN'T TAKE THE TIME TO TRAIN THOROUGHLY ON THIS DURING THE FIRST ORIENTATION TRAINING SESSIONS.
AAH... YOU'RE PROBABLY RIGHT... HM...
WOULD IT BE POSSIBLE TO GATHER THE NEW EMPLOYEES ONCE MORE TO REVIEW THIS TOPIC?
HMMM...
I UNDERSTAND YOUR POINT, BUT...THE TIME IT WOULD TAKE TO GATHER THEM ALL...
WITH THE END OF THE MONTH, ALL THE DEPARTMENTS ARE IN A CRUNCH...
I UNDERSTAND THAT, BUUUT...
...THAT'S PRECISELY THE REASON WHY THEY NEED TO DO A GOOD JOB ON THIS. OR ELSE WE CAN'T DO OUR JOB EITHER.
HMMMM. QUITE THE PICKLE, ISN'T IT...? HM...

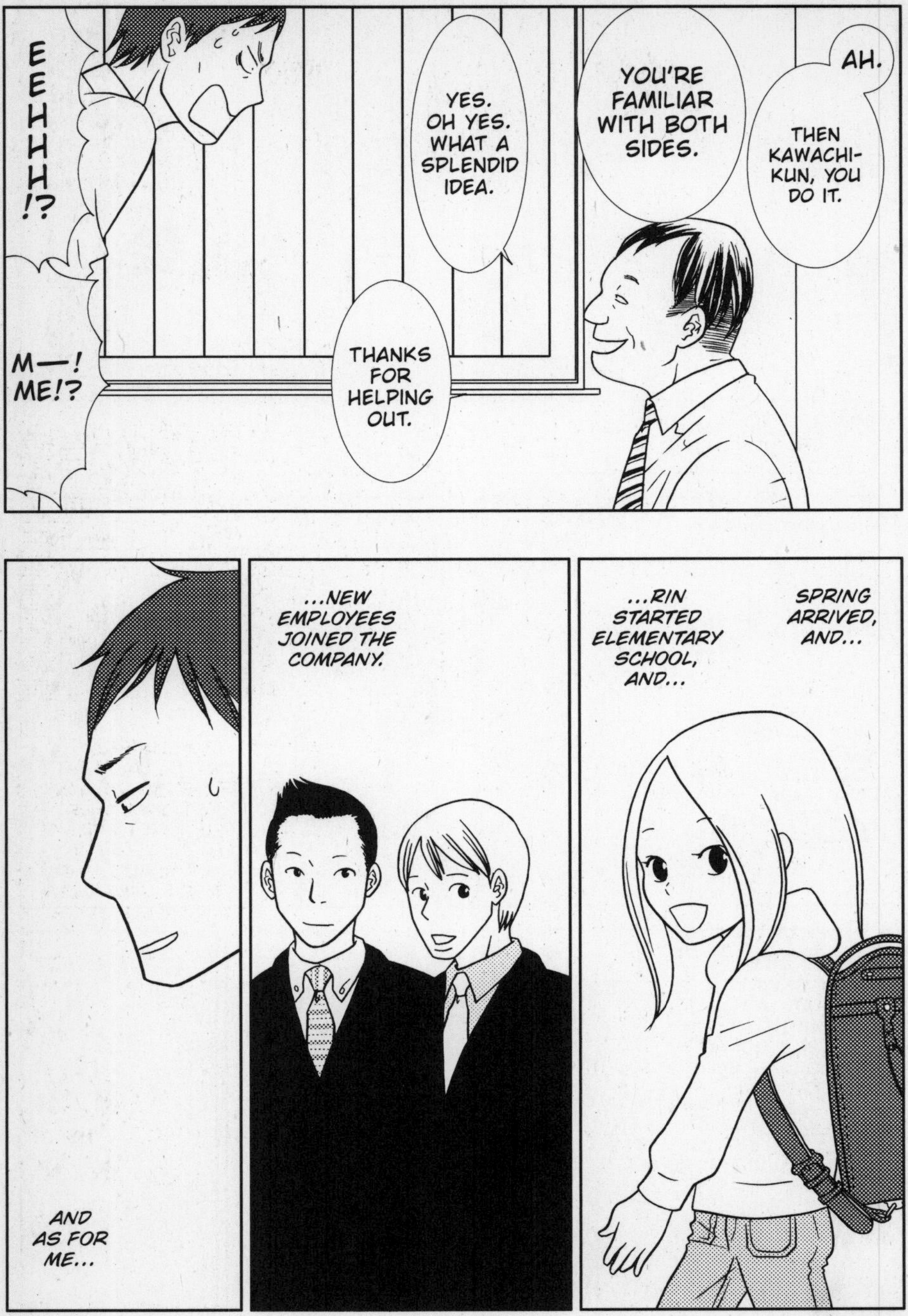
AH.
THEN KAWACHI-KUN, YOU DO IT.
YOU'RE FAMILIAR WITH BOTH SIDES.
YES. OH YES. WHAT A SPLENDID IDEA.
THANKS FOR HELPING OUT.
EEHHHH!?
M—! ME!?
SPRING ARRIVED, AND...
...RIN STARTED ELEMENTARY SCHOOL, AND...
...NEW EMPLOYEES JOINED THE COMPANY.
AND AS FOR ME...

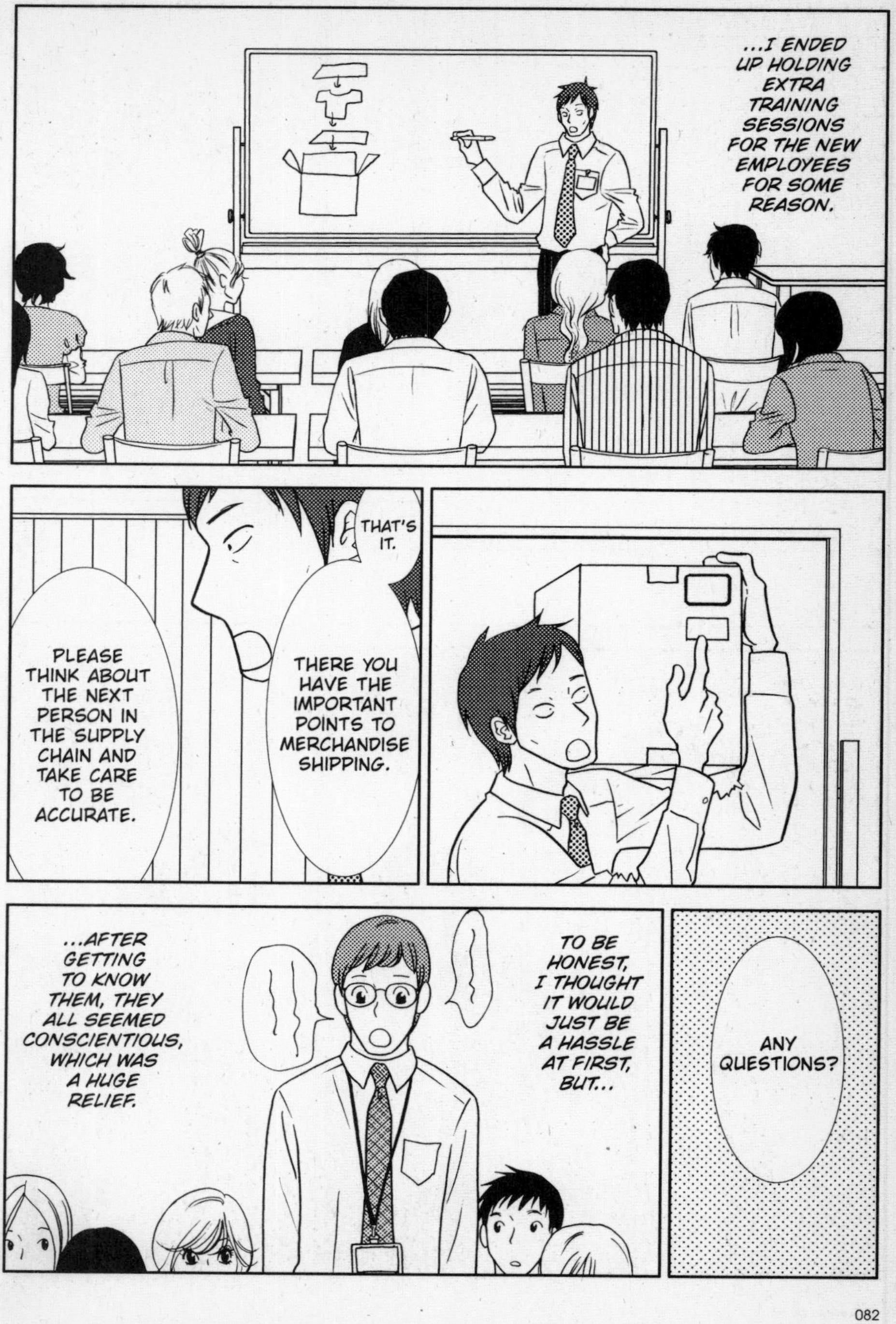
...I ENDED UP HOLDING EXTRA TRAINING SESSIONS FOR THE NEW EMPLOYEES FOR SOME REASON.
THAT'S IT.
THERE YOU HAVE THE IMPORTANT POINTS TO MERCHANDISE SHIPPING.
PLEASE THINK ABOUT THE NEXT PERSON IN THE SUPPLY CHAIN AND TAKE CARE TO BE ACCURATE.
ANY QUESTIONS?
TO BE HONEST, I THOUGHT IT WOULD JUST BE A HASSLE AT FIRST, BUT...
...AFTER GETTING TO KNOW THEM, THEY ALL SEEMED CONSCIENTIOUS, WHICH WAS A HUGE RELIEF.

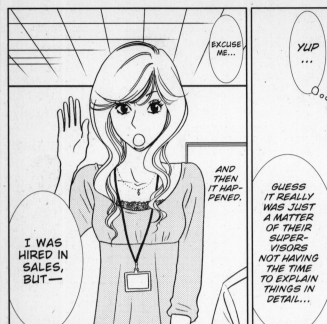

TO HELP WITH WORKFLOW EFFICIENCY, IT WAS AN EASY ENOUGH THING TO DO.
YUP ...
GUESS IT REALLY WAS JUST A MATTER OF THEIR SUPER-VISORS NOT HAVING THE TIME TO EXPLAIN THINGS IN DETAIL...
EXCUSE ME...
AND THEN IT HAP-PENED.
I WAS HIRED IN SALES, BUT—
...IT SEEMS LIKE I'M SPENDING EVERY DAY PACKING AND UNPACKING THE SAME KINDS OF THINGS.
EVEN MY HANDS ARE FEELING HORRIBLY ROUGH LATELY...
ZAWA (MURMUR)
ざわ…
HOW LONG IS THIS WORK GOING TO LAST?
THAT QUESTION DOESN'T REALLY HAVE ANYTHING TO DO WITH THIS SUBJECT...
PLUS, THE REST OF THEM ARE CLEARLY LOOKING UNCOM-FORTABLE ...
WELL ...

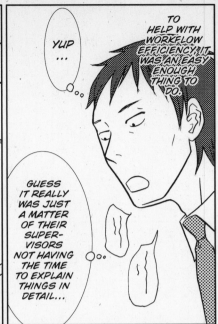

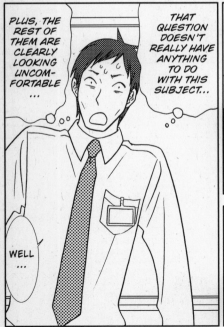

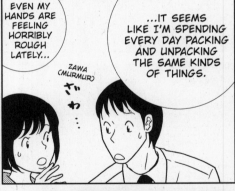

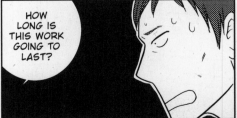

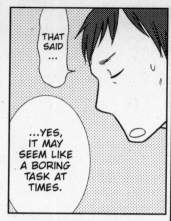

...THE JOB OF HANDLING BOXES PROBABLY ISN'T GOING TO GO AWAY ANYTIME SOON AT THIS COM-PANY.
WHEN IT'S REALLY BUSY, EVEN THE DIRECTORS HELP WITH PACKING AND DELIVERY.
THAT SAID ...
...YES, IT MAY SEEM LIKE A BORING TASK AT TIMES.
BUT THIS IS NO SIMPLE TASK.
FROM PACKAGES SHIPPED TO OUR CUSTOMERS, TO THOSE RETURNED FROM OUR CUS-TOMERS...FROM THOSE SENT TO US FROM OUR MANUFACTUR-ERS, TO THOSE RETURNED TO OUR MANUFAC-TURERS...
FROM PHOTO PROOFS TO SAMPLES FOR MEET-INGS...
AT FIRST GLANCE, THEY MAY ALL LOOK LIKE THE SAME CARD-BOARD BOX, BUT ...
...THE SIGNIFI-CANCE OF THEIR CONTENTS IS ALWAYS DIFFERENT.

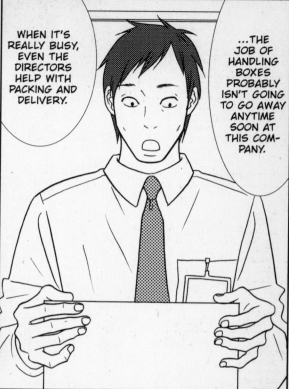

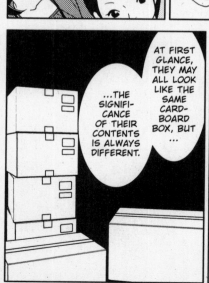

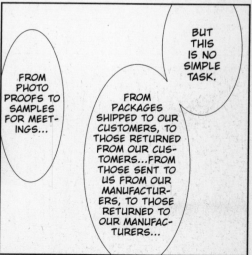

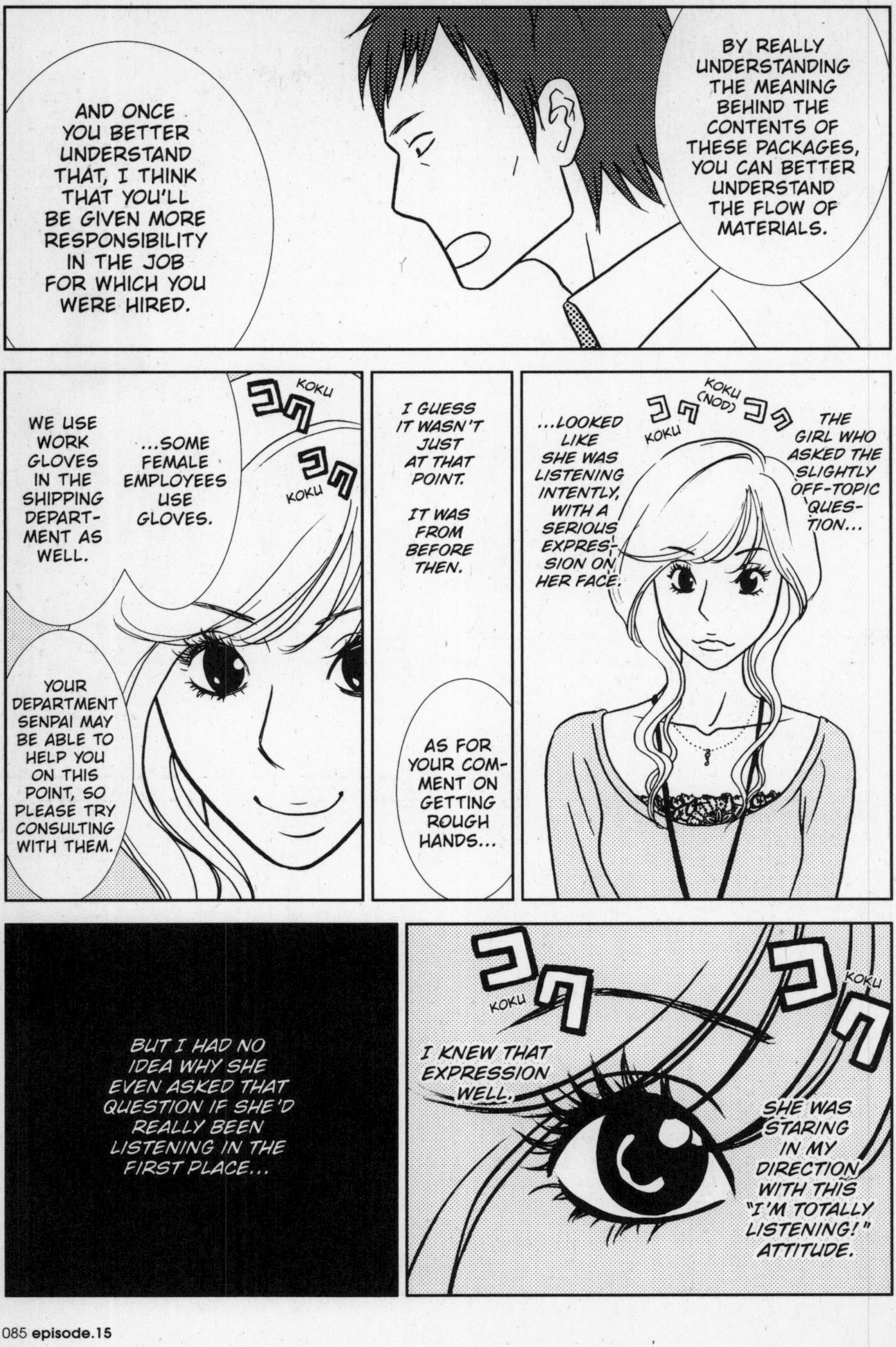
BY REALLY UNDERSTANDING THE MEANING BEHIND THE CONTENTS OF THESE PACKAGES, YOU CAN BETTER UNDERSTAND THE FLOW OF MATERIALS.
AND ONCE YOU BETTER UNDERSTAND THAT, I THINK THAT YOU'LL BE GIVEN MORE RESPONSIBILITY IN THE JOB FOR WHICH YOU WERE HIRED.
THE GIRL WHO ASKED THE SLIGHTLY OFF-TOPIC QUESTION...
KOKU (NOD)
KOKU
...LOOKED LIKE SHE WAS LISTENING INTENTLY, WITH A SERIOUS EXPRESSION ON HER FACE.
I GUESS IT WASN'T JUST AT THAT POINT.
IT WAS FROM BEFORE THEN.
AS FOR YOUR COMMENT ON GETTING ROUGH HANDS...
KOKU
KOKU
...SOME FEMALE EMPLOYEES USE GLOVES.
WE USE WORK GLOVES IN THE SHIPPING DEPARTMENT AS WELL.
YOUR DEPARTMENT SENPAI MAY BE ABLE TO HELP YOU ON THIS POINT, SO PLEASE TRY CONSULTING WITH THEM.
KOKU
KOKU
I KNEW THAT EXPRESSION WELL.
SHE WAS STARING IN MY DIRECTION WITH THIS "I'M TOTALLY LISTENING!" ATTITUDE.
BUT I HAD NO IDEA WHY SHE EVEN ASKED THAT QUESTION IF SHE'D REALLY BEEN LISTENING IN THE FIRST PLACE...

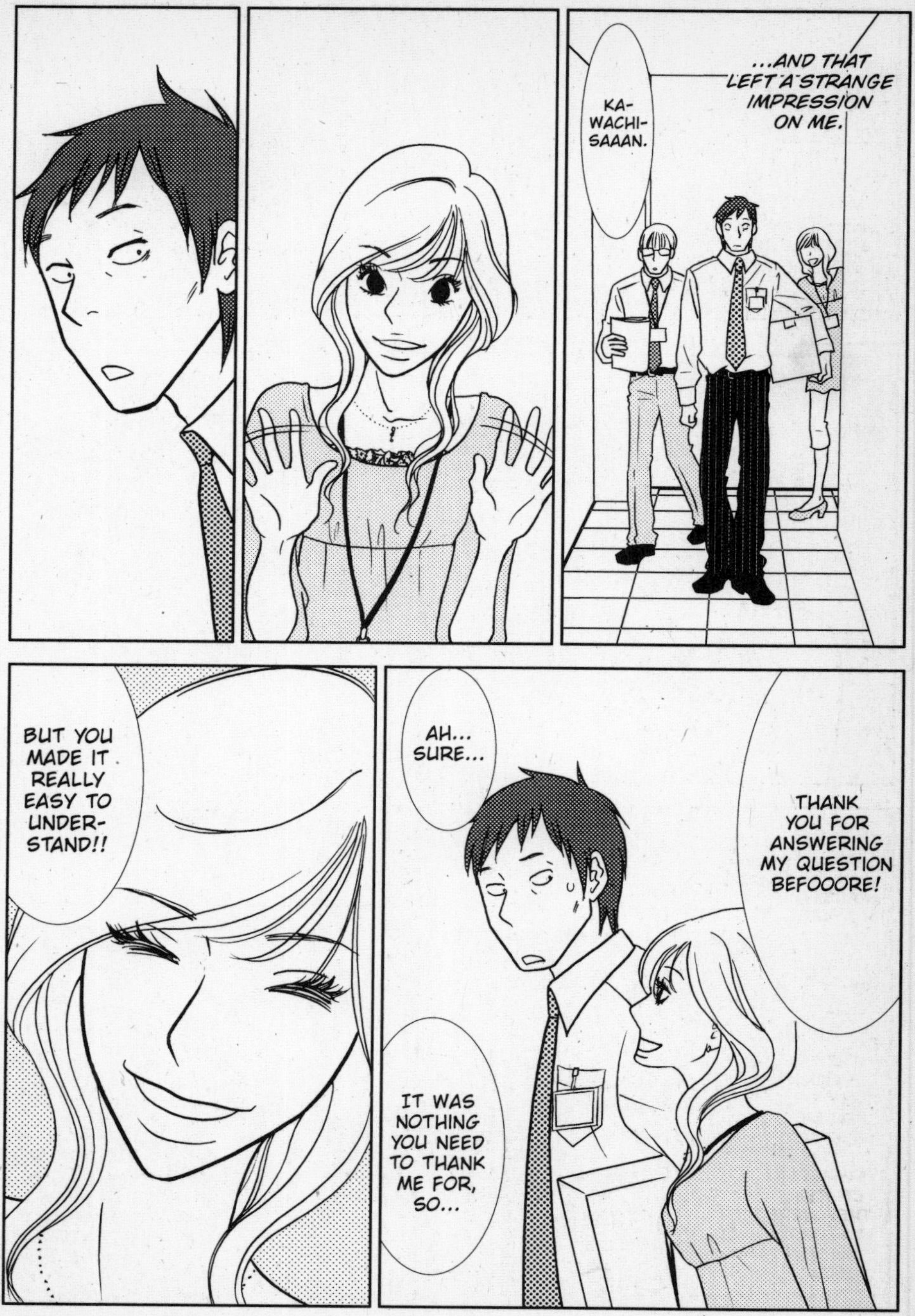
...AND THAT LEFT A STRANGE IMPRESSION ON ME.
KA-WACHI-SAAAN.
THANK YOU FOR ANSWERING MY QUESTION BEFOOORE!
AH... SURE...
IT WAS NOTHING YOU NEED TO THANK ME FOR, SO...
BUT YOU MADE IT REALLY EASY TO UNDER-STAND!!

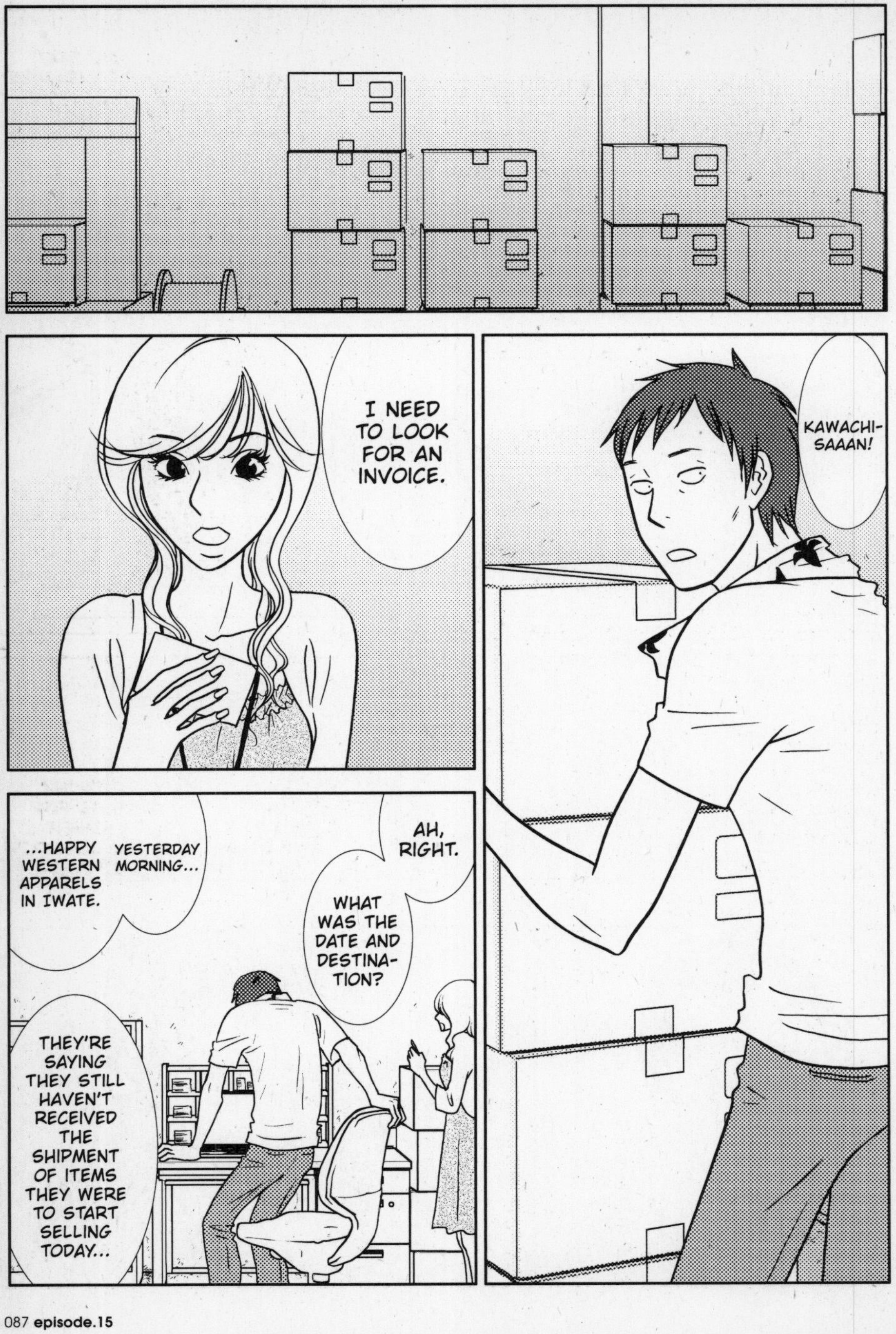
KAWACHI-SAAAN!
I NEED TO LOOK FOR AN INVOICE.
AH, RIGHT.
WHAT WAS THE DATE AND DESTINATION?
YESTERDAY MORNING...
...HAPPY WESTERN APPARELS IN IWATE.
THEY'RE SAYING THEY STILL HAVEN'T RECEIVED THE SHIPMENT OF ITEMS THEY WERE TO START SELLING TODAY...

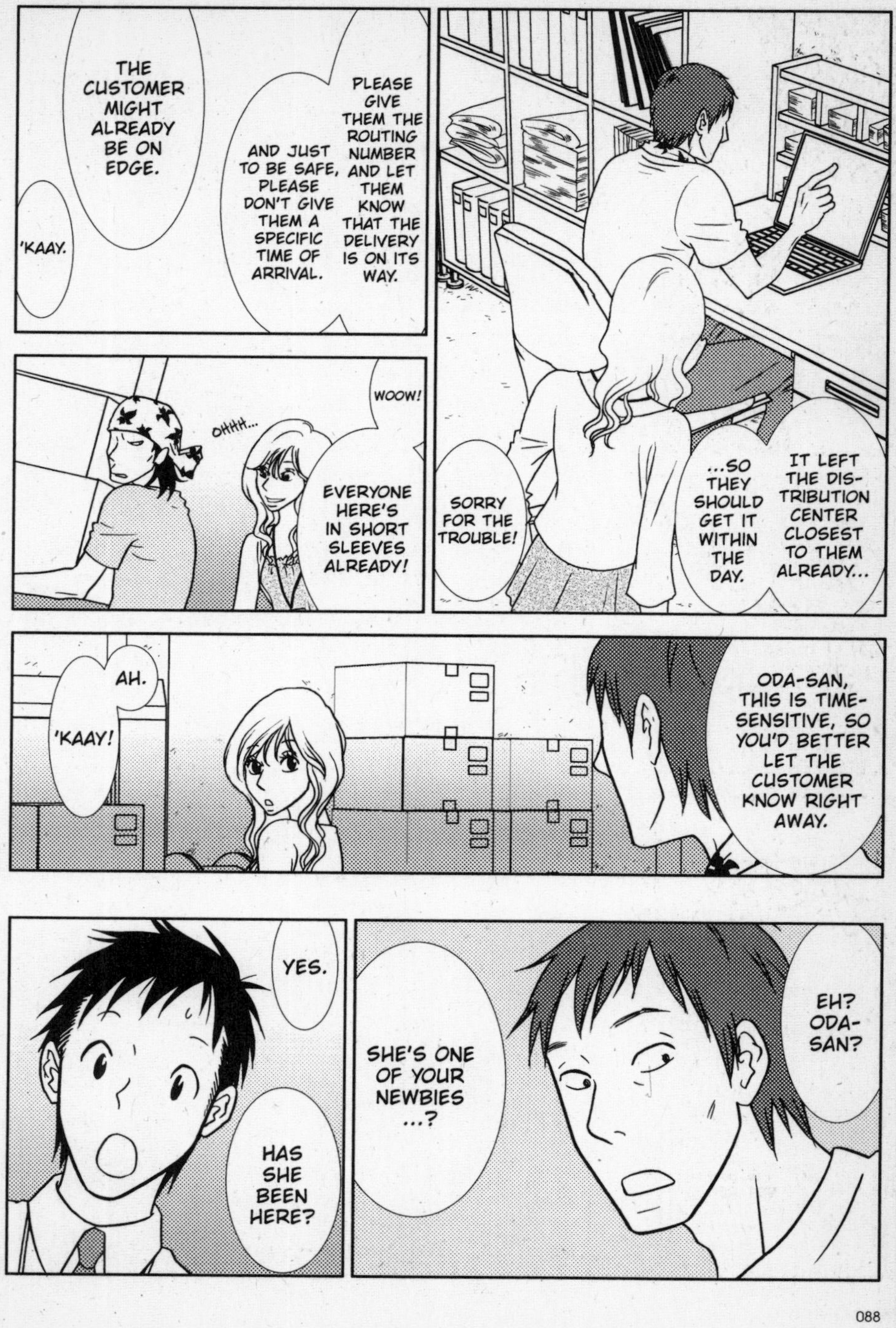
IT LEFT THE DIS-TRIBUTION CENTER CLOSEST TO THEM ALREADY...
...SO THEY SHOULD GET IT WITHIN THE DAY.
SORRY FOR THE TROUBLE!
PLEASE GIVE THEM THE ROUTING NUMBER AND LET THEM KNOW THAT THE DELIVERY IS ON ITS WAY.
AND JUST TO BE SAFE, PLEASE DON'T GIVE THEM A SPECIFIC TIME OF ARRIVAL.
THE CUSTOMER MIGHT ALREADY BE ON EDGE.
'KAAY.
WOOW!
EVERYONE HERE'S IN SHORT SLEEVES ALREADY!
OHHH...
ODA-SAN, THIS IS TIME-SENSITIVE, SO YOU'D BETTER LET THE CUSTOMER KNOW RIGHT AWAY.
AH.
'KAAY!
EH? ODA-SAN?
SHE'S ONE OF YOUR NEWBIES ...?
YES.
HAS SHE BEEN HERE?

AHHH, YEAH, SHE COMES HERE EVERY SO OFTEN...
I KNEW IT...
SHE MAKES UP EXCUSES AND JUST WANDERS OFF—!
AND ONCE SHE LEAVES, IT TAKES HER FOREVER TO COME BACK.
I HAVEN'T SEEN HER YET TODAY...
THANK YOU. I'LL TRY PAGING HER.
HANG IN THERE, SENPAI.
GEEZ, KAWACHI-SAN!!
WHY DO YOU HAVE TO BRING THAT UP EVERY SINGLE YEAR?
ARE YOU GOING TO TEASE ME ABOUT THIS EVERY TIME WE HAVE NEW EMPLOYEES!!?
WELL!
NIYA (SMIRK)
ニヤニヤ
NIYA
REALLY!
THE FACT THAT YOU'RE A SENPAI...IT JUST NEVER GETS OLD.
......
IT'S PROBABLY NOT REALLY MY PLACE TO SAY THIS, BUT...

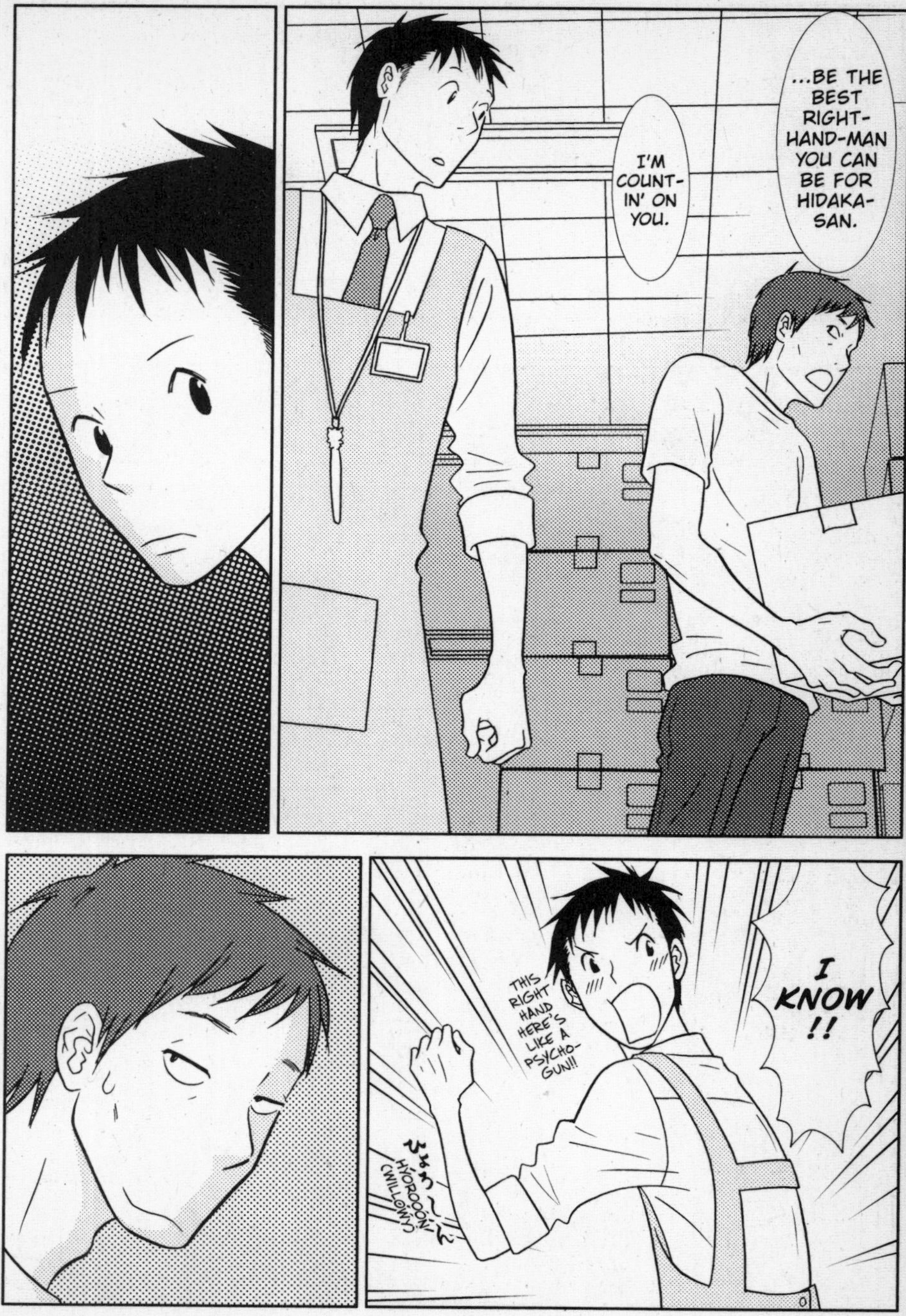
...BE THE BEST RIGHT-HAND-MAN YOU CAN BE FOR HIDAKA-SAN.
I'M COUNTIN' ON YOU.
I KNOW!!
THIS RIGHT HAND HERE'S LIKE A PSYCHO-GUN!!
ひょろ〜〜ん
HYOROOON! (WILLOWY)

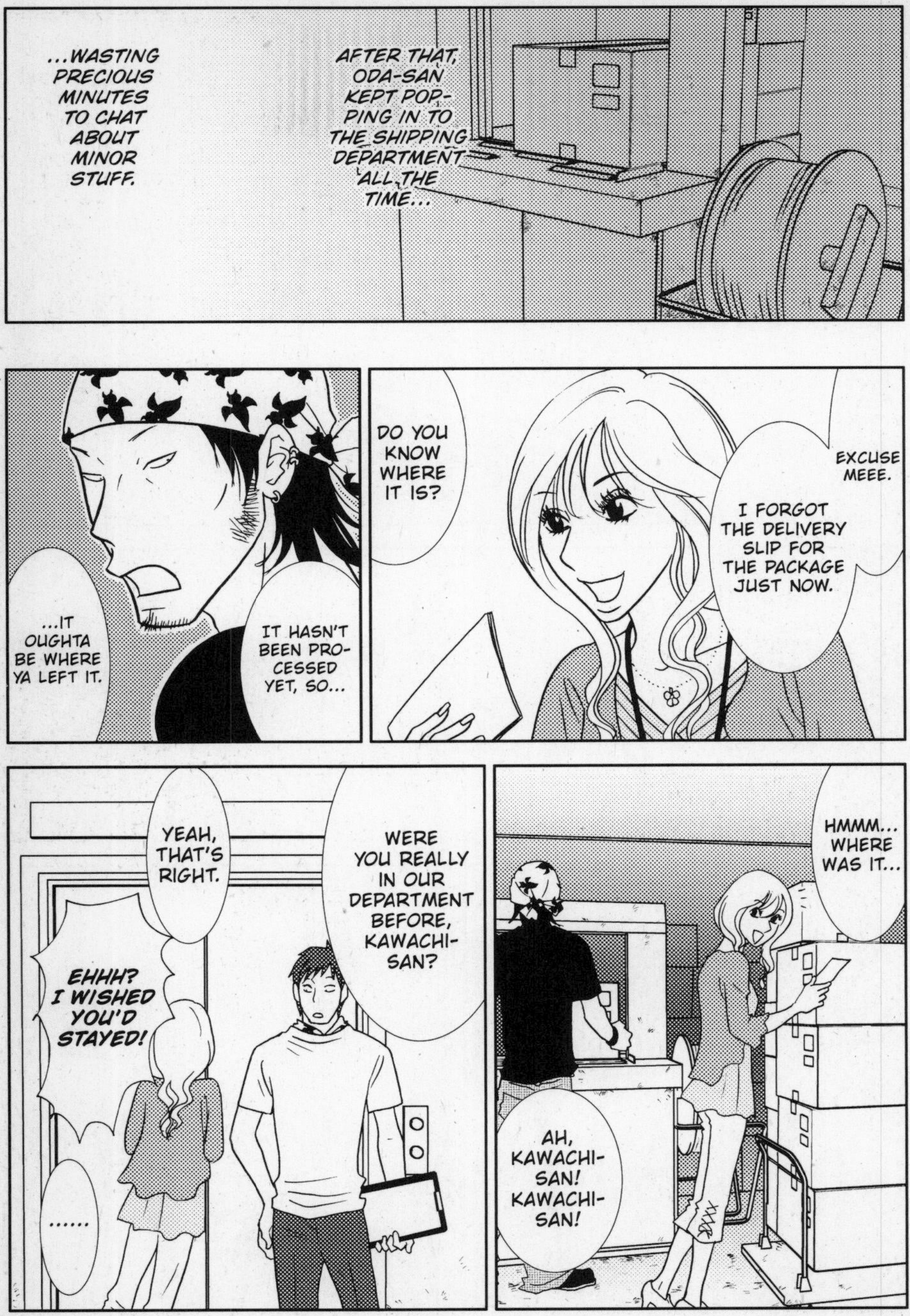
AFTER THAT, ODA-SAN KEPT POP-PING IN TO THE SHIPPING DEPARTMENT ALL THE TIME...
...WASTING PRECIOUS MINUTES TO CHAT ABOUT MINOR STUFF.
EXCUSE MEEE.
I FORGOT THE DELIVERY SLIP FOR THE PACKAGE JUST NOW.
DO YOU KNOW WHERE IT IS?
IT HASN'T BEEN PRO-CESSED YET, SO...
...IT OUGHTA BE WHERE YA LEFT IT.
HMMM... WHERE WAS IT...
AH, KAWACHI-SAN! KAWACHI-SAN!
WERE YOU REALLY IN OUR DEPARTMENT BEFORE, KAWACHI-SAN?
YEAH, THAT'S RIGHT.
EHHH? I WISHED YOU'D STAYED!
......

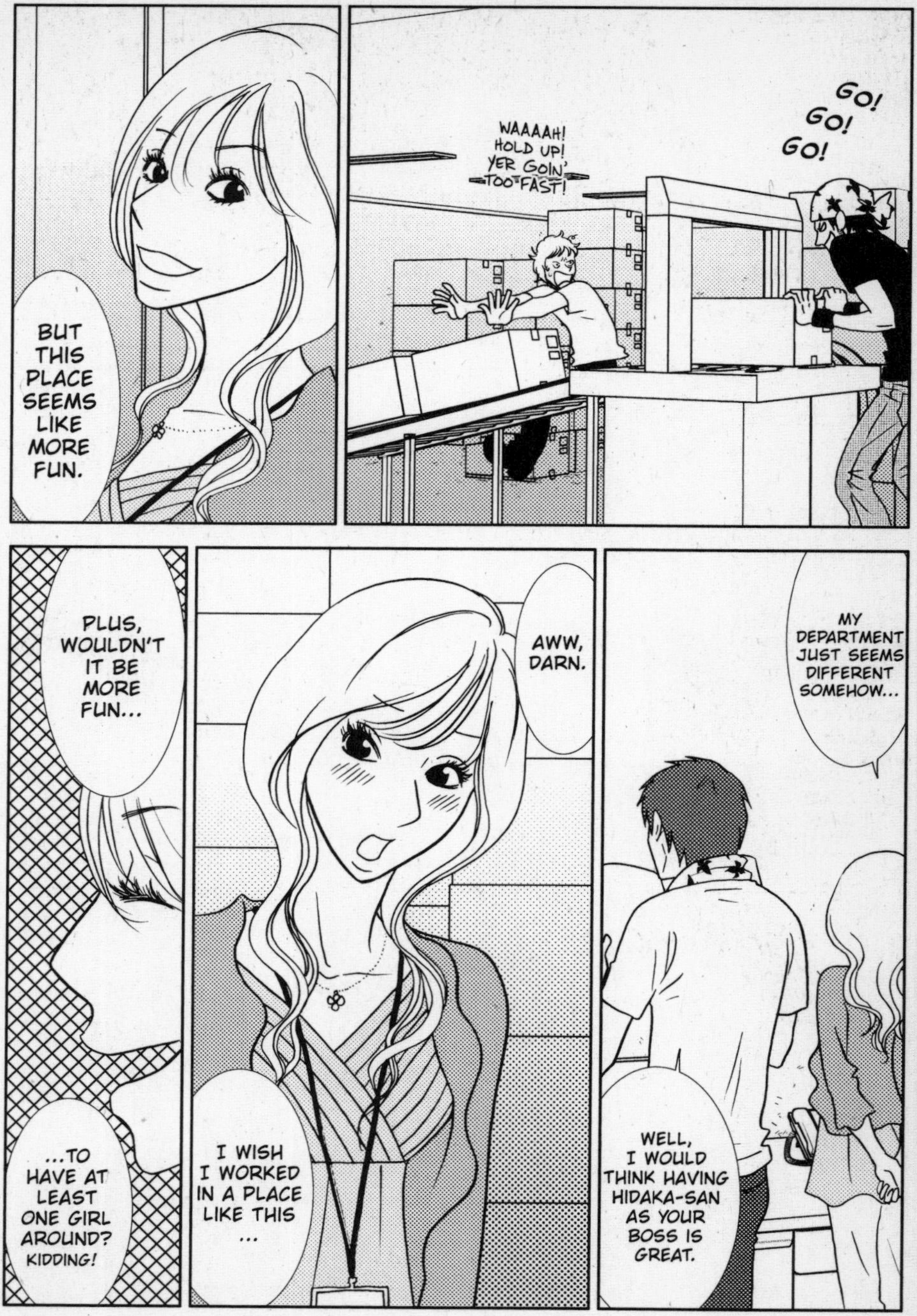
GO! GO! GO!
WAAAAH! HOLD UP! YER GOIN' TOO FAST!
BUT THIS PLACE SEEMS LIKE MORE FUN.
MY DEPARTMENT JUST SEEMS DIFFERENT SOMEHOW...
WELL, I WOULD THINK HAVING HIDAKA-SAN AS YOUR BOSS IS GREAT.
AWW, DARN.
I WISH I WORKED IN A PLACE LIKE THIS ...
PLUS, WOULDN'T IT BE MORE FUN...
...TO HAVE AT LEAST ONE GIRL AROUND?
KIDDING!

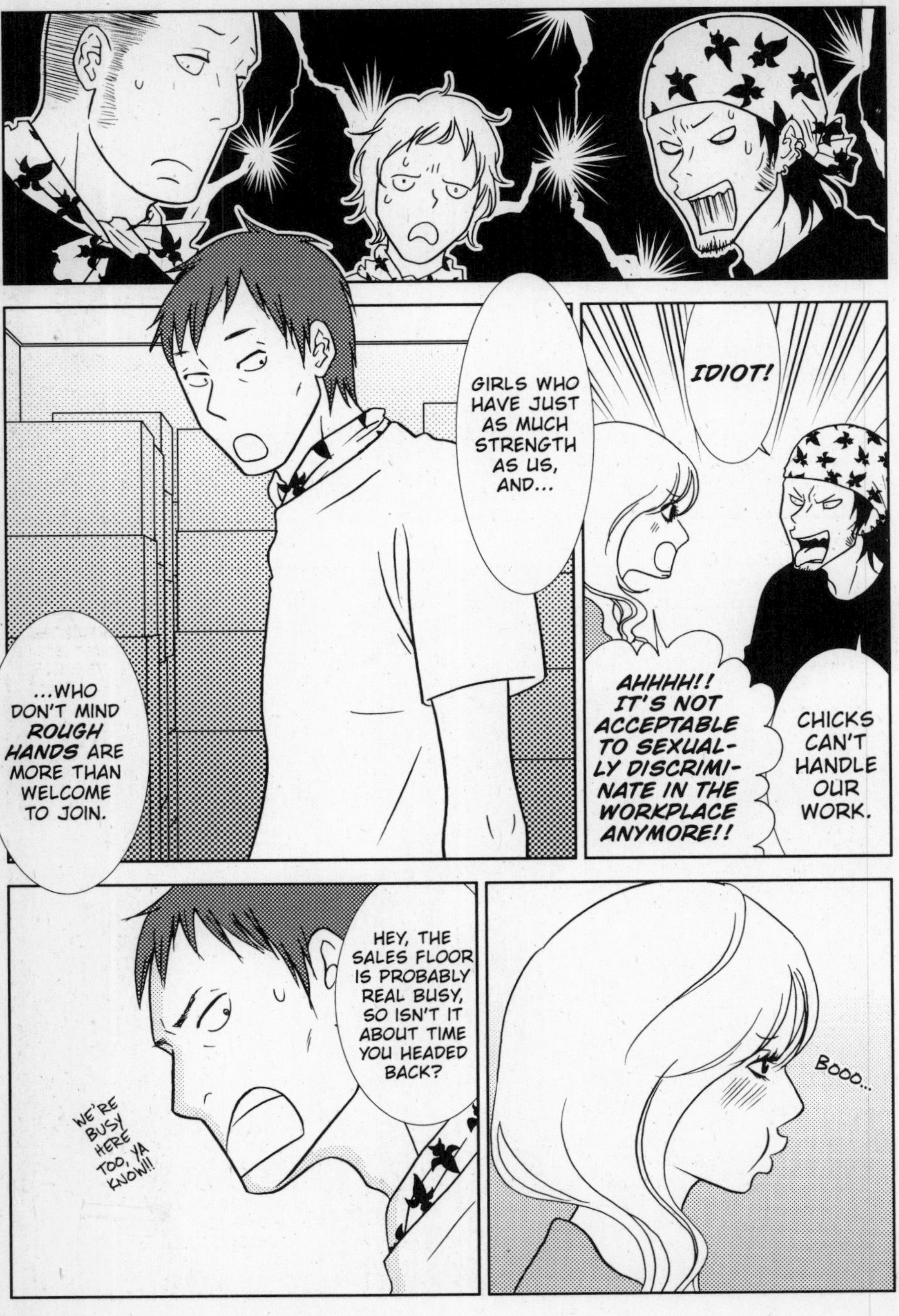
IDIOT!
CHICKS CAN'T HANDLE OUR WORK.
AHHHH!! IT'S NOT ACCEPTABLE TO SEXUALLY DISCRIMINATE IN THE WORKPLACE ANYMORE!!
GIRLS WHO HAVE JUST AS MUCH STRENGTH AS US, AND...
...WHO DON'T MIND ROUGH HANDS ARE MORE THAN WELCOME TO JOIN.
BOOO...
HEY, THE SALES FLOOR IS PROBABLY REAL BUSY, SO ISN'T IT ABOUT TIME YOU HEADED BACK?
WE'RE BUSY HERE TOO, YA KNOW!!

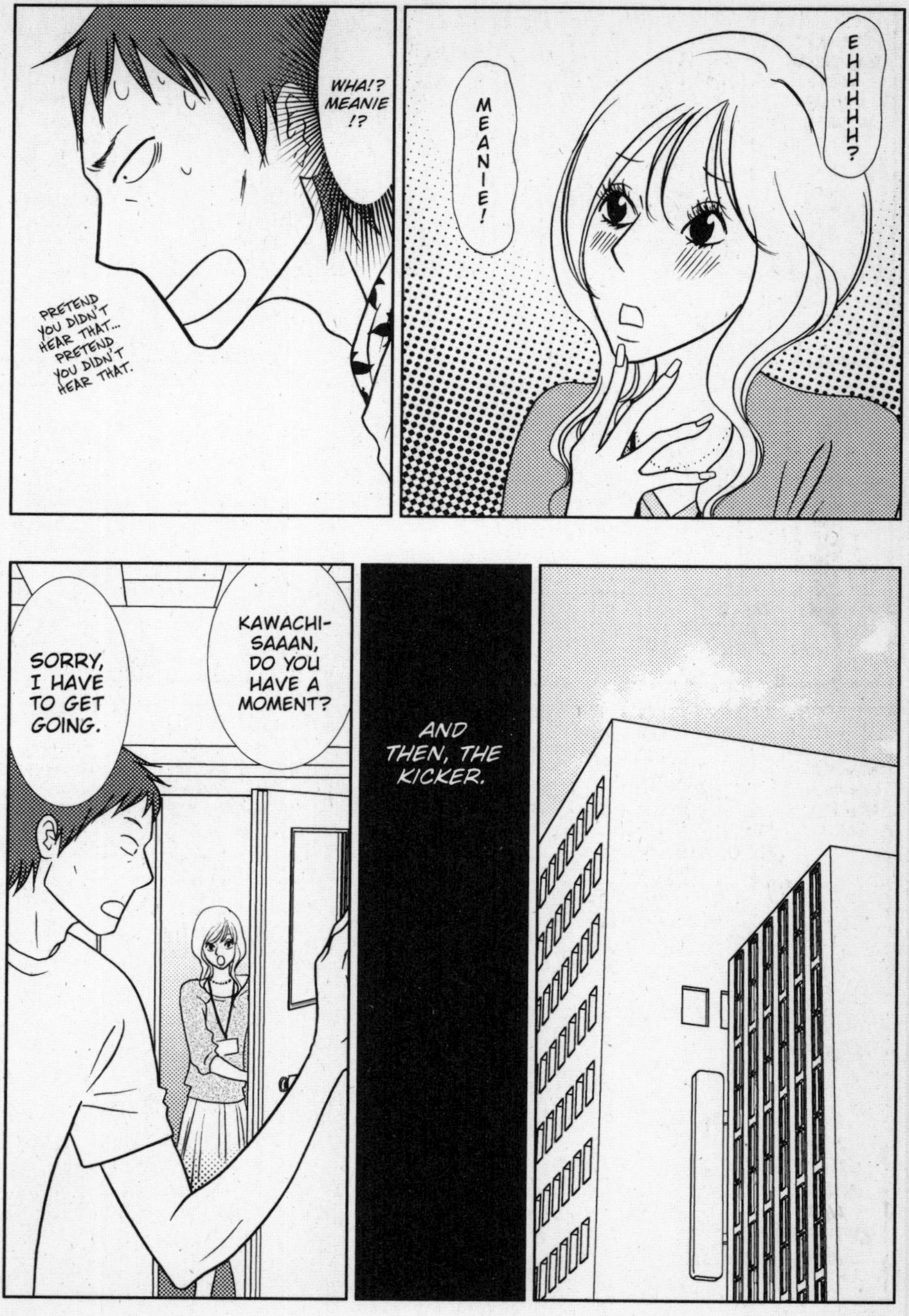
EHHHHHH?
MEANIE!
WHA!? MEANIE!?
PRETEND YOU DIDN'T HEAR THAT... PRETEND YOU DIDN'T HEAR THAT.
AND THEN, THE KICKER.
KAWACHI-SAAAN, DO YOU HAVE A MOMENT?
SORRY, I HAVE TO GET GOING.

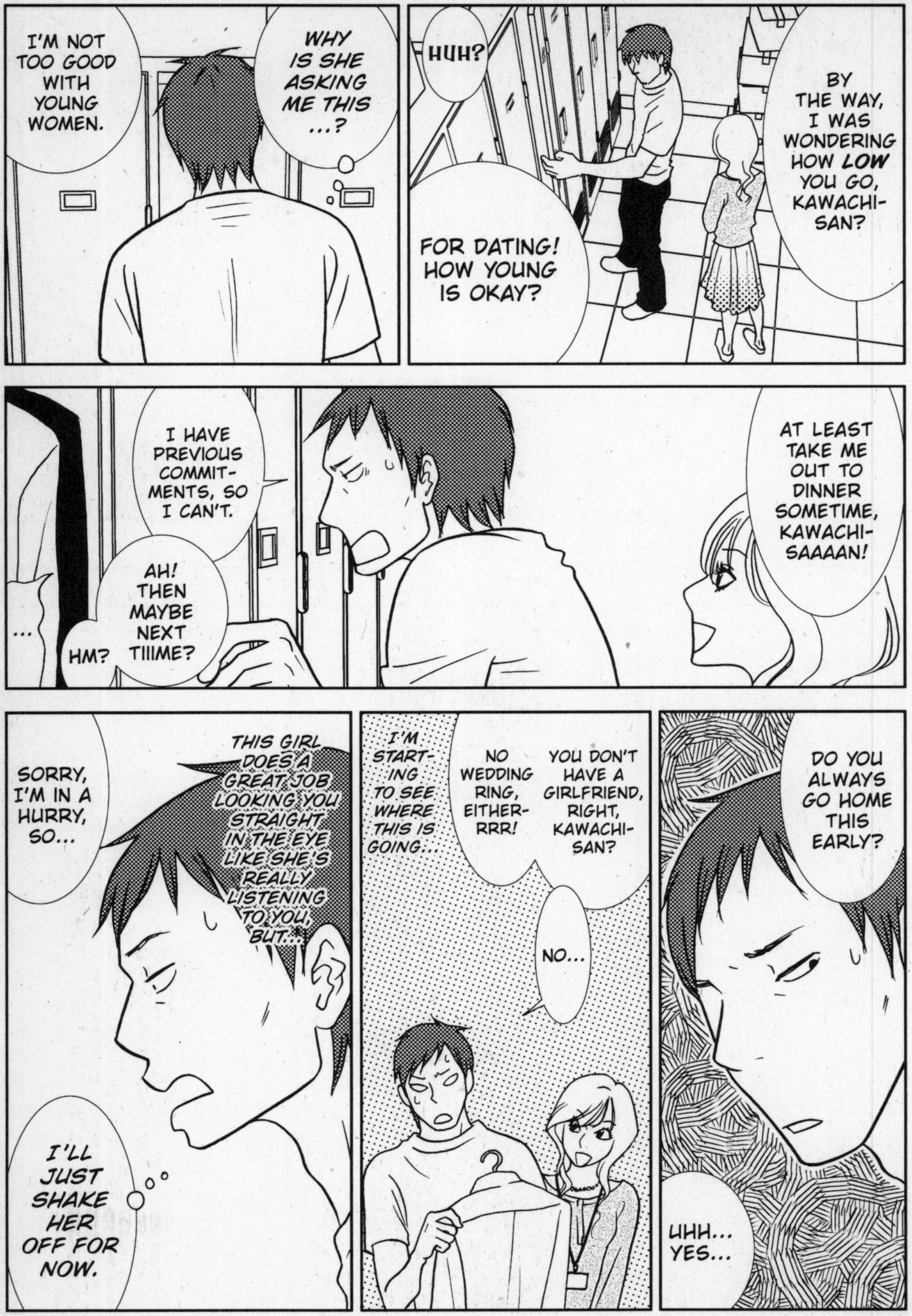
BY THE WAY, I WAS WONDERING HOW LOW YOU GO, KAWACHI-SAN?
HUH?
FOR DATING! HOW YOUNG IS OKAY?
WHY IS SHE ASKING ME THIS ...?
I'M NOT TOO GOOD WITH YOUNG WOMEN.
AT LEAST TAKE ME OUT TO DINNER SOMETIME, KAWACHI-SAAAAN!
I HAVE PREVIOUS COMMIT-MENTS, SO I CAN'T.
AH! THEN MAYBE NEXT TIIIME?
HM?
...
DO YOU ALWAYS GO HOME THIS EARLY?
UHH... YES...
YOU DON'T HAVE A GIRLFRIEND, RIGHT, KAWACHI-SAN?
NO WEDDING RING, EITHER-RRR!
I'M START-ING TO SEE WHERE THIS IS GOING...
NO...
SORRY, I'M IN A HURRY, SO...
THIS GIRL DOES A GREAT JOB LOOKING YOU STRAIGHT IN THE EYE LIKE SHE'S REALLY LISTENING TO YOU, BUT...
I'LL JUST SHAKE HER OFF FOR NOW.

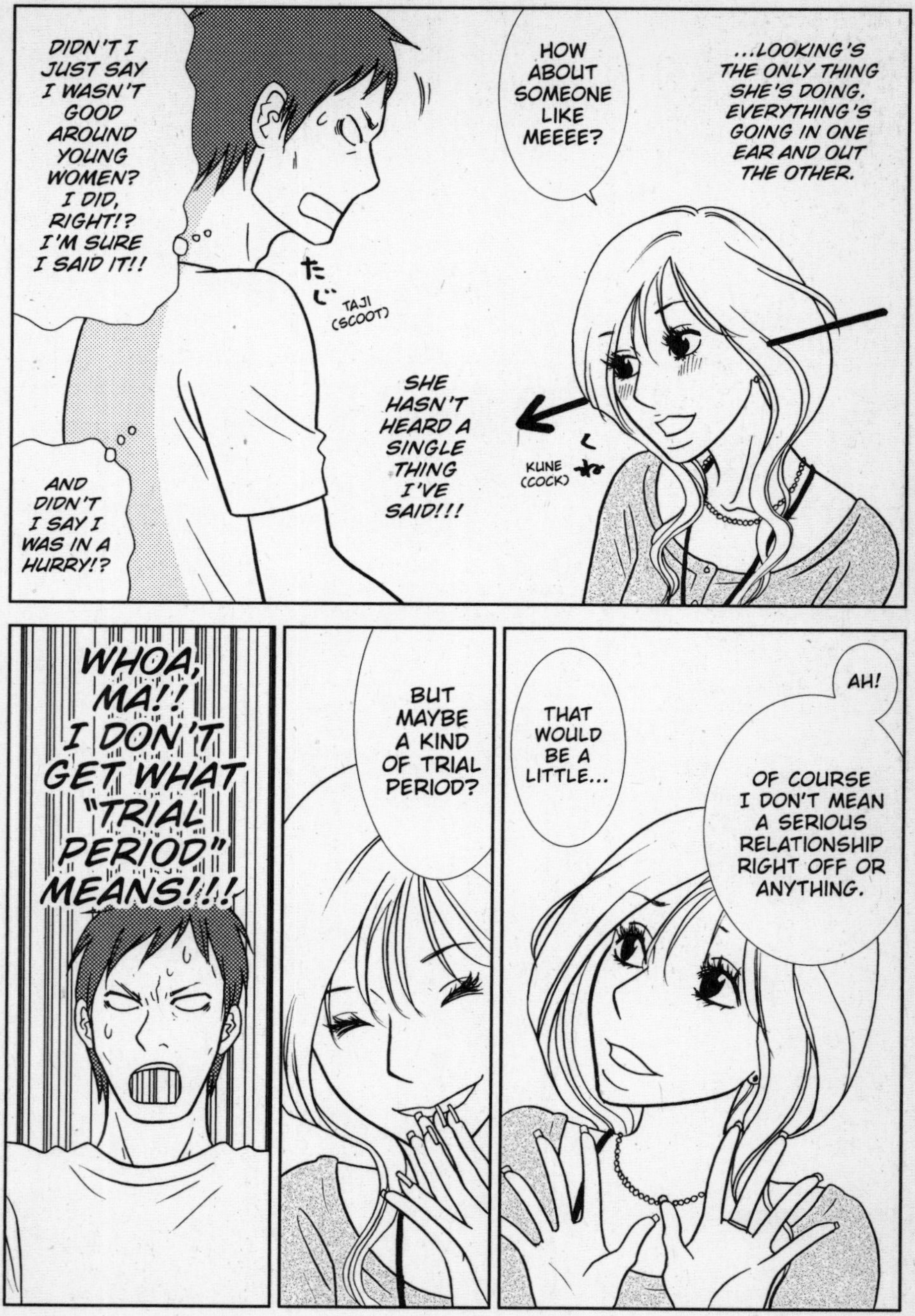
...LOOKING'S THE ONLY THING SHE'S DOING. EVERYTHING'S GOING IN ONE EAR AND OUT THE OTHER.
HOW ABOUT SOMEONE LIKE MEEEE?
DIDN'T I JUST SAY I WASN'T GOOD AROUND YOUNG WOMEN? I DID, RIGHT!? I'M SURE I SAID IT!!
くね
KUNE (COCK)
SHE HASN'T HEARD A SINGLE THING I'VE SAID!!!
たじ
TAJI (SCOOT)
AND DIDN'T I SAY I WAS IN A HURRY!?
AH!
OF COURSE I DON'T MEAN A SERIOUS RELATIONSHIP RIGHT OFF OR ANYTHING.
THAT WOULD BE A LITTLE...
BUT MAYBE A KIND OF TRIAL PERIOD?
WHOA, MA!! I DON'T GET WHAT "TRIAL PERIOD" MEANS!!!

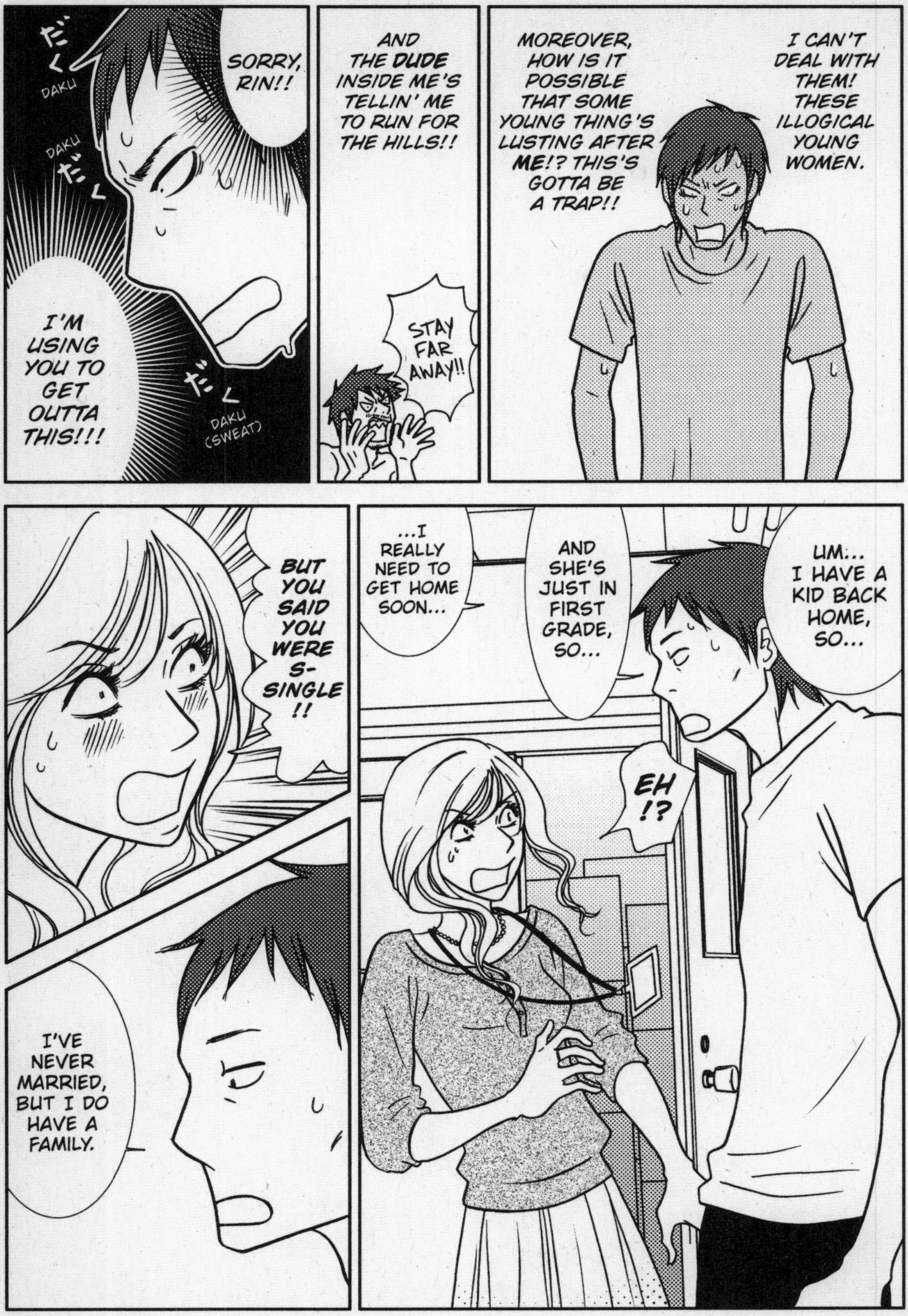
I CAN'T DEAL WITH THEM! THESE ILLOGICAL YOUNG WOMEN.
MOREOVER, HOW IS IT POSSIBLE THAT SOME YOUNG THING'S LUSTING AFTER ME!? THIS'S GOTTA BE A TRAP!!
AND THE DUDE INSIDE ME'S TELLIN' ME TO RUN FOR THE HILLS!!
STAY FAR AWAY!!
SORRY, RIN!!
だく
DAKU
DAKU
だく
I'M USING YOU TO GET OUTTA THIS!!!
だく
DAKU (SWEAT)
UM... I HAVE A KID BACK HOME, SO...
AND SHE'S JUST IN FIRST GRADE, SO...
...I REALLY NEED TO GET HOME SOON...
EH!?
BUT YOU SAID YOU WERE S-SINGLE!!
I'VE NEVER MARRIED, BUT I DO HAVE A FAMILY.

AH ...
EH ...?
YOU KNOW WHAT? FORGET I SAID ANY-THING.
EH?
SORRYYY!
POTSUUUN (STUNNED)
ぽつーん
FORGET?
......
THAT'S FINE WITH ME, BUT...

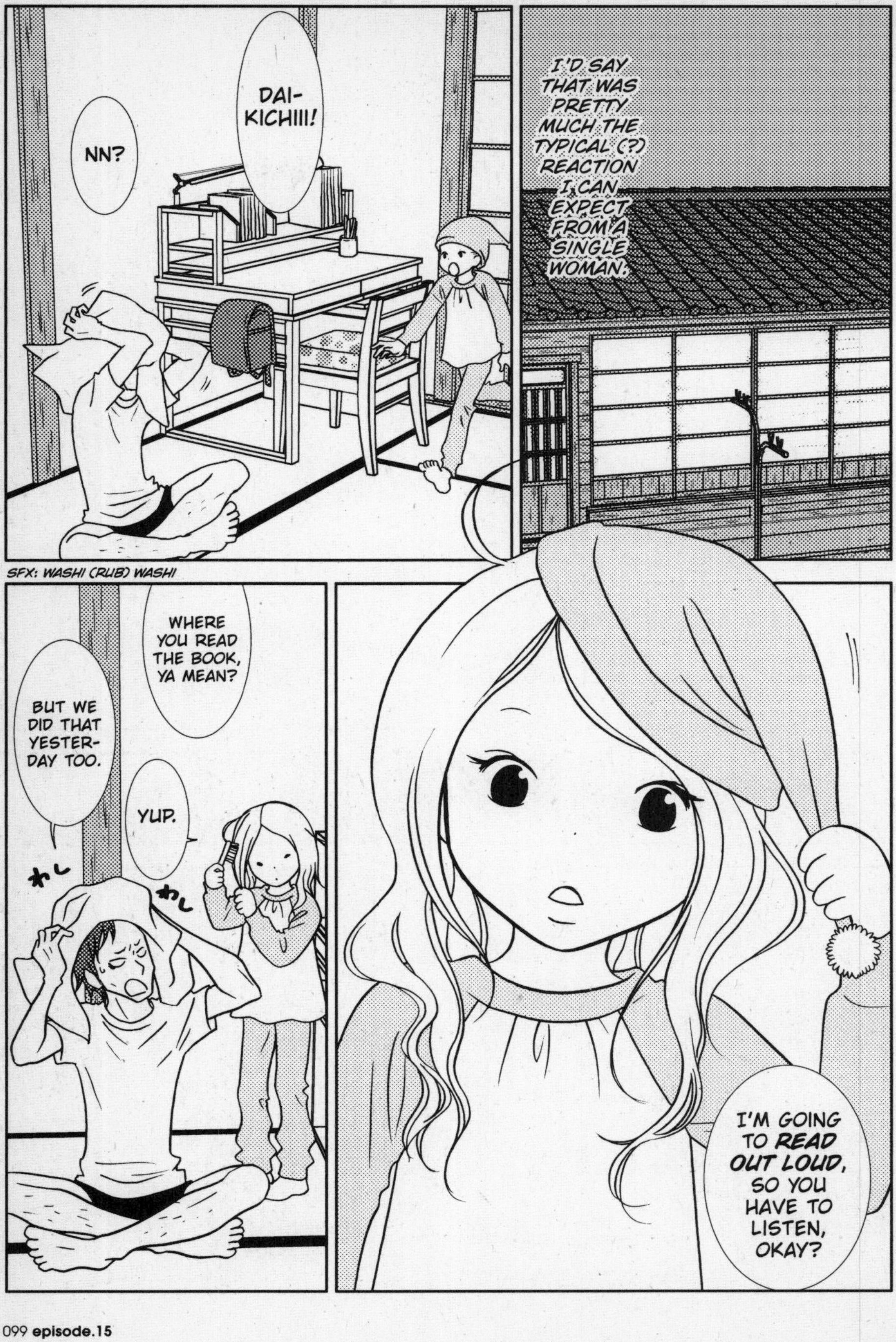
I'D SAY THAT WAS PRETTY MUCH THE TYPICAL (?) REACTION I CAN EXPECT FROM A SINGLE WOMAN.
DAI-KICHIII!
NN?
SFX: WASHI (RUB) WASHI
I'M GOING TO **READ OUT LOUD**, SO YOU HAVE TO LISTEN, OKAY?
WHERE YOU READ THE BOOK, YA MEAN?
BUT WE DID THAT YESTER-DAY TOO.
YUP.
わし
わし

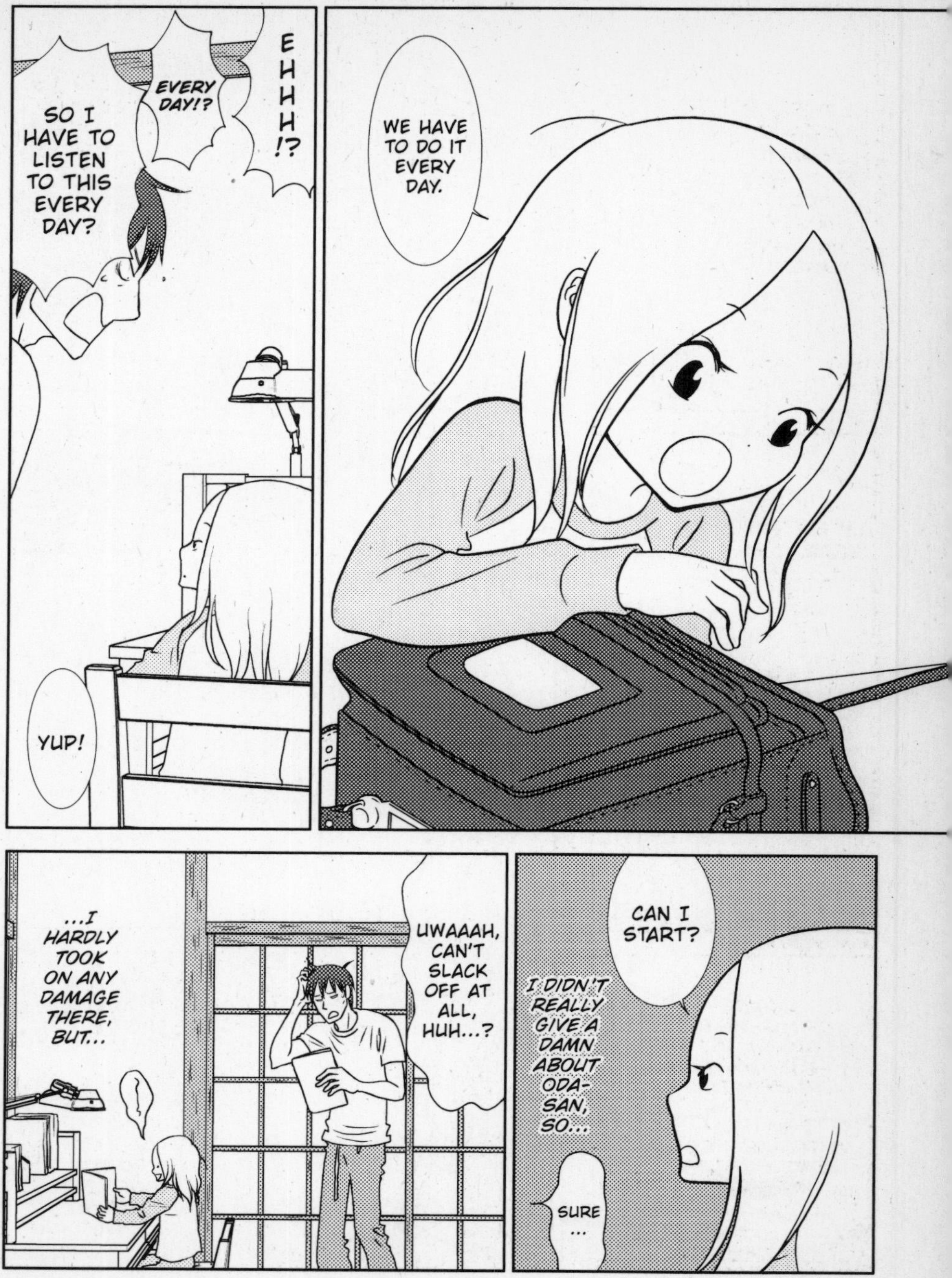
WE HAVE TO DO IT EVERY DAY.
EHHHH!?
EVERY DAY!?
SO I HAVE TO LISTEN TO THIS EVERY DAY?
YUP!
CAN I START?
I DIDN'T REALLY GIVE A DAMN ABOUT ODA-SAN, SO...
SURE ...
UWAAAH, CAN'T SLACK OFF AT ALL, HUH...?
...I HARDLY TOOK ON ANY DAMAGE THERE, BUT...

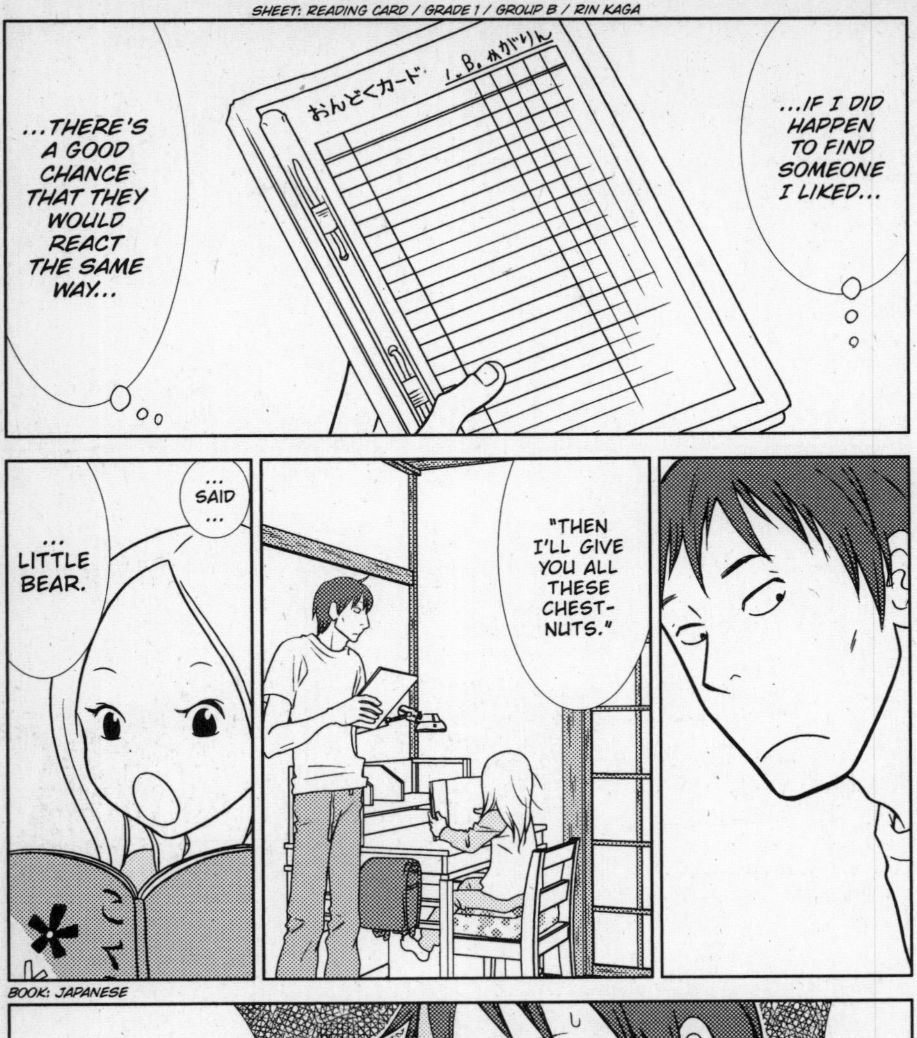
SHEET: READING CARD / GRADE 1 / GROUP B / RIN KAGA
...IF I DID HAPPEN TO FIND SOMEONE I LIKED...
おんどくカード
...THERE'S A GOOD CHANCE THAT THEY WOULD REACT THE SAME WAY...
"THEN I'LL GIVE YOU ALL THESE CHEST-NUTS."
...SAID...
...LITTLE BEAR.
BOOK: JAPANESE
"THANK YOU."
MISTER RABBIT WAS VERY HAPPY.
I GOTTA SAY, RATHER THAN HAVING A DIFFICULT DINNER WITH A DIFFICULT GIRL, I THINK I'D RATHER BE HERE, EATING CURRY WITH RIN...

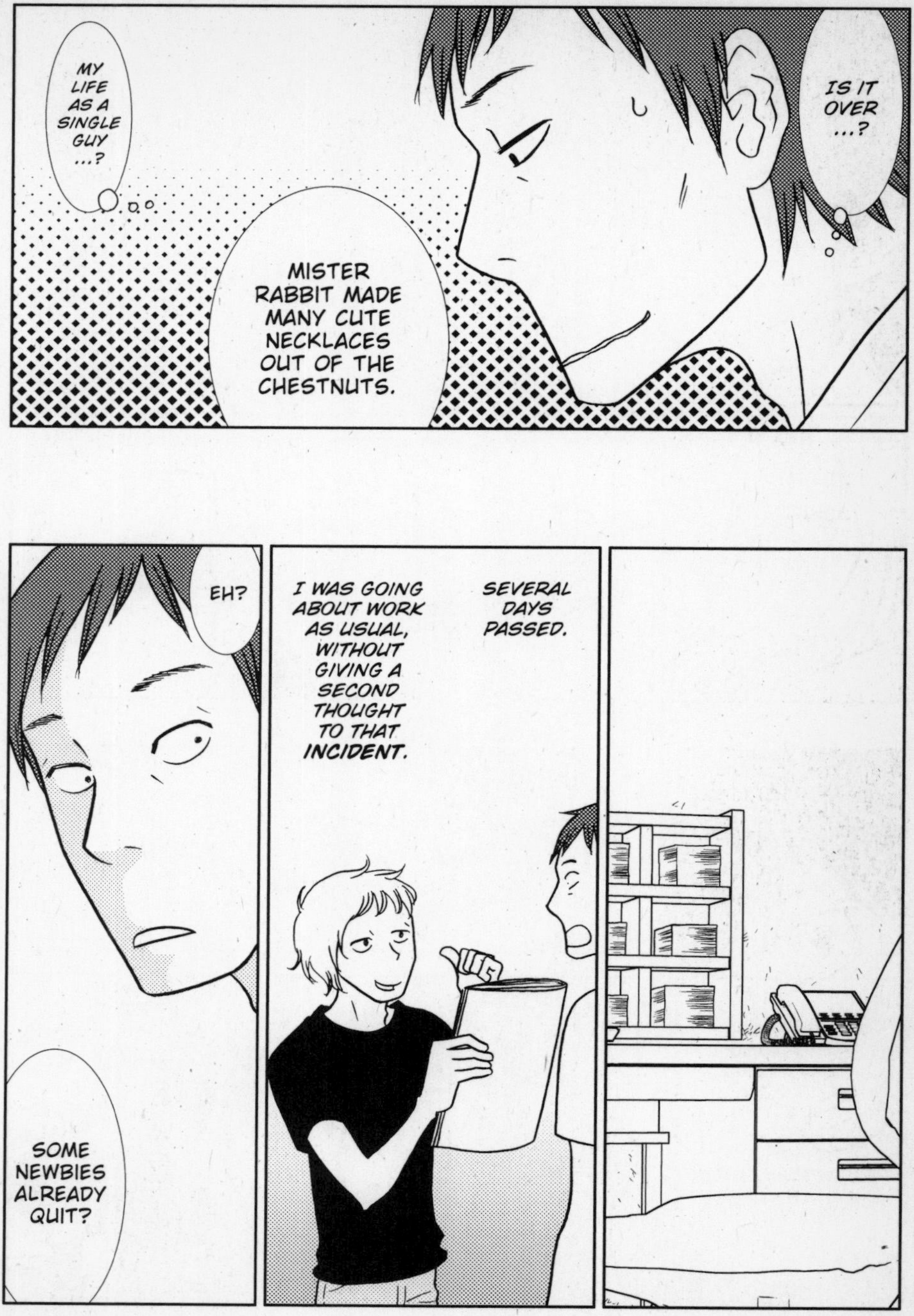
IS IT OVER ...?
MY LIFE AS A SINGLE GUY ...?
MISTER RABBIT MADE MANY CUTE NECKLACES OUT OF THE CHESTNUTS.
SEVERAL DAYS PASSED.
I WAS GOING ABOUT WORK AS USUAL, WITHOUT GIVING A SECOND THOUGHT TO THAT INCIDENT.
EH?
SOME NEWBIES ALREADY QUIT?

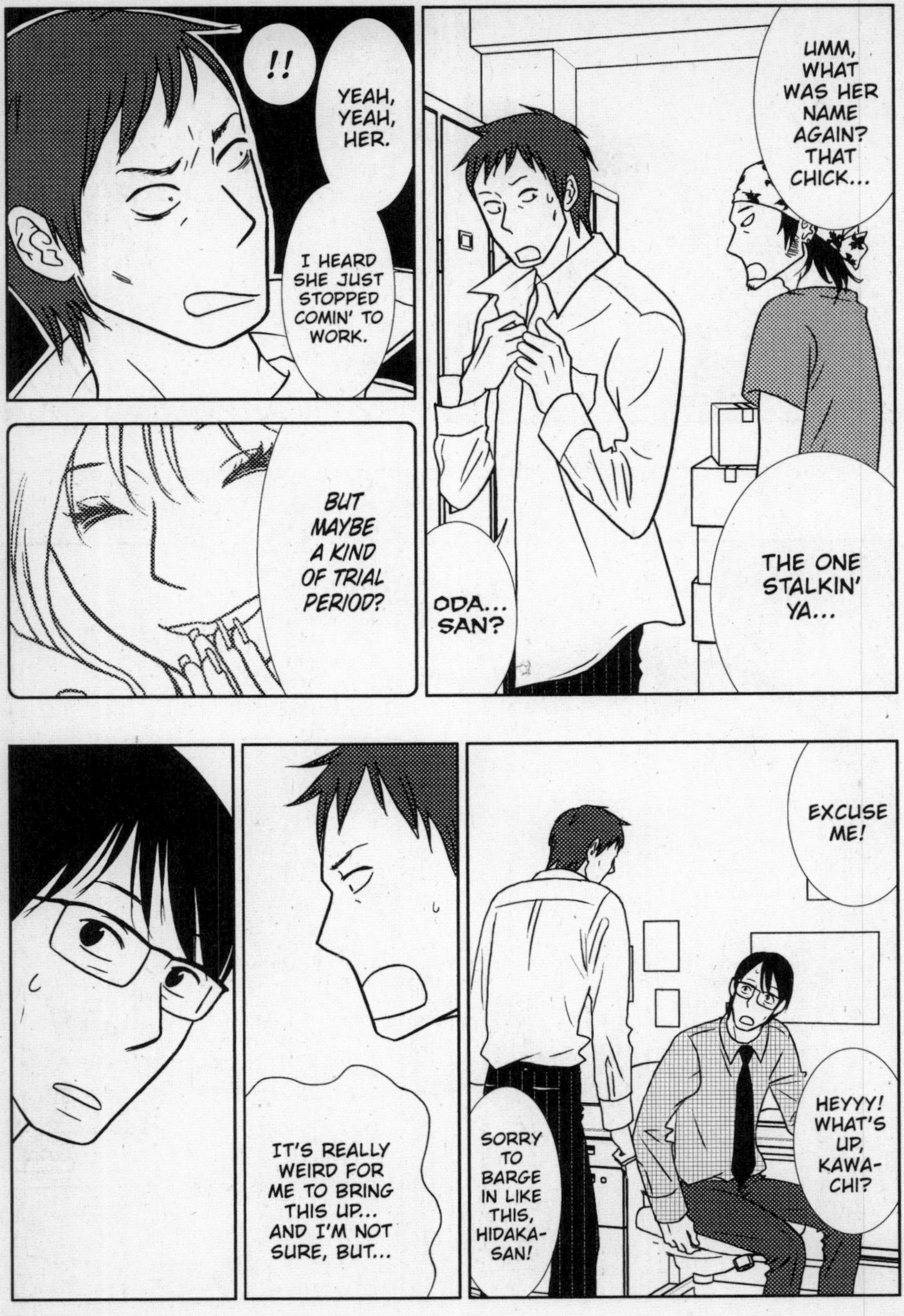
UMM, WHAT WAS HER NAME AGAIN? THAT CHICK...
THE ONE STALKIN' YA...
ODA... SAN?
!!
YEAH, YEAH, HER.
I HEARD SHE JUST STOPPED COMIN' TO WORK.
BUT MAYBE A KIND OF TRIAL PERIOD?
EXCUSE ME!
HEYYY! WHAT'S UP, KAWA-CHI?
SORRY TO BARGE IN LIKE THIS, HIDAKA-SAN!
IT'S REALLY WEIRD FOR ME TO BRING THIS UP... AND I'M NOT SURE, BUT...

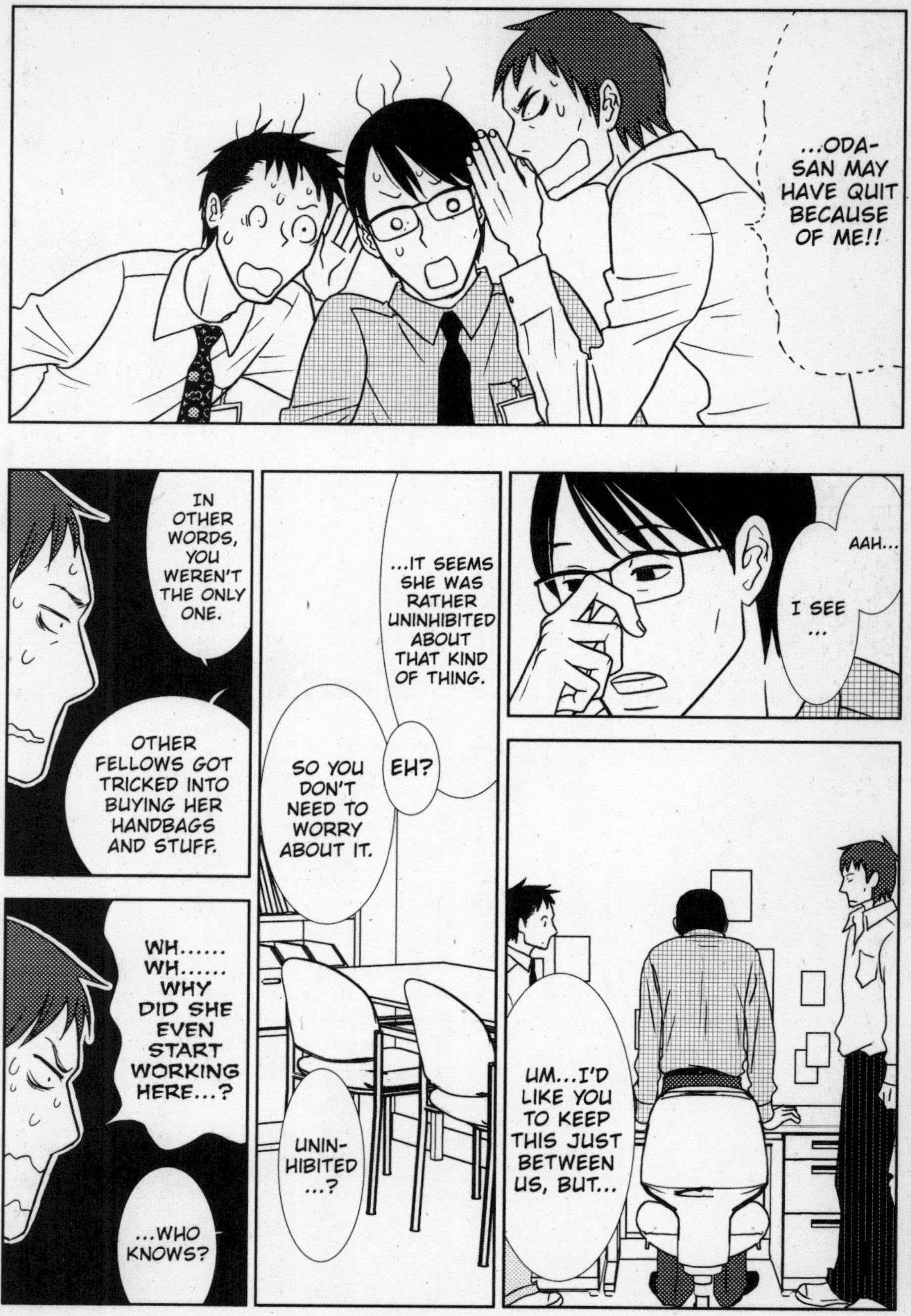
...ODA-SAN MAY HAVE QUIT BECAUSE OF ME!!
AAH... I SEE ...
UM...I'D LIKE YOU TO KEEP THIS JUST BETWEEN US, BUT...
...IT SEEMS SHE WAS RATHER UNINHIBITED ABOUT THAT KIND OF THING.
EH?
SO YOU DON'T NEED TO WORRY ABOUT IT.
UNIN-HIBITED ...?
IN OTHER WORDS, YOU WEREN'T THE ONLY ONE.
OTHER FELLOWS GOT TRICKED INTO BUYING HER HANDBAGS AND STUFF.
WH...... WH...... WHY DID SHE EVEN START WORKING HERE...?
...WHO KNOWS?

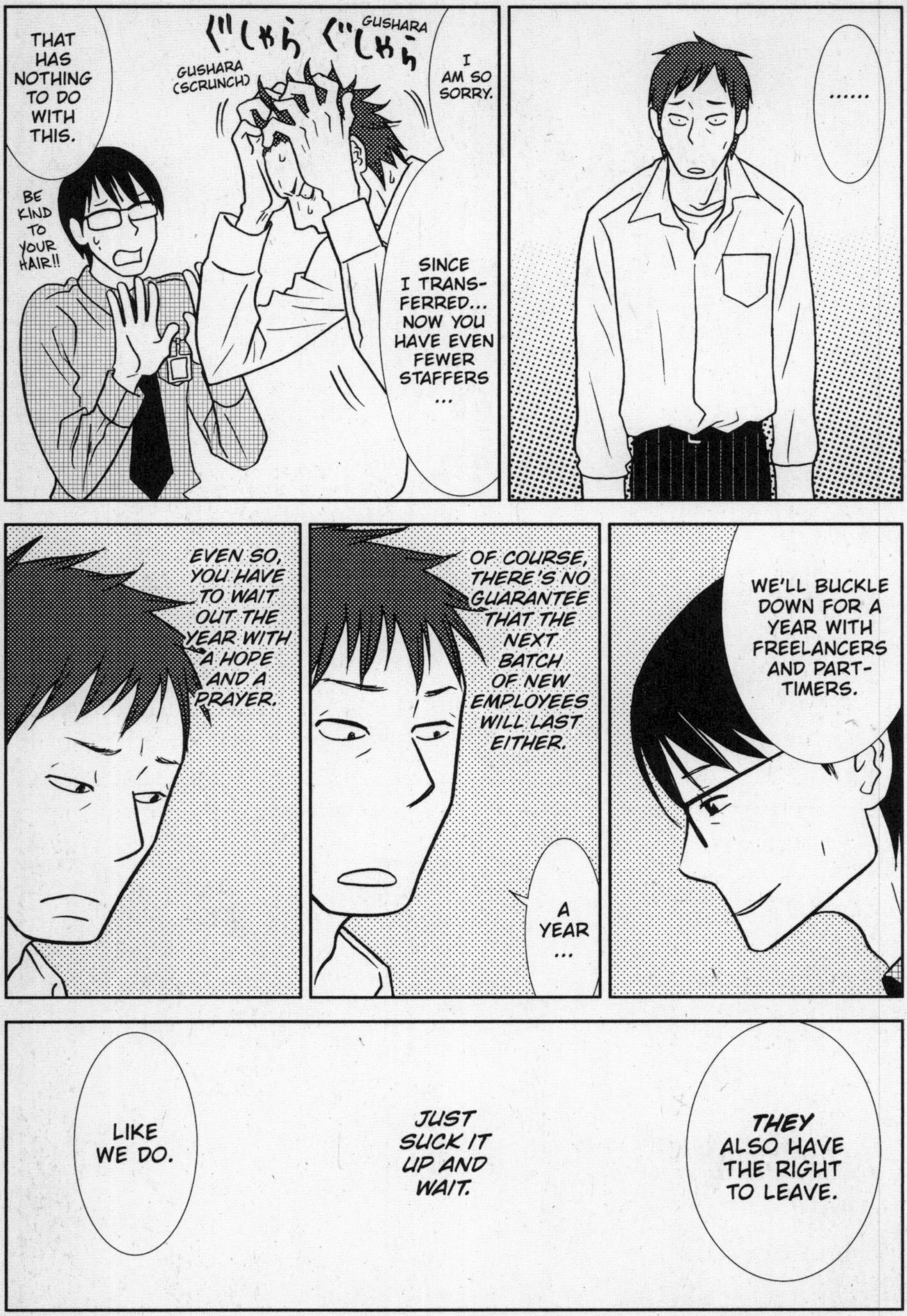
......
I AM SO SORRY.
SINCE I TRANSFERRED... NOW YOU HAVE EVEN FEWER STAFFERS ...
ぐしゃら ぐしゃら
GUSHARA
GUSHARA (SCRUNCH)
THAT HAS NOTHING TO DO WITH THIS.
BE KIND TO YOUR HAIR!!
WE'LL BUCKLE DOWN FOR A YEAR WITH FREELANCERS AND PART-TIMERS.
OF COURSE, THERE'S NO GUARANTEE THAT THE NEXT BATCH OF NEW EMPLOYEES WILL LAST EITHER.
A YEAR ...
EVEN SO, YOU HAVE TO WAIT OUT THE YEAR WITH A HOPE AND A PRAYER.
THEY ALSO HAVE THE RIGHT TO LEAVE.
JUST SUCK IT UP AND WAIT.
LIKE WE DO.

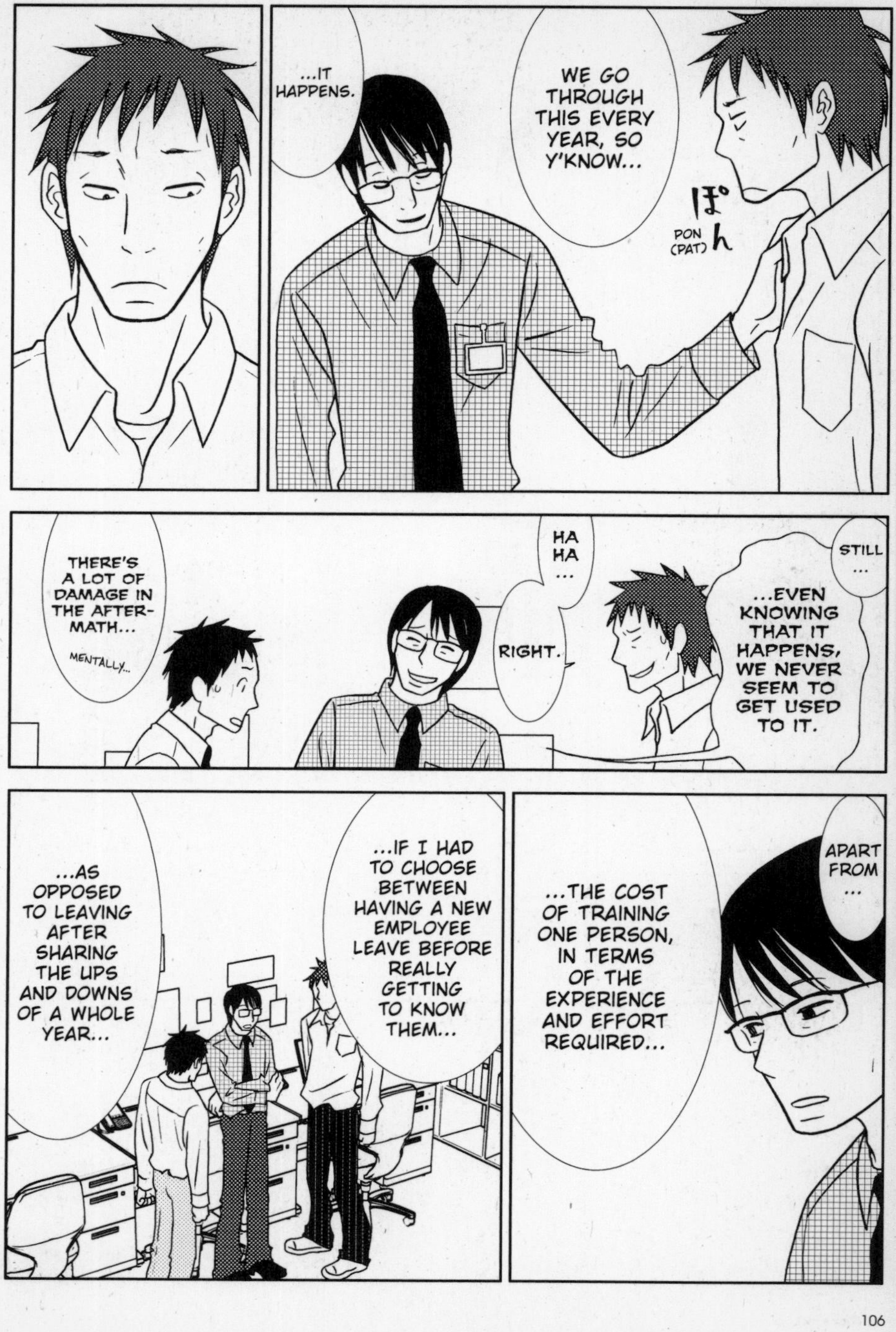
WE GO THROUGH THIS EVERY YEAR, SO Y'KNOW...
...IT HAPPENS.
ぽん
PON (PAT)
STILL...
...EVEN KNOWING THAT IT HAPPENS, WE NEVER SEEM TO GET USED TO IT.
HA HA...
RIGHT.
THERE'S A LOT OF DAMAGE IN THE AFTER-MATH...
MENTALLY...
APART FROM...
...THE COST OF TRAINING ONE PERSON, IN TERMS OF THE EXPERIENCE AND EFFORT REQUIRED...
...IF I HAD TO CHOOSE BETWEEN HAVING A NEW EMPLOYEE LEAVE BEFORE REALLY GETTING TO KNOW THEM...
...AS OPPOSED TO LEAVING AFTER SHARING THE UPS AND DOWNS OF A WHOLE YEAR...

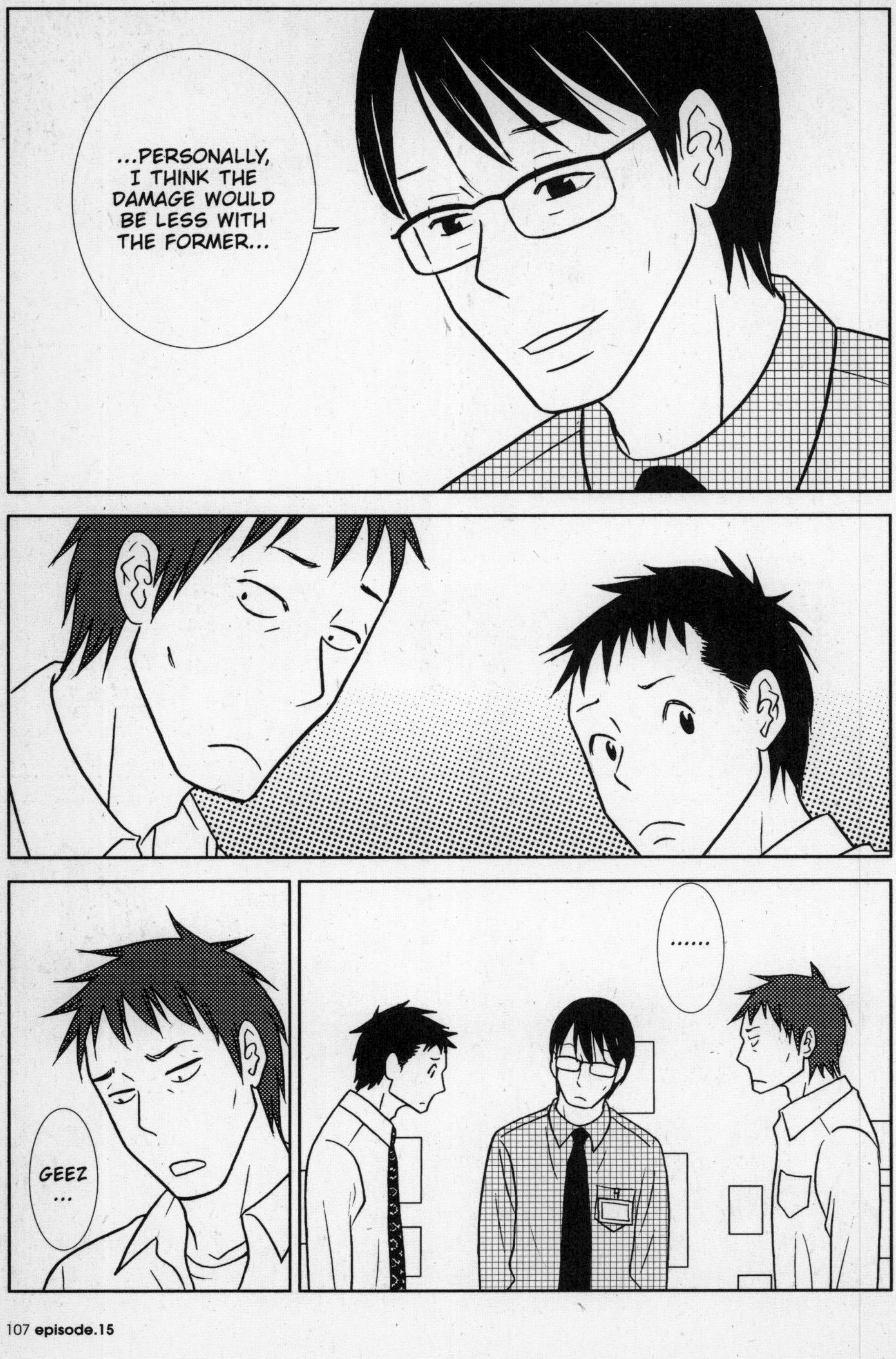
...PERSONALLY, I THINK THE DAMAGE WOULD BE LESS WITH THE FORMER...
......
GEEZ ...

WHY ARE FEMALE EMPLOYEES SO HARD TO DEAL WITH...?
HAAAH...
WELL, IT'S NOT ALL OF THEM...
...I WISH THEY WERE ALL LIKE GOTOU-SAN.
H-HEY, KAWACHI... YOU CAN THINK *THAT*, BUT YOU SHOULDN'T SAY IT OUT LOUD...
YOU'RE GONNA GIVE ME MORE GRAY HAIR...
SHH!
THAT'S SEXUAL HARASS-MENT!!
YOU CAN'T SAY STUFF LIKE THAT N-N-NOWA-DAYS!!
THAT'S NOT WHAT I MEAN.
I'M SAYING THAT THEY'RE HARD TO DEAL WITH 'COS THEY MAKE YOU NERVOUS LIKE THIS EVERY DAY.
BESIDES, I'VE NEVER BEEN GOOD AROUND GIRLS AND WOMEN TO BEGIN WITH, NOT EVEN AT HOME.
HA-HA... HA...
I GUESS WE'LL JUST HAVE TO LEAVE IT AT THAT...
AH-HA-HA...
UH, I'M GOING BACK TO THE SALES FLOOR.

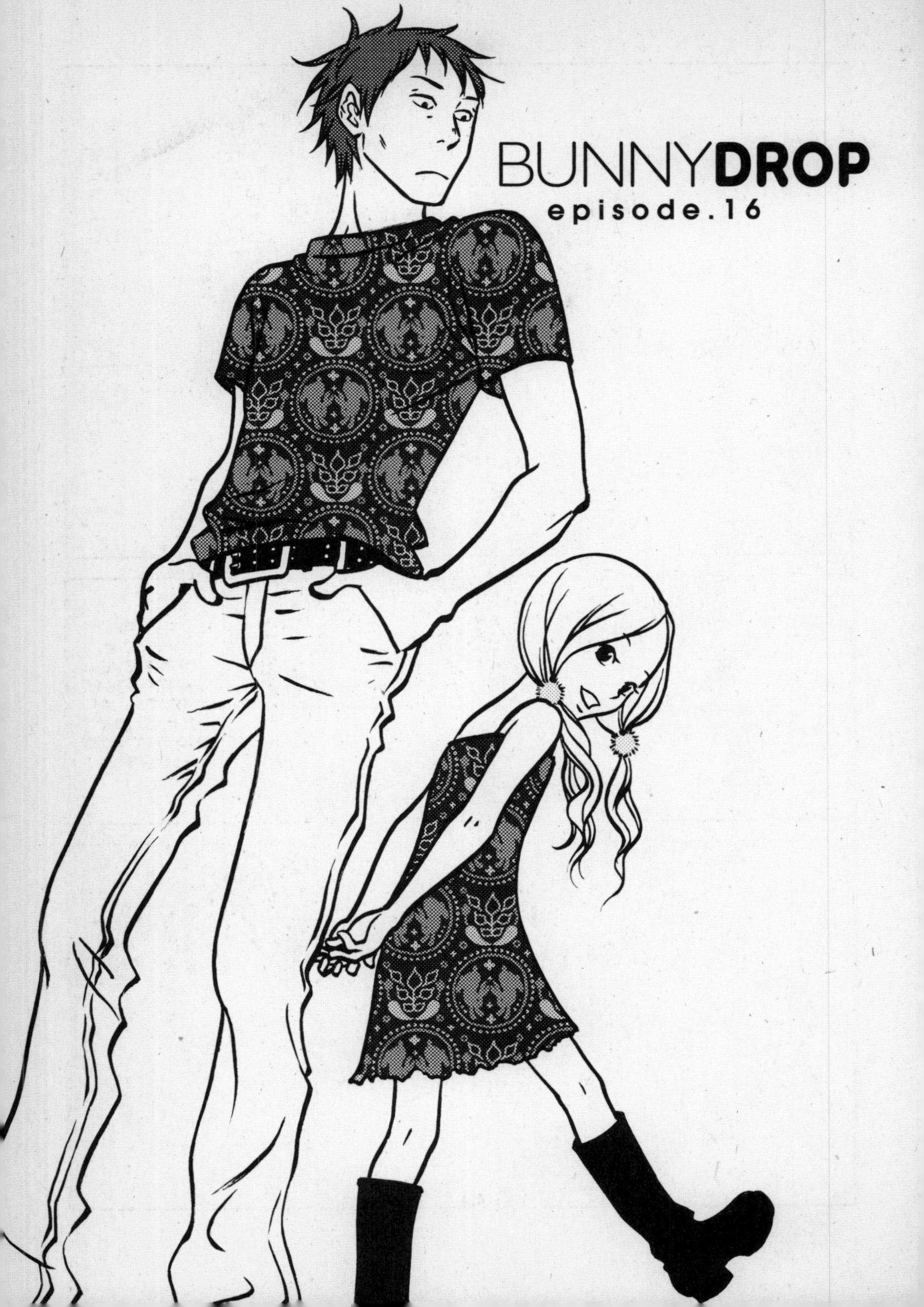
BUNNYDROP
episode.16

DAIKICHI, DAIKICHI !!

WHAT D'YOU WANT ...?

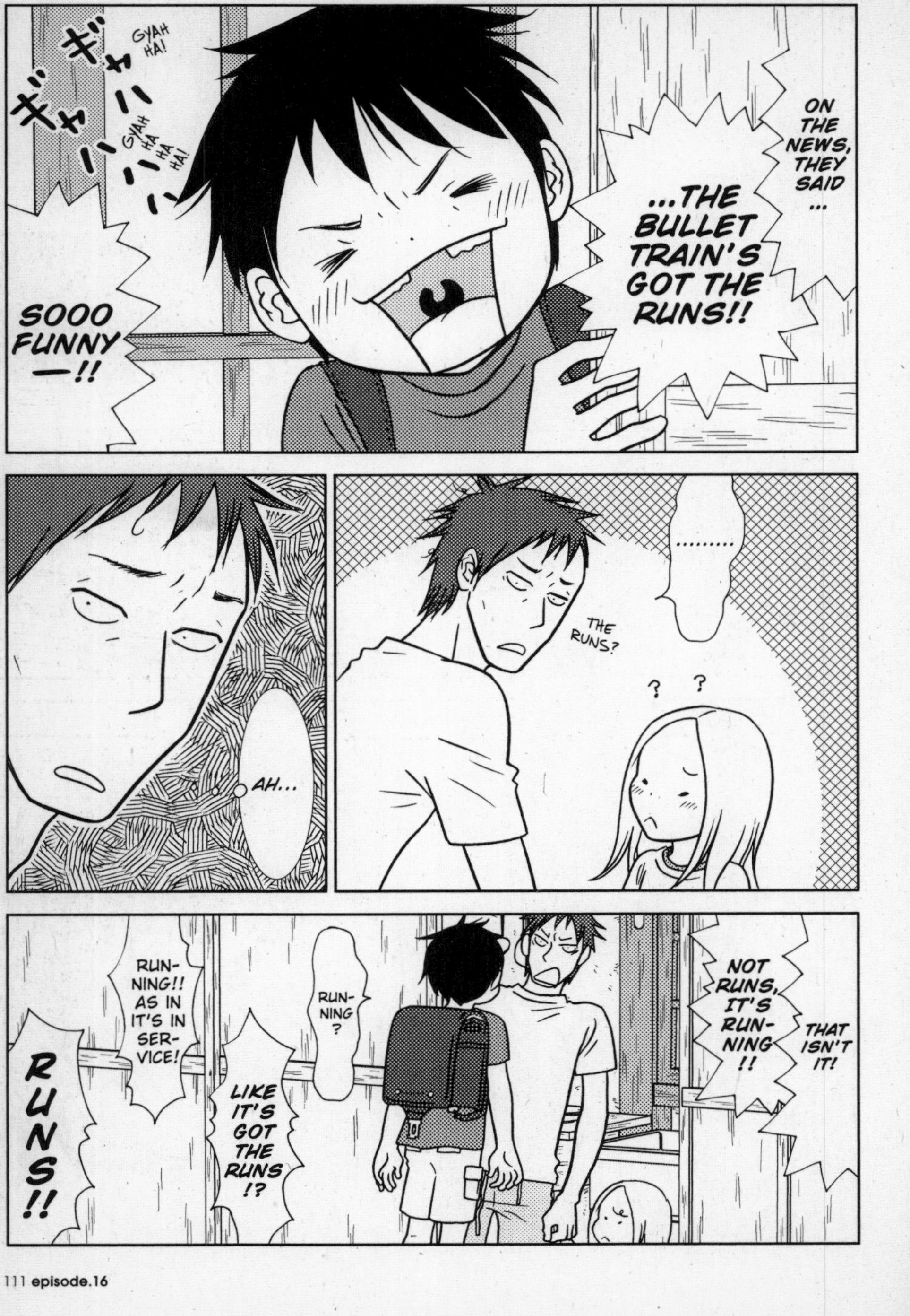
ON THE NEWS, THEY SAID ...
...THE BULLET TRAIN'S GOT THE RUNS!!
GYAH HA!
GYAH HA HA HA!
SOOO FUNNY—!!
....
THE RUNS?
? ?
AH...
NOT RUNS, IT'S RUNNING!!
THAT ISN'T IT!
RUNNING?
RUNNING!! AS IN IT'S IN SERVICE!
LIKE IT'S GOT THE RUNS!?
RUNS!!

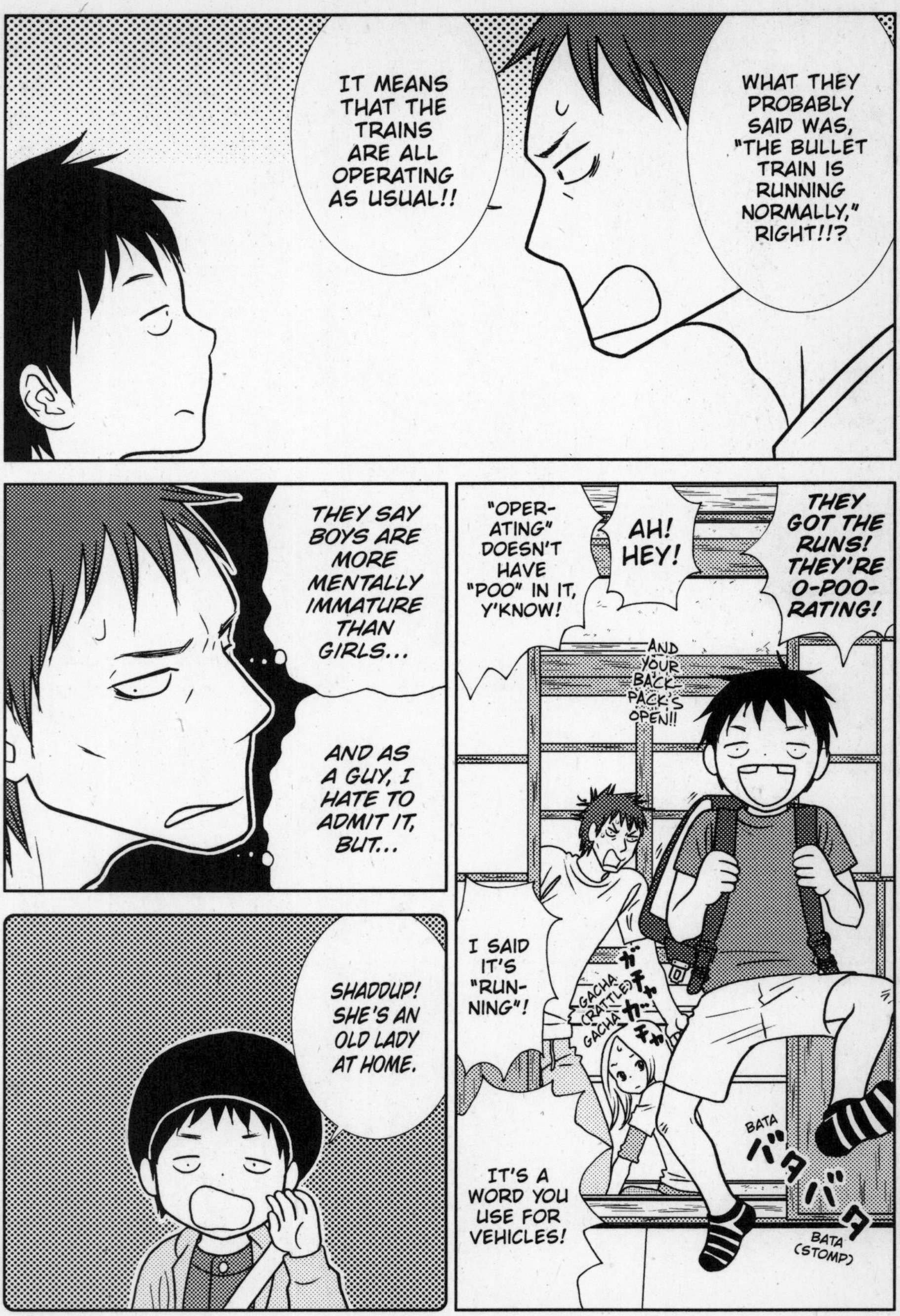
WHAT THEY PROBABLY SAID WAS, "THE BULLET TRAIN IS RUNNING NORMALLY," RIGHT!!?
IT MEANS THAT THE TRAINS ARE ALL OPERATING AS USUAL!!
THEY GOT THE RUNS! THEY'RE O-POO-RATING!
AH! HEY!
"OPER-ATING" DOESN'T HAVE "POO" IN IT, Y'KNOW!
AND YOUR BACK PACK'S OPEN!!
I SAID IT'S "RUN-NING"!
GACHA GACHA (RATTLE)
IT'S A WORD YOU USE FOR VEHICLES!
BATA BATA (STOMP)
THEY SAY BOYS ARE MORE MENTALLY IMMATURE THAN GIRLS...
AND AS A GUY, I HATE TO ADMIT IT, BUT...
SHADDUP! SHE'S AN OLD LADY AT HOME.

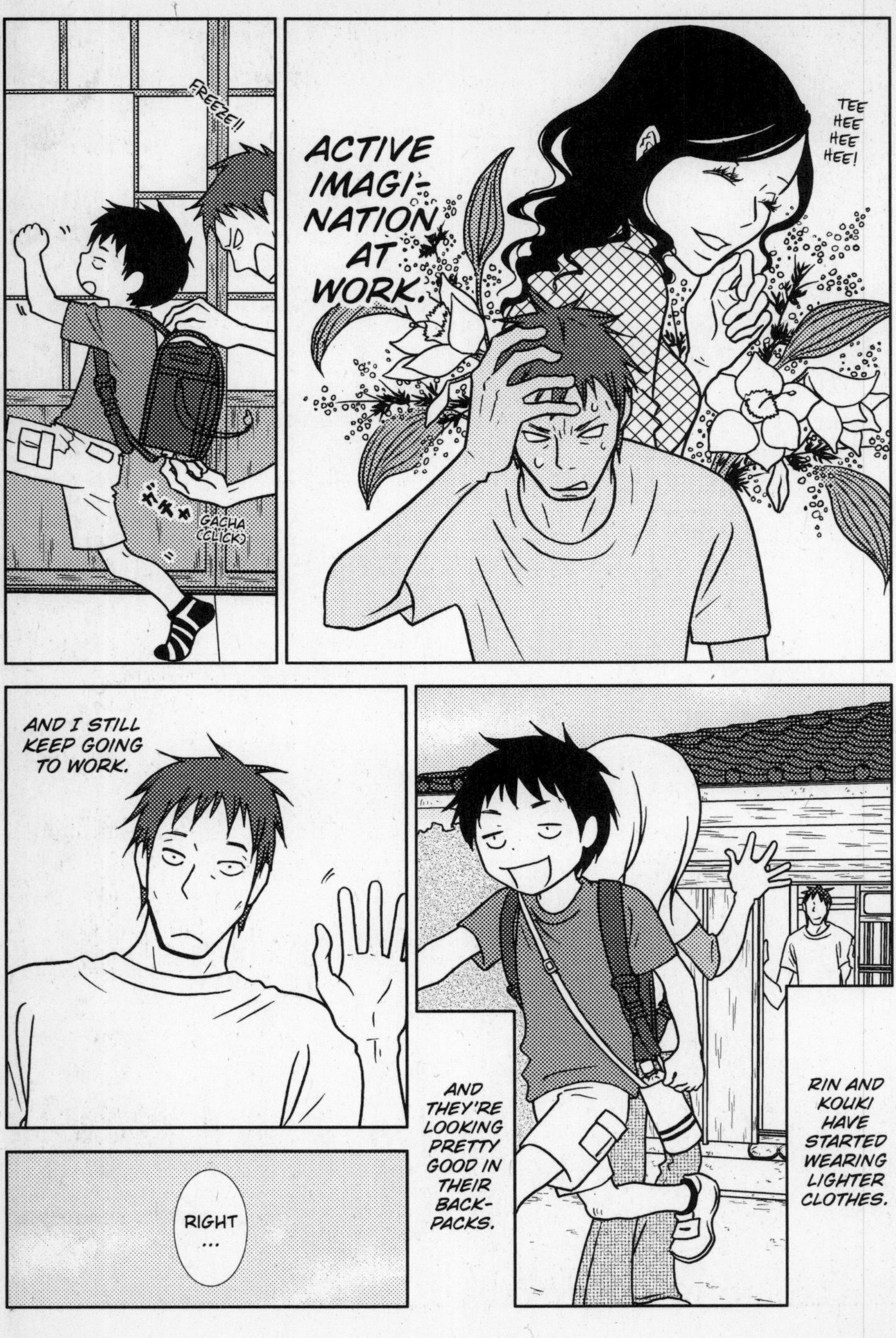
ACTIVE IMAGINATION AT WORK.
TEE HEE HEE HEE!
FREEZE!!
ガチャ
GACHA (CLICK)
RIN AND KOUKI HAVE STARTED WEARING LIGHTER CLOTHES.
AND THEY'RE LOOKING PRETTY GOOD IN THEIR BACKPACKS.
AND I STILL KEEP GOING TO WORK.
RIGHT ...

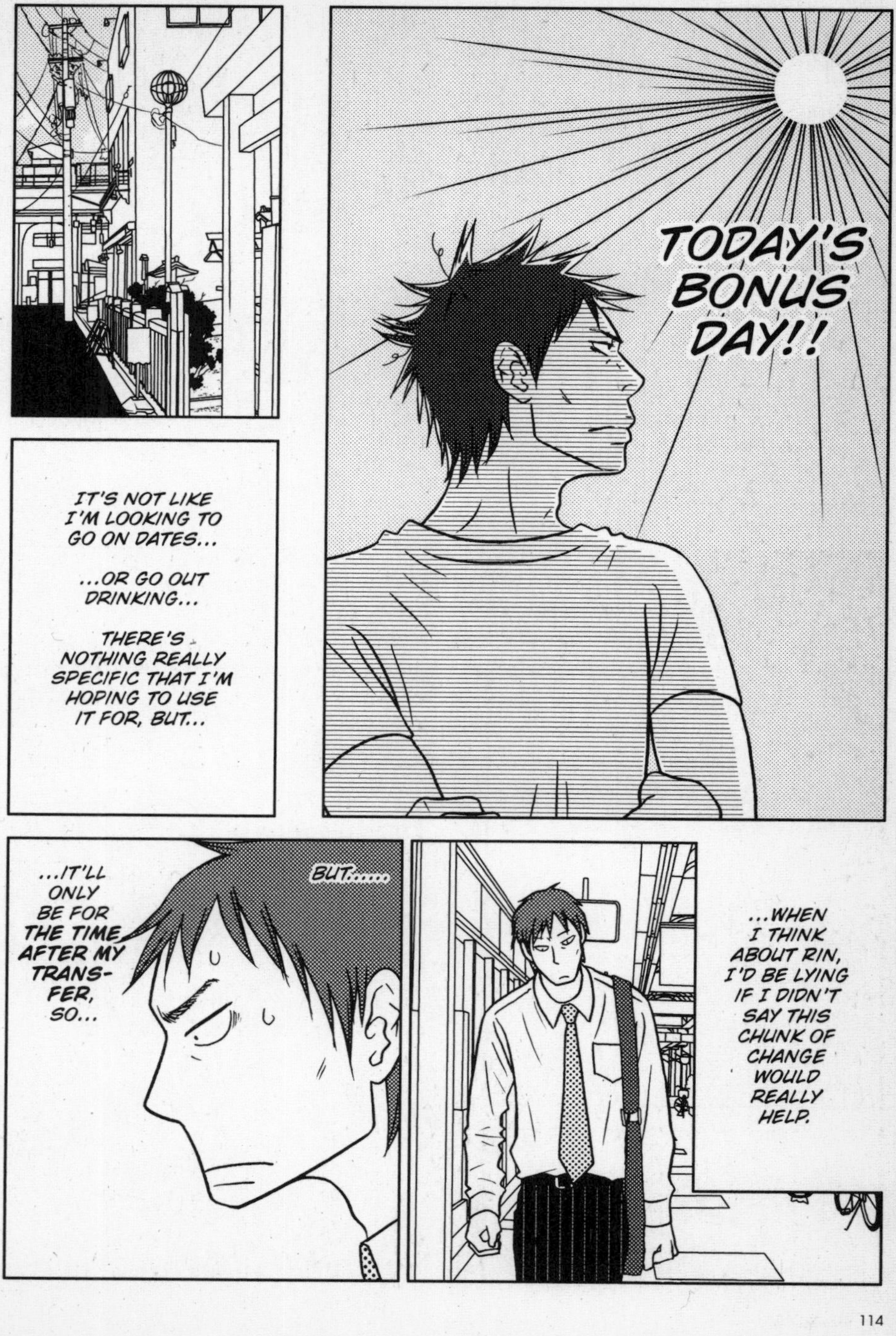
TODAY'S BONUS DAY!!
IT'S NOT LIKE I'M LOOKING TO GO ON DATES...
...OR GO OUT DRINKING...
THERE'S NOTHING REALLY SPECIFIC THAT I'M HOPING TO USE IT FOR, BUT...
...WHEN I THINK ABOUT RIN, I'D BE LYING IF I DIDN'T SAY THIS CHUNK OF CHANGE WOULD REALLY HELP.
BUT......
...IT'LL ONLY BE FOR THE TIME AFTER MY TRANSFER, SO...

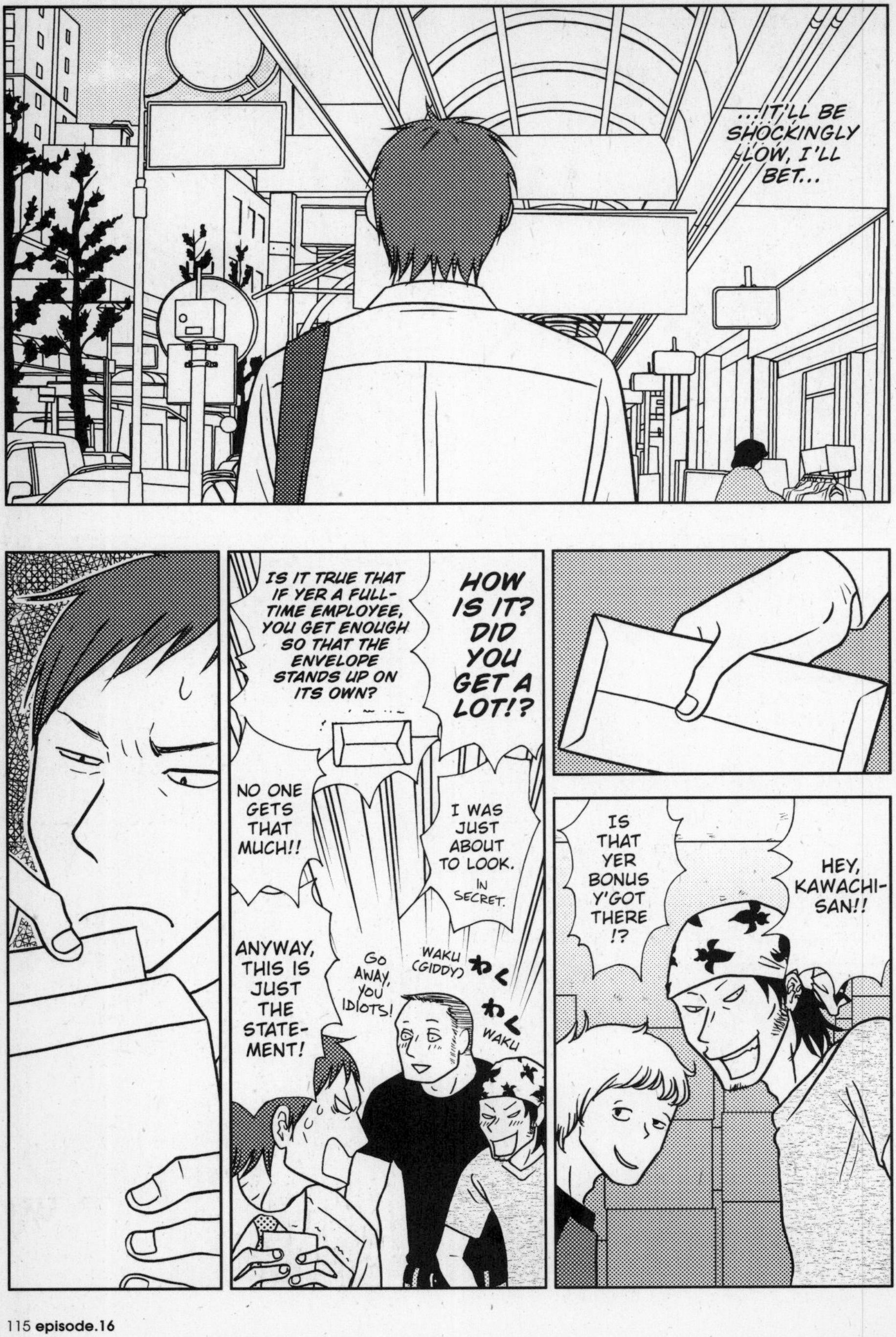
...IT'LL BE SHOCKINGLY LOW, I'LL BET...
HEY, KAWACHI-SAN!!
IS THAT YER BONUS Y'GOT THERE!?
HOW IS IT? DID YOU GET A LOT!?
IS IT TRUE THAT IF YER A FULL-TIME EMPLOYEE, YOU GET ENOUGH SO THAT THE ENVELOPE STANDS UP ON ITS OWN?
I WAS JUST ABOUT TO LOOK. IN SECRET.
NO ONE GETS THAT MUCH!!
WAKU (GIDDY) わく
わく WAKU
GO AWAY, YOU IDIOTS!
ANYWAY, THIS IS JUST THE STATEMENT!

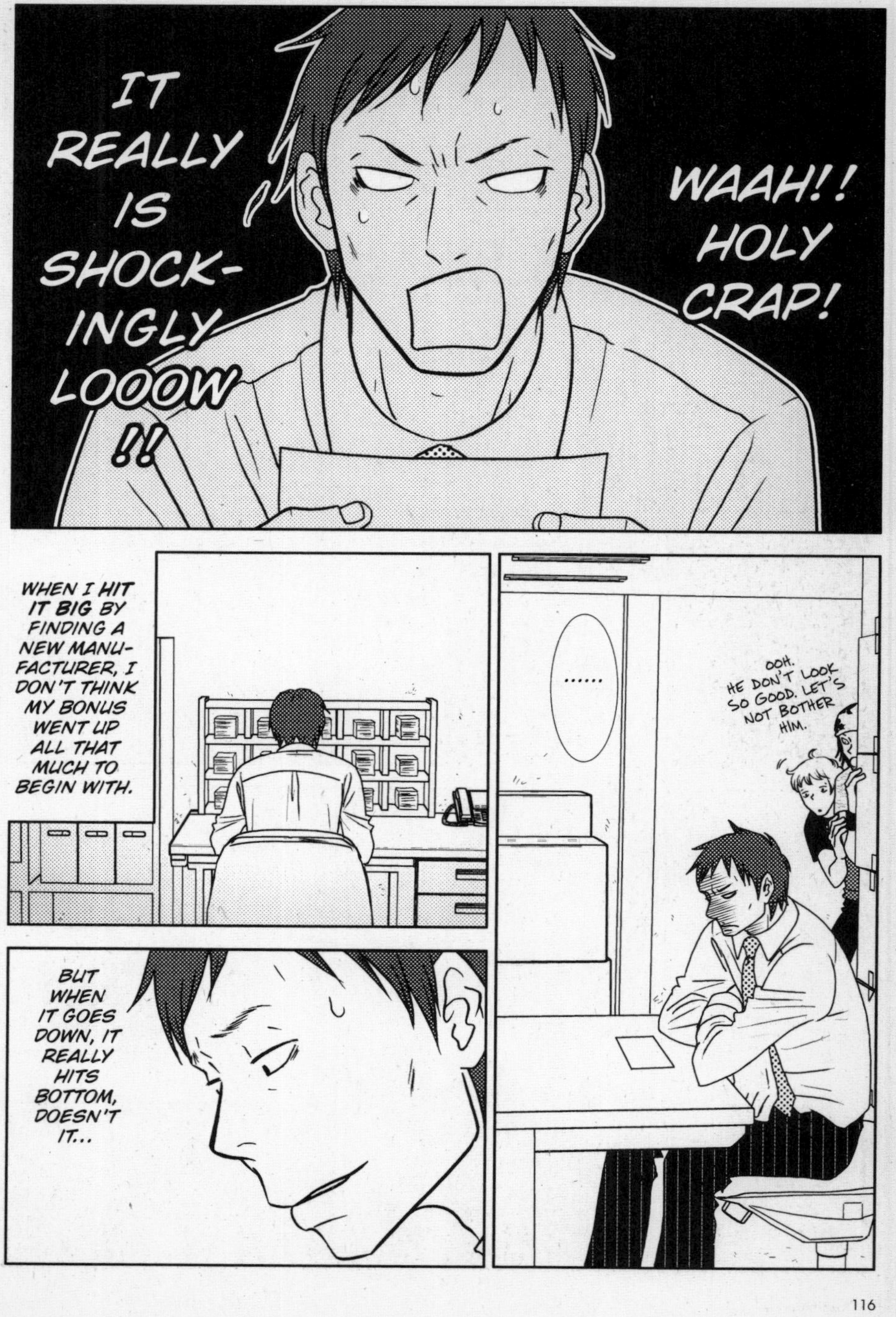
WAAH!! HOLY CRAP!
IT REALLY IS SHOCK-INGLY LOOOW!!
OOH. HE DON'T LOOK SO GOOD. LET'S NOT BOTHER HIM.
......
WHEN I HIT IT BIG BY FINDING A NEW MANU-FACTURER, I DON'T THINK MY BONUS WENT UP ALL THAT MUCH TO BEGIN WITH.
BUT WHEN IT GOES DOWN, IT REALLY HITS BOTTOM, DOESN'T IT...

HOW BITTER-SWEET...
YOU HAVE TO WORK TO MAKE A LIVING.
IF YOU TRY TO RAISE A CHILD, YOUR TIME ON THE CLOCK GETS CUT...
...AND THEN YOUR PAY GOES DOWN.
HOW THE HECK DOES EVERYONE BALANCE THEIR CHECK-BOOKS ...!?
EVEN THOUGH MY CURRENT MONTHLY PAY WENT DOWN, MY BASE SALARY IS STILL WEIGHTED BY MY NINE YEARS OF SERVICE HERE AT THE COMPANY...
IT'S EASY ENOUGH TO KEEP RIN FED AND CLOTHED, BUT...
SURE, YOU CAN GET IT.
...I WONDER WHAT IT'S LIKE FOR A YOUNG SINGLE MOM RAISING A CHILD BY HERSELF...?

BAG: SWEET BUNS

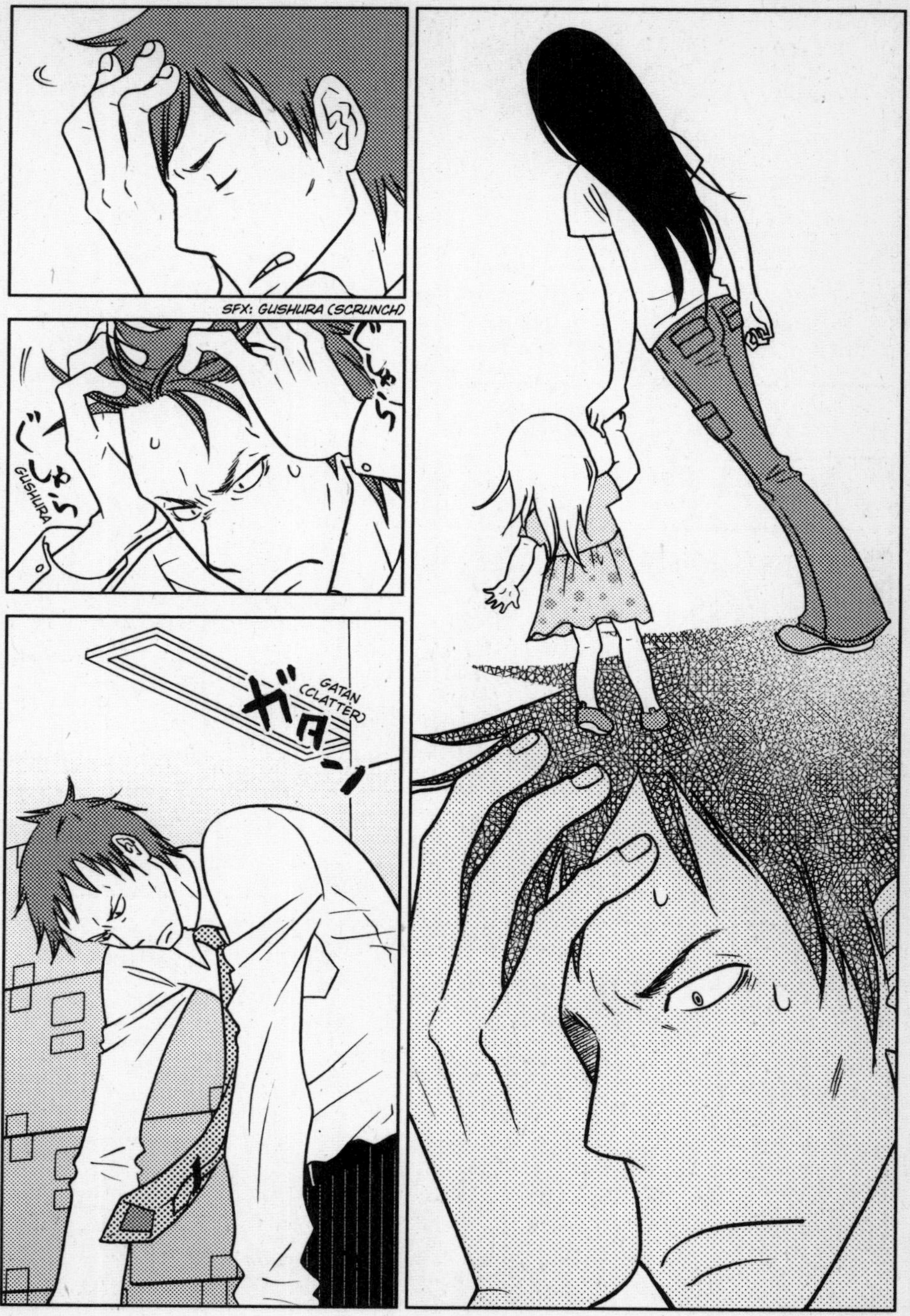
SFX: GUSHURA (SCRUNCH)
ぐしゃら
ぐしゃら
GUSHURA
ガタン
GATAN (CLATTER)

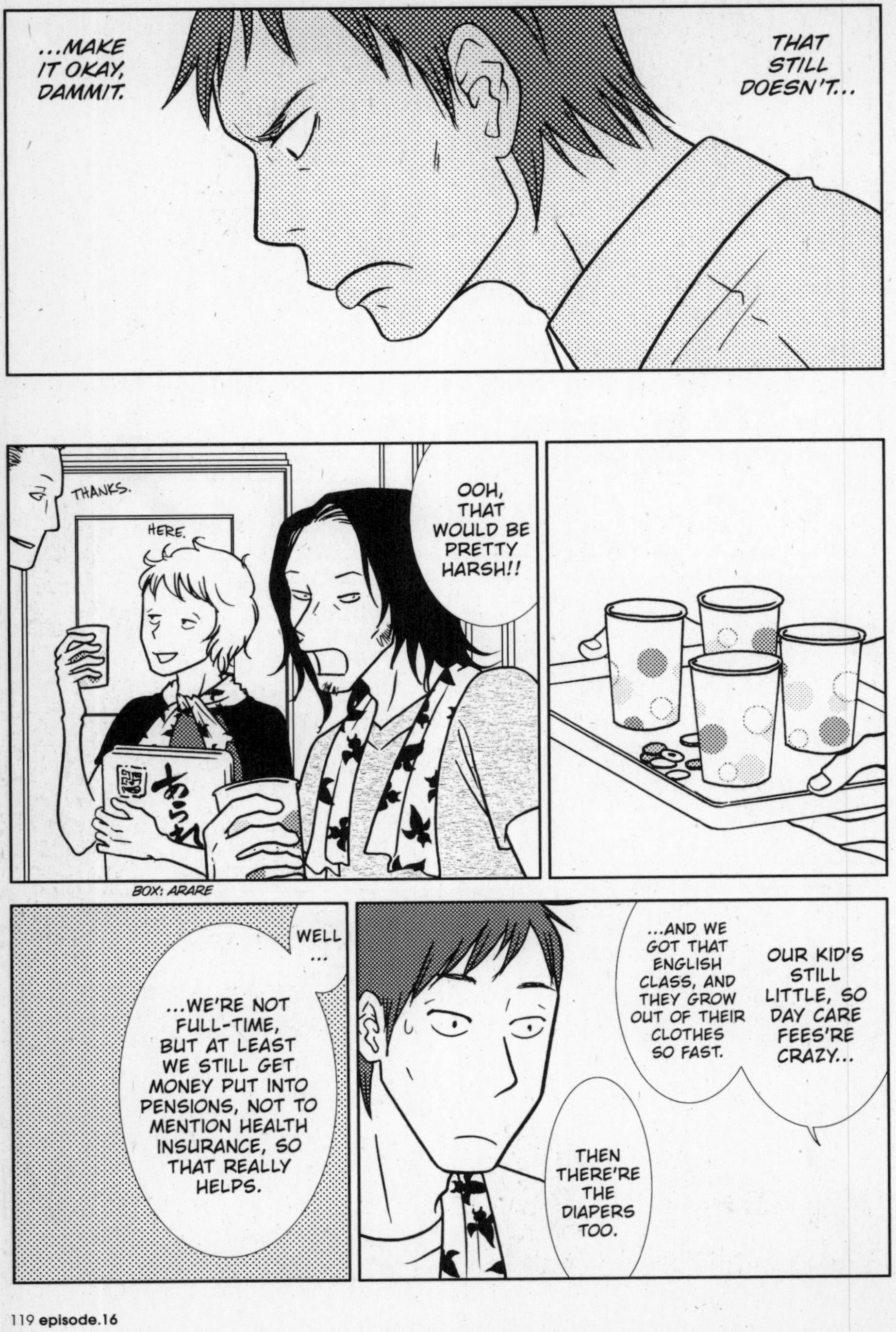
THAT STILL DOESN'T...
...MAKE IT OKAY, DAMMIT.
OOH, THAT WOULD BE PRETTY HARSH!!
HERE.
THANKS.
あられ
BOX: ARARE
OUR KID'S STILL LITTLE, SO DAY CARE FEES'RE CRAZY...
...AND WE GOT THAT ENGLISH CLASS, AND THEY GROW OUT OF THEIR CLOTHES SO FAST.
THEN THERE'RE THE DIAPERS TOO.
WELL ...
...WE'RE NOT FULL-TIME, BUT AT LEAST WE STILL GET MONEY PUT INTO PENSIONS, NOT TO MENTION HEALTH INSURANCE, SO THAT REALLY HELPS.

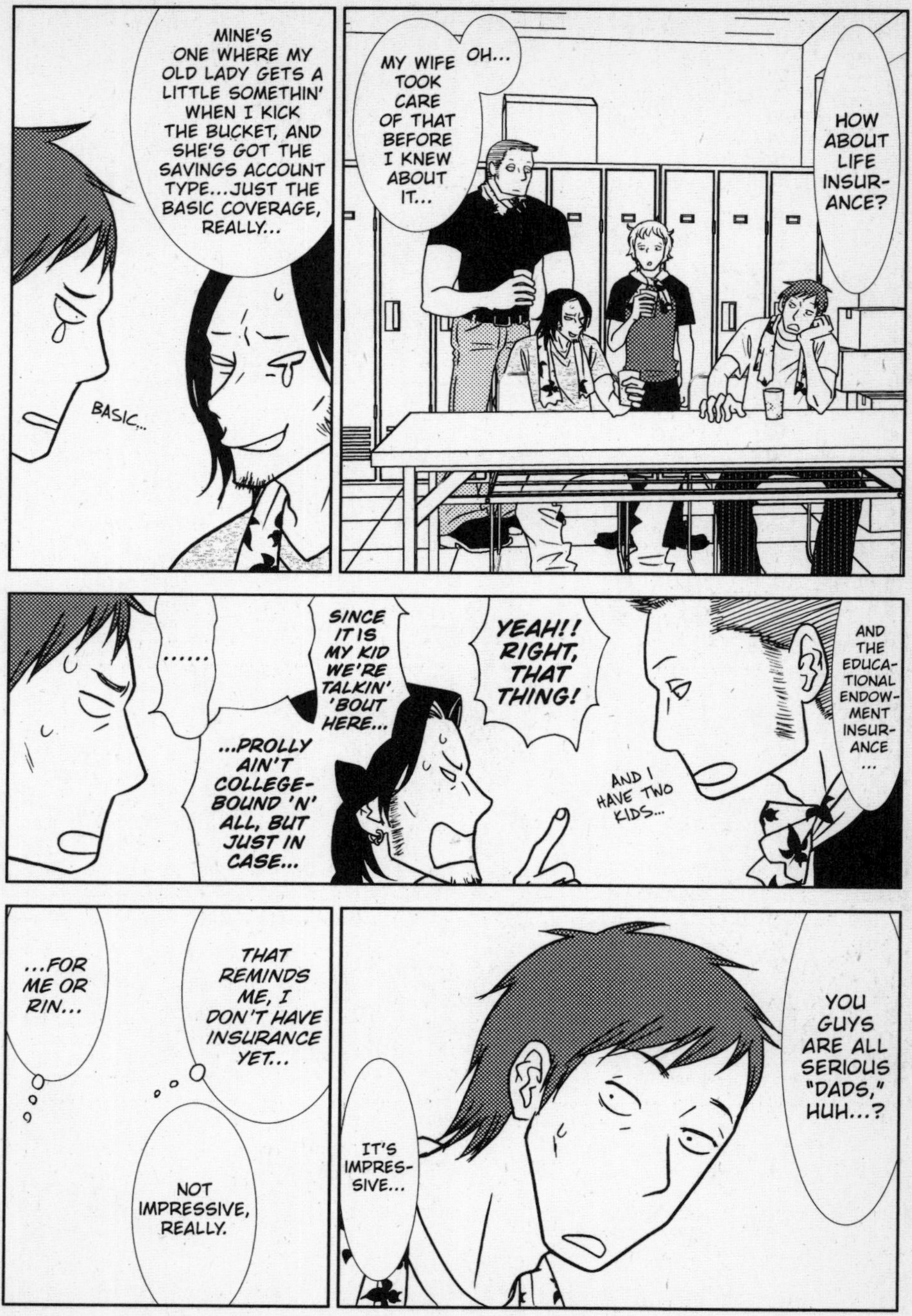
HOW ABOUT LIFE INSURANCE?
OH...
MY WIFE TOOK CARE OF THAT BEFORE I KNEW ABOUT IT...
MINE'S ONE WHERE MY OLD LADY GETS A LITTLE SOMETHIN' WHEN I KICK THE BUCKET, AND SHE'S GOT THE SAVINGS ACCOUNT TYPE...JUST THE BASIC COVERAGE, REALLY...
BASIC...
AND THE EDUCATIONAL ENDOWMENT INSURANCE...
AND I HAVE TWO KIDS...
YEAH!! RIGHT, THAT THING!
SINCE IT IS MY KID WE'RE TALKIN' 'BOUT HERE...
...PROLLY AIN'T COLLEGE-BOUND 'N' ALL, BUT JUST IN CASE...
......
YOU GUYS ARE ALL SERIOUS "DADS," HUH...?
IT'S IMPRESSIVE...
THAT REMINDS ME, I DON'T HAVE INSURANCE YET...
...FOR ME OR RIN...
NOT IMPRESSIVE, REALLY.

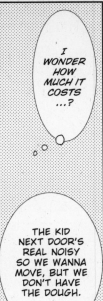

I WONDER HOW MUCH IT COSTS ...?
THE KID NEXT DOOR'S REAL NOISY SO WE WANNA MOVE, BUT WE DON'T HAVE THE DOUGH.
I SERIOUSLY DON'T EVEN KNOW WHY I WORK.
YOU, WATCH OUT!! THIS IS WHAT HAPPENS WHEN YOU GET MARRIED!!
OH, I'M SAFE. I DON'T EVEN HAVE A GIRL-FRIEND.
SAFE?
AS MUCH AS THESE GUYS COMPLAIN ...
... THEY HAVE A SENSE OF SECU-RITY ABOUT THEM.
...I CAN'T SEE THEM TURNING INTO...
...SOMEONE LIKE RIN'S MOTHER AT ALL.

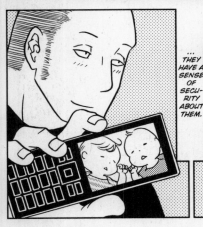

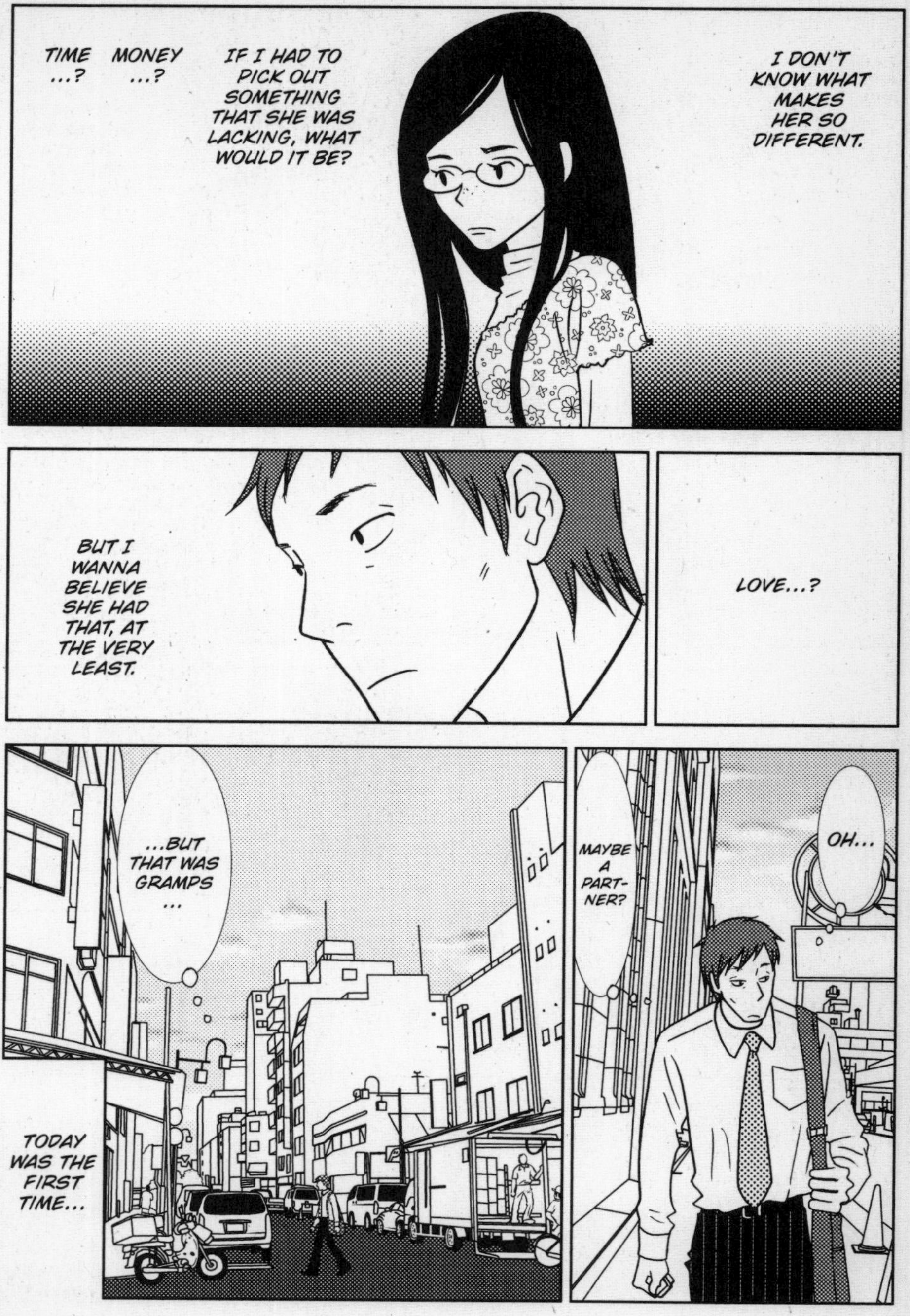
I DON'T KNOW WHAT MAKES HER SO DIFFERENT.
IF I HAD TO PICK OUT SOMETHING THAT SHE WAS LACKING, WHAT WOULD IT BE?
MONEY ...?
TIME ...?
LOVE...?
BUT I WANNA BELIEVE SHE HAD THAT, AT THE VERY LEAST.
OH...
MAYBE A PART-NER?
...BUT THAT WAS GRAMPS ...
TODAY WAS THE FIRST TIME...

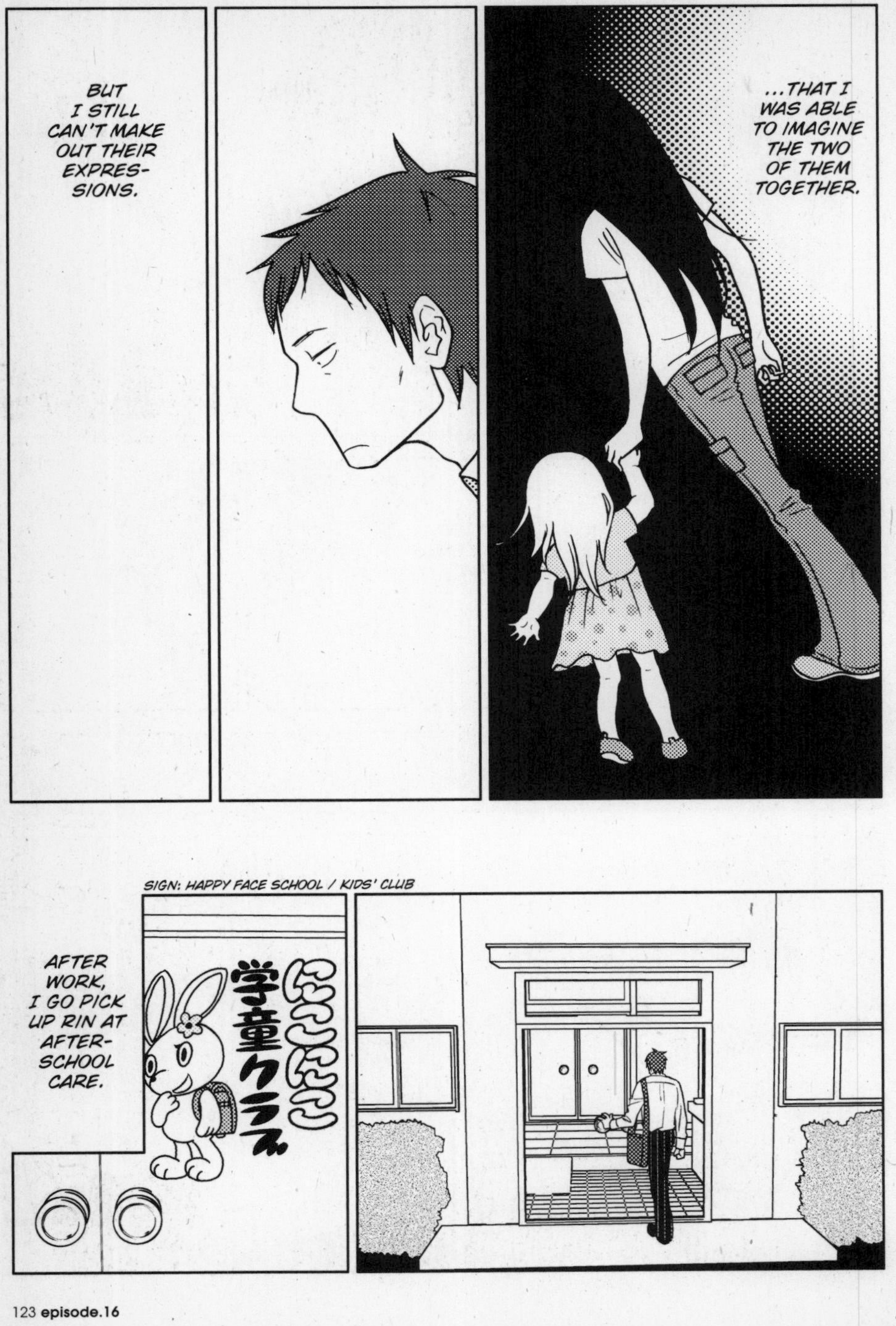
...THAT I WAS ABLE TO IMAGINE THE TWO OF THEM TOGETHER.
BUT I STILL CAN'T MAKE OUT THEIR EXPRES-SIONS.
SIGN: HAPPY FACE SCHOOL / KIDS' CLUB
AFTER WORK, I GO PICK UP RIN AT AFTER-SCHOOL CARE.
にこにこ学童クラブ

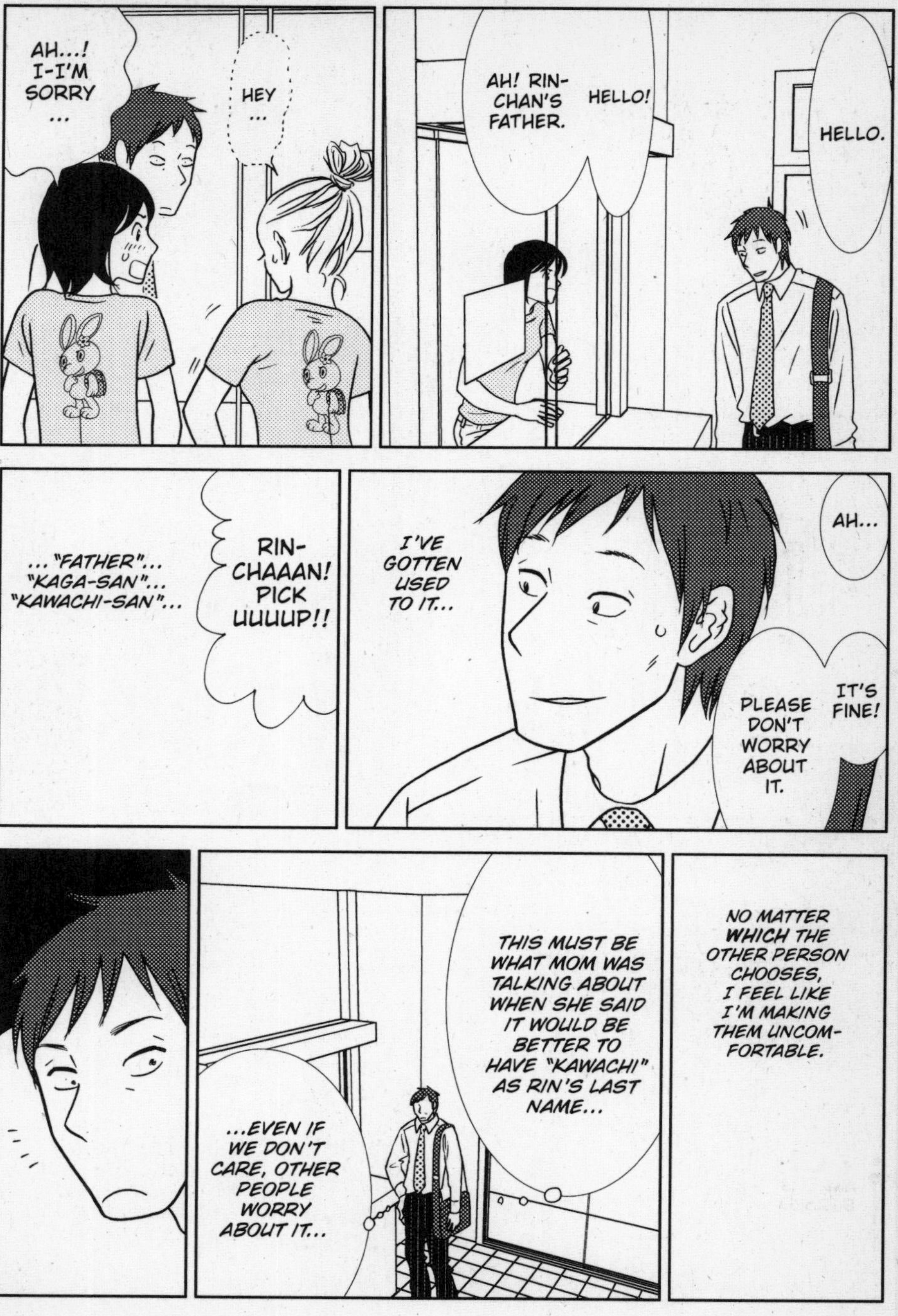
HELLO.
HELLO!
AH! RIN-CHAN'S FATHER.
HEY ...
AH...! I-I'M SORRY ...
AH...
I'VE GOTTEN USED TO IT...
IT'S FINE!
PLEASE DON'T WORRY ABOUT IT.
RIN-CHAAAN! PICK UUUUP!!
... "FATHER"... "KAGA-SAN"... "KAWACHI-SAN"...
NO MATTER WHICH THE OTHER PERSON CHOOSES, I FEEL LIKE I'M MAKING THEM UNCOM-FORTABLE.
THIS MUST BE WHAT MOM WAS TALKING ABOUT WHEN SHE SAID IT WOULD BE BETTER TO HAVE "KAWACHI" AS RIN'S LAST NAME...
...EVEN IF WE DON'T CARE, OTHER PEOPLE WORRY ABOUT IT...

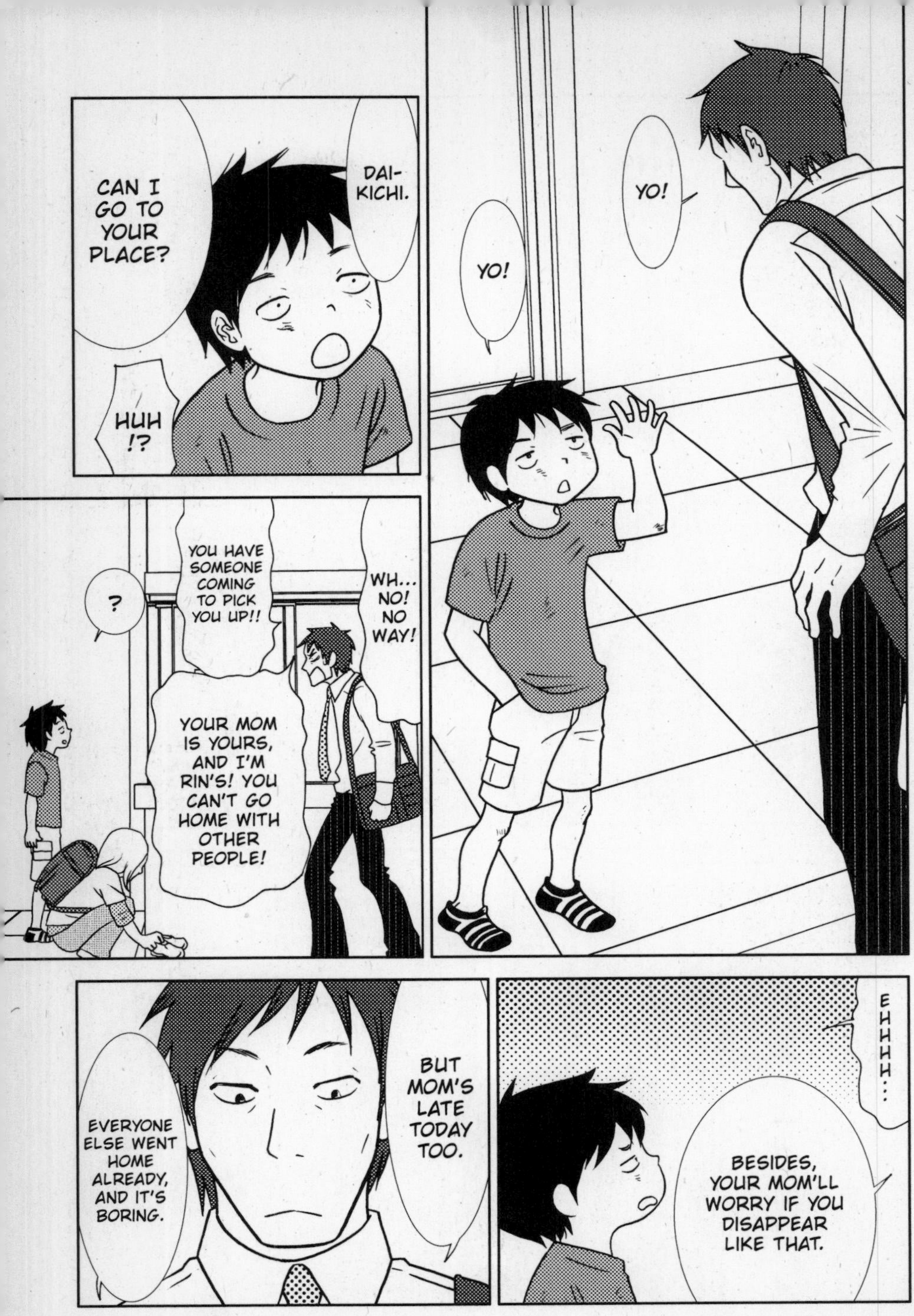
YO!
YO!
DAI-KICHI.
CAN I GO TO YOUR PLACE?
HUH!?
WH... NO! NO WAY!
YOU HAVE SOMEONE COMING TO PICK YOU UP!!
?
YOUR MOM IS YOURS, AND I'M RIN'S! YOU CAN'T GO HOME WITH OTHER PEOPLE!
EHHHHH...
BESIDES, YOUR MOM'LL WORRY IF YOU DISAPPEAR LIKE THAT.
BUT MOM'S LATE TODAY TOO.
EVERYONE ELSE WENT HOME ALREADY, AND IT'S BORING.

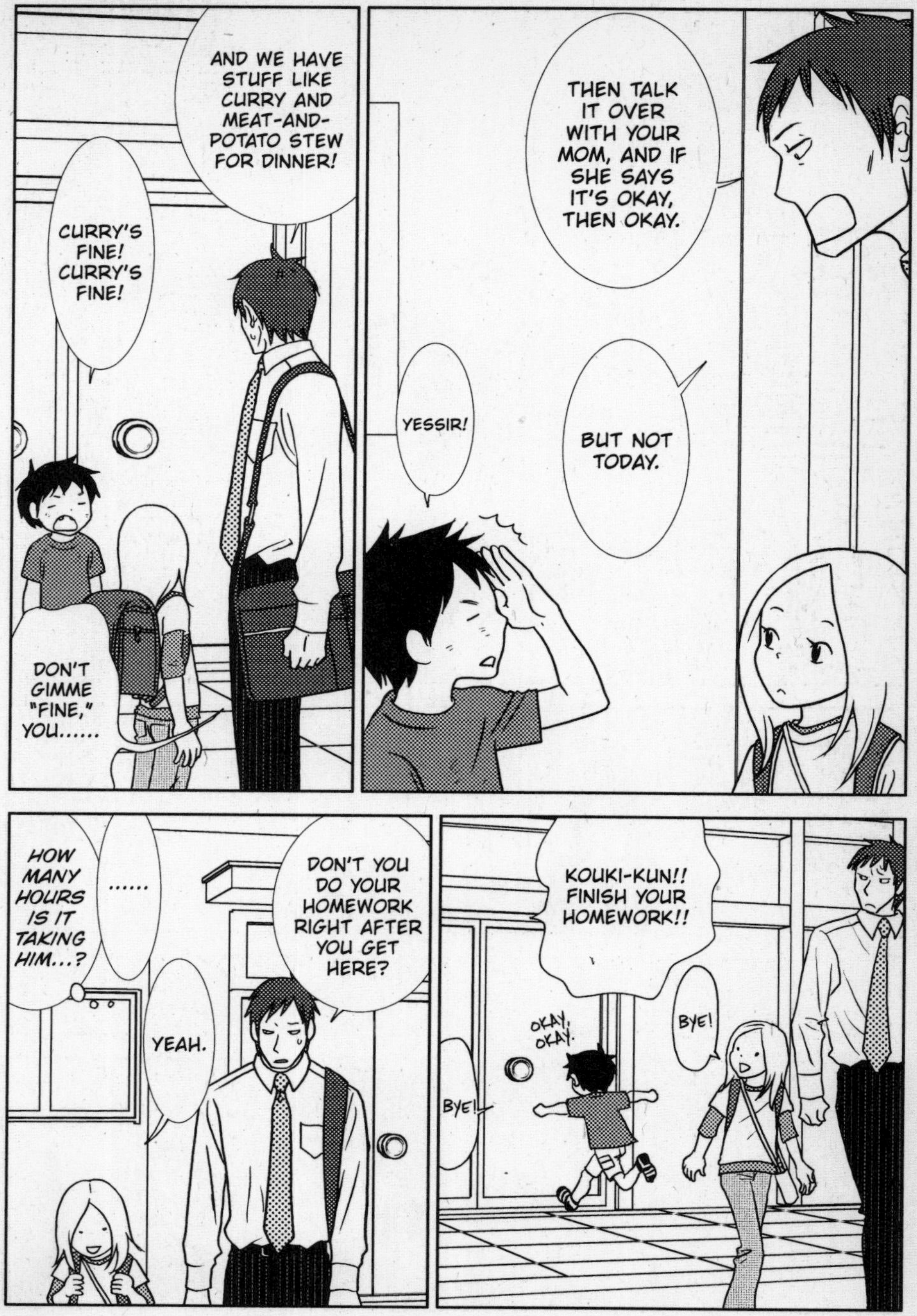
THEN TALK IT OVER WITH YOUR MOM, AND IF SHE SAYS IT'S OKAY, THEN OKAY.
YESSIR!
BUT NOT TODAY.
AND WE HAVE STUFF LIKE CURRY AND MEAT-AND-POTATO STEW FOR DINNER!
CURRY'S FINE! CURRY'S FINE!
DON'T GIMME "FINE," YOU......
KOUKI-KUN!! FINISH YOUR HOMEWORK!!
BYE!
OKAY, OKAY.
BYE!
DON'T YOU DO YOUR HOMEWORK RIGHT AFTER YOU GET HERE?
YEAH.
......
HOW MANY HOURS IS IT TAKING HIM...?

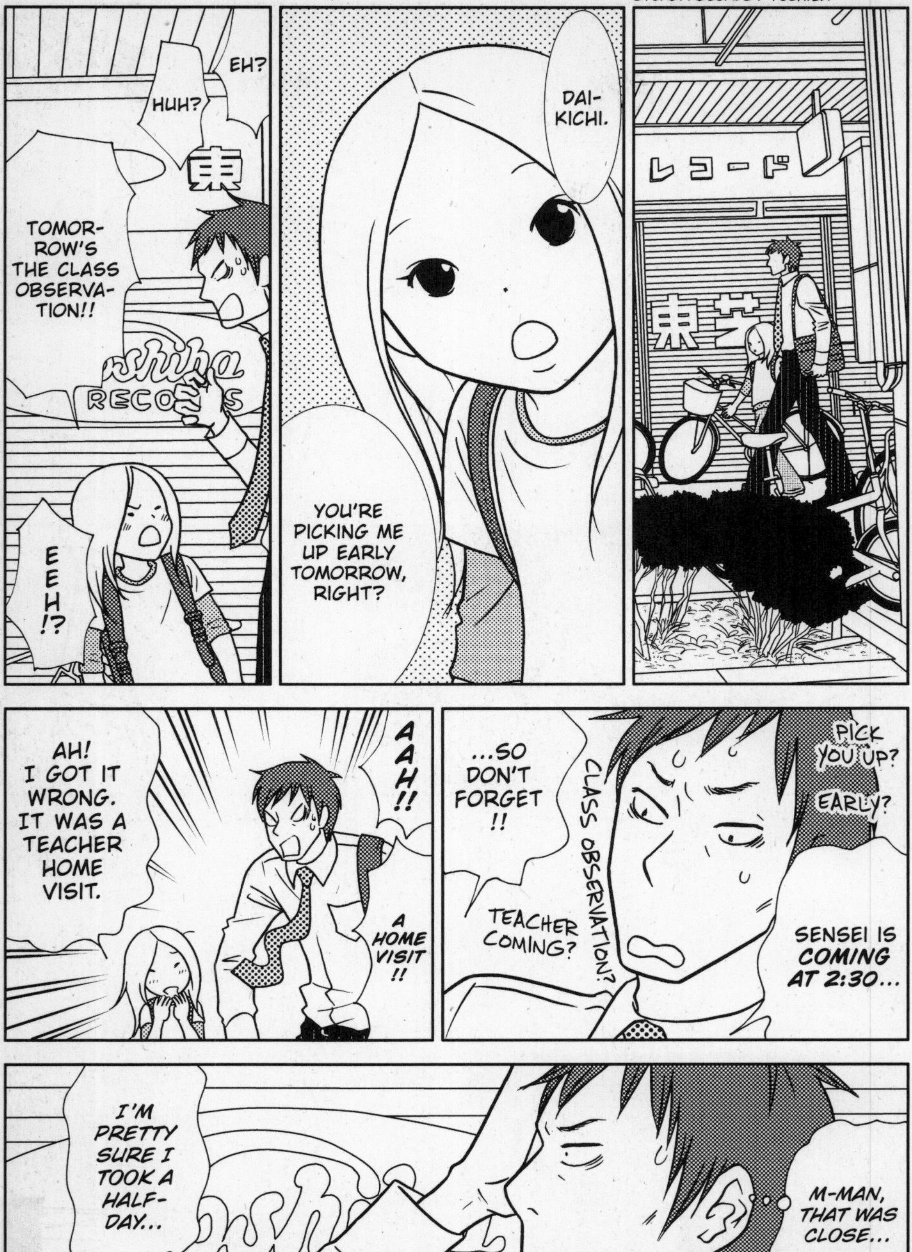
レコード
DAI-KICHI.
YOU'RE PICKING ME UP EARLY TOMORROW, RIGHT?
EH?
HUH?
TOMORROW'S THE CLASS OBSERVATION!!
EEEH!?
PICK YOU UP? EARLY?
SENSEI IS COMING AT 2:30...
...SO DON'T FORGET!!
CLASS OBSERVATION?
TEACHER COMING?
AAH!!
A HOME VISIT!!
AH! I GOT IT WRONG. IT WAS A TEACHER HOME VISIT.
M-MAN, THAT WAS CLOSE...
WHEW...
I'M PRETTY SURE I TOOK A HALF-DAY...

PAPER: INFORMATION ABOUT THE TEACHER HOME VISIT

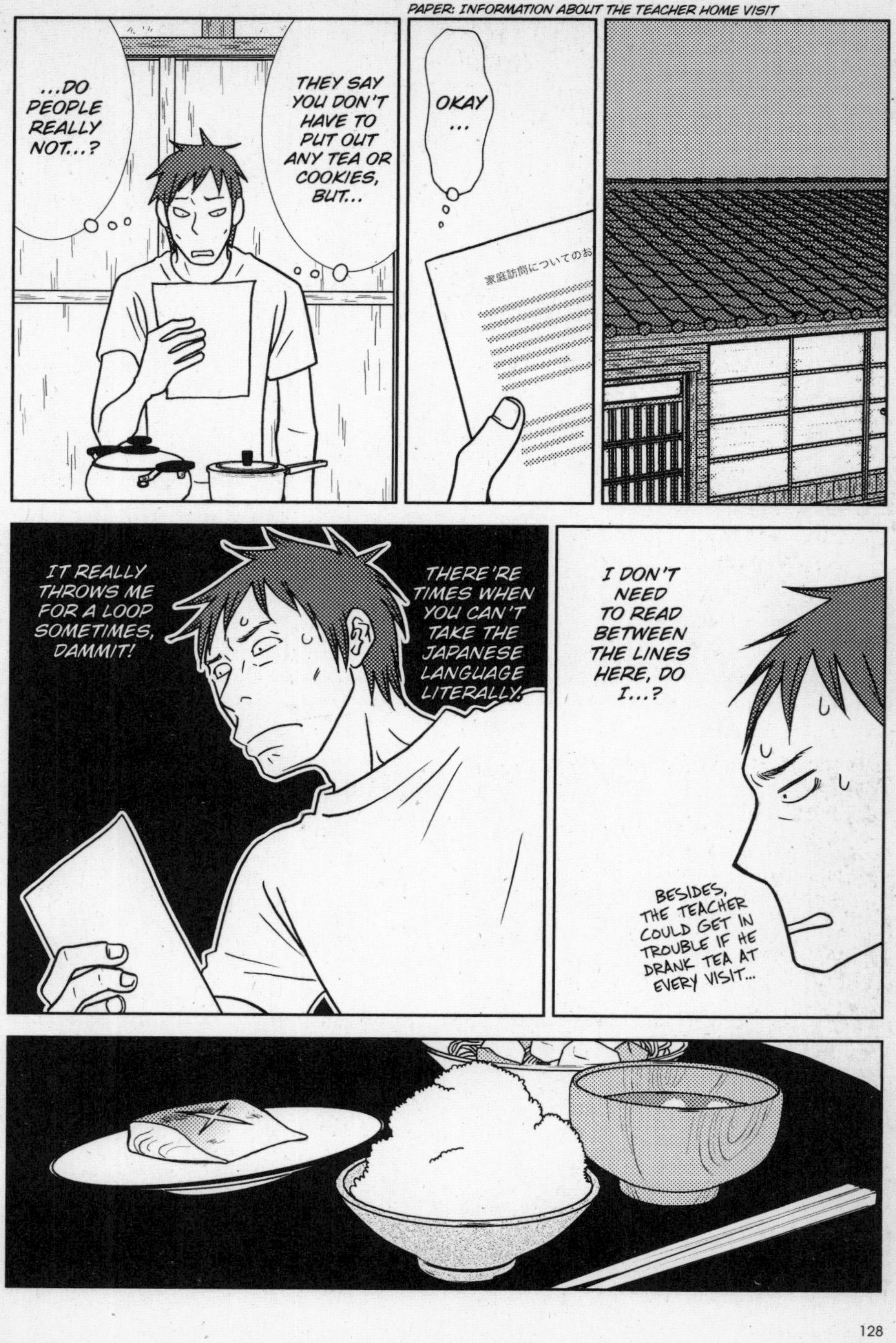
OKAY ...
家庭訪問についてのお
THEY SAY YOU DON'T HAVE TO PUT OUT ANY TEA OR COOKIES, BUT...
...DO PEOPLE REALLY NOT...?
I DON'T NEED TO READ BETWEEN THE LINES HERE, DO I...?
BESIDES, THE TEACHER COULD GET IN TROUBLE IF HE DRANK TEA AT EVERY VISIT...
THERE'RE TIMES WHEN YOU CAN'T TAKE THE JAPANESE LANGUAGE LITERALLY.
IT REALLY THROWS ME FOR A LOOP SOMETIMES, DAMMIT!

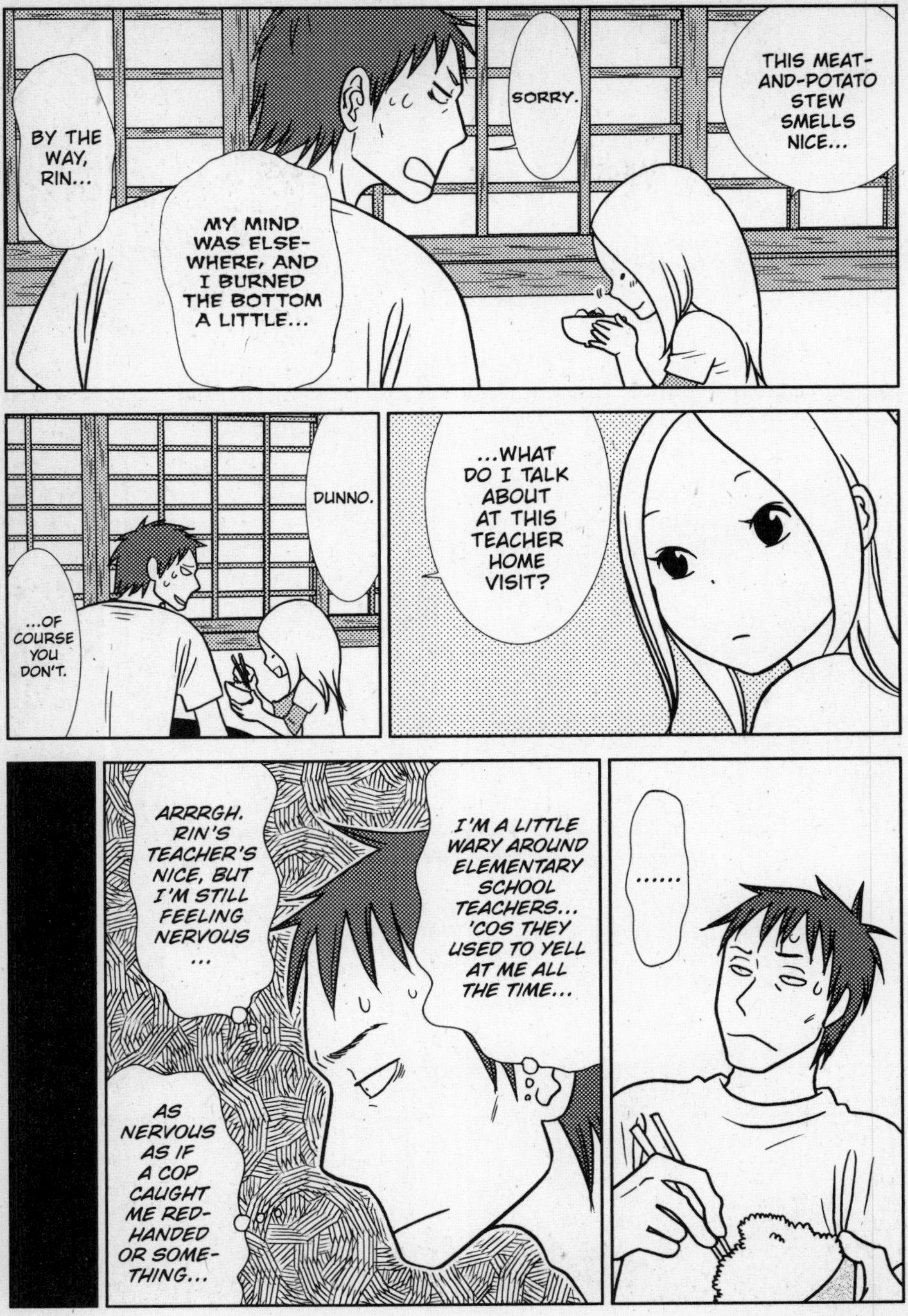
THIS MEAT-AND-POTATO STEW SMELLS NICE...
SORRY.
MY MIND WAS ELSEWHERE, AND I BURNED THE BOTTOM A LITTLE...
BY THE WAY, RIN...
...WHAT DO I TALK ABOUT AT THIS TEACHER HOME VISIT?
DUNNO.
...OF COURSE YOU DON'T.
......
I'M A LITTLE WARY AROUND ELEMENTARY SCHOOL TEACHERS... 'COS THEY USED TO YELL AT ME ALL THE TIME...
ARRRGH. RIN'S TEACHER'S NICE, BUT I'M STILL FEELING NERVOUS...
AS NERVOUS AS IF A COP CAUGHT ME RED-HANDED OR SOMETHING...

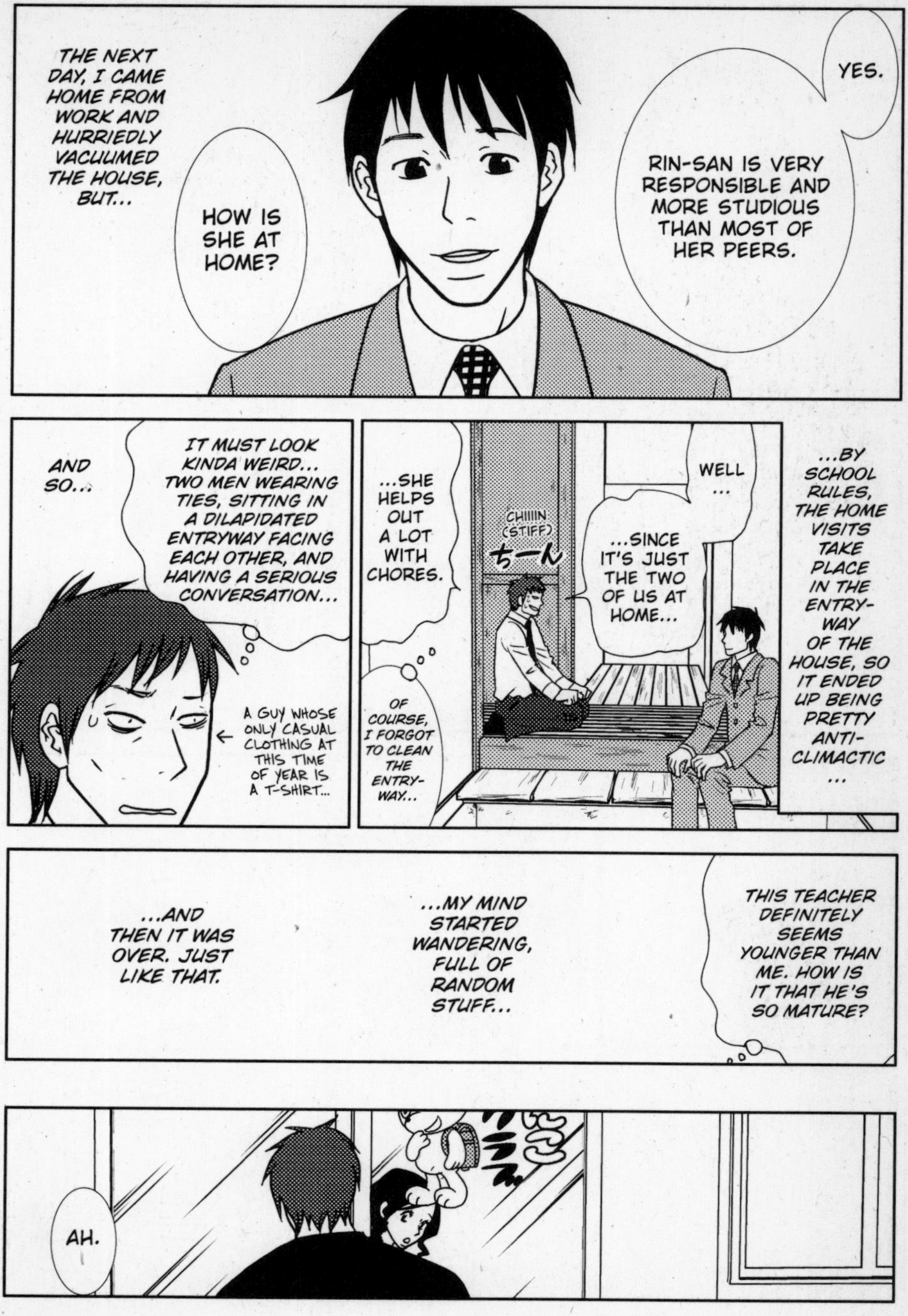
YES.
RIN-SAN IS VERY RESPONSIBLE AND MORE STUDIOUS THAN MOST OF HER PEERS.
HOW IS SHE AT HOME?
THE NEXT DAY, I CAME HOME FROM WORK AND HURRIEDLY VACUUMED THE HOUSE, BUT...
...BY SCHOOL RULES, THE HOME VISITS TAKE PLACE IN THE ENTRY-WAY OF THE HOUSE, SO IT ENDED UP BEING PRETTY ANTI-CLIMACTIC ...
WELL ...
...SINCE IT'S JUST THE TWO OF US AT HOME...
CHIIIIN (STIFF)
ちーん
...SHE HELPS OUT A LOT WITH CHORES.
OF COURSE, I FORGOT TO CLEAN THE ENTRY-WAY...
IT MUST LOOK KINDA WEIRD... TWO MEN WEARING TIES, SITTING IN A DILAPIDATED ENTRYWAY FACING EACH OTHER, AND HAVING A SERIOUS CONVERSATION...
AND SO...
A GUY WHOSE ONLY CASUAL CLOTHING AT THIS TIME OF YEAR IS A T-SHIRT...
THIS TEACHER DEFINITELY SEEMS YOUNGER THAN ME. HOW IS IT THAT HE'S SO MATURE?
...MY MIND STARTED WANDERING, FULL OF RANDOM STUFF...
...AND THEN IT WAS OVER. JUST LIKE THAT.
AH.

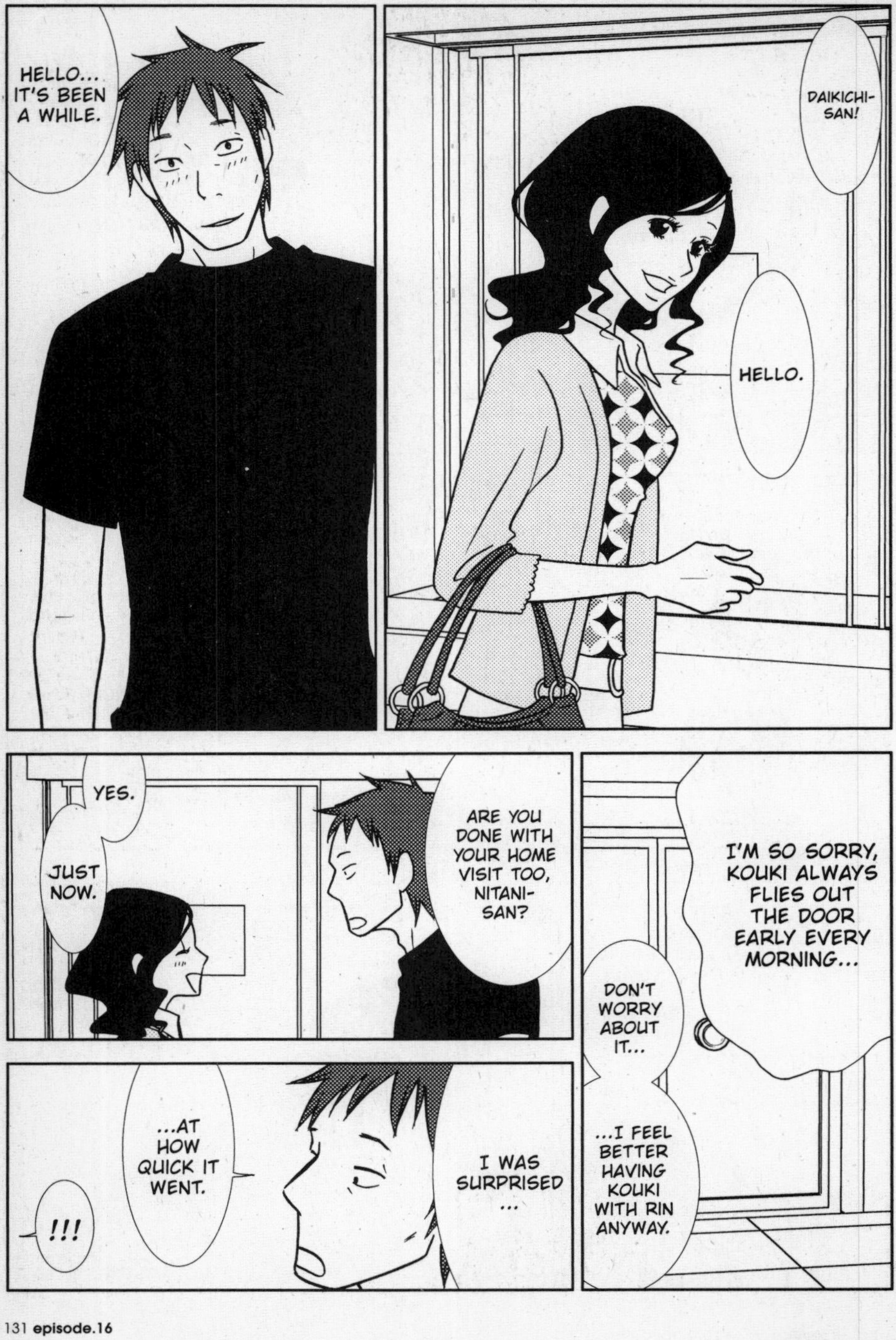
DAIKICHI-SAN!
HELLO.
HELLO... IT'S BEEN A WHILE.
I'M SO SORRY, KOUKI ALWAYS FLIES OUT THE DOOR EARLY EVERY MORNING...
DON'T WORRY ABOUT IT...
...I FEEL BETTER HAVING KOUKI WITH RIN ANYWAY.
ARE YOU DONE WITH YOUR HOME VISIT TOO, NITANI-SAN?
YES.
JUST NOW.
I WAS SURPRISED...
...AT HOW QUICK IT WENT.
!!!

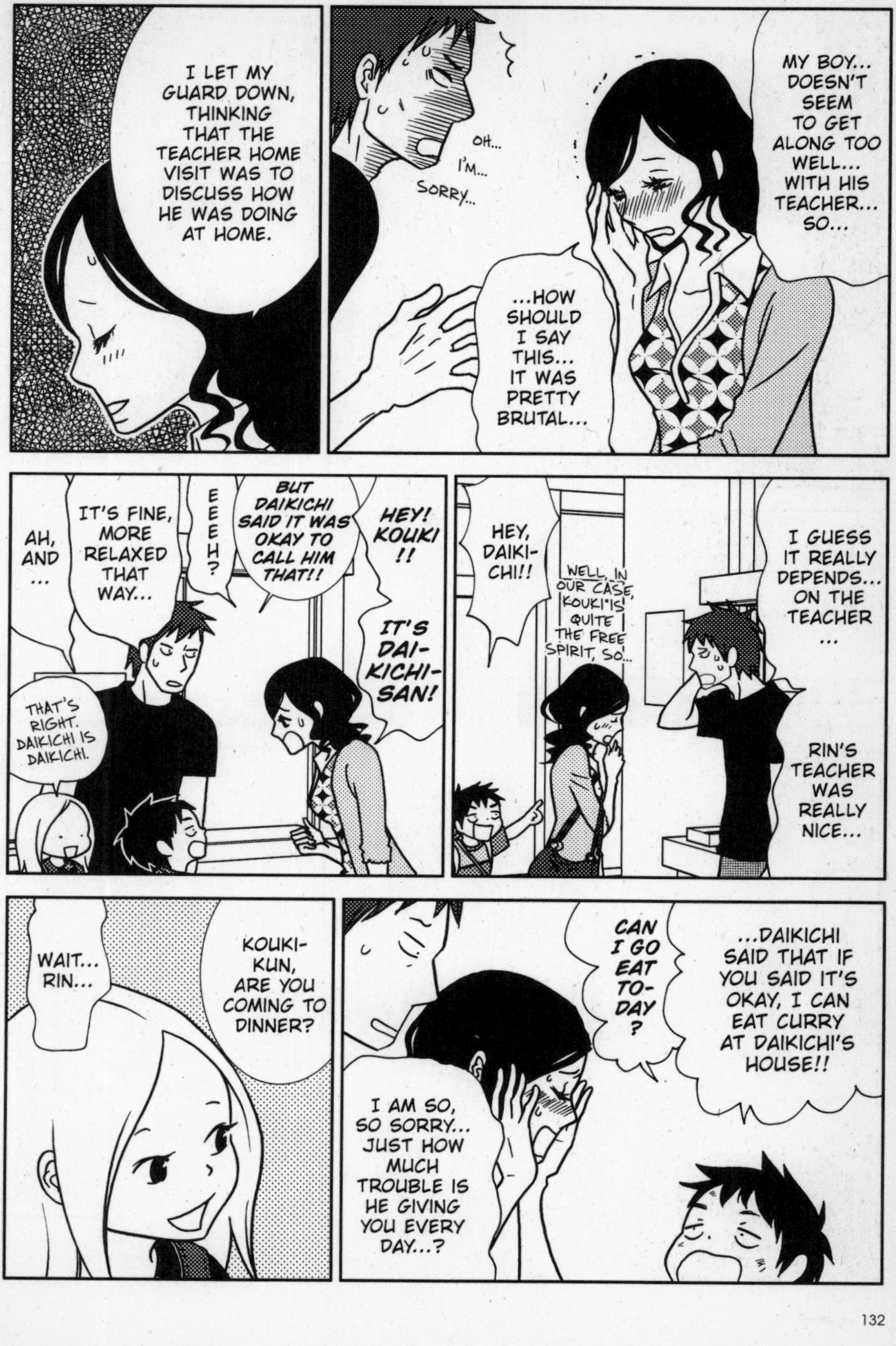
MY BOY... DOESN'T SEEM TO GET ALONG TOO WELL... WITH HIS TEACHER... SO...
OH... I'M... SORRY...
...HOW SHOULD I SAY THIS... IT WAS PRETTY BRUTAL...
I LET MY GUARD DOWN, THINKING THAT THE TEACHER HOME VISIT WAS TO DISCUSS HOW HE WAS DOING AT HOME.
I GUESS IT REALLY DEPENDS... ON THE TEACHER...
RIN'S TEACHER WAS REALLY NICE...
HEY, DAIKI-CHI!!
WELL, IN OUR CASE, KOUKI IS QUITE THE FREE SPIRIT, SO...
HEY! KOUKI!!
IT'S DAI-KICHI-SAN!
BUT DAIKICHI SAID IT WAS OKAY TO CALL HIM THAT!!
EEEEH?
IT'S FINE, MORE RELAXED THAT WAY...
AH, AND...
THAT'S RIGHT. DAIKICHI IS DAIKICHI.
...DAIKICHI SAID THAT IF YOU SAID IT'S OKAY, I CAN EAT CURRY AT DAIKICHI'S HOUSE!!
CAN I GO EAT TO-DAY?
I AM SO, SO SORRY... JUST HOW MUCH TROUBLE IS HE GIVING YOU EVERY DAY...?
KOUKI-KUN, ARE YOU COMING TO DINNER?
WAIT... RIN...

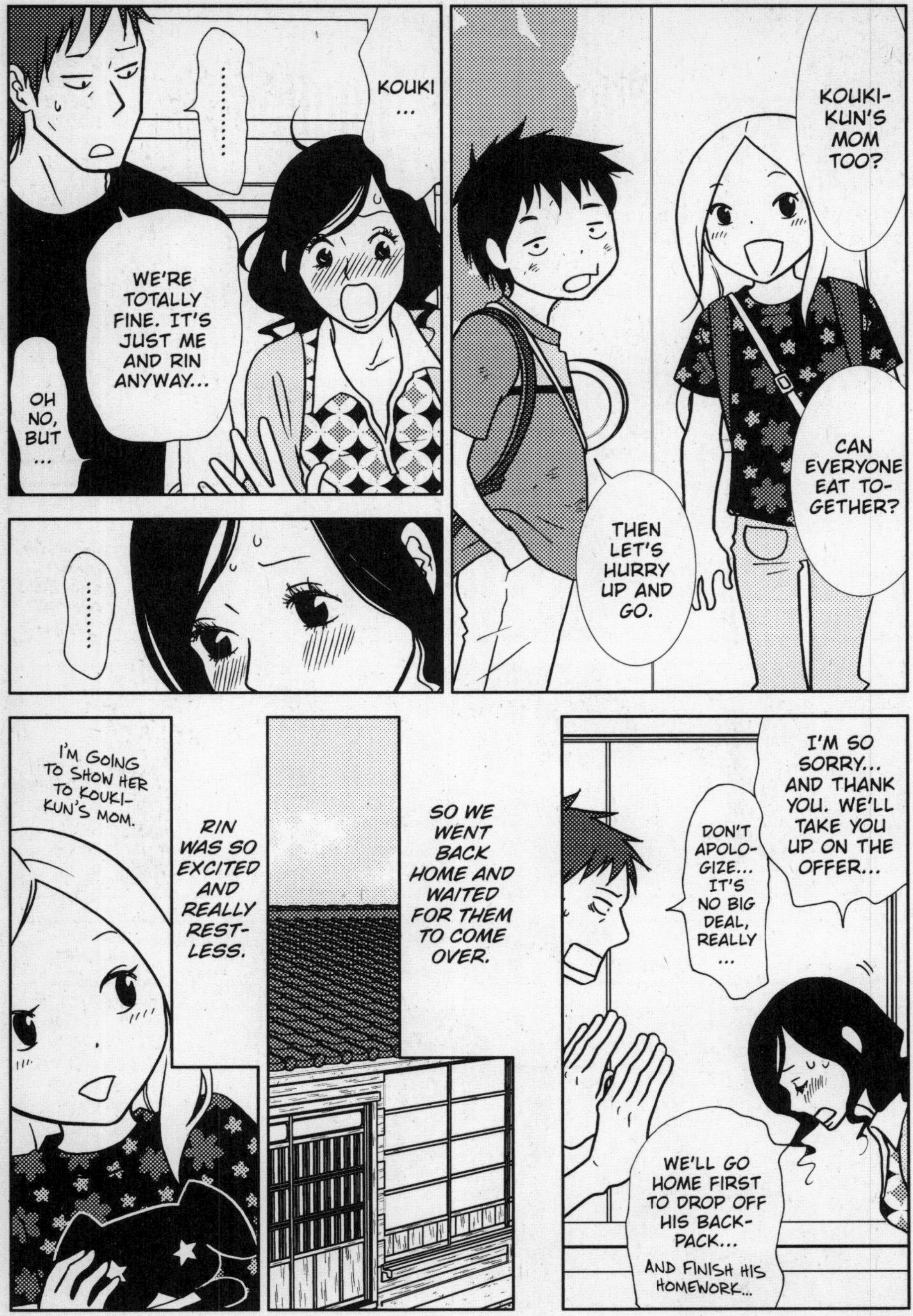
KOUKI-KUN'S MOM TOO?
CAN EVERYONE EAT TO-GETHER?
THEN LET'S HURRY UP AND GO.
KOUKI ...
......
WE'RE TOTALLY FINE. IT'S JUST ME AND RIN ANYWAY...
OH NO, BUT ...
......
I'M SO SORRY... AND THANK YOU. WE'LL TAKE YOU UP ON THE OFFER...
DON'T APOLO-GIZE... IT'S NO BIG DEAL, REALLY ...
WE'LL GO HOME FIRST TO DROP OFF HIS BACK-PACK...
AND FINISH HIS HOMEWORK...
SO WE WENT BACK HOME AND WAITED FOR THEM TO COME OVER.
RIN WAS SO EXCITED AND REALLY REST-LESS.
I'M GOING TO SHOW HER TO KOUKI-KUN'S MOM.

THANK YOU SO MUCH FOR HAVING US.
COME ON, KOUKI, SAY THANK YOU!
I BROUGHT MY DS. LET'S PLAY!!
I DON'T HAVE ONE!
AFTER A LITTLE WHILE, THEY CAME OVER, EVEN BRINGING SOME GROCERIES ALONG.
AH-HA-HA! I CAN'T DO THIS.
GIVE IT HERE.
I HAVEN'T BEEN ABLE TO DO THINGS LIKE THIS FOR HIM, SO...
I'M REALLY HAPPY ABOUT TODAY.
THANK YOU SO MUCH.
DON'T MENTION IT...I'M GRATE-FUL TOO.

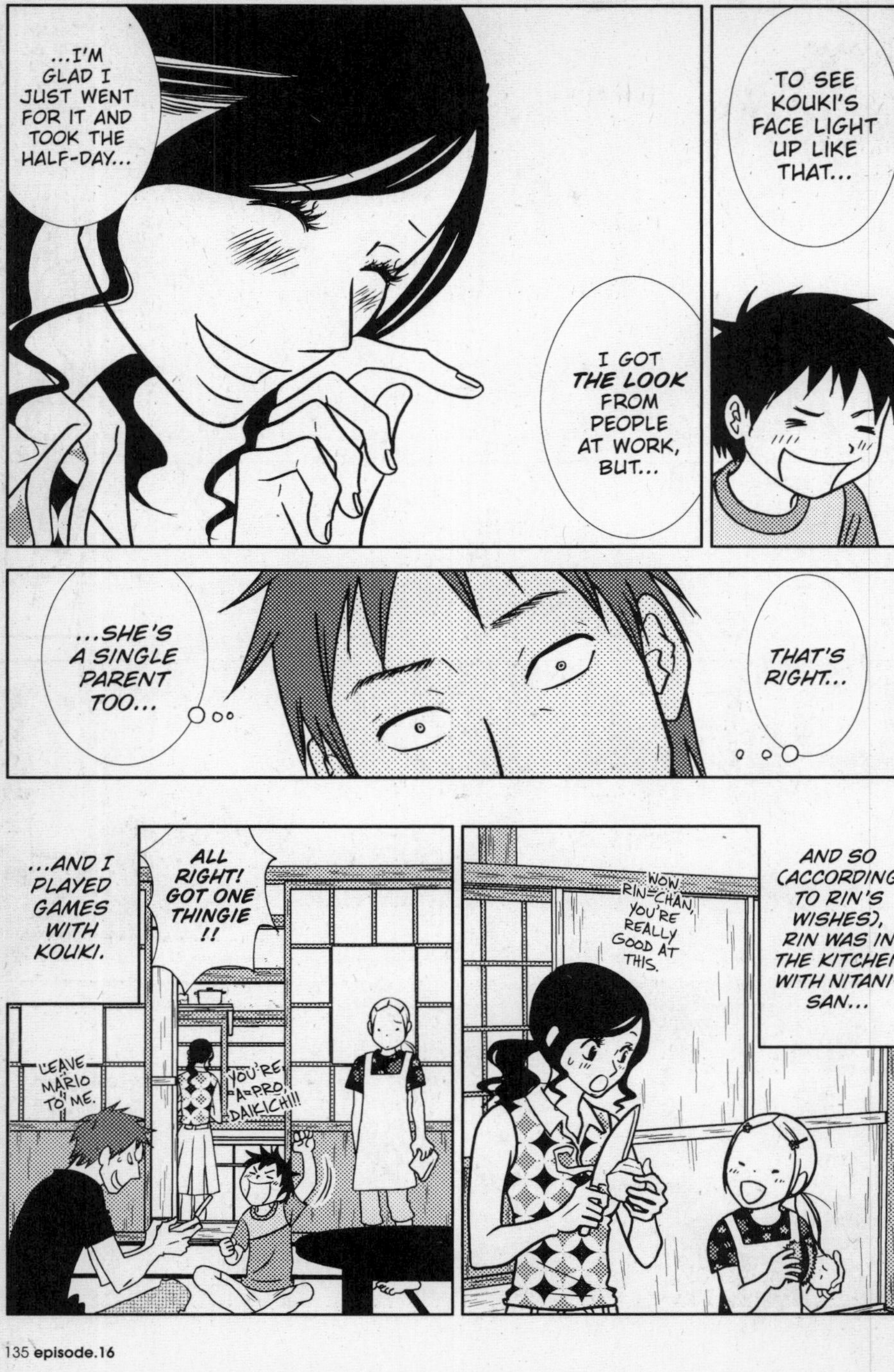
TO SEE KOUKI'S FACE LIGHT UP LIKE THAT...
I GOT **THE LOOK** FROM PEOPLE AT WORK, BUT...
...I'M GLAD I JUST WENT FOR IT AND TOOK THE HALF-DAY...
THAT'S RIGHT...
...SHE'S A SINGLE PARENT TOO...
AND SO (ACCORDING TO RIN'S WISHES), RIN WAS IN THE KITCHEN WITH NITANI-SAN...
WOW, RIN-CHAN, YOU'RE REALLY GOOD AT THIS.
...AND I PLAYED GAMES WITH KOUKI.
ALL RIGHT! GOT ONE THINGIE !!
YOU'RE A PRO, DAIKICHI!!!
LEAVE MARIO TO ME.

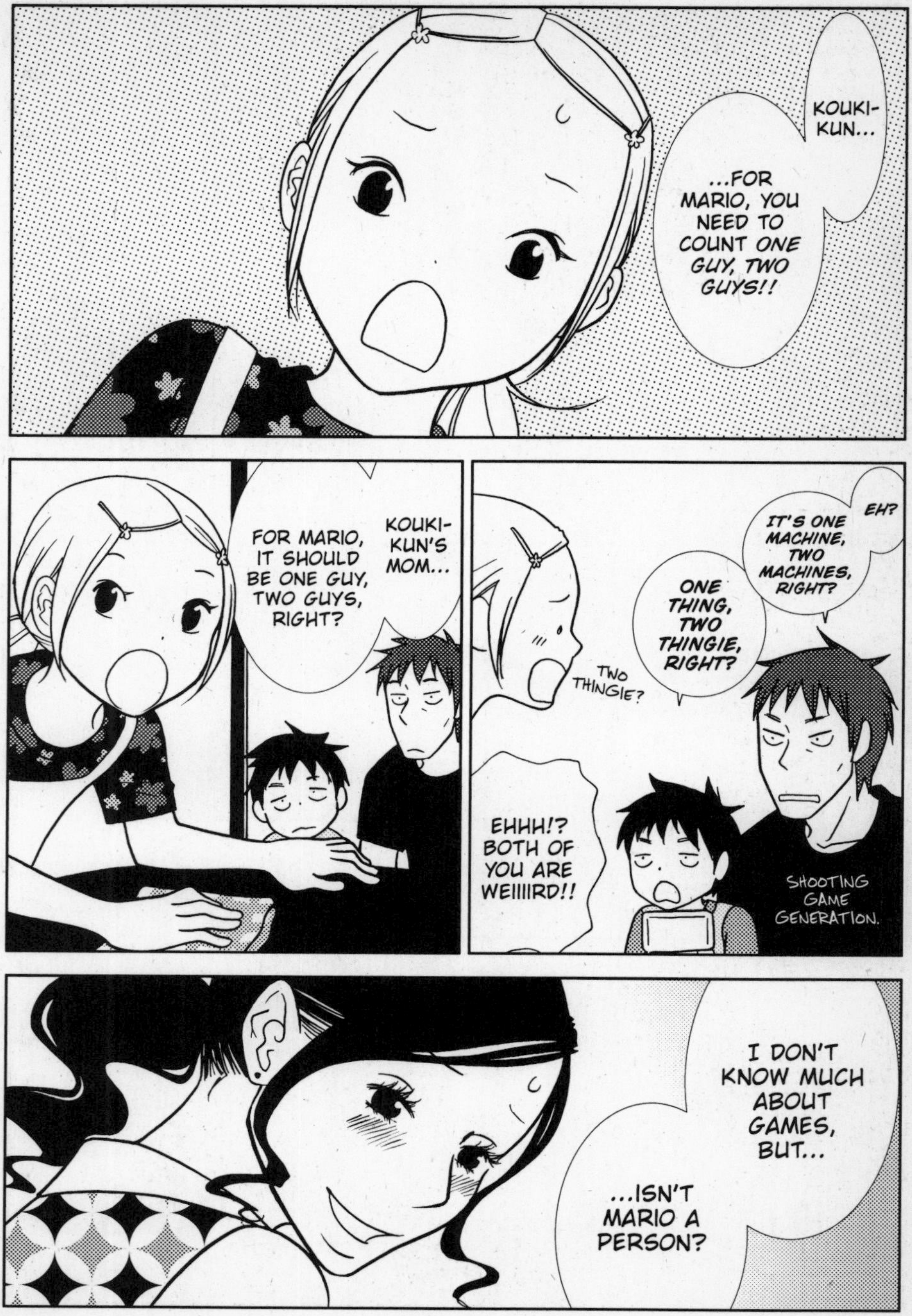
KOUKI-KUN...
...FOR MARIO, YOU NEED TO COUNT ONE GUY, TWO GUYS!!
EH?
IT'S ONE MACHINE, TWO MACHINES, RIGHT?
ONE THING, TWO THINGIE, RIGHT?
TWO THINGIE?
EHHH!? BOTH OF YOU ARE WEIIIIRD!!
SHOOTING GAME GENERATION.
KOUKI-KUN'S MOM...
FOR MARIO, IT SHOULD BE ONE GUY, TWO GUYS, RIGHT?
I DON'T KNOW MUCH ABOUT GAMES, BUT...
...ISN'T MARIO A PERSON?

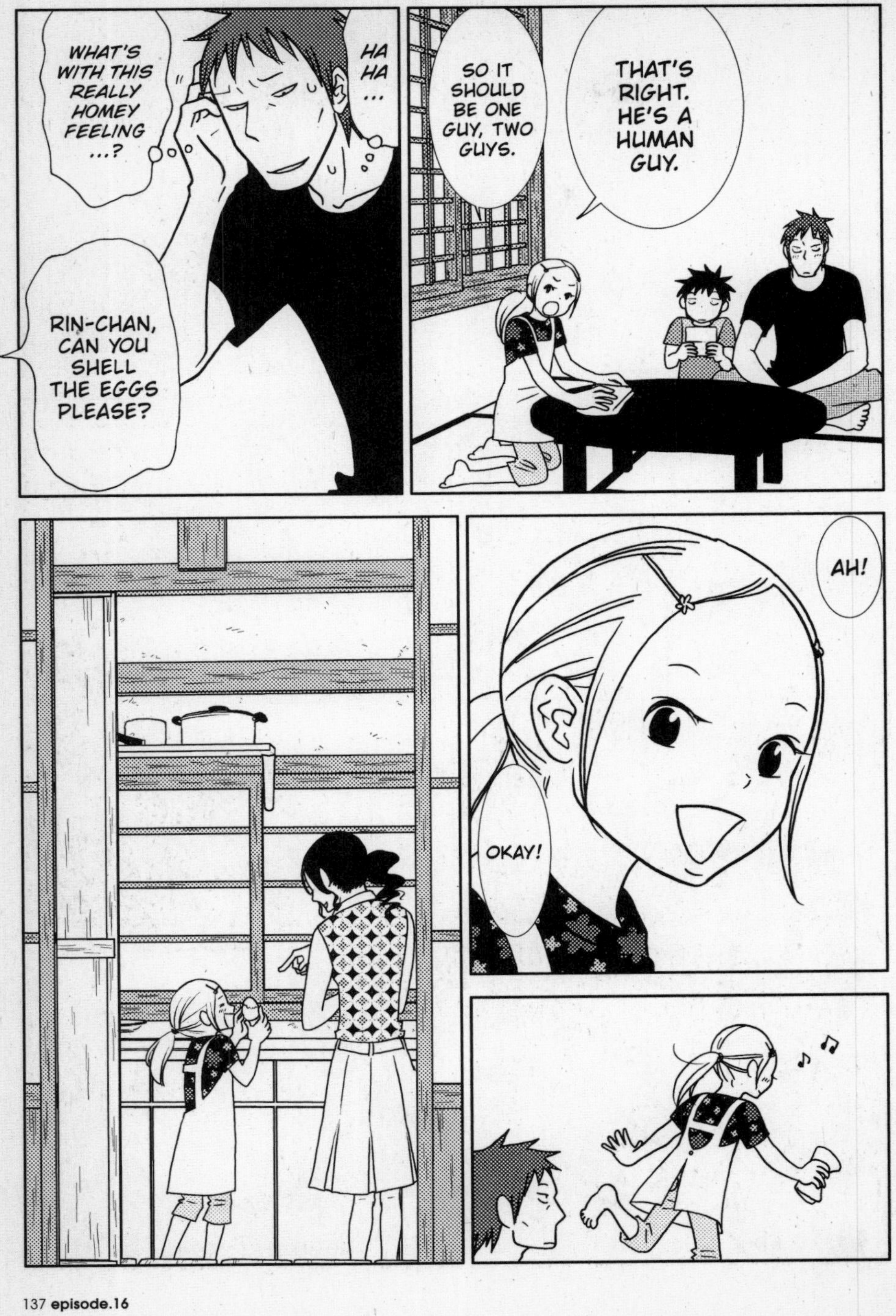
THAT'S RIGHT. HE'S A HUMAN GUY.
SO IT SHOULD BE ONE GUY, TWO GUYS.
HA HA ...
WHAT'S WITH THIS REALLY HOMEY FEELING ...?
RIN-CHAN, CAN YOU SHELL THE EGGS PLEASE?
AH!
OKAY!

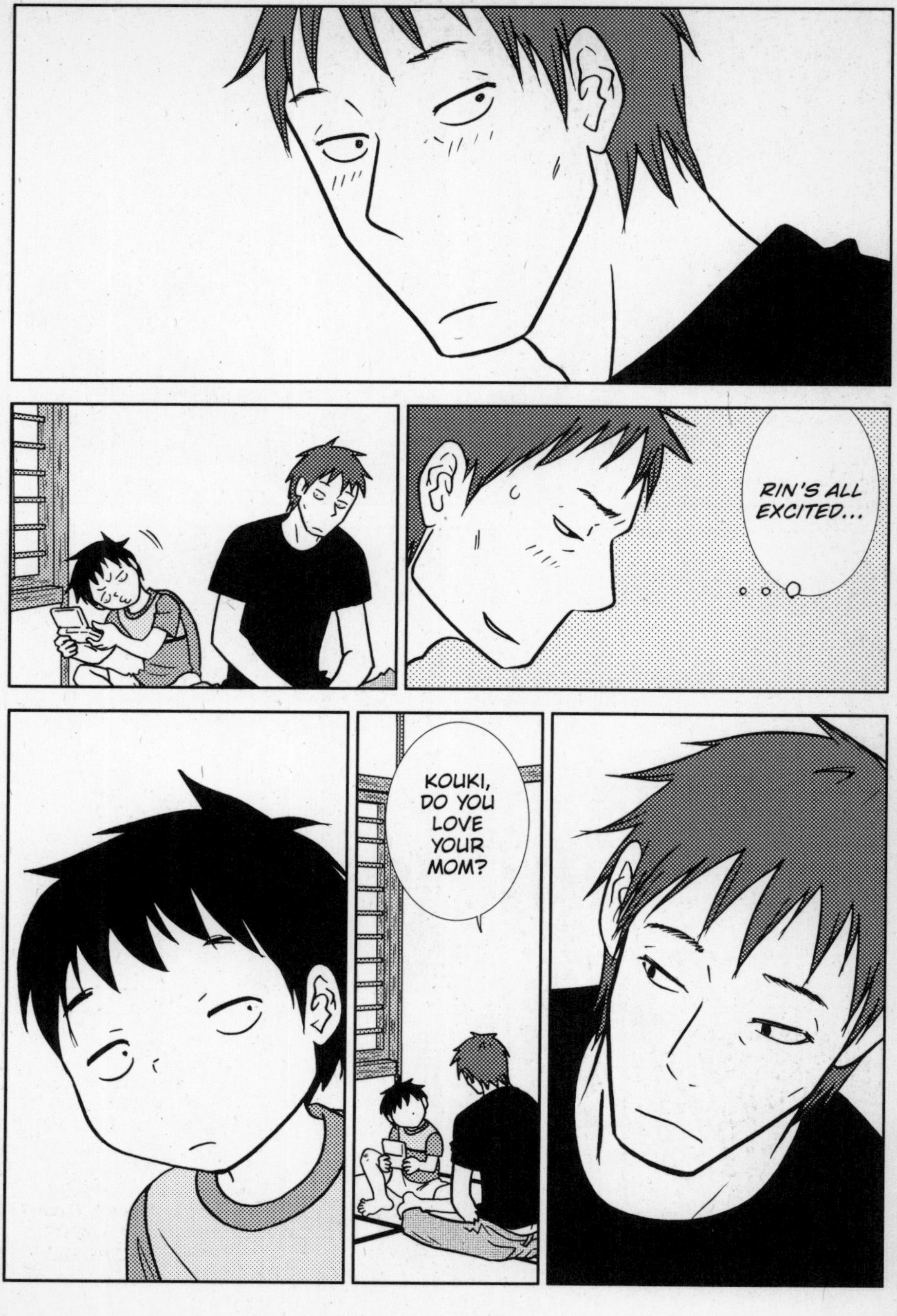
RIN'S ALL EXCITED...
KOUKI, DO YOU LOVE YOUR MOM?

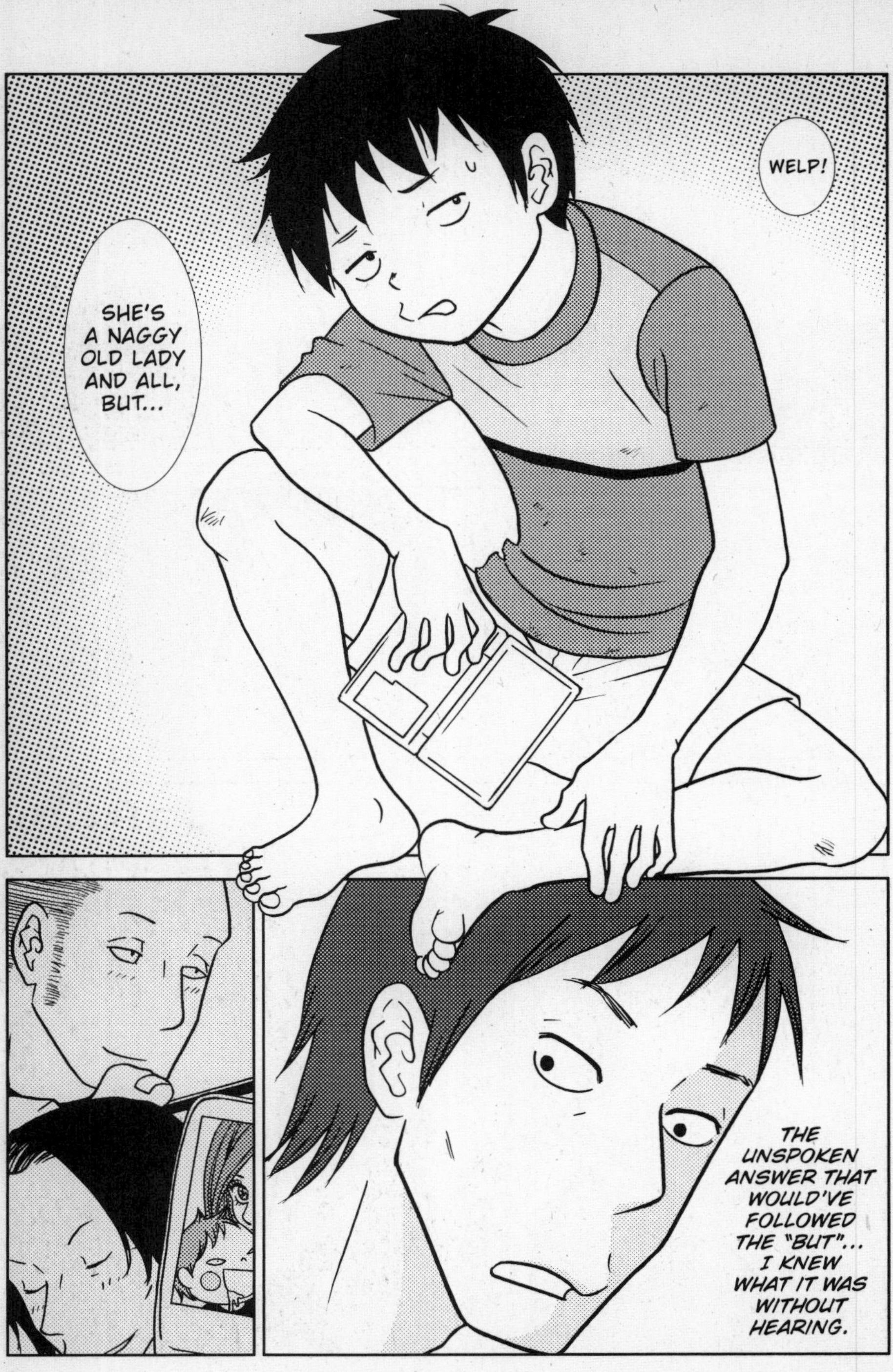
WELP!
SHE'S A NAGGY OLD LADY AND ALL, BUT...
THE UNSPOKEN ANSWER THAT WOULD'VE FOLLOWED THE "BUT"... I KNEW WHAT IT WAS WITHOUT HEARING.

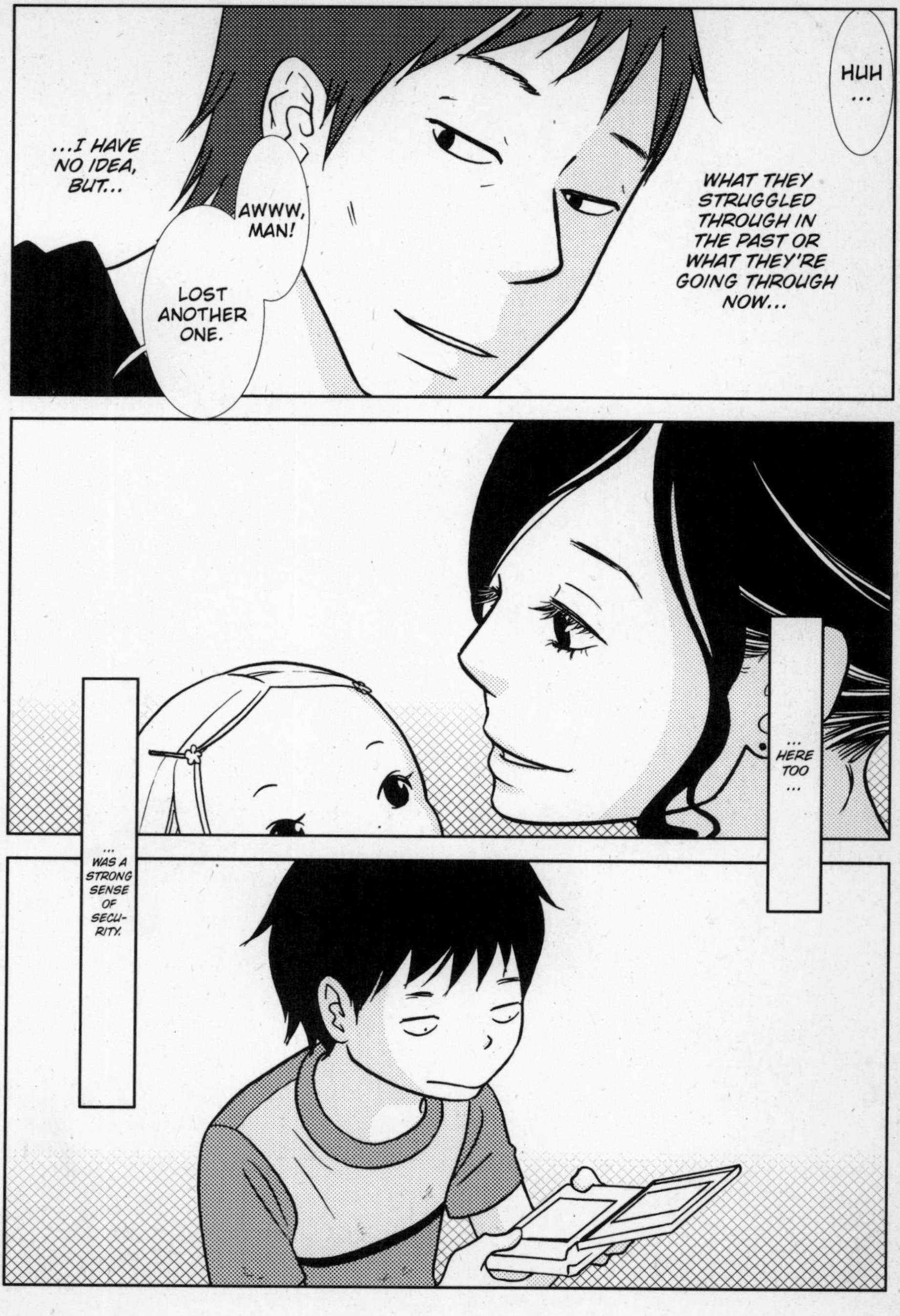
HUH ...
WHAT THEY STRUGGLED THROUGH IN THE PAST OR WHAT THEY'RE GOING THROUGH NOW...
...I HAVE NO IDEA, BUT...
AWWW, MAN!
LOST ANOTHER ONE.
... HERE TOO ...
... WAS A STRONG SENSE OF SECU- RITY.

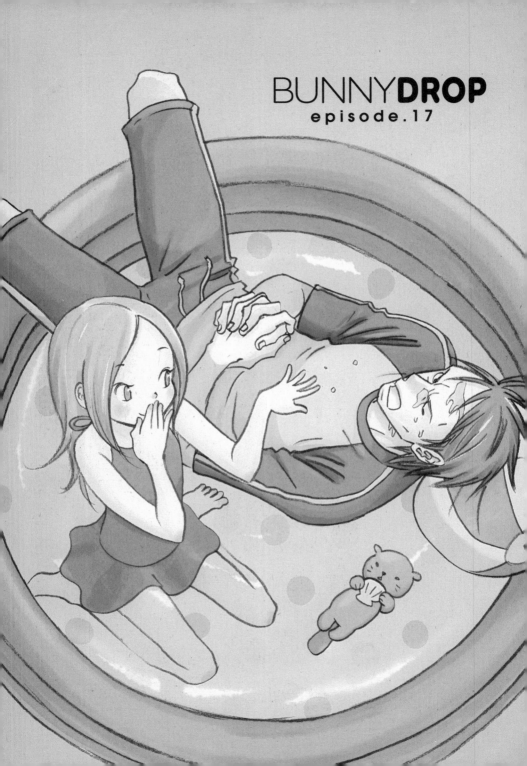

BUNNY**DROP**
episode.17

BUNNY**DROP**

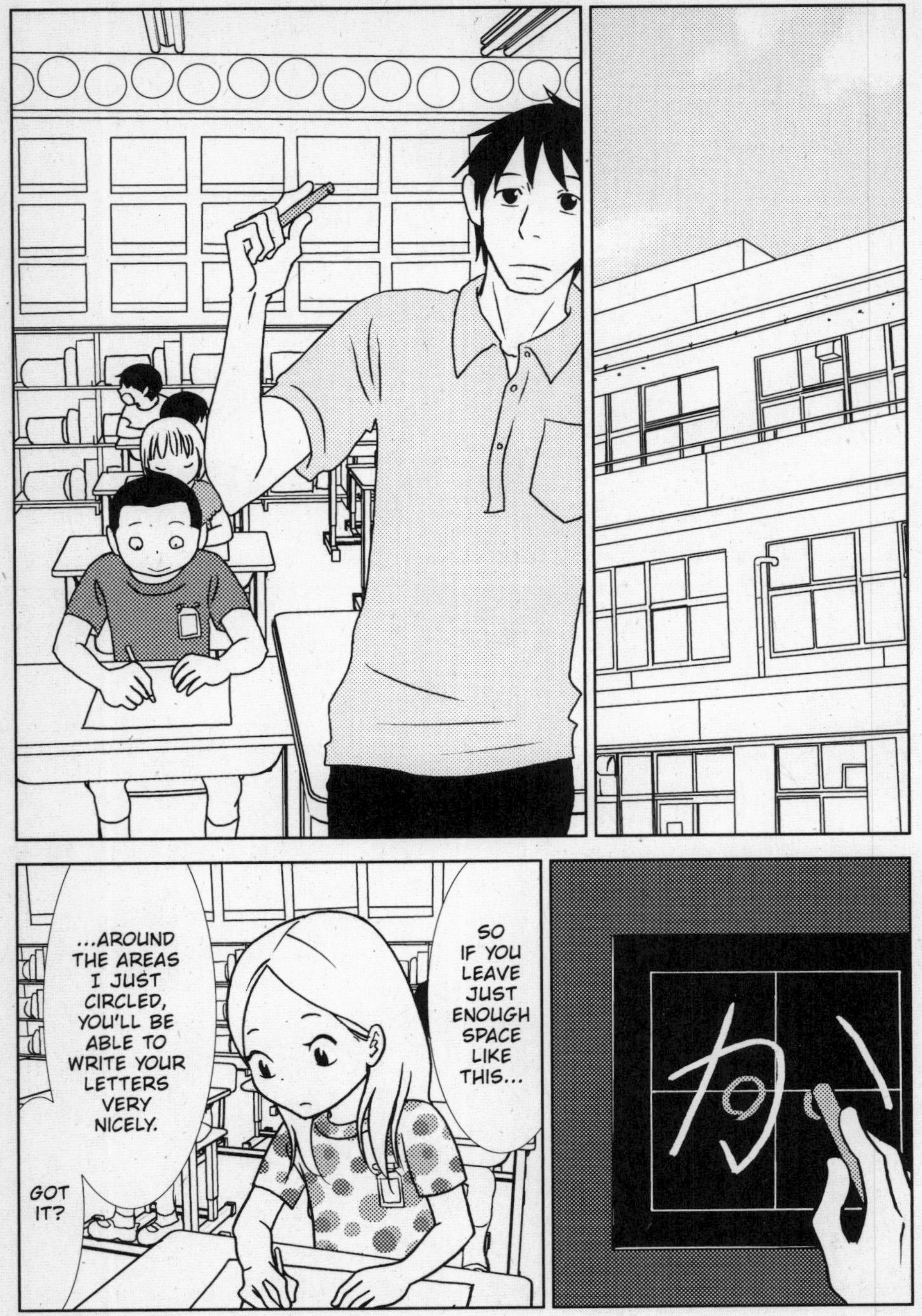
SO IF YOU LEAVE JUST ENOUGH SPACE LIKE THIS...
...AROUND THE AREAS I JUST CIRCLED, YOU'LL BE ABLE TO WRITE YOUR LETTERS VERY NICELY.
GOT IT?

SENSEEEH, WHAT'S "JUST ENOUGH"?
UHHHH...
HOW MANY CENTI-METERS?
HOW MANY MILLI-METERS?
HOW WOULD I KNOW IN MILLI-METERS...?
THIS MUCH IS JUST ENOUGH!!
WRITE WITH CONFI-DENCE, EVERY-ONE!
AND BE CAREFUL HOW YOU HOLD YOUR PENCIL!!
YOU DON'T NEED TO WRITE THESE CIRCLES!!
OKAY?
OKAAAY!!
AH.
WE'RE OUT OF TIME, SO PLEASE FINISH THE REST FOR HOMEWORK, ALL RIIIGHT!?

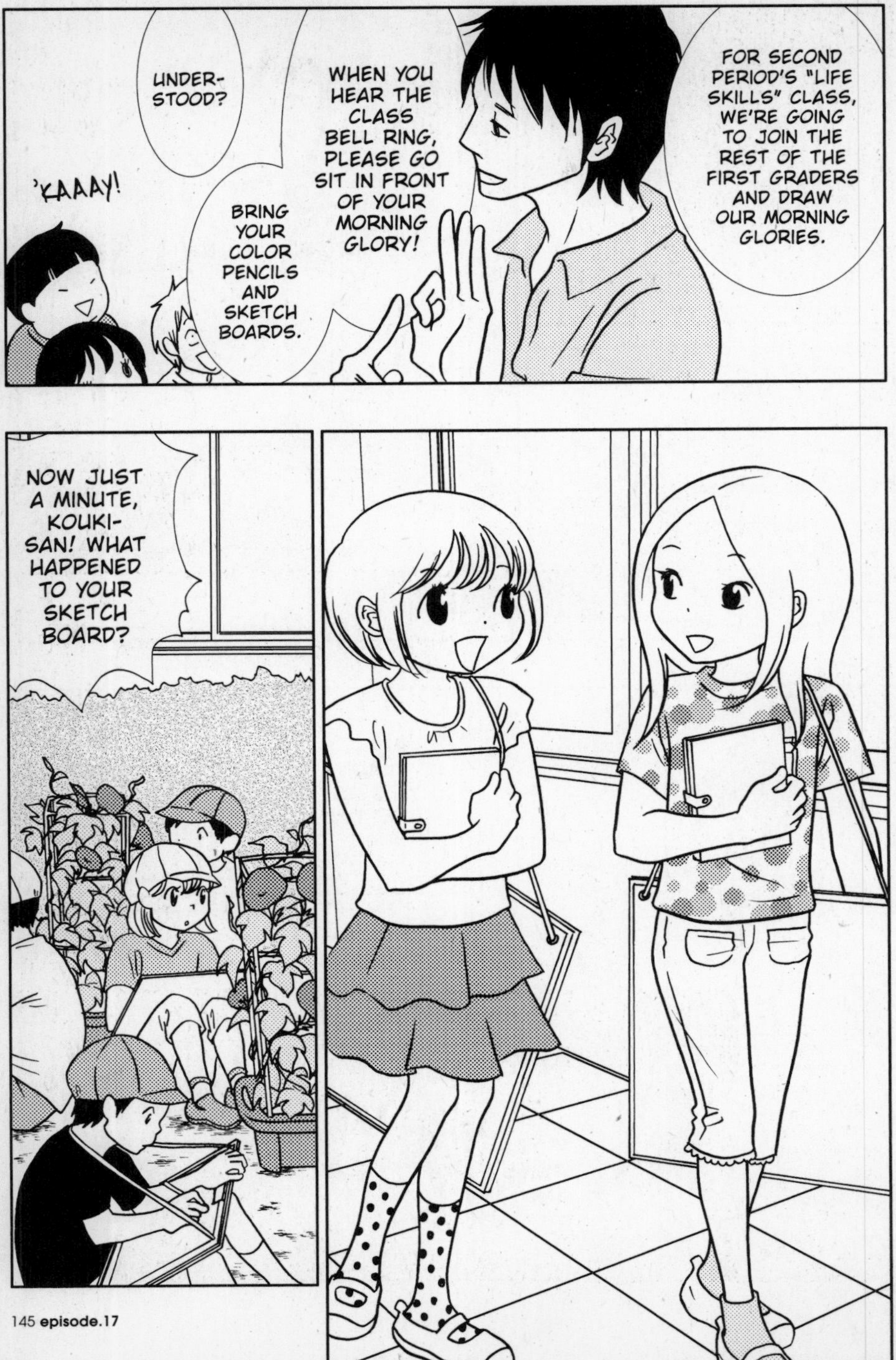
FOR SECOND PERIOD'S "LIFE SKILLS" CLASS, WE'RE GOING TO JOIN THE REST OF THE FIRST GRADERS AND DRAW OUR MORNING GLORIES.
WHEN YOU HEAR THE CLASS BELL RING, PLEASE GO SIT IN FRONT OF YOUR MORNING GLORY!
BRING YOUR COLOR PENCILS AND SKETCH BOARDS.
UNDER-STOOD?
'KAAAY!
NOW JUST A MINUTE, KOUKI-SAN! WHAT HAPPENED TO YOUR SKETCH BOARD?

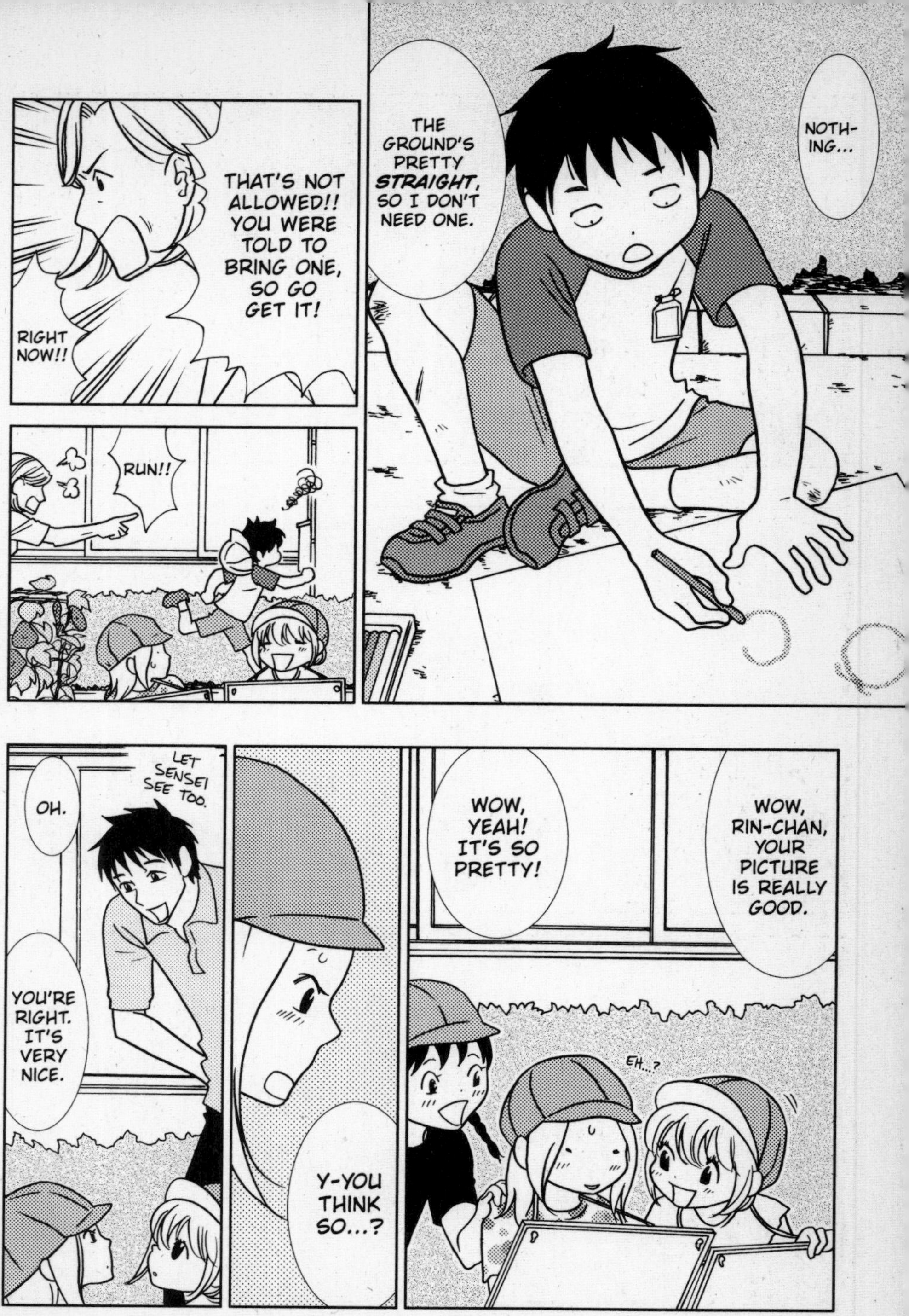
NOTH-ING...
THE GROUND'S PRETTY **STRAIGHT**, SO I DON'T NEED ONE.
THAT'S NOT ALLOWED!! YOU WERE TOLD TO BRING ONE, SO GO GET IT!
RIGHT NOW!!
RUN!!
WOW, RIN-CHAN, YOUR PICTURE IS REALLY GOOD.
WOW, YEAH! IT'S SO PRETTY!
EH...?
Y-YOU THINK SO...?
LET SENSEI SEE TOO.
OH.
YOU'RE RIGHT. IT'S VERY NICE.

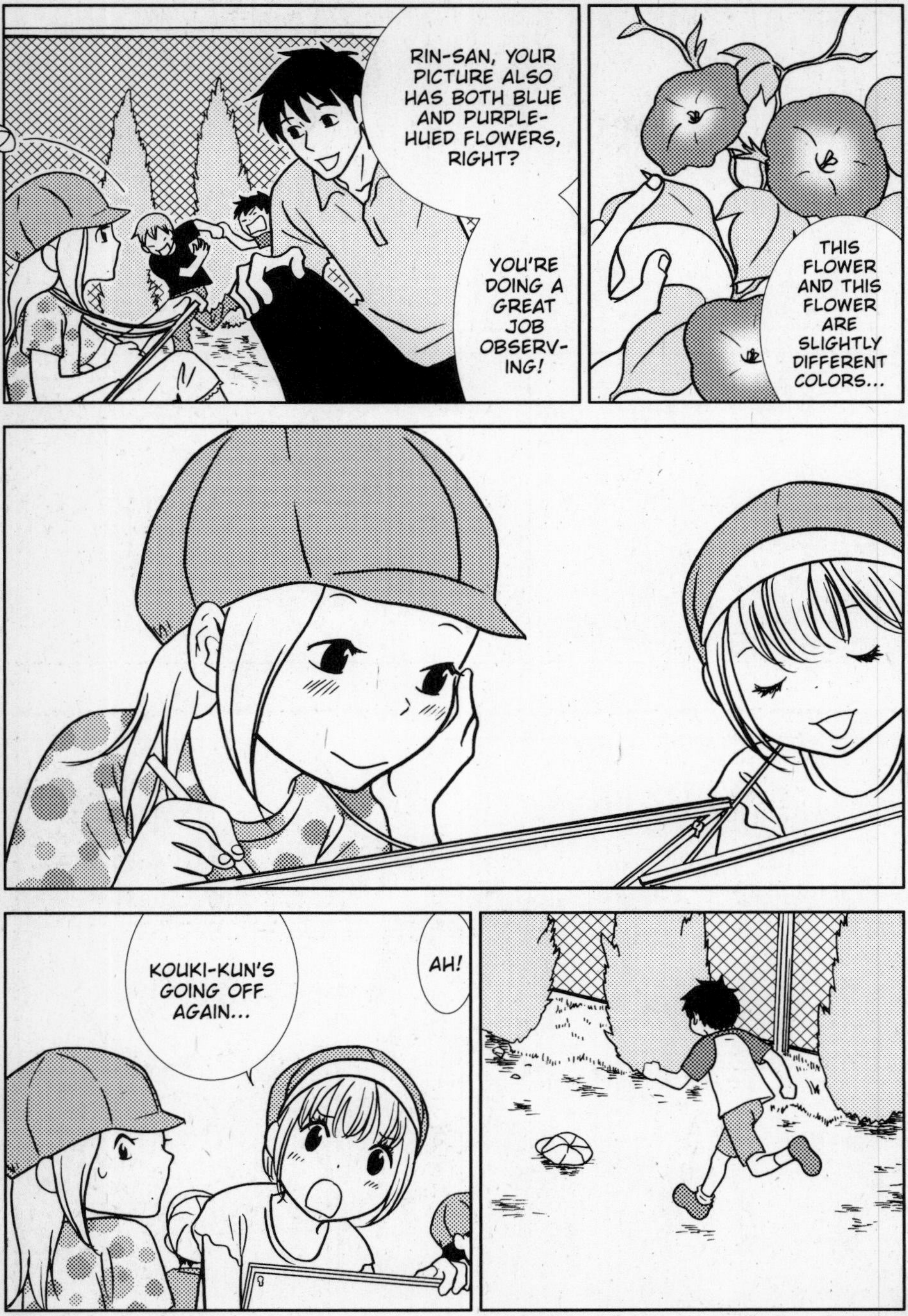
THIS FLOWER AND THIS FLOWER ARE SLIGHTLY DIFFERENT COLORS...
RIN-SAN, YOUR PICTURE ALSO HAS BOTH BLUE AND PURPLE-HUED FLOWERS, RIGHT?
YOU'RE DOING A GREAT JOB OBSERV-ING!
AH!
KOUKI-KUN'S GOING OFF AGAIN...

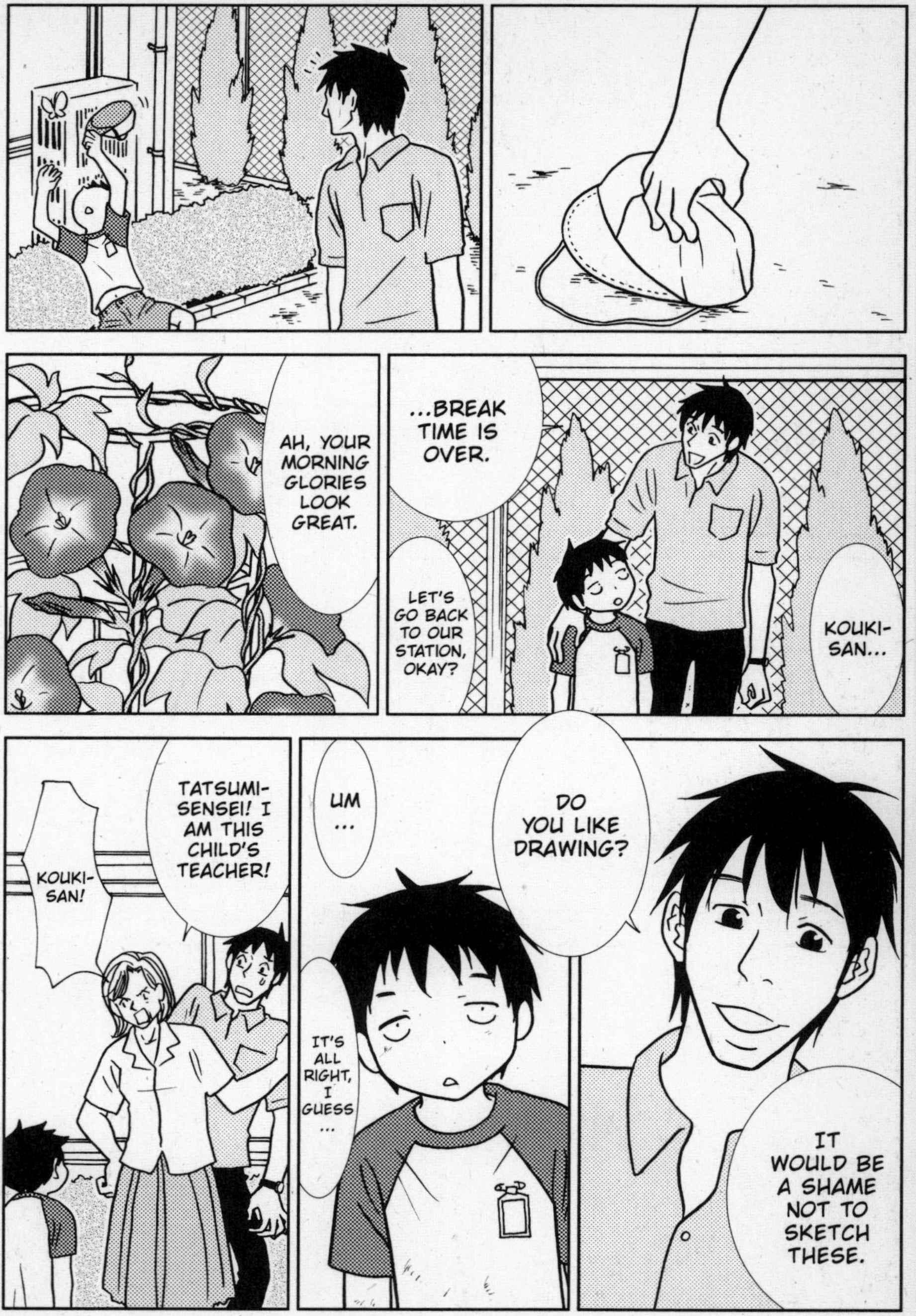
KOUKI-SAN...
...BREAK TIME IS OVER.
LET'S GO BACK TO OUR STATION, OKAY?
AH, YOUR MORNING GLORIES LOOK GREAT.
DO YOU LIKE DRAWING?
UM...
IT'S ALL RIGHT, I GUESS...
IT WOULD BE A SHAME NOT TO SKETCH THESE.
TATSUMI-SENSEI! I AM THIS CHILD'S TEACHER!
KOUKI-SAN!

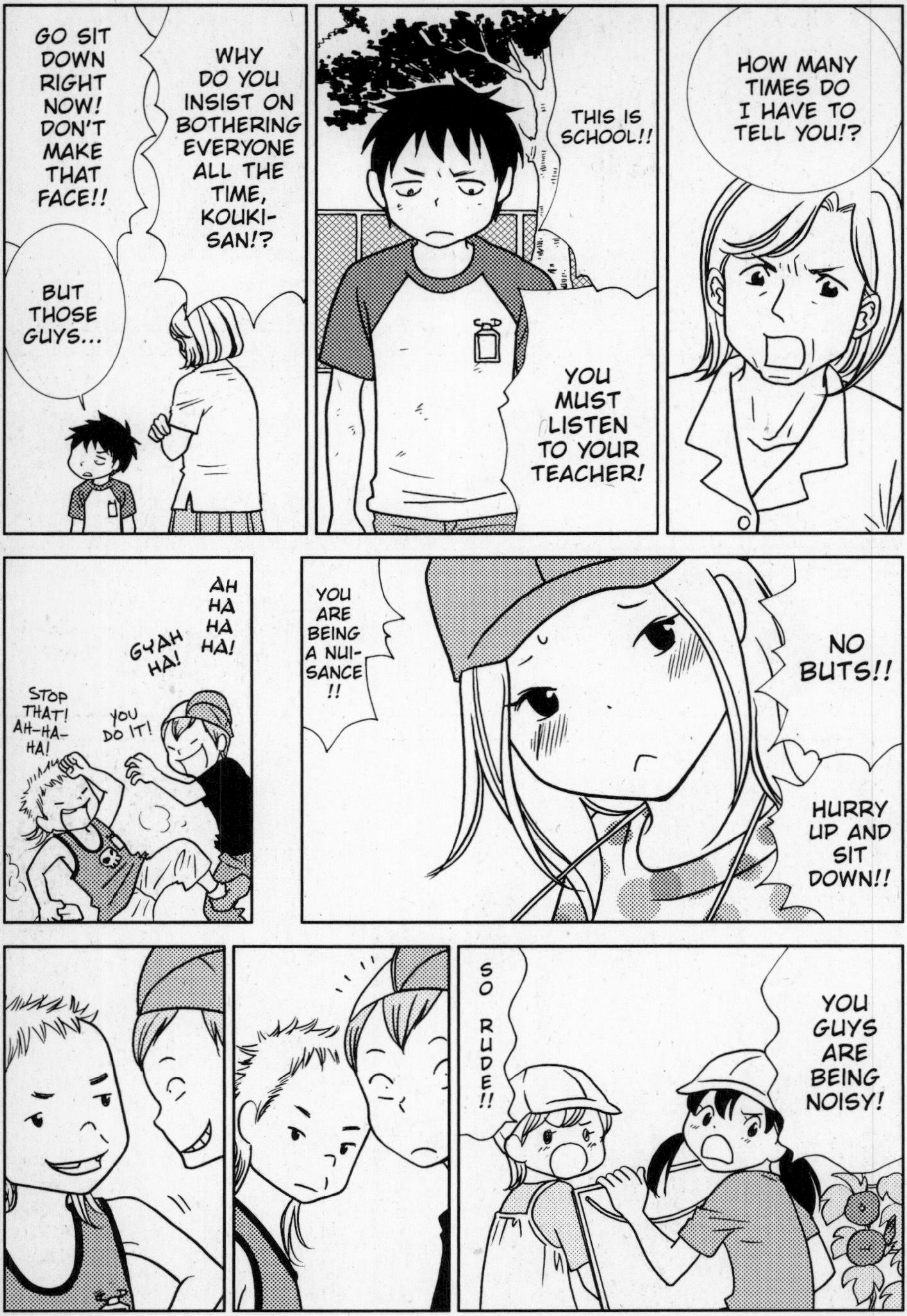
HOW MANY TIMES DO I HAVE TO TELL YOU!?
THIS IS SCHOOL!!
YOU MUST LISTEN TO YOUR TEACHER!
WHY DO YOU INSIST ON BOTHERING EVERYONE ALL THE TIME, KOUKI-SAN!?
GO SIT DOWN RIGHT NOW! DON'T MAKE THAT FACE!!
BUT THOSE GUYS...
NO BUTS!!
HURRY UP AND SIT DOWN!!
YOU ARE BEING A NUI-SANCE!!
AH HA HA HA!
GYAH HA!
YOU DO IT!
STOP THAT! AH-HA-HA!
YOU GUYS ARE BEING NOISY!
SO RUDE!!

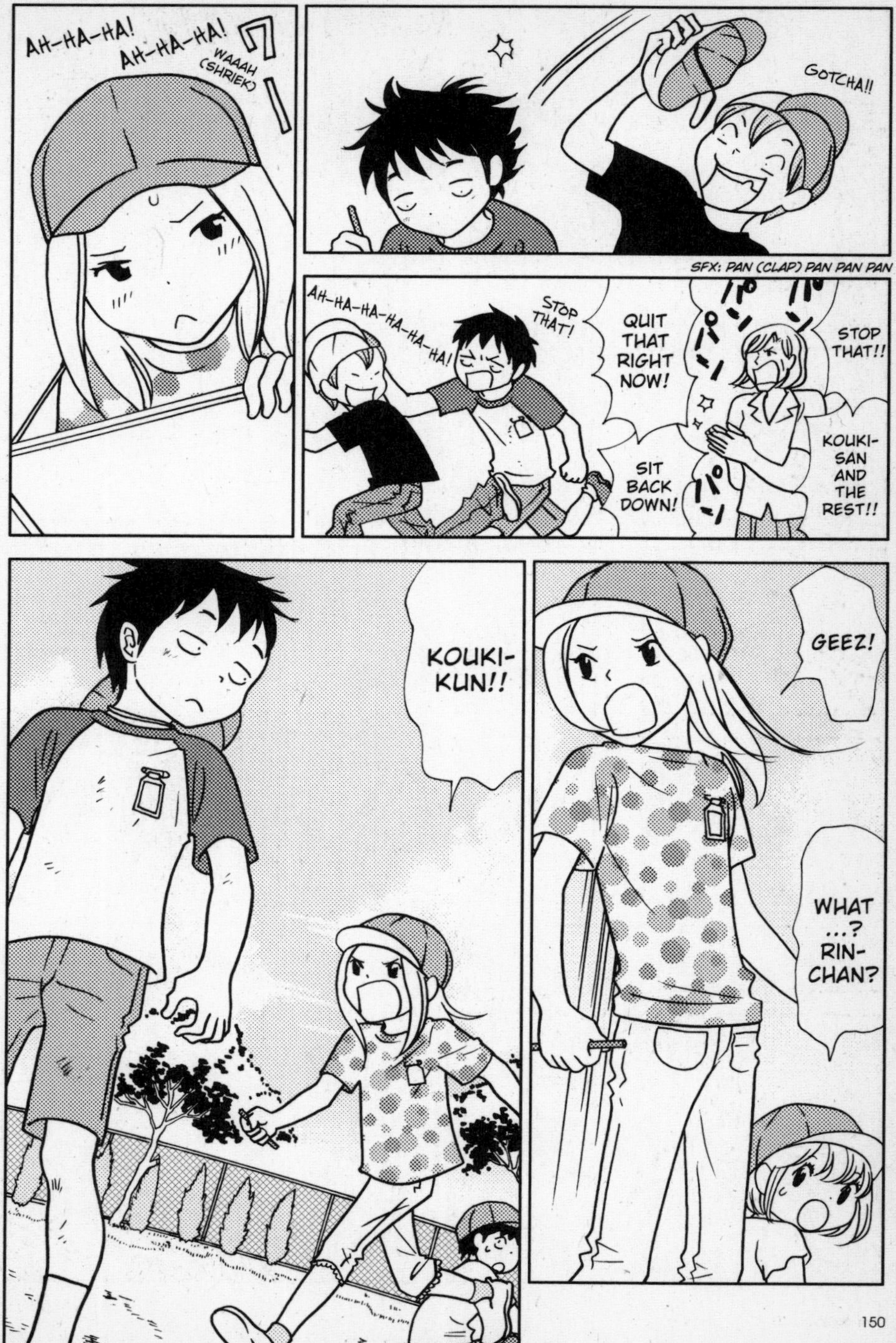
GOTCHA!!
SFX: PAN (CLAP) PAN PAN PAN
STOP THAT!!
KOUKI-SAN AND THE REST!!
QUIT THAT RIGHT NOW!
SIT BACK DOWN!
STOP THAT!
AH-HA-HA-HA-HA-HA!
AH-HA-HA!
AH-HA-HA!
WAAAH (SHRIEK)
GEEZ!
WHAT ...? RIN-CHAN?
KOUKI-KUN!!

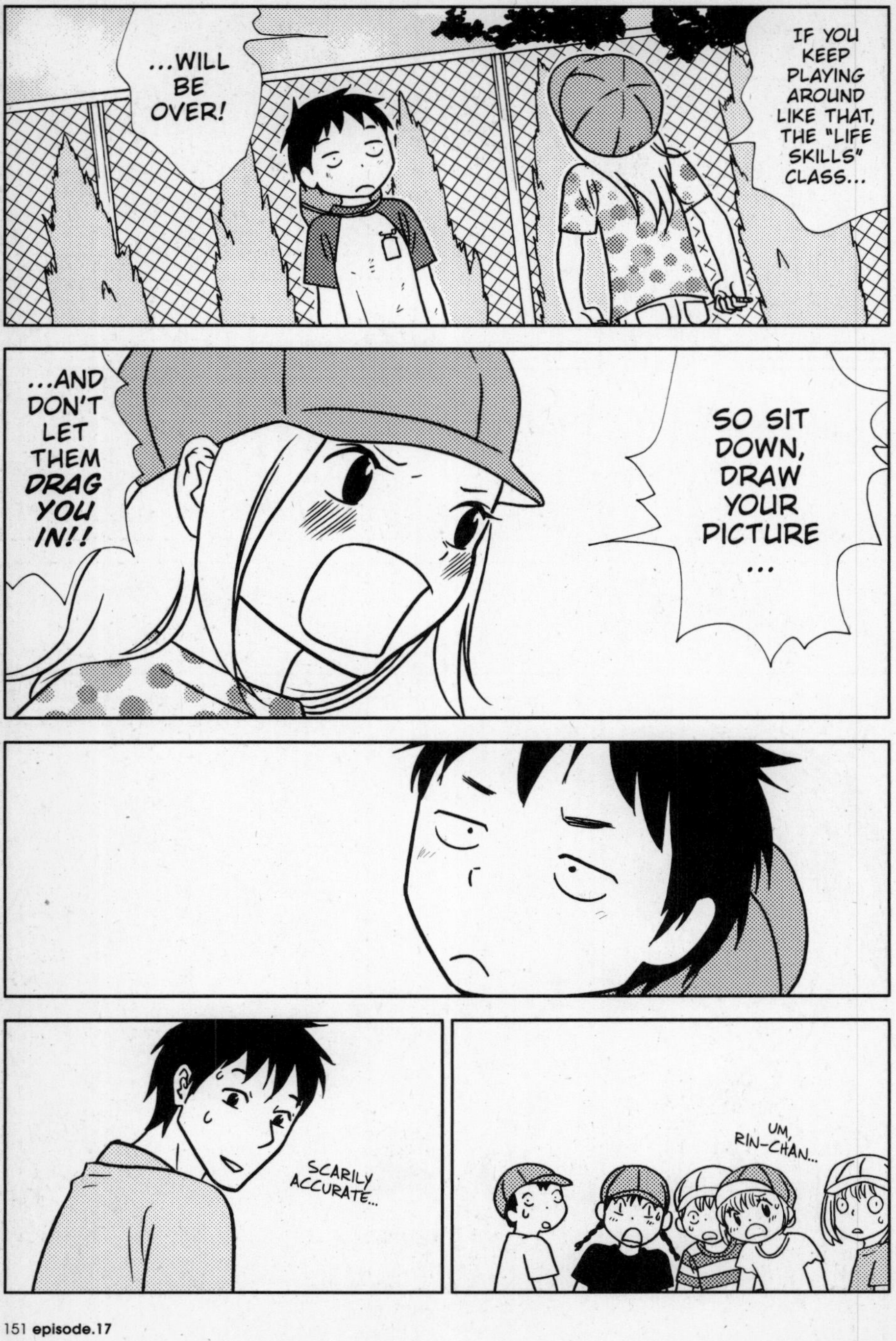
IF YOU KEEP PLAYING AROUND LIKE THAT, THE "LIFE SKILLS" CLASS...
...WILL BE OVER!
SO SIT DOWN, DRAW YOUR PICTURE ...
...AND DON'T LET THEM DRAG YOU IN!!
UM, RIN-CHAN...
SCARILY ACCURATE...

OKAY.

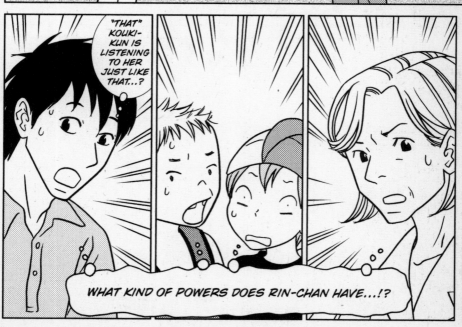

"THAT" KOUKI-KUN IS LISTENING TO HER JUST LIKE THAT...?

WHAT KIND OF POWERS DOES RIN-CHAN HAVE....!?

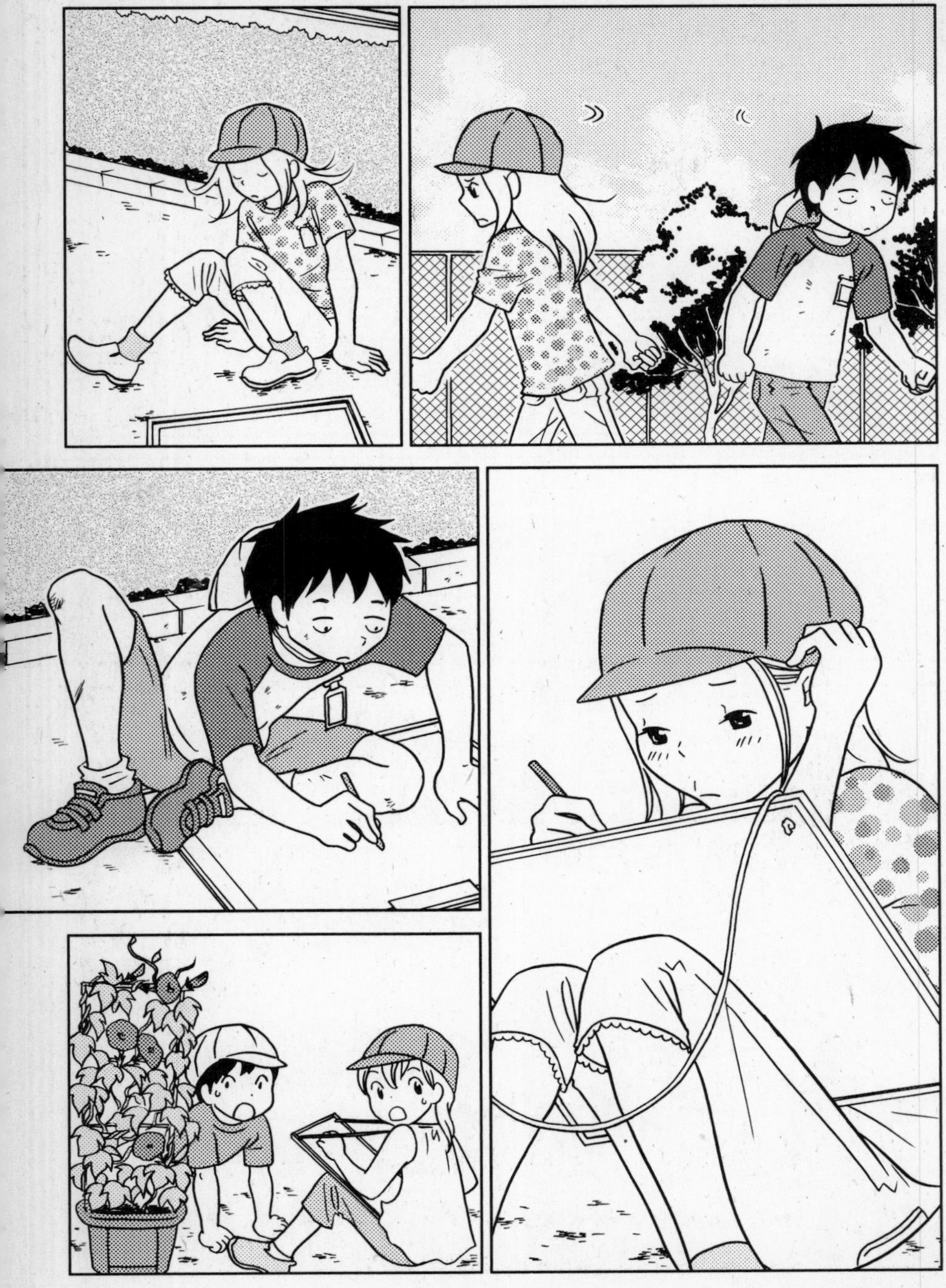

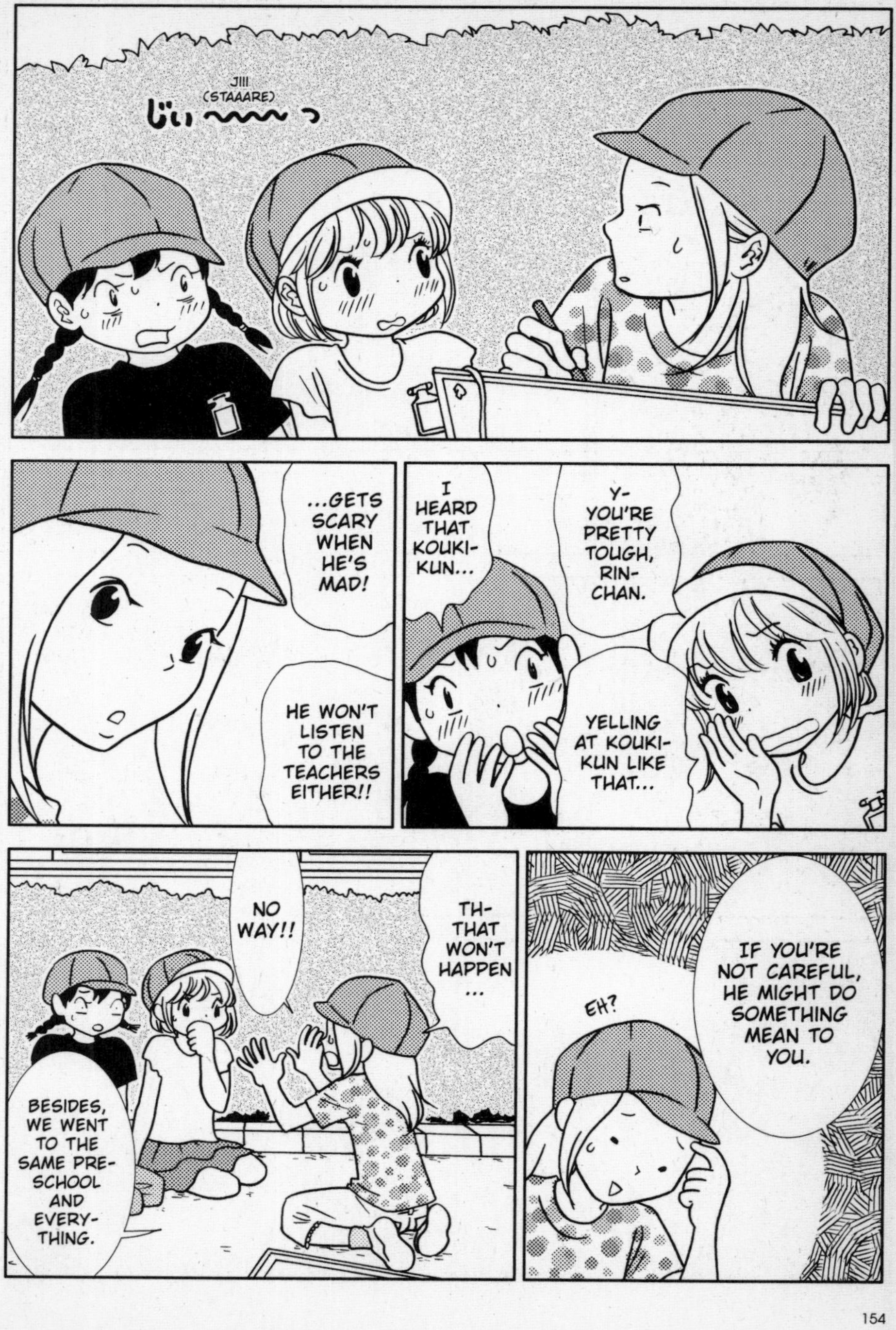
JIII
(STAAARE)
じぃ〜〜〜っ
Y- YOU'RE PRETTY TOUGH, RIN-CHAN.
YELLING AT KOUKI-KUN LIKE THAT...
I HEARD THAT KOUKI-KUN...
...GETS SCARY WHEN HE'S MAD!
HE WON'T LISTEN TO THE TEACHERS EITHER!!
IF YOU'RE NOT CAREFUL, HE MIGHT DO SOMETHING MEAN TO YOU.
EH?
TH- THAT WON'T HAPPEN ...
NO WAY!!
BESIDES, WE WENT TO THE SAME PRE-SCHOOL AND EVERY-THING.

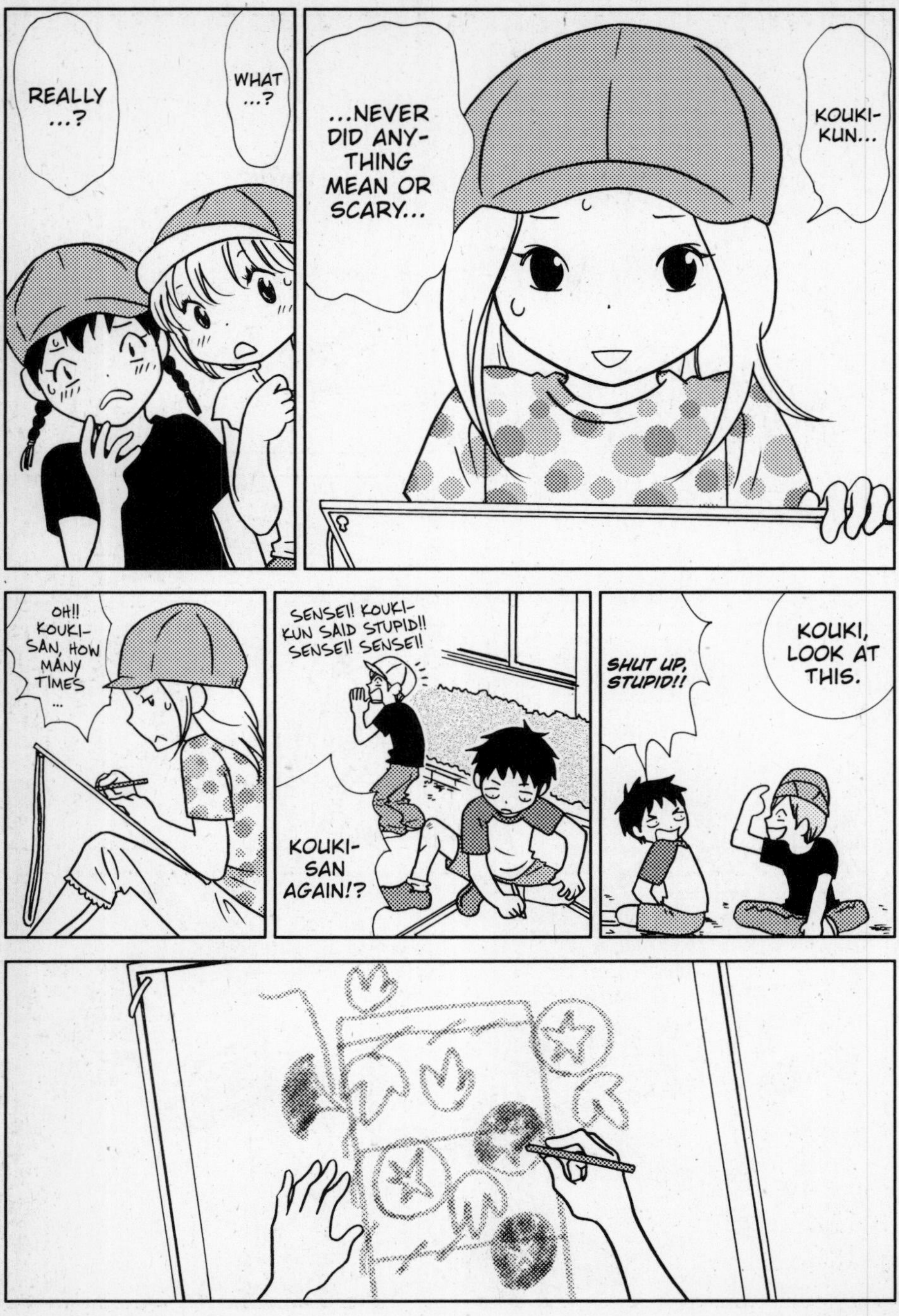
KOUKI-KUN...
...NEVER DID ANY-THING MEAN OR SCARY...
WHAT ...?
REALLY ...?
KOUKI, LOOK AT THIS.
SHUT UP, STUPID!!
SENSEI! KOUKI-KUN SAID STUPID!! SENSEI! SENSEI!
KOUKI-SAN AGAIN!?
OH!! KOUKI-SAN, HOW MANY TIMES ...

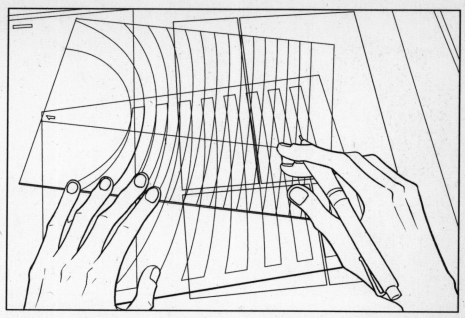

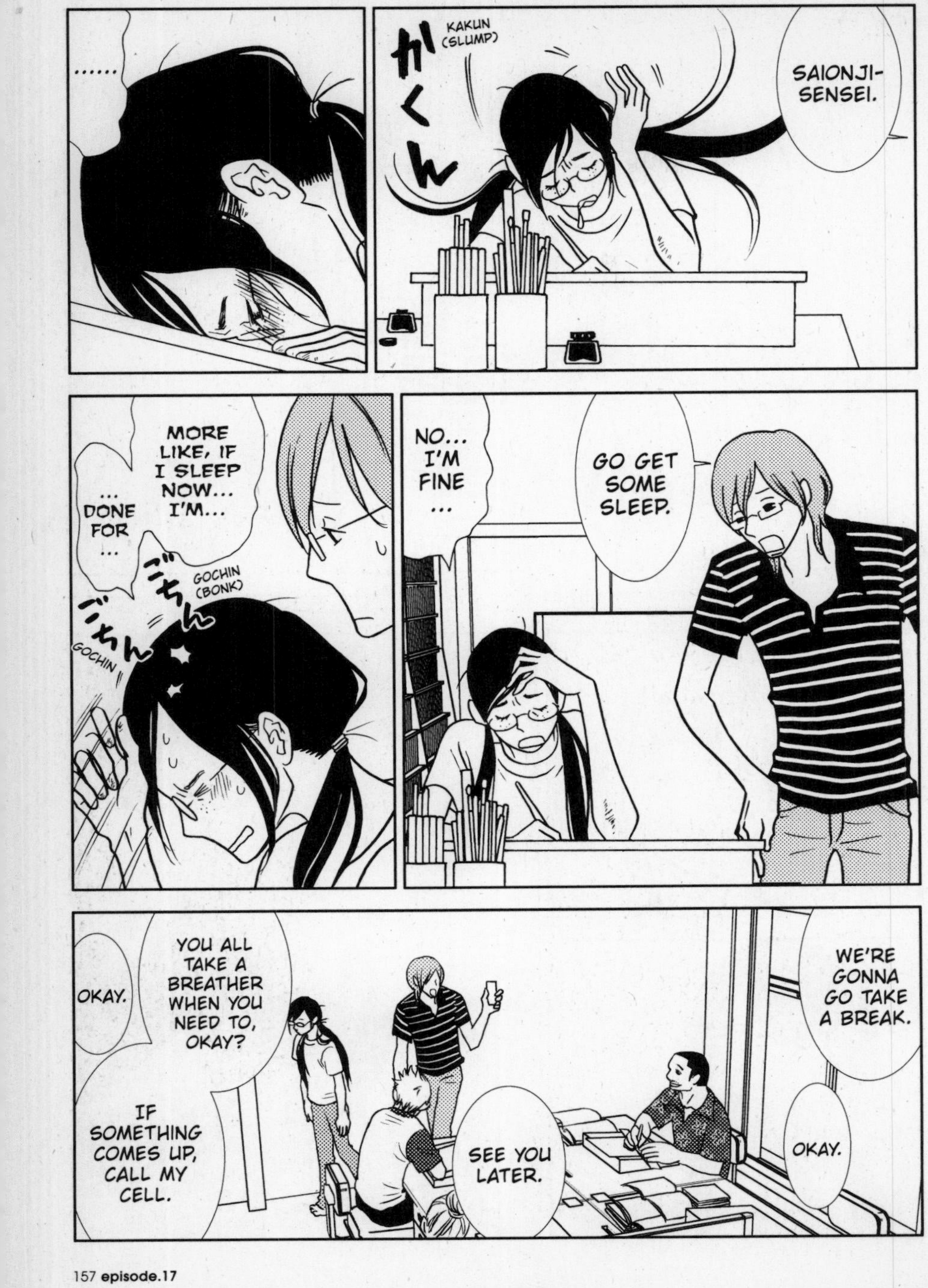
SAIONJI-SENSEI.
かくん
KAKUN (SLUMP)
......
GO GET SOME SLEEP.
NO... I'M FINE ...
MORE LIKE, IF I SLEEP NOW... I'M...
... DONE FOR ...
ごちん
GOCHIN (BONK)
ごちん
GOCHIN
WE'RE GONNA GO TAKE A BREAK.
OKAY.
SEE YOU LATER.
YOU ALL TAKE A BREATHER WHEN YOU NEED TO, OKAY?
IF SOMETHING COMES UP, CALL MY CELL.
OKAY.

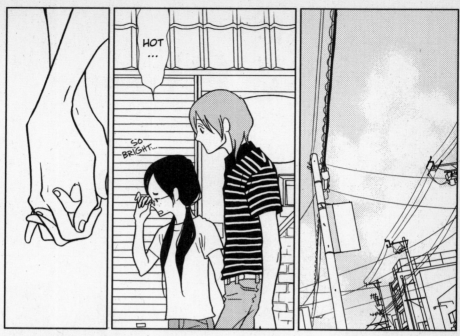

HOT ...
SO BRIGHT...
BUT YOUR HANDS ARE LIKE ICE.
THE TEMP'S DOWN TOO LOW IN THERE.
BUT IF WE CUT THE A.C., THE GUYS'LL SWEAT ALL OVER THE MANU-SCRIPTS...
I HEARD STRESS CAN LOWER YOUR BODY TEMPERA-TURE TOO.
HUH ...

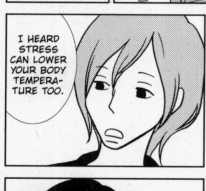

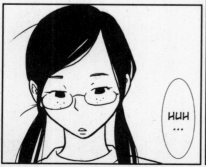

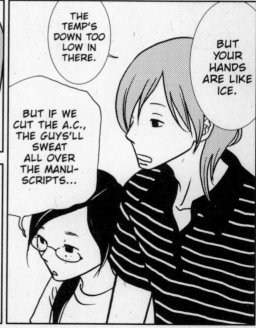

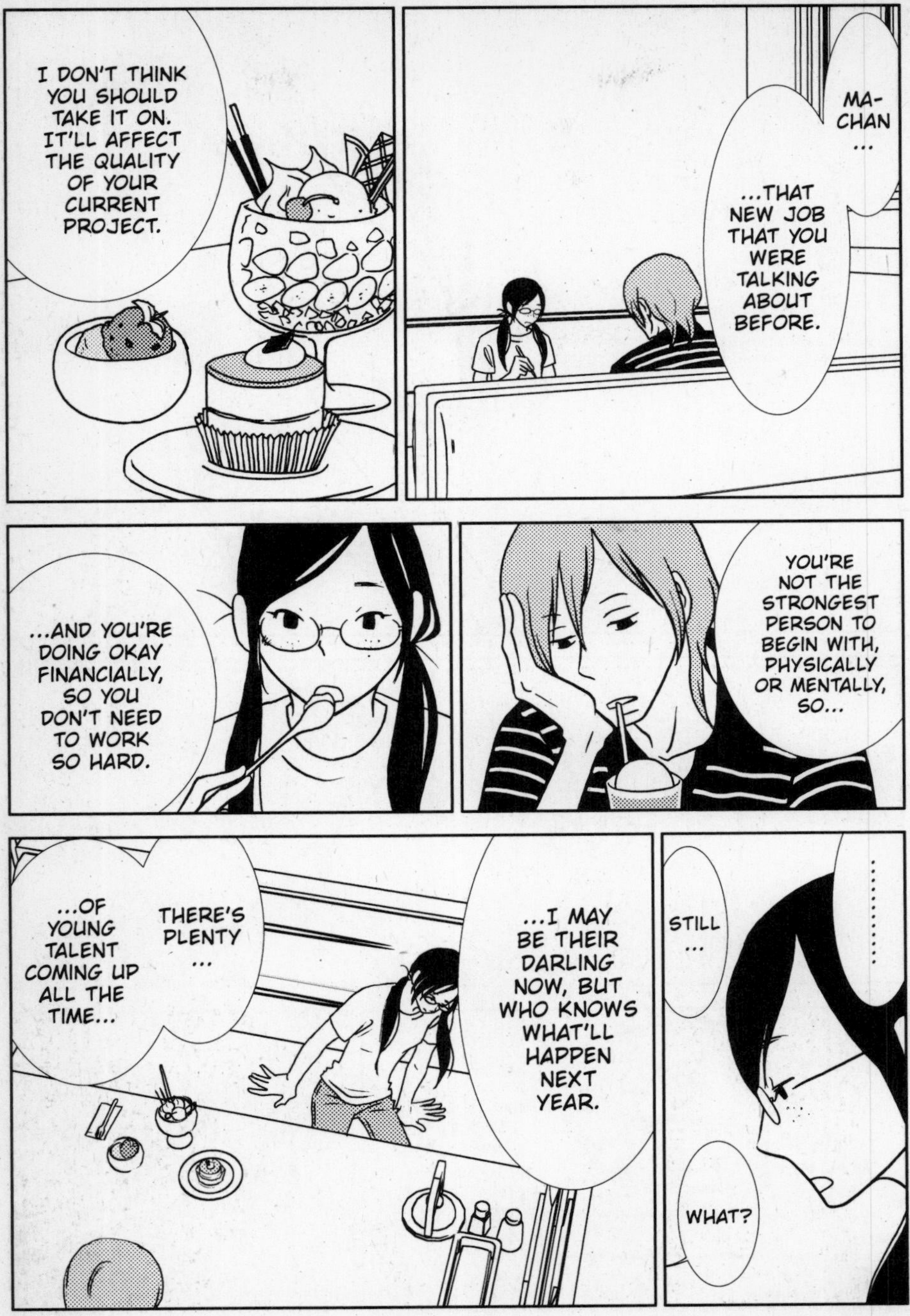
MA-CHAN...
...THAT NEW JOB THAT YOU WERE TALKING ABOUT BEFORE.
I DON'T THINK YOU SHOULD TAKE IT ON. IT'LL AFFECT THE QUALITY OF YOUR CURRENT PROJECT.
YOU'RE NOT THE STRONGEST PERSON TO BEGIN WITH, PHYSICALLY OR MENTALLY, SO...
...AND YOU'RE DOING OKAY FINANCIALLY, SO YOU DON'T NEED TO WORK SO HARD.
......
STILL...
WHAT?
...I MAY BE THEIR DARLING NOW, BUT WHO KNOWS WHAT'LL HAPPEN NEXT YEAR.
THERE'S PLENTY...
...OF YOUNG TALENT COMING UP ALL THE TIME...

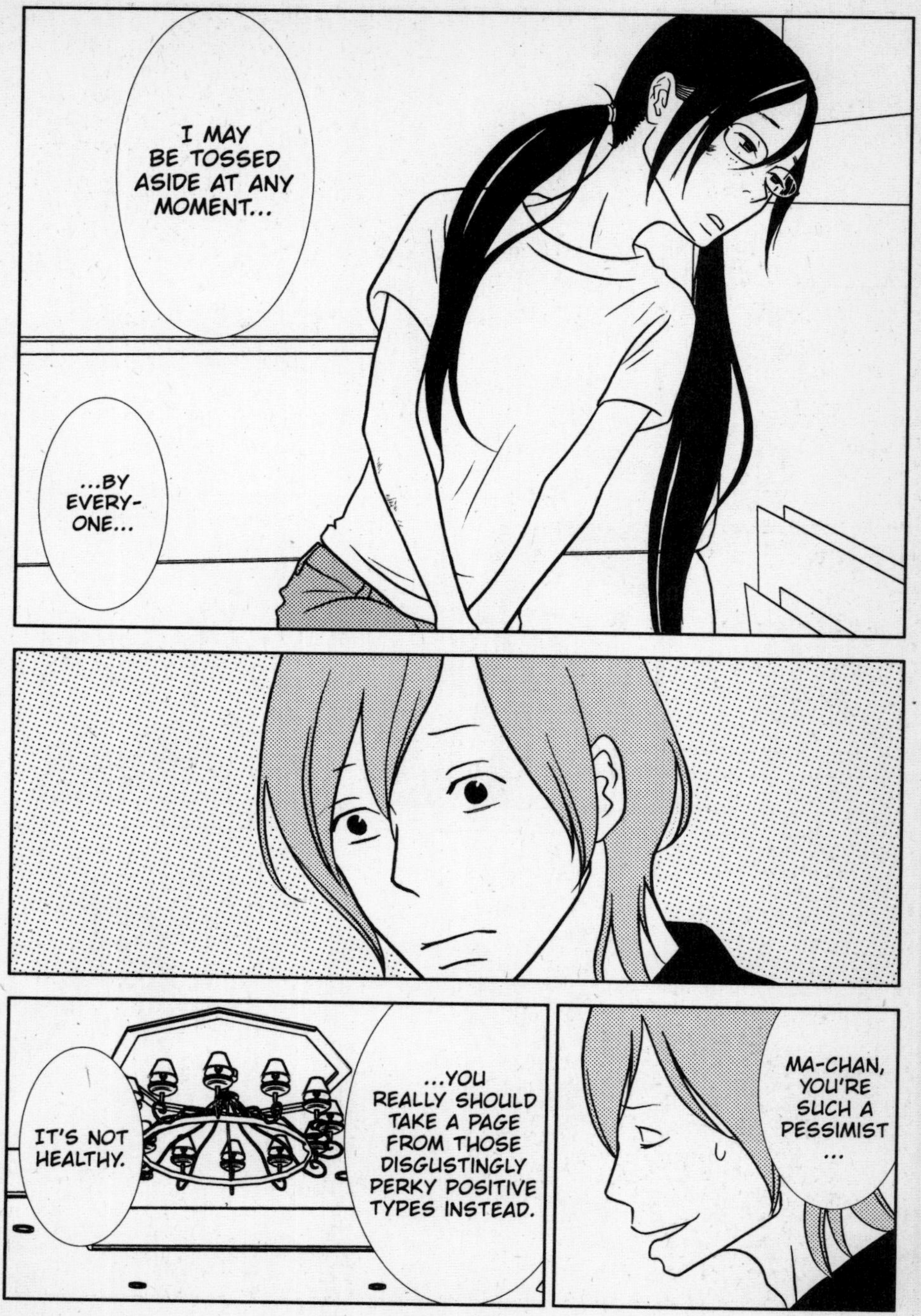
I MAY BE TOSSED ASIDE AT ANY MOMENT...
...BY EVERY-ONE...
MA-CHAN, YOU'RE SUCH A PESSIMIST ...
...YOU REALLY SHOULD TAKE A PAGE FROM THOSE DISGUSTINGLY PERKY POSITIVE TYPES INSTEAD.
IT'S NOT HEALTHY.

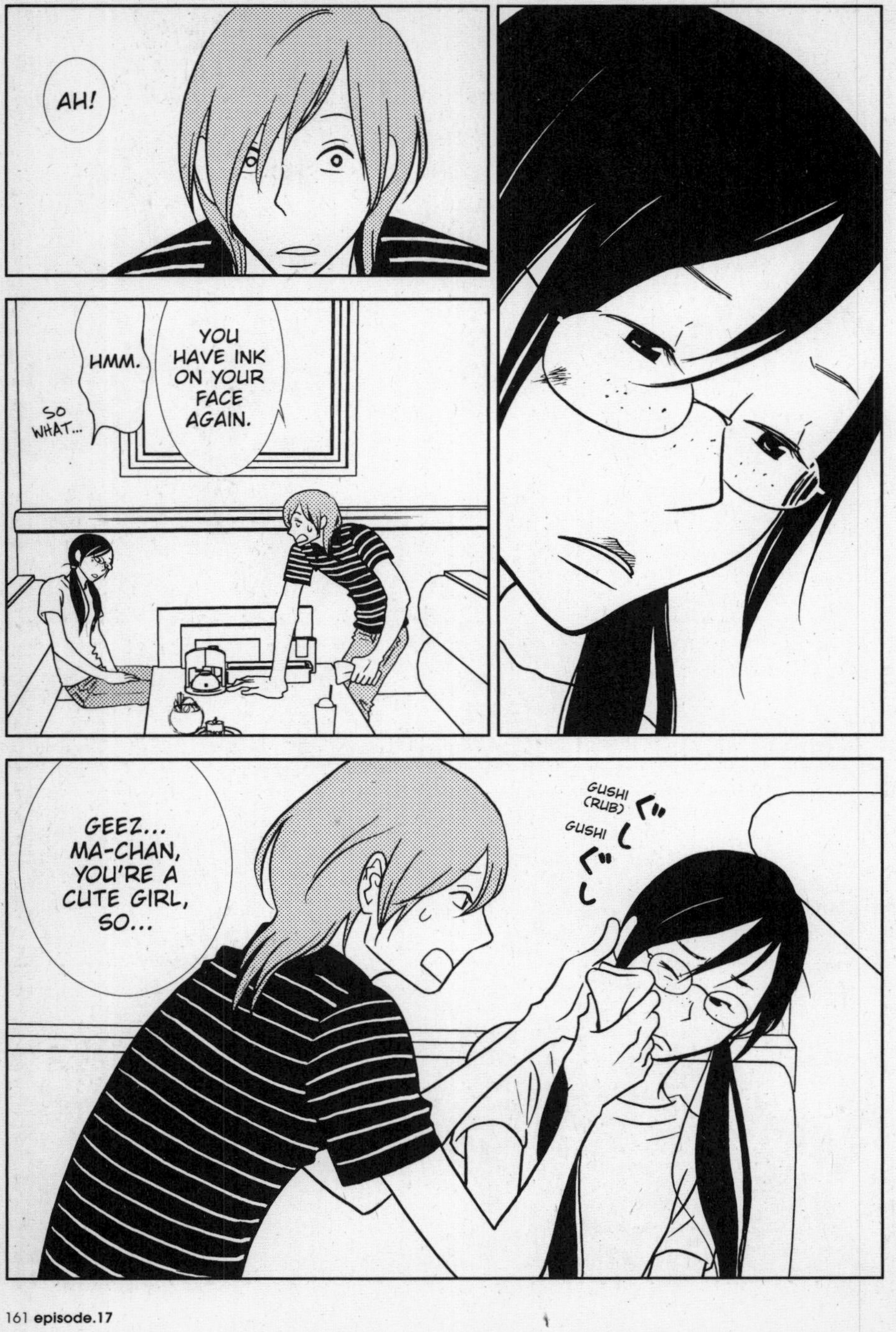
AH!
YOU HAVE INK ON YOUR FACE AGAIN.
HMM.
SO WHAT...
GUSHI (RUB) GUSHI
ぐしぐし
GEEZ... MA-CHAN, YOU'RE A CUTE GIRL, SO...

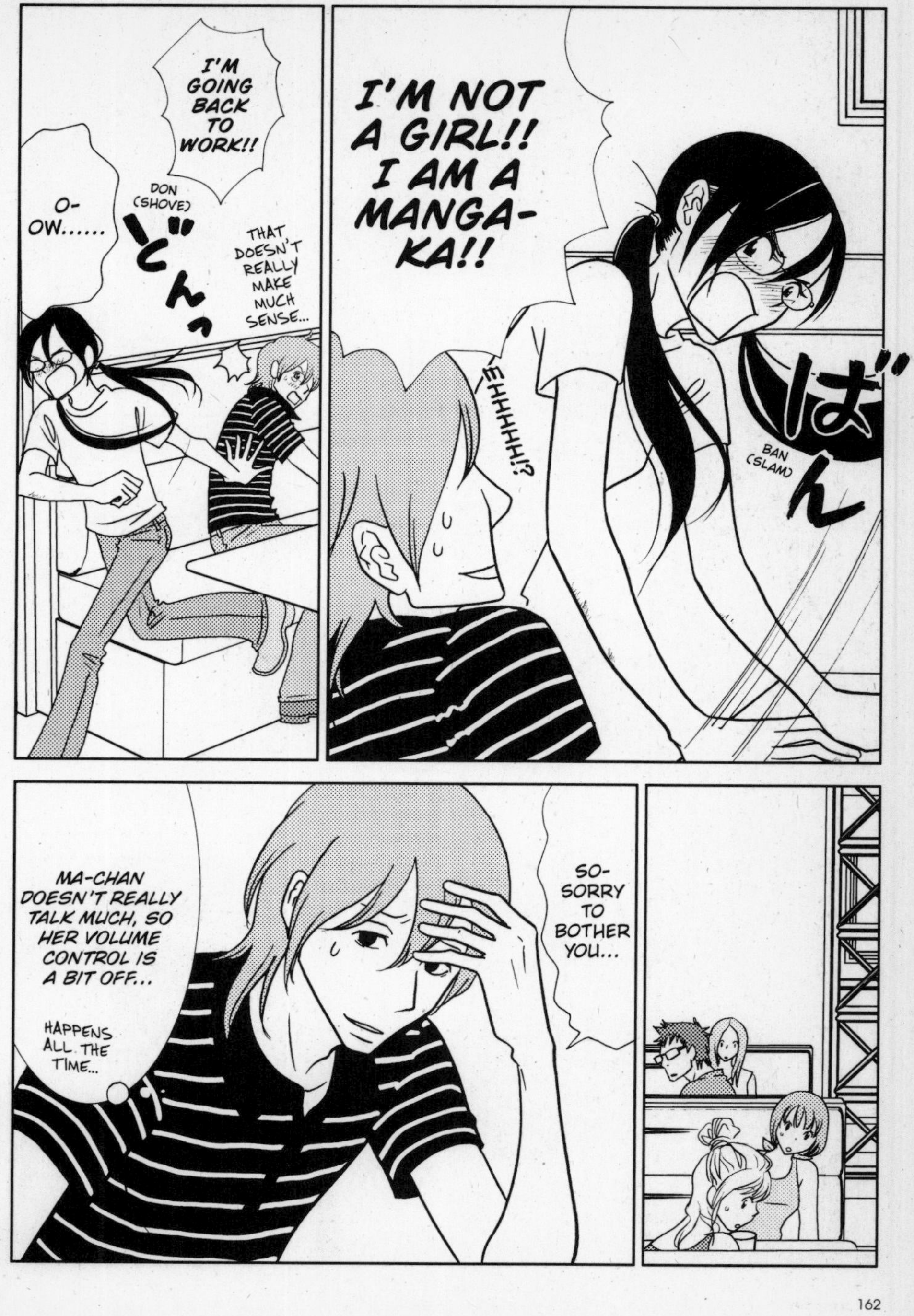
I'M NOT A GIRL!! I AM A MANGA-KA!!
EHHHHH!?
ばん
BAN (SLAM)
I'M GOING BACK TO WORK!!
どんっ
DON (SHOVE)
O-OW......
THAT DOESN'T REALLY MAKE MUCH SENSE...
SO-SORRY TO BOTHER YOU...
MA-CHAN DOESN'T REALLY TALK MUCH, SO HER VOLUME CONTROL IS A BIT OFF...
HAPPENS ALL THE TIME...

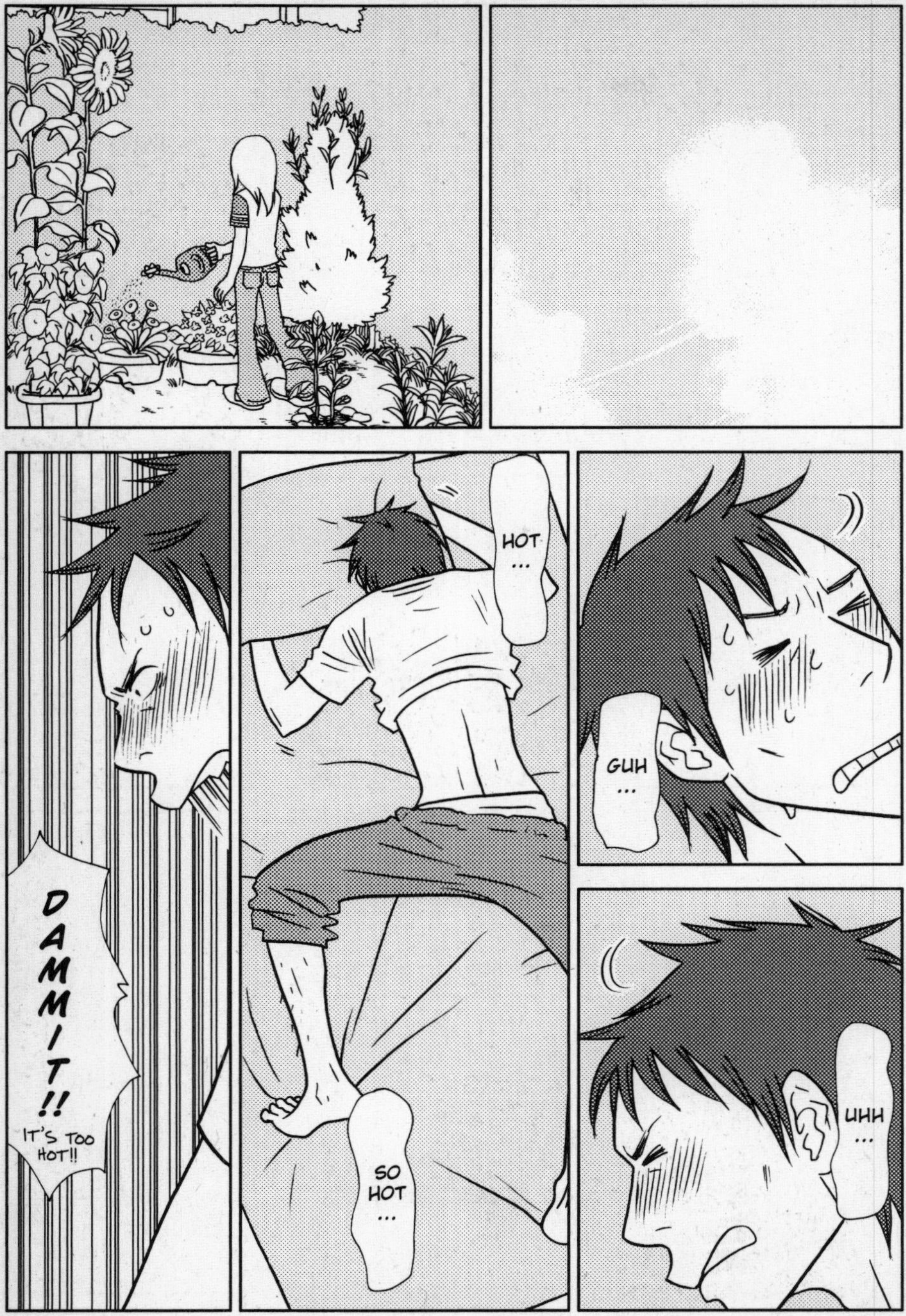
GUH ...
UHH ...
HOT ...
SO HOT ...
DAMMIT!!
IT'S TOO HOT!!

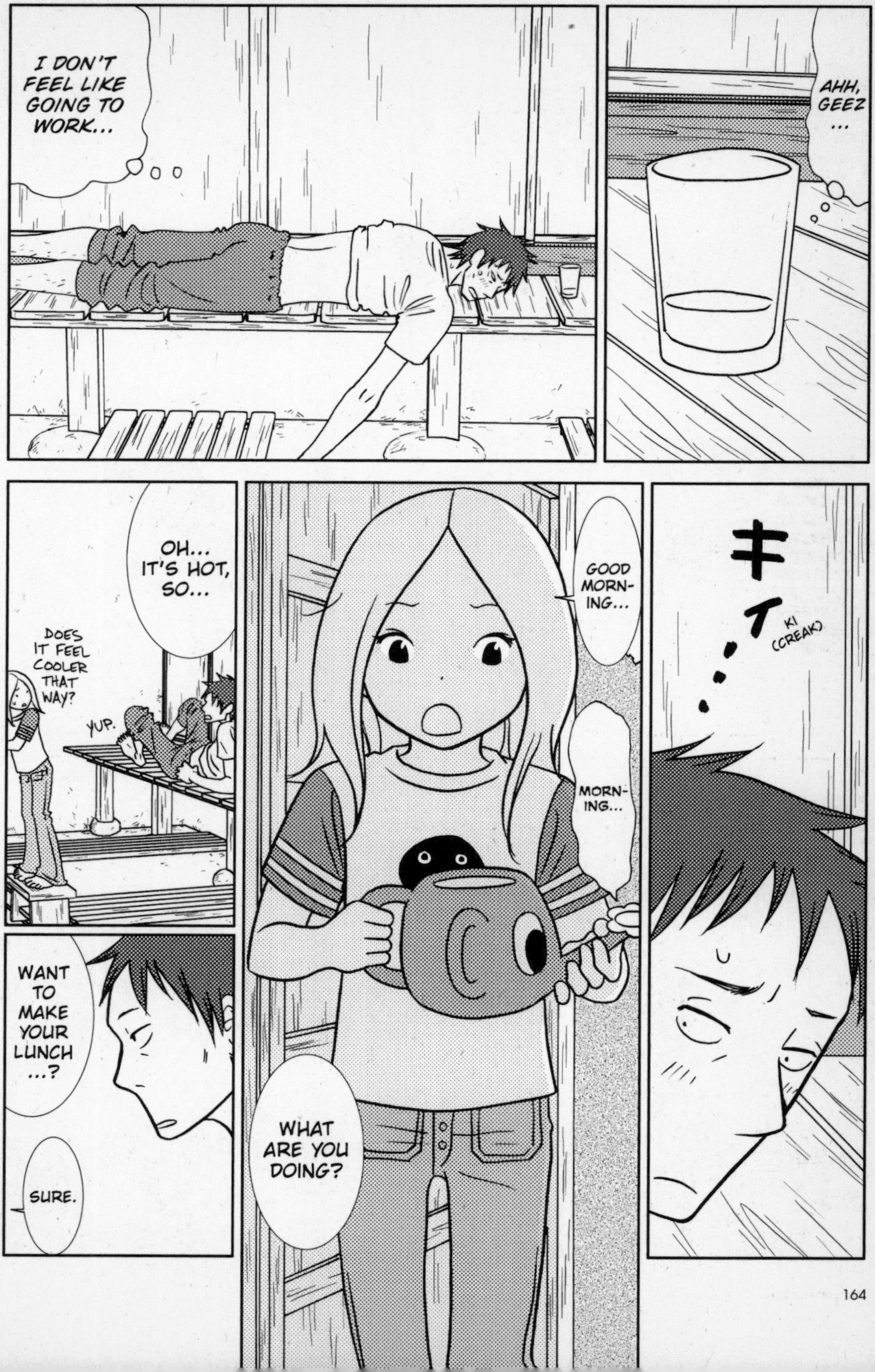
AHH, GEEZ ...
I DON'T FEEL LIKE GOING TO WORK...
キィ...
KI (CREAK)
GOOD MORNING...
MORNING...
WHAT ARE YOU DOING?
OH... IT'S HOT, SO...
DOES IT FEEL COOLER THAT WAY?
YUP.
WANT TO MAKE YOUR LUNCH ...?
SURE.

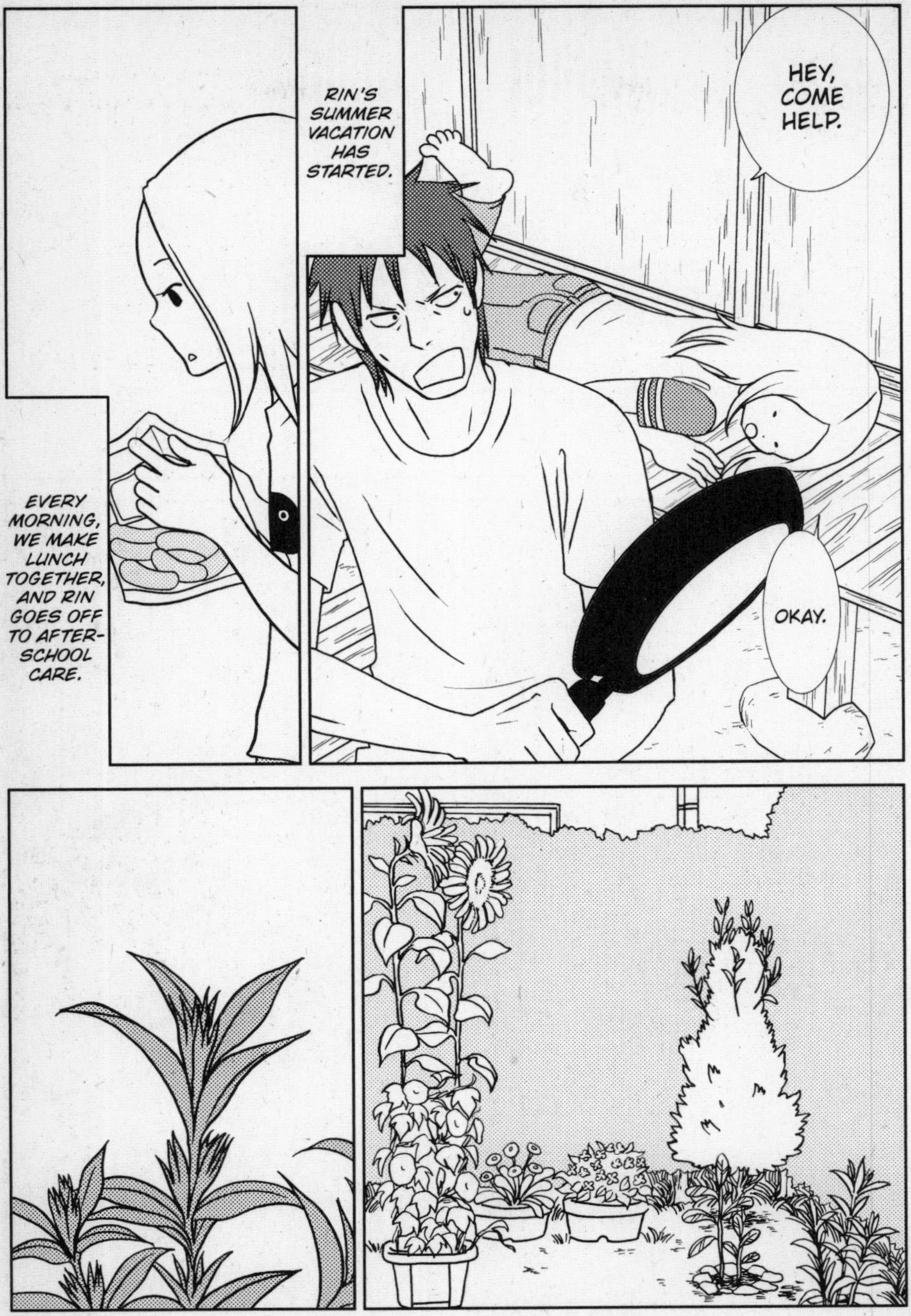
HEY, COME HELP.
RIN'S SUMMER VACATION HAS STARTED.
OKAY.
EVERY MORNING, WE MAKE LUNCH TOGETHER, AND RIN GOES OFF TO AFTER-SCHOOL CARE.

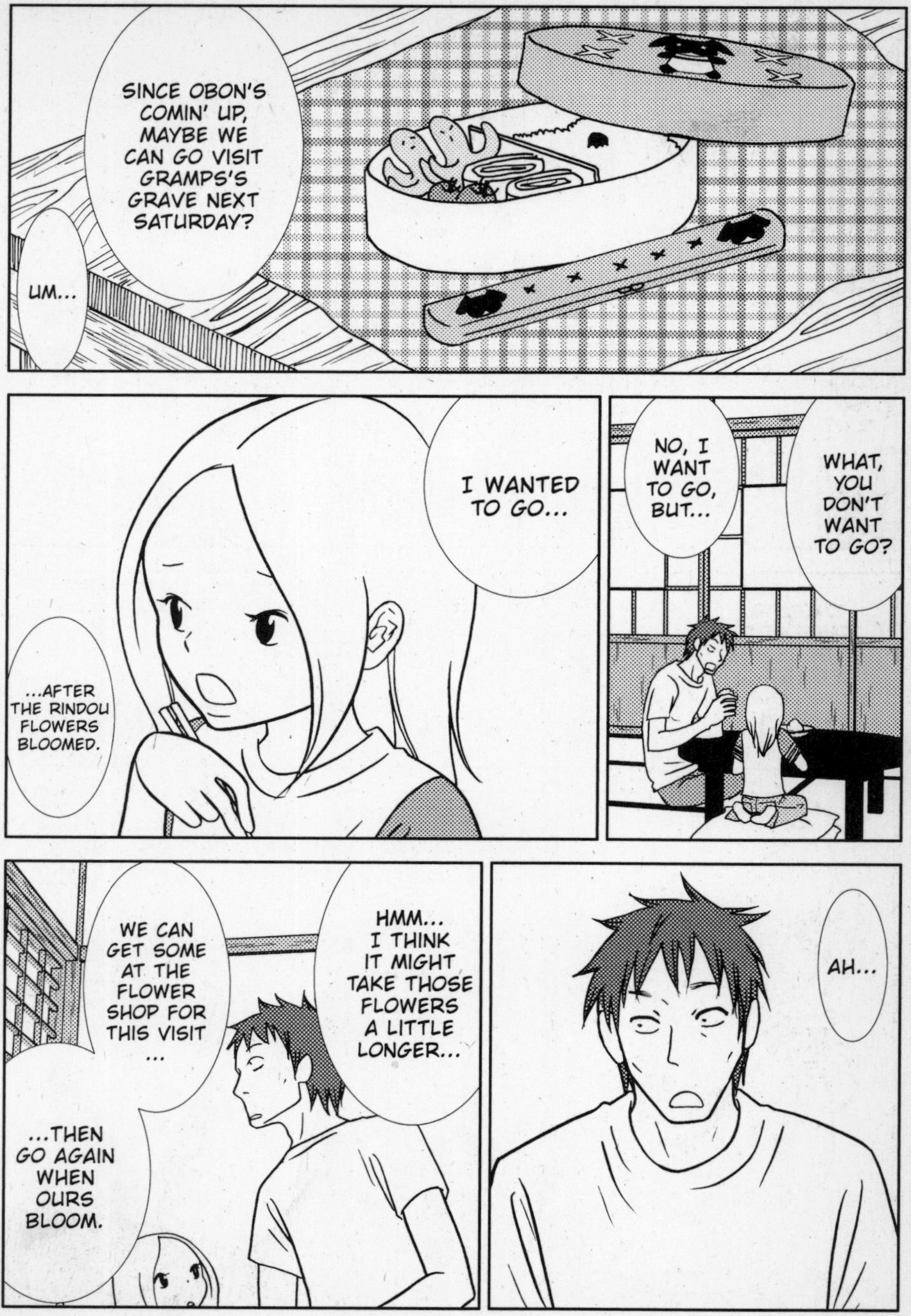
SINCE OBON'S COMIN' UP, MAYBE WE CAN GO VISIT GRAMPS'S GRAVE NEXT SATURDAY?
UM...
WHAT, YOU DON'T WANT TO GO?
NO, I WANT TO GO, BUT...
I WANTED TO GO...
...AFTER THE RINDOU FLOWERS BLOOMED.
AH...
HMM... I THINK IT MIGHT TAKE THOSE FLOWERS A LITTLE LONGER...
WE CAN GET SOME AT THE FLOWER SHOP FOR THIS VISIT ...
...THEN GO AGAIN WHEN OURS BLOOM.

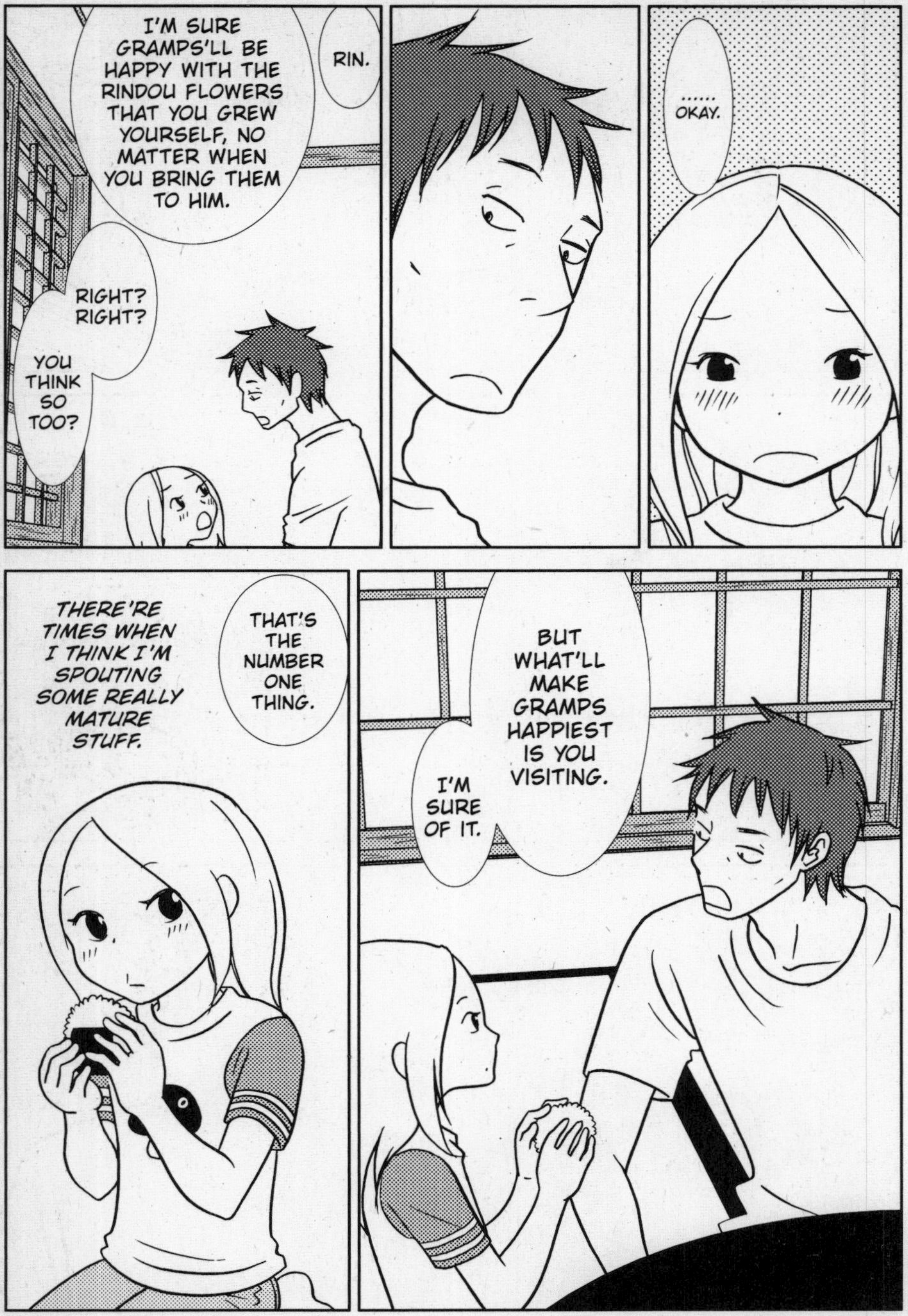
......OKAY.
RIN.
I'M SURE GRAMPS'LL BE HAPPY WITH THE RINDOU FLOWERS THAT YOU GREW YOURSELF, NO MATTER WHEN YOU BRING THEM TO HIM.
RIGHT? RIGHT?
YOU THINK SO TOO?
BUT WHAT'LL MAKE GRAMPS HAPPIEST IS YOU VISITING.
I'M SURE OF IT.
THAT'S THE NUMBER ONE THING.
THERE'RE TIMES WHEN I THINK I'M SPOUTING SOME REALLY MATURE STUFF.

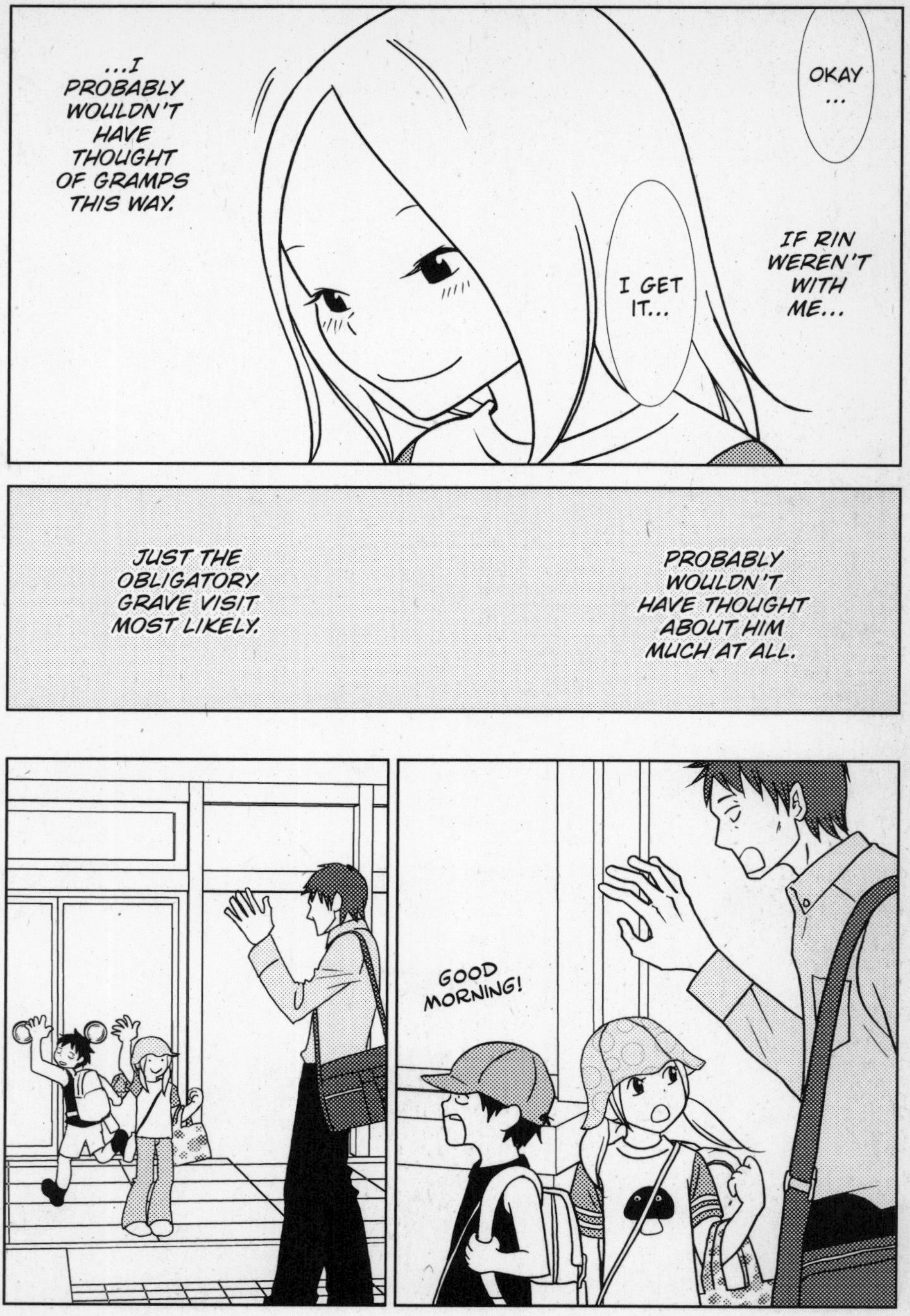
OKAY...
IF RIN WEREN'T WITH ME...
I GET IT...
...I PROBABLY WOULDN'T HAVE THOUGHT OF GRAMPS THIS WAY.
PROBABLY WOULDN'T HAVE THOUGHT ABOUT HIM MUCH AT ALL.
JUST THE OBLIGATORY GRAVE VISIT MOST LIKELY.
GOOD MORNING!

SO, FEELING LIKE I'M GRASPING AT CLOUDS, I KEEP PRETENDING TO ACT THE ADULT.

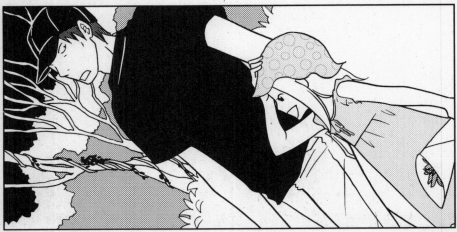

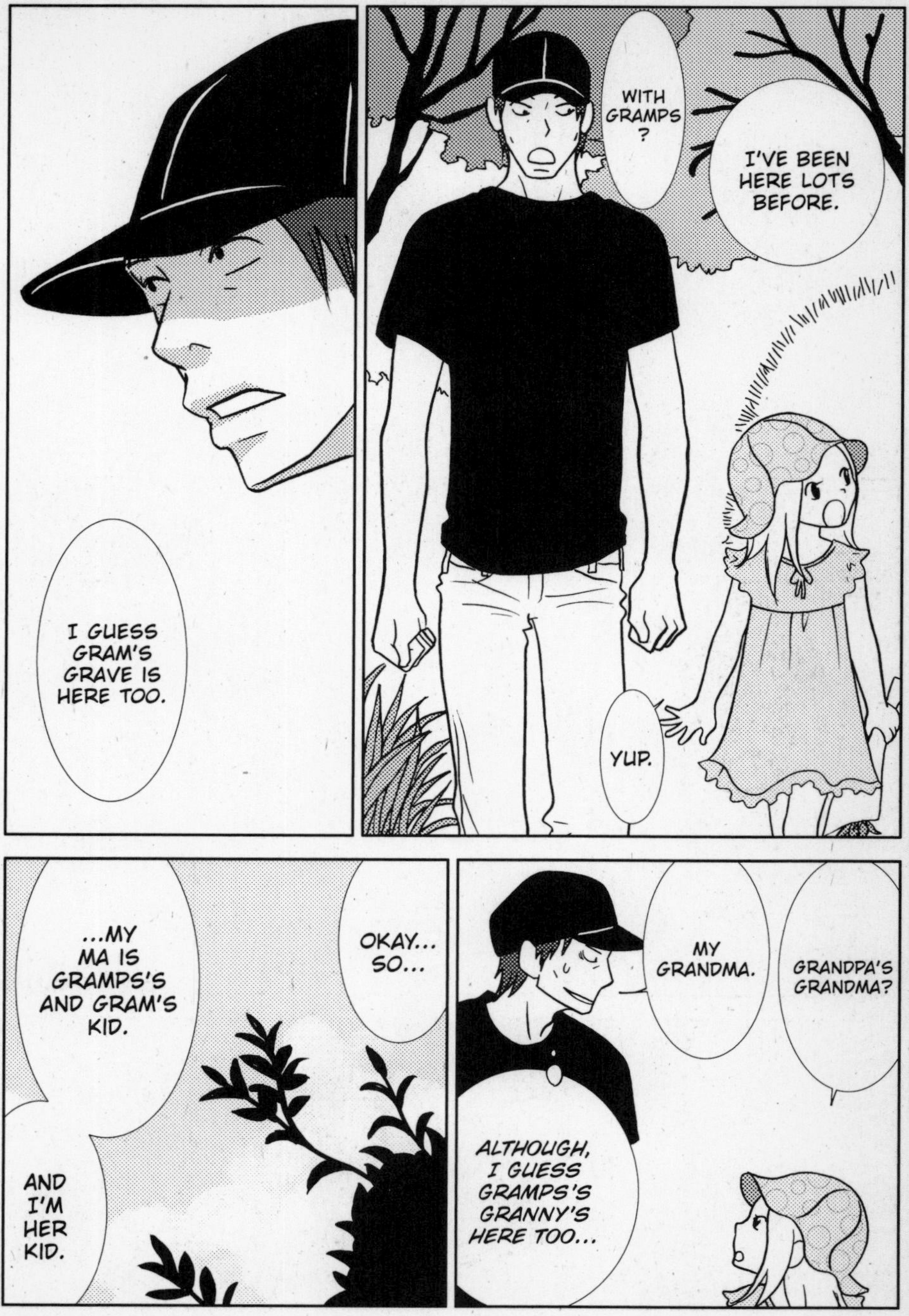
I'VE BEEN HERE LOTS BEFORE.
WITH GRAMPS?
YUP.
I GUESS GRAM'S GRAVE IS HERE TOO.
GRANDPA'S GRANDMA?
MY GRANDMA.
ALTHOUGH, I GUESS GRAMPS'S GRANNY'S HERE TOO...
OKAY... SO...
...MY MA IS GRAMPS'S AND GRAM'S KID.
AND I'M HER KID.

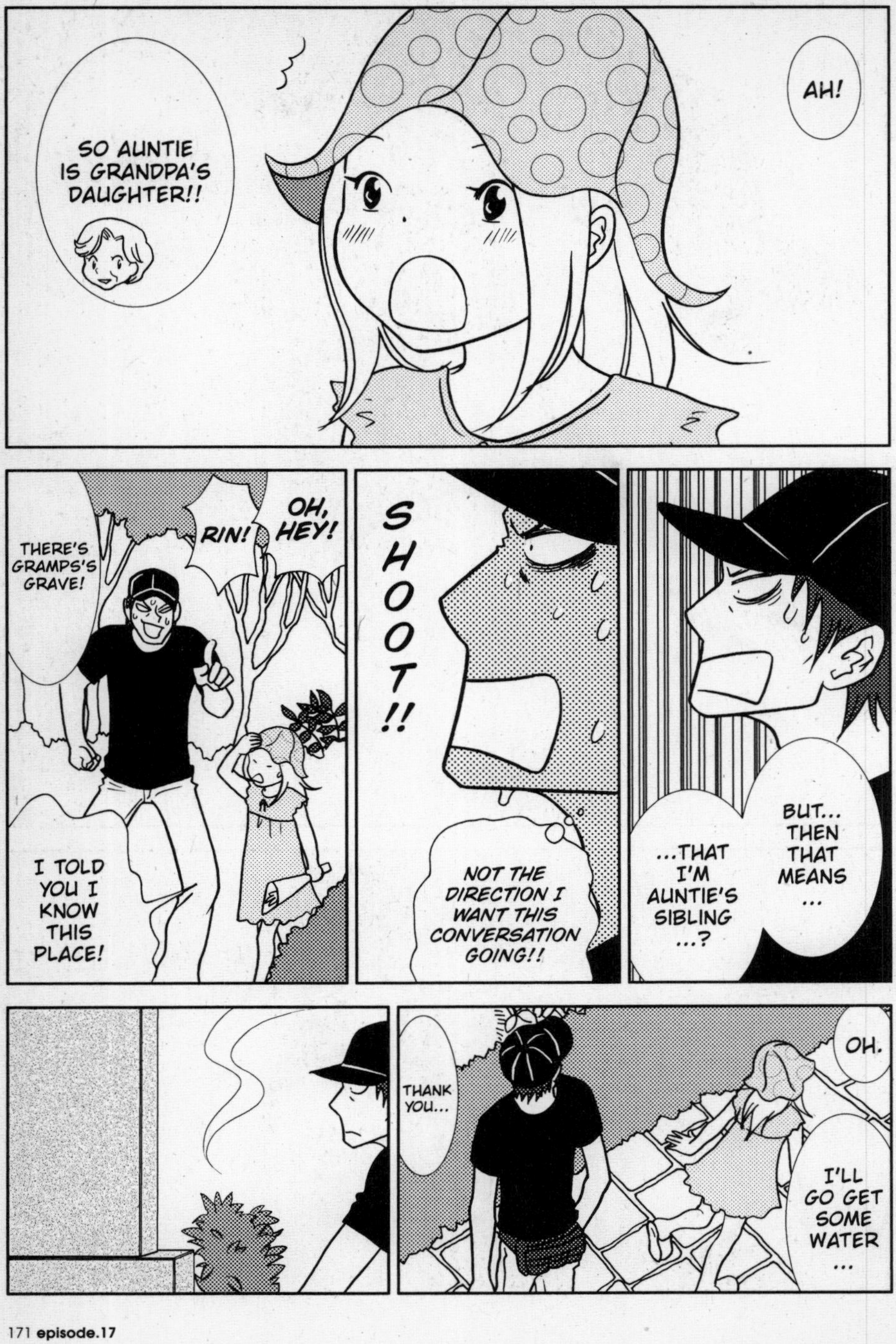
AH!
SO AUNTIE IS GRANDPA'S DAUGHTER!!
BUT... THEN THAT MEANS ...
...THAT I'M AUNTIE'S SIBLING ...?
SHOOOT!!
NOT THE DIRECTION I WANT THIS CONVERSATION GOING!!
OH, HEY!
RIN!
THERE'S GRAMPS'S GRAVE!
I TOLD YOU I KNOW THIS PLACE!
OH.
I'LL GO GET SOME WATER ...
THANK YOU...

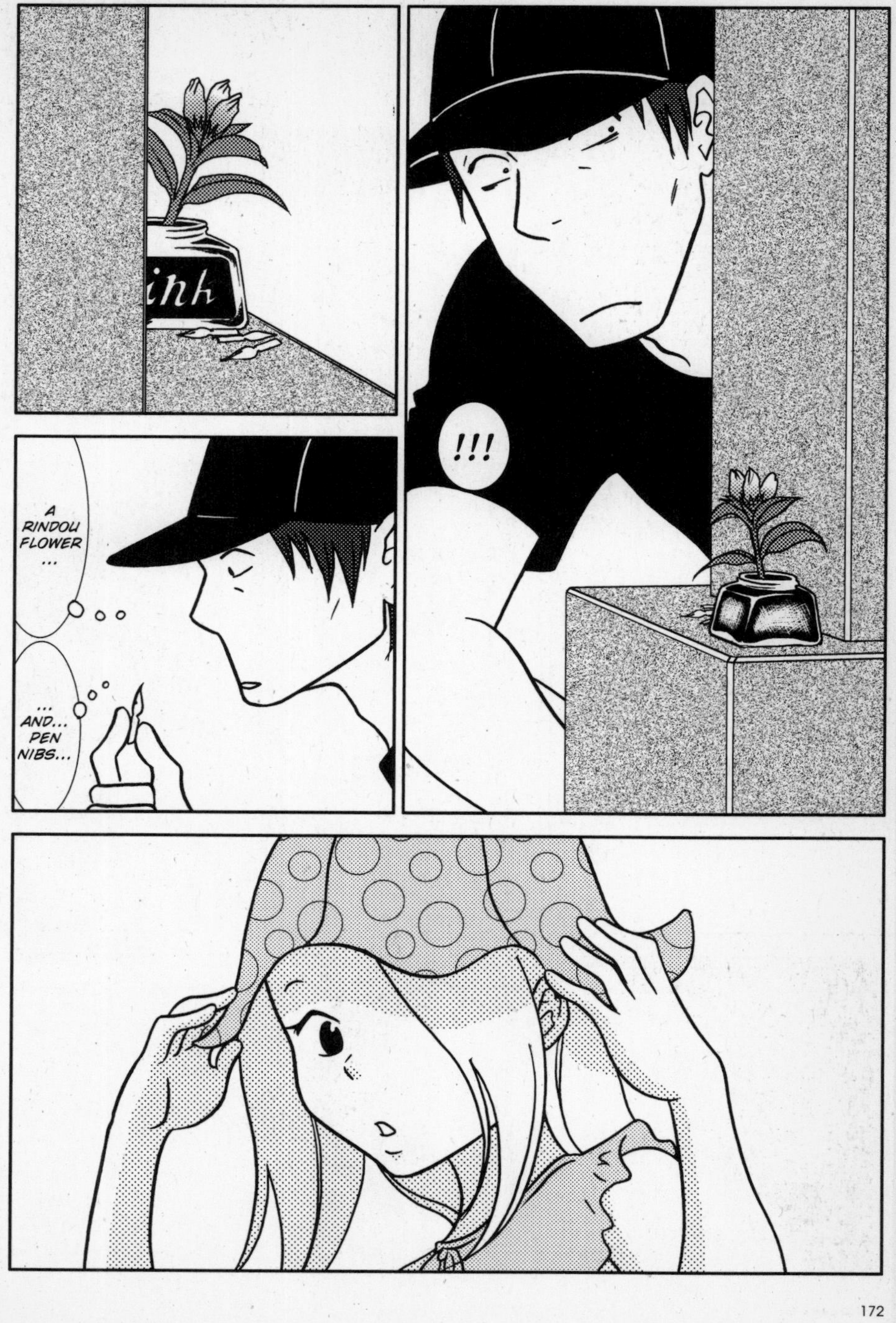
!!!
ink
A RINDOU FLOWER ...
... AND... PEN NIBS...

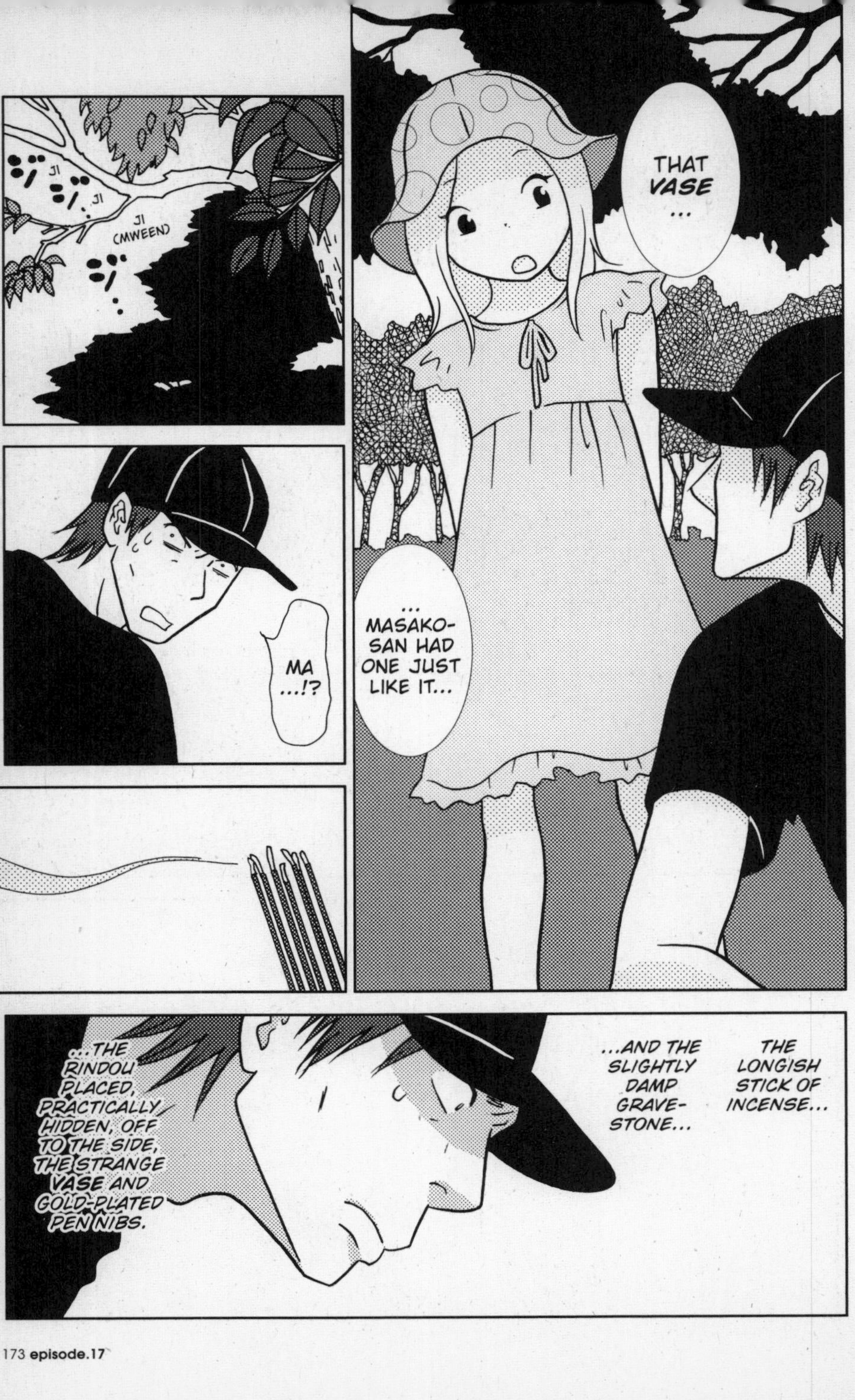
THAT VASE ...
... MASAKO-SAN HAD ONE JUST LIKE IT...
JI
JI
JI (MWEEN)
MA ...!?
THE LONGISH STICK OF INCENSE...
...AND THE SLIGHTLY DAMP GRAVE-STONE...
...THE RINDOU PLACED, PRACTICALLY HIDDEN, OFF TO THE SIDE, THE STRANGE VASE AND GOLD-PLATED PEN NIBS.

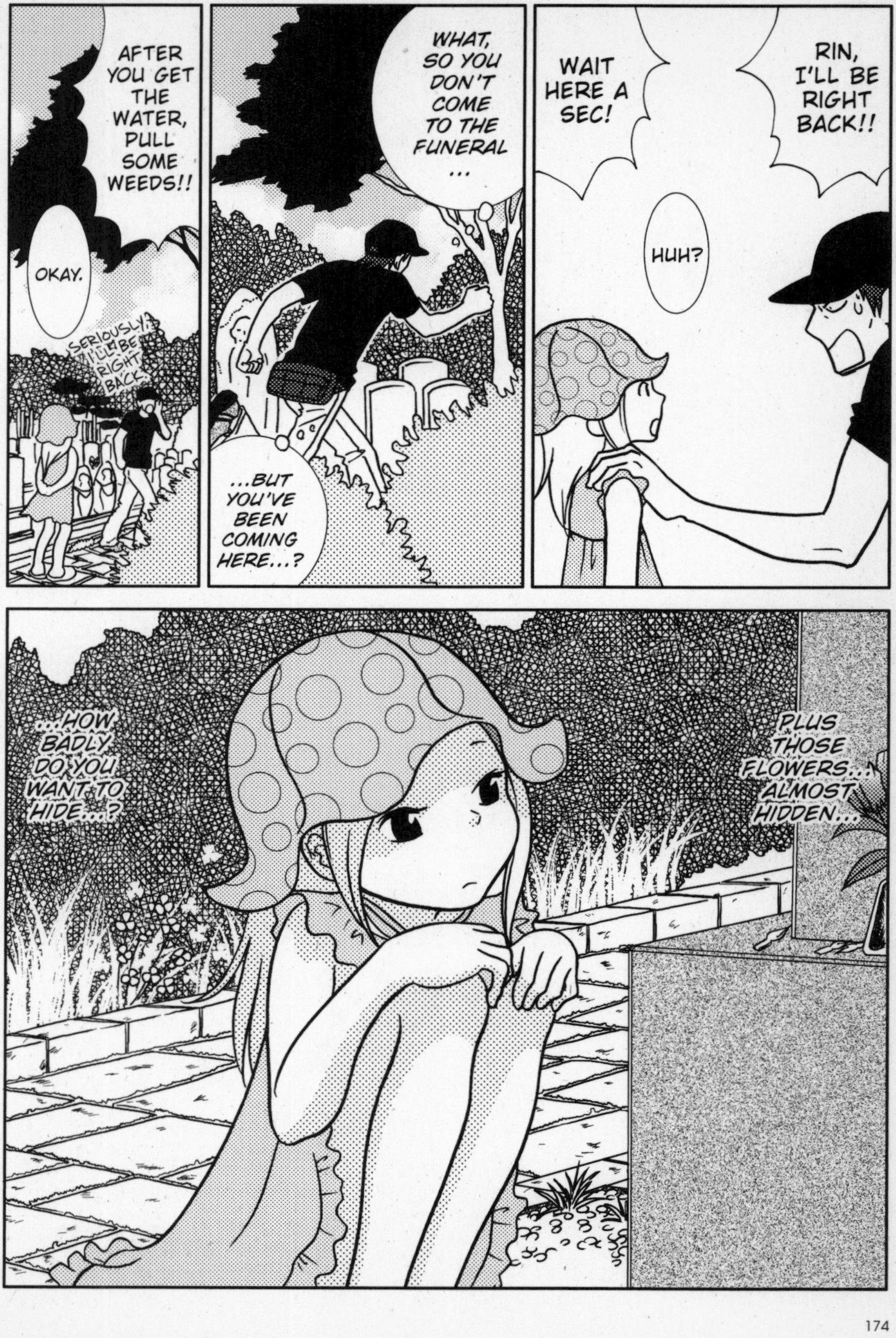
RIN, I'LL BE RIGHT BACK!!
WAIT HERE A SEC!
HUH?
WHAT, SO YOU DON'T COME TO THE FUNERAL ...
...BUT YOU'VE BEEN COMING HERE...?
AFTER YOU GET THE WATER, PULL SOME WEEDS!!
OKAY.
SERIOUSLY, I'LL BE RIGHT BACK.
PLUS THOSE FLOWERS... ALMOST HIDDEN...
...HOW BADLY DO YOU WANT TO HIDE...?

BUNNY**DROP**

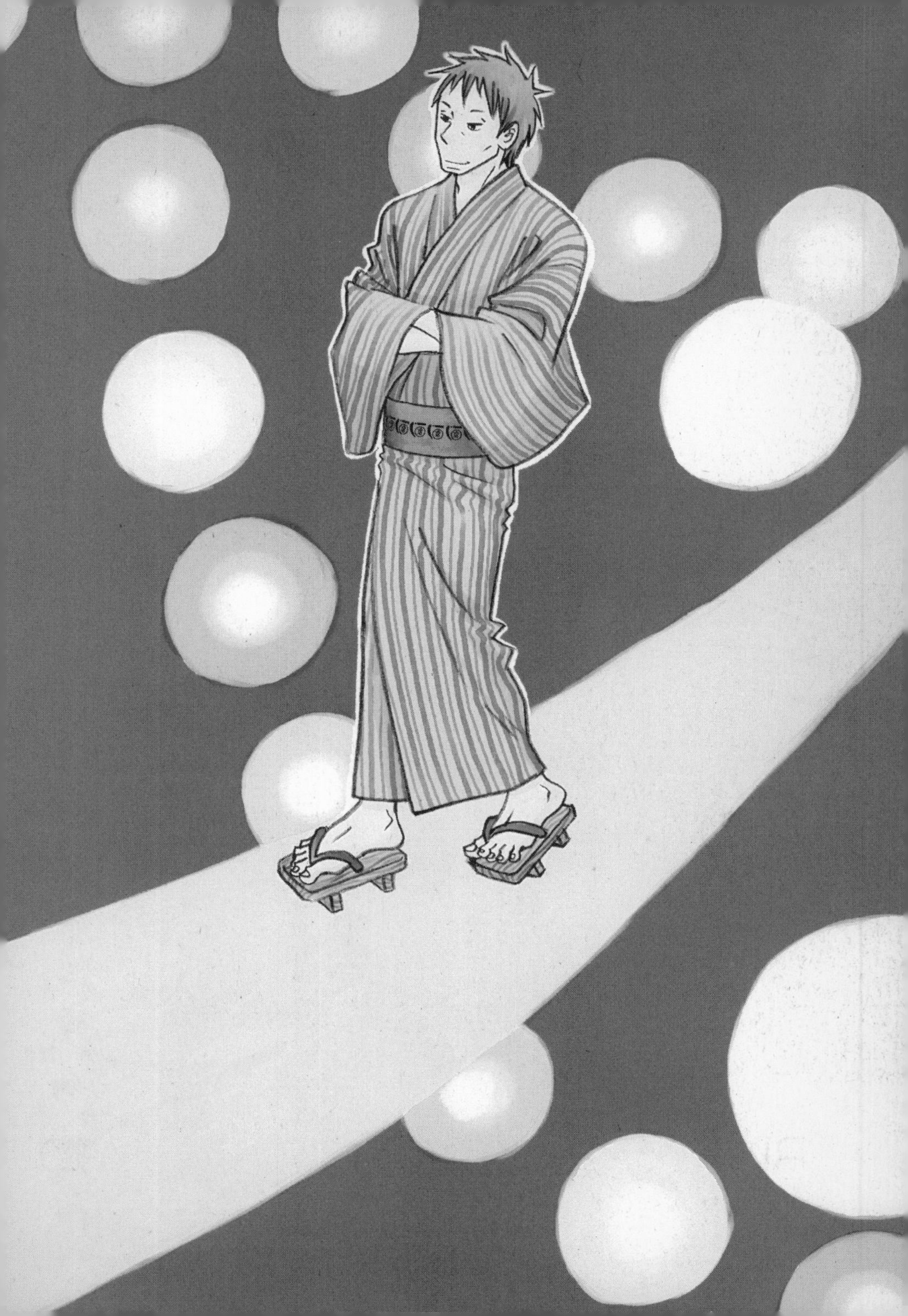

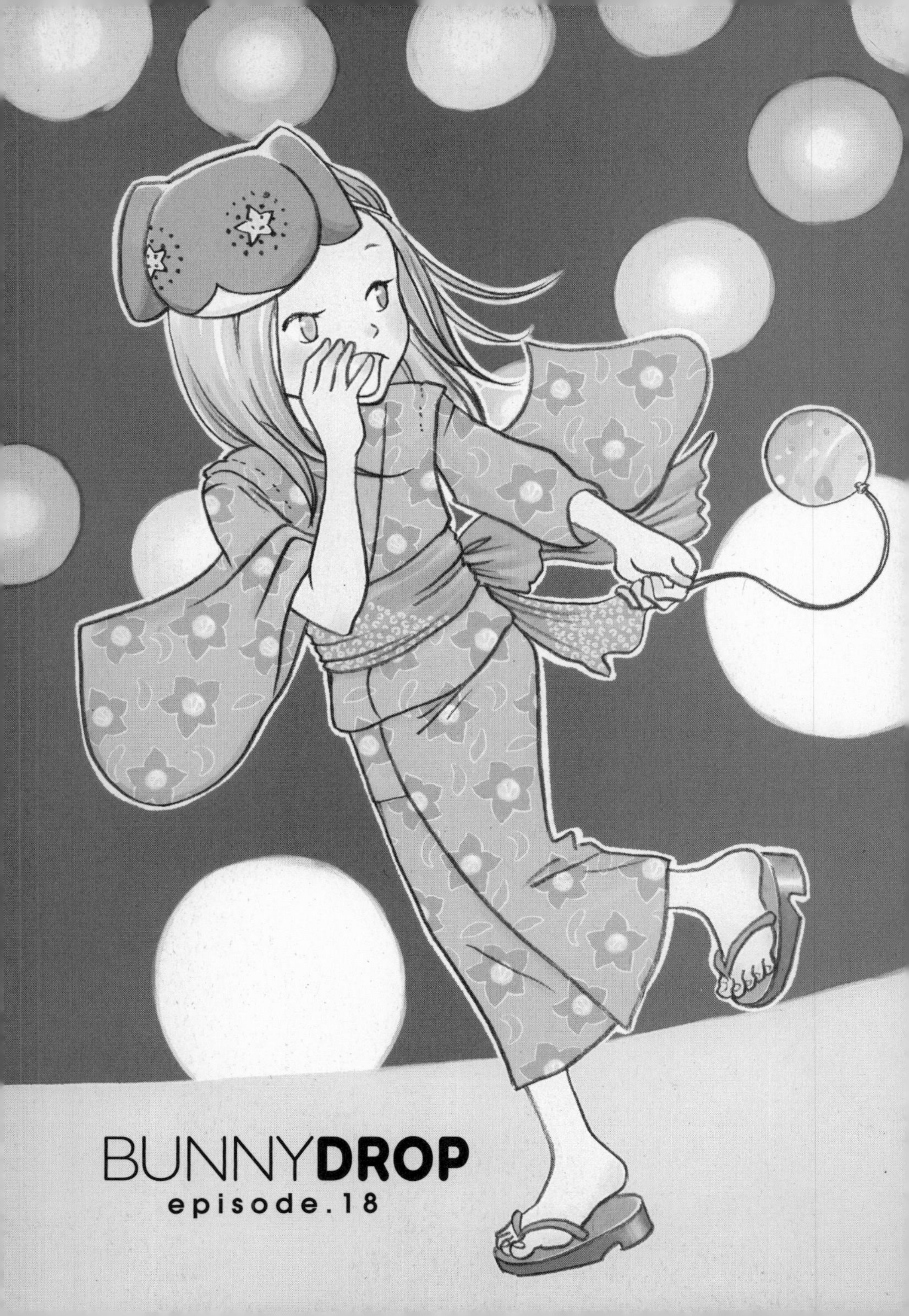
BUNNY**DROP**
episode.18

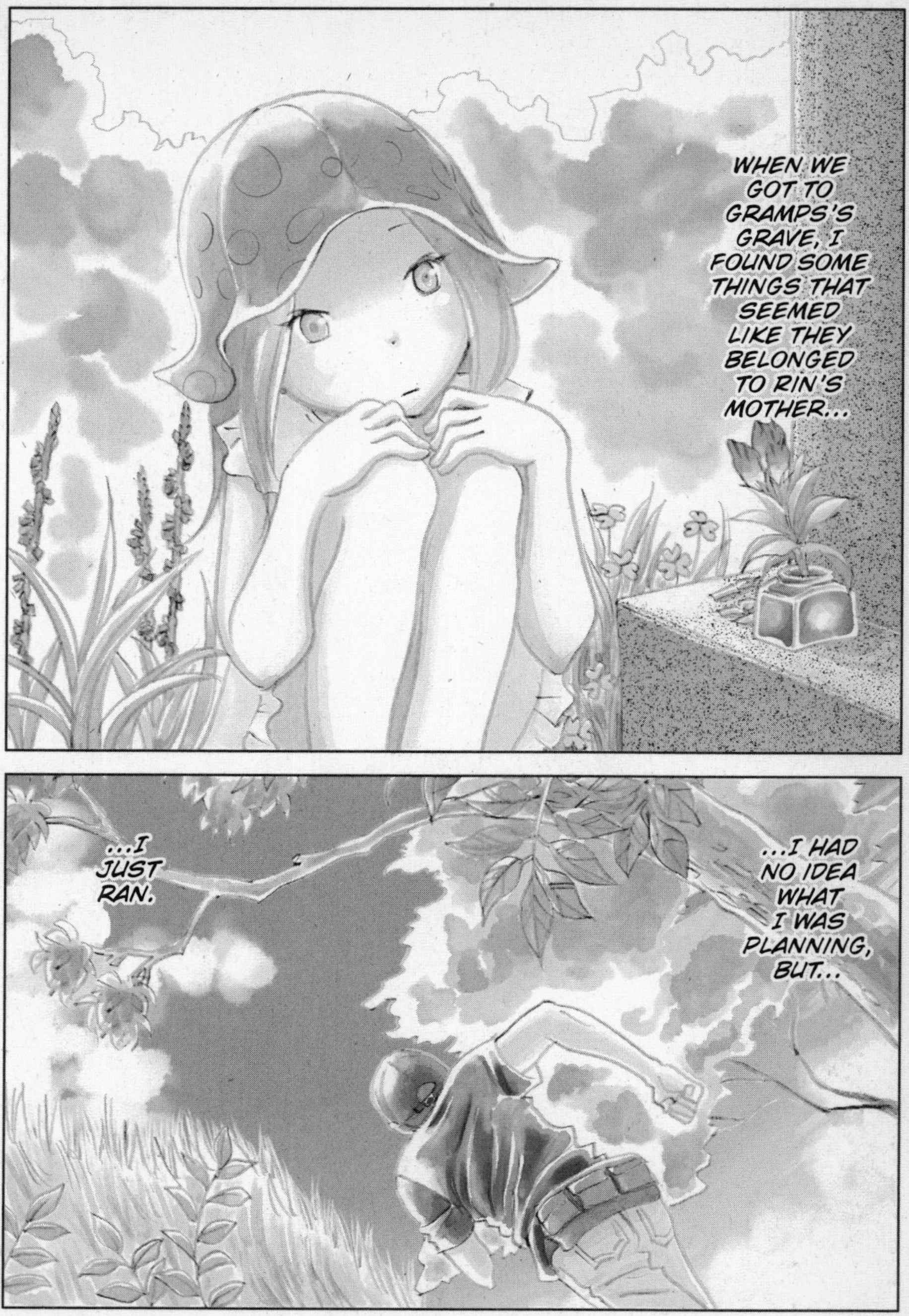
WHEN WE GOT TO GRAMPS'S GRAVE, I FOUND SOME THINGS THAT SEEMED LIKE THEY BELONGED TO RIN'S MOTHER...
...I HAD NO IDEA WHAT I WAS PLANNING, BUT...
...I JUST RAN.

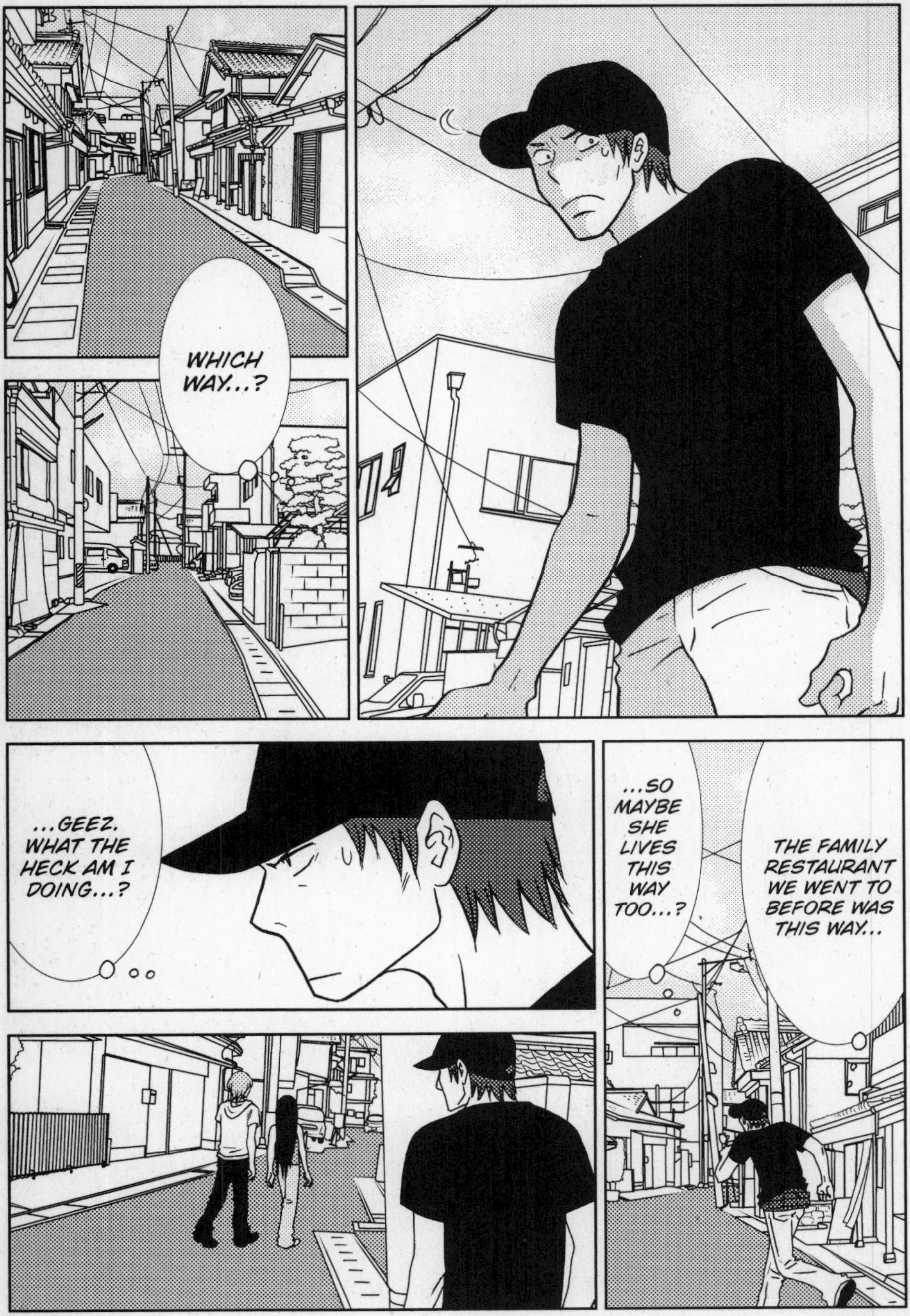
WHICH WAY...?
THE FAMILY RESTAURANT WE WENT TO BEFORE WAS THIS WAY...
...SO MAYBE SHE LIVES THIS WAY TOO...?
...GEEZ. WHAT THE HECK AM I DOING...?

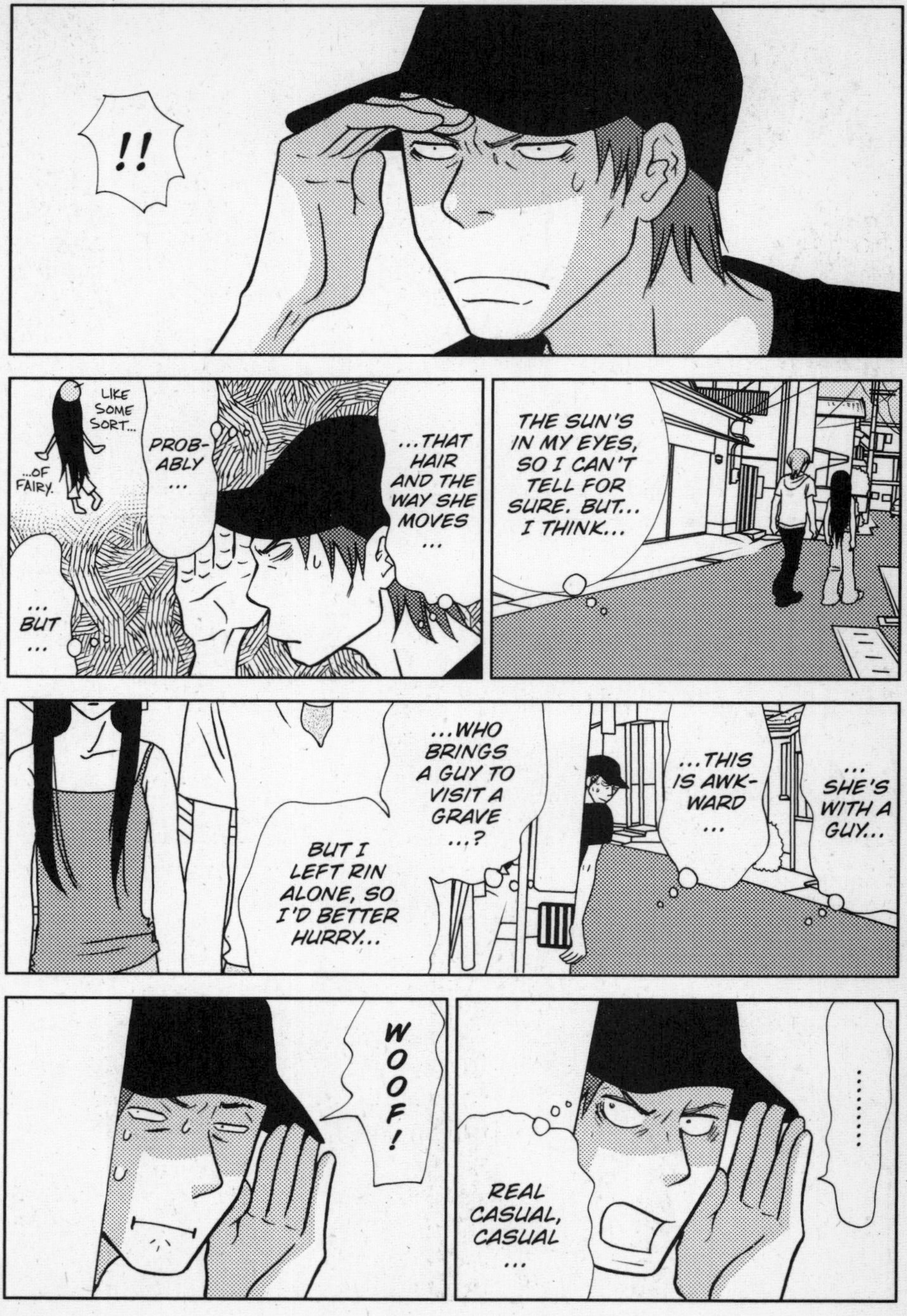
!!
THE SUN'S IN MY EYES, SO I CAN'T TELL FOR SURE. BUT... I THINK...
...THAT HAIR AND THE WAY SHE MOVES ...
PROB-ABLY ...
LIKE SOME SORT...
...OF FAIRY.
... BUT ...
... SHE'S WITH A GUY...
...THIS IS AWK-WARD ...
...WHO BRINGS A GUY TO VISIT A GRAVE ...?
BUT I LEFT RIN ALONE, SO I'D BETTER HURRY...
....
REAL CASUAL, CASUAL ...
WOOF!

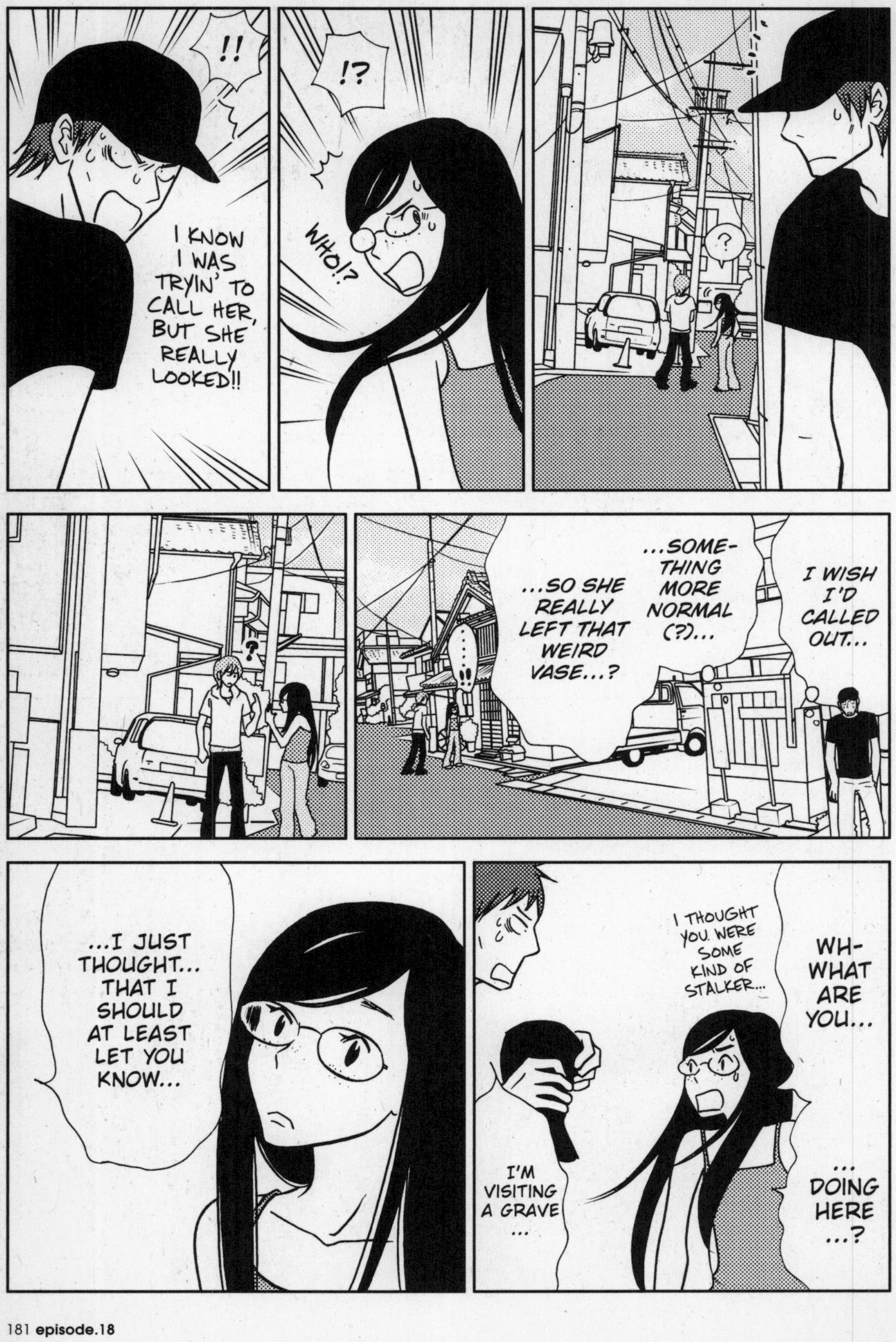
!?
?
WHO!?
!!
I KNOW I WAS TRYIN' TO CALL HER, BUT SHE REALLY LOOKED!!
I WISH I'D CALLED OUT...
...SOMETHING MORE NORMAL (?)...
...SO SHE REALLY LEFT THAT WEIRD VASE...?
?
WH-WHAT ARE YOU...
...DOING HERE...?
I THOUGHT YOU WERE SOME KIND OF STALKER...
I'M VISITING A GRAVE...
...I JUST THOUGHT... THAT I SHOULD AT LEAST LET YOU KNOW...

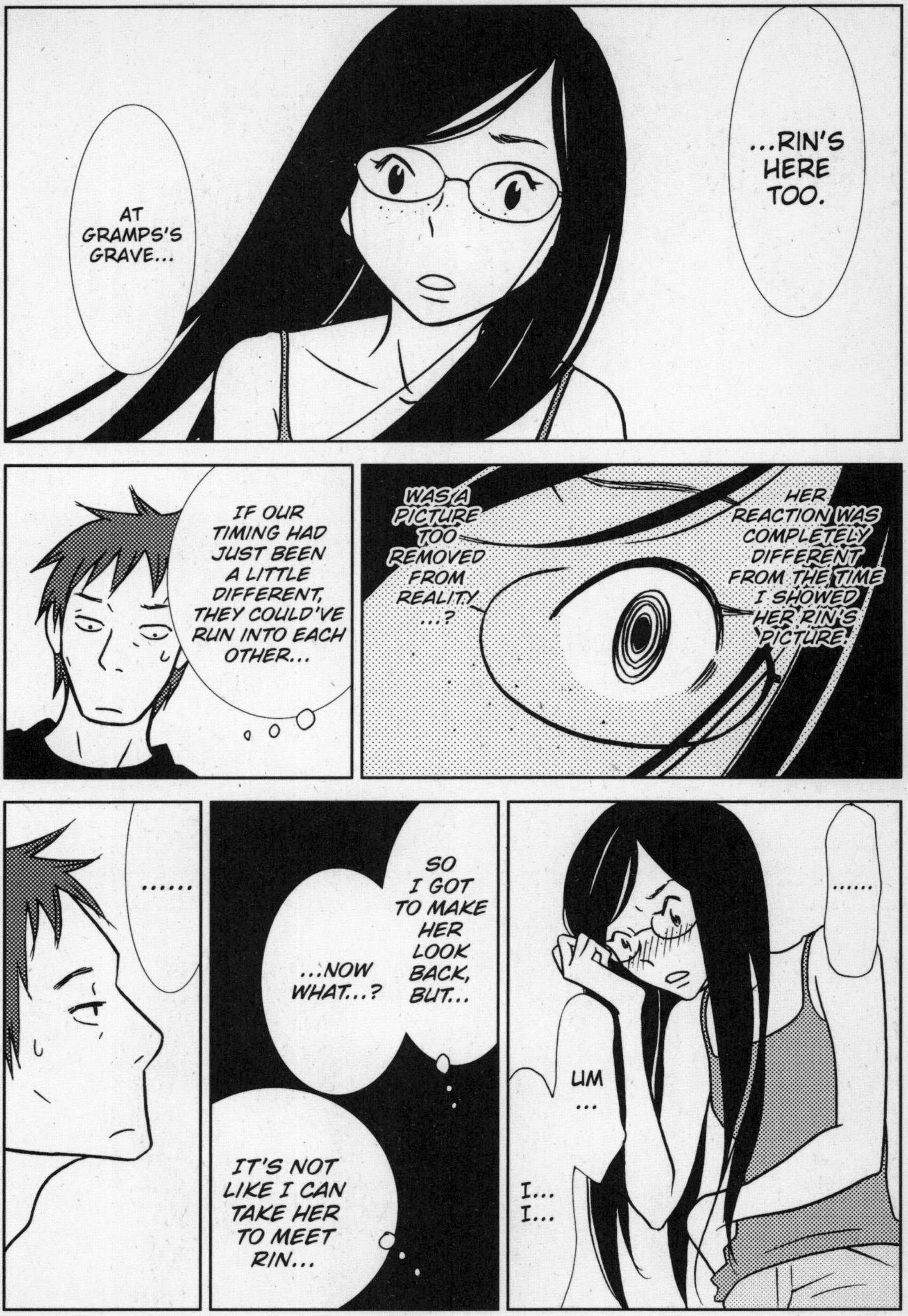
...RIN'S HERE TOO.
AT GRAMPS'S GRAVE...
HER REACTION WAS COMPLETELY DIFFERENT FROM THE TIME I SHOWED HER RIN'S PICTURE.
WAS A PICTURE TOO REMOVED FROM REALITY ...?
IF OUR TIMING HAD JUST BEEN A LITTLE DIFFERENT, THEY COULD'VE RUN INTO EACH OTHER...
......
UM ...
I... I...
SO I GOT TO MAKE HER LOOK BACK, BUT...
...NOW WHAT...?
IT'S NOT LIKE I CAN TAKE HER TO MEET RIN...
......

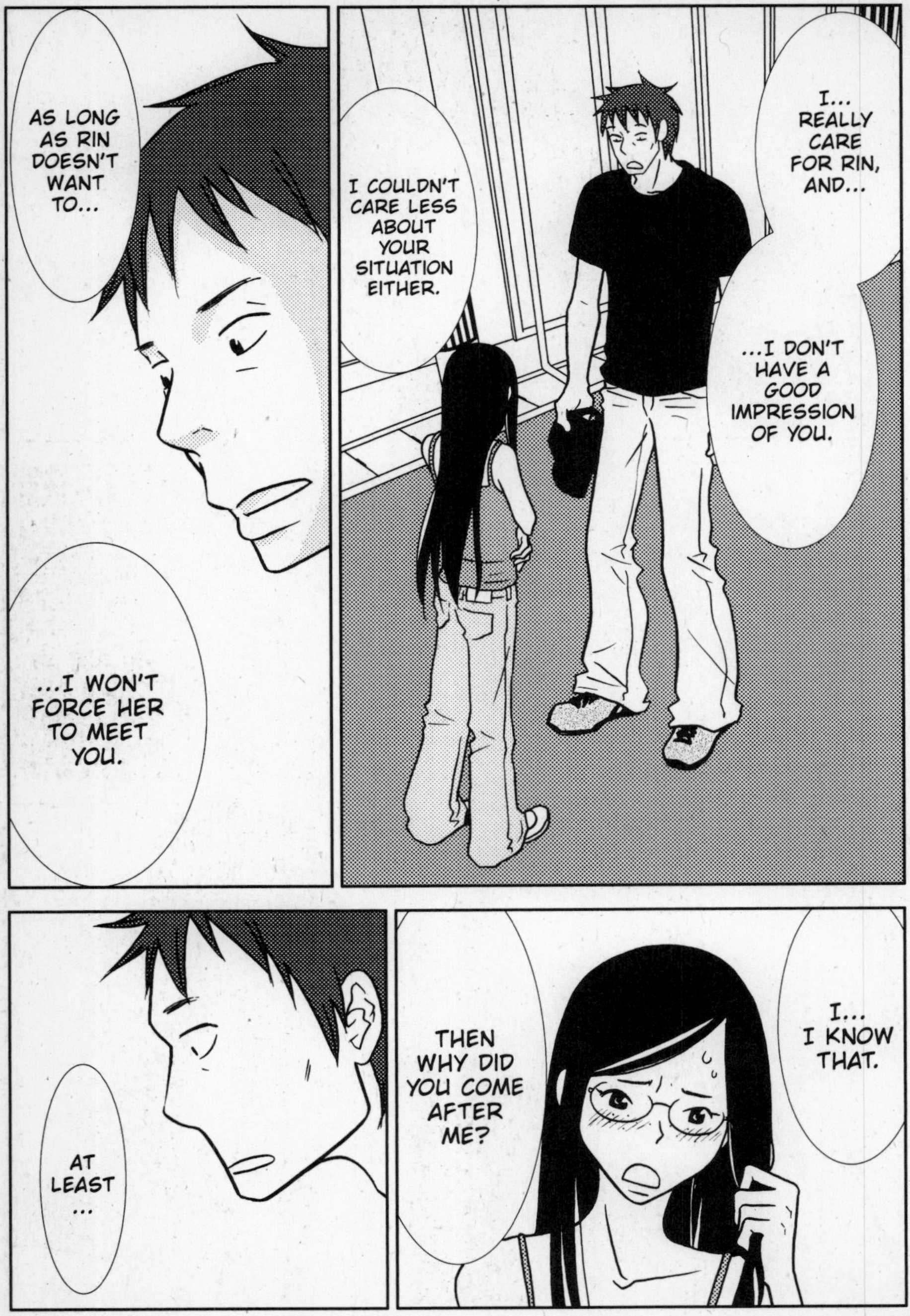
I... REALLY CARE FOR RIN, AND...
...I DON'T HAVE A GOOD IMPRESSION OF YOU.
I COULDN'T CARE LESS ABOUT YOUR SITUATION EITHER.
AS LONG AS RIN DOESN'T WANT TO...
...I WON'T FORCE HER TO MEET YOU.
I... I KNOW THAT.
THEN WHY DID YOU COME AFTER ME?
AT LEAST ...

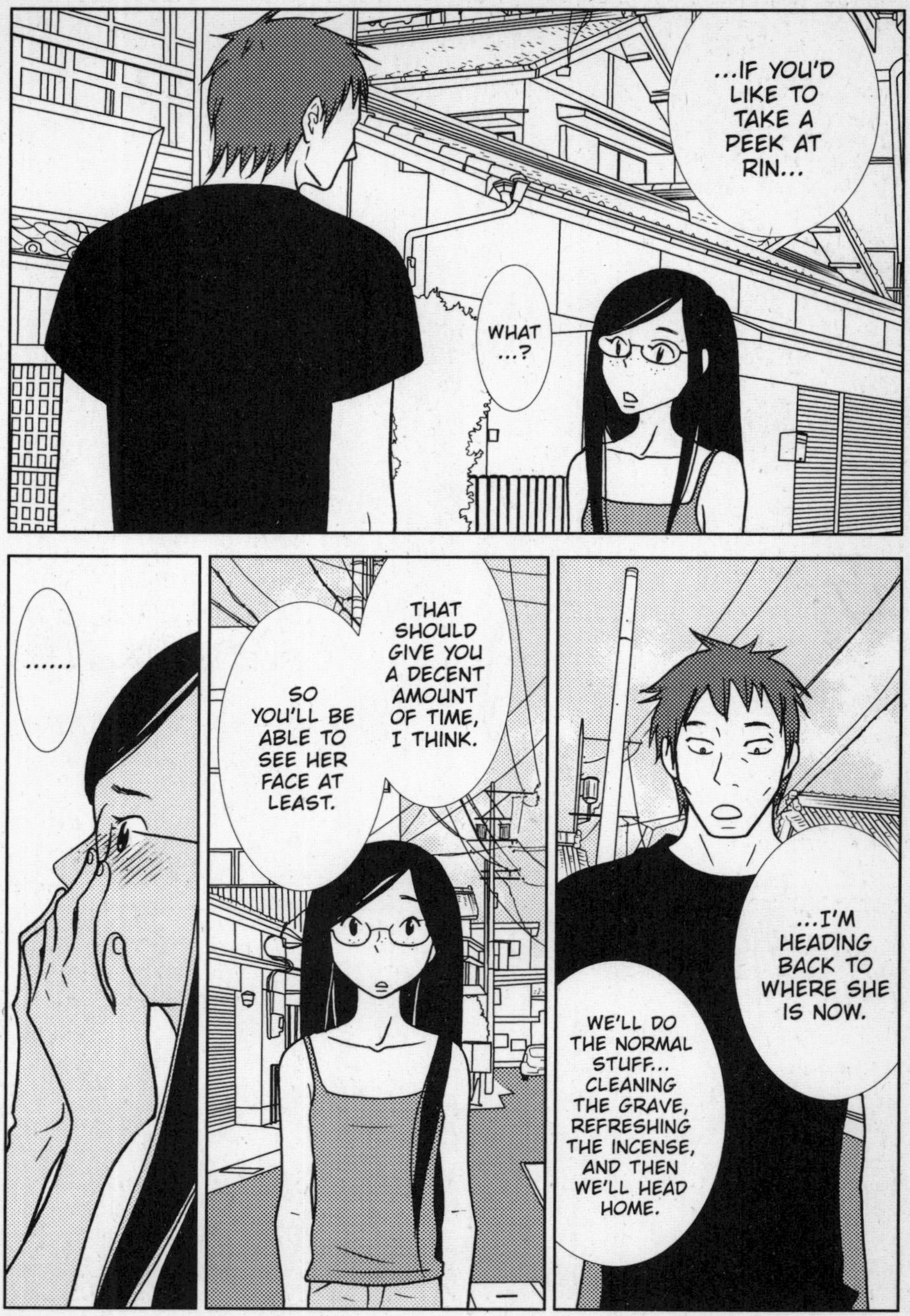
...IF YOU'D LIKE TO TAKE A PEEK AT RIN...
WHAT ...?
...I'M HEADING BACK TO WHERE SHE IS NOW.
WE'LL DO THE NORMAL STUFF... CLEANING THE GRAVE, REFRESHING THE INCENSE, AND THEN WE'LL HEAD HOME.
THAT SHOULD GIVE YOU A DECENT AMOUNT OF TIME, I THINK.
SO YOU'LL BE ABLE TO SEE HER FACE AT LEAST.
......

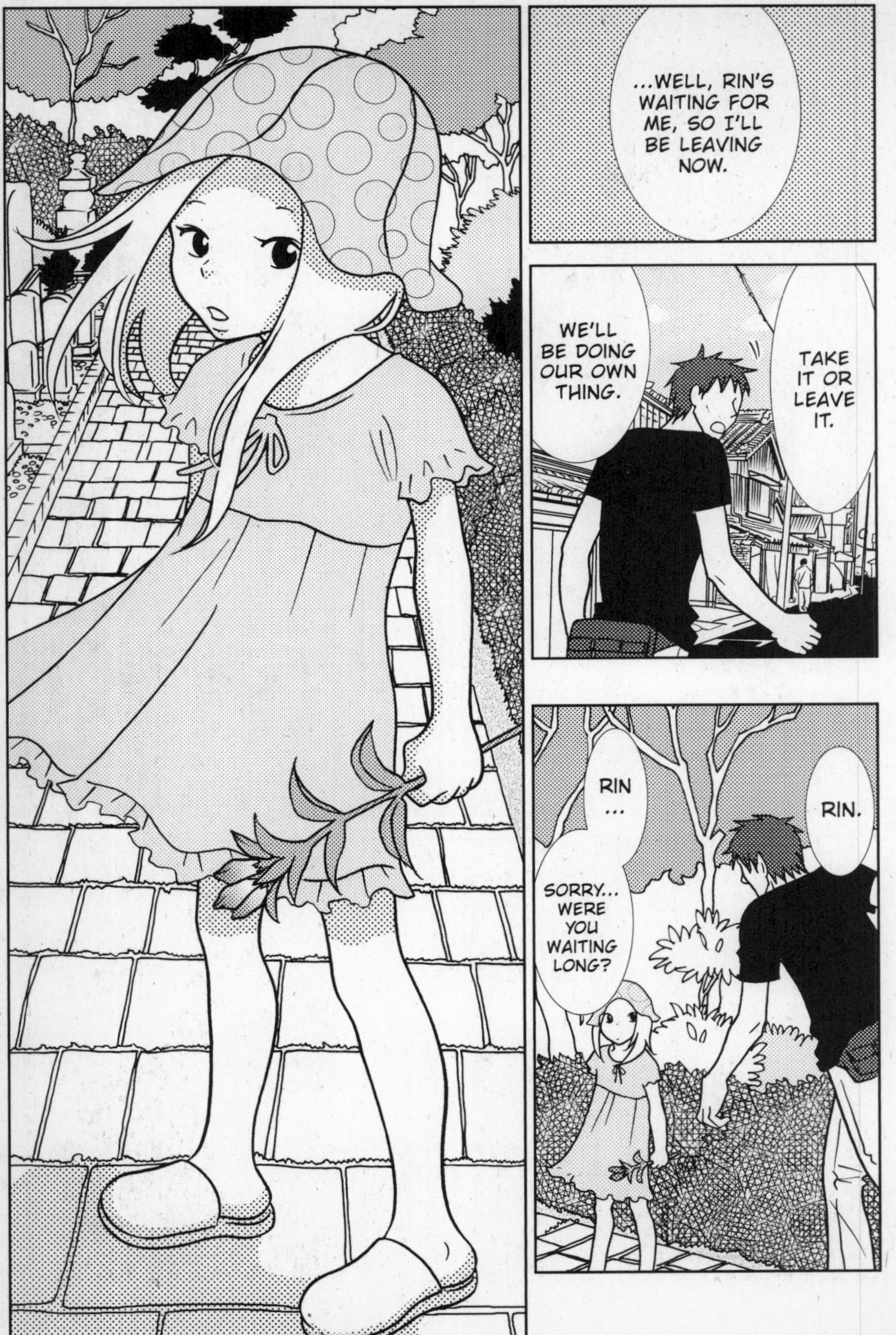
...WELL, RIN'S WAITING FOR ME, SO I'LL BE LEAVING NOW.
TAKE IT OR LEAVE IT.
WE'LL BE DOING OUR OWN THING.
RIN.
RIN ...
SORRY... WERE YOU WAITING LONG?

AH!
ずきん
ZUKIN (STING)
OH, UM... ...YOU OKAY...?
EH?
NO...
...UH, DID YOU WAIT LONG?
UM...I NEEDED TO PAY MY RESPECTS TO THE PRIESTS (OR SOMETHING), SO...
NAH.
YOU WEREN'T LONELY...?
AH HA HA.

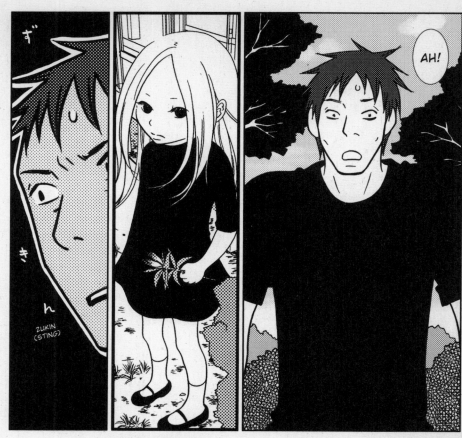

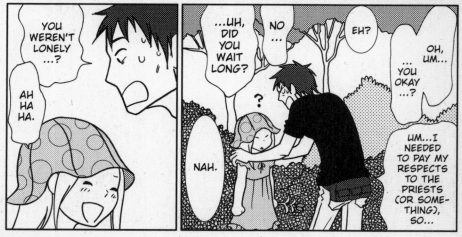

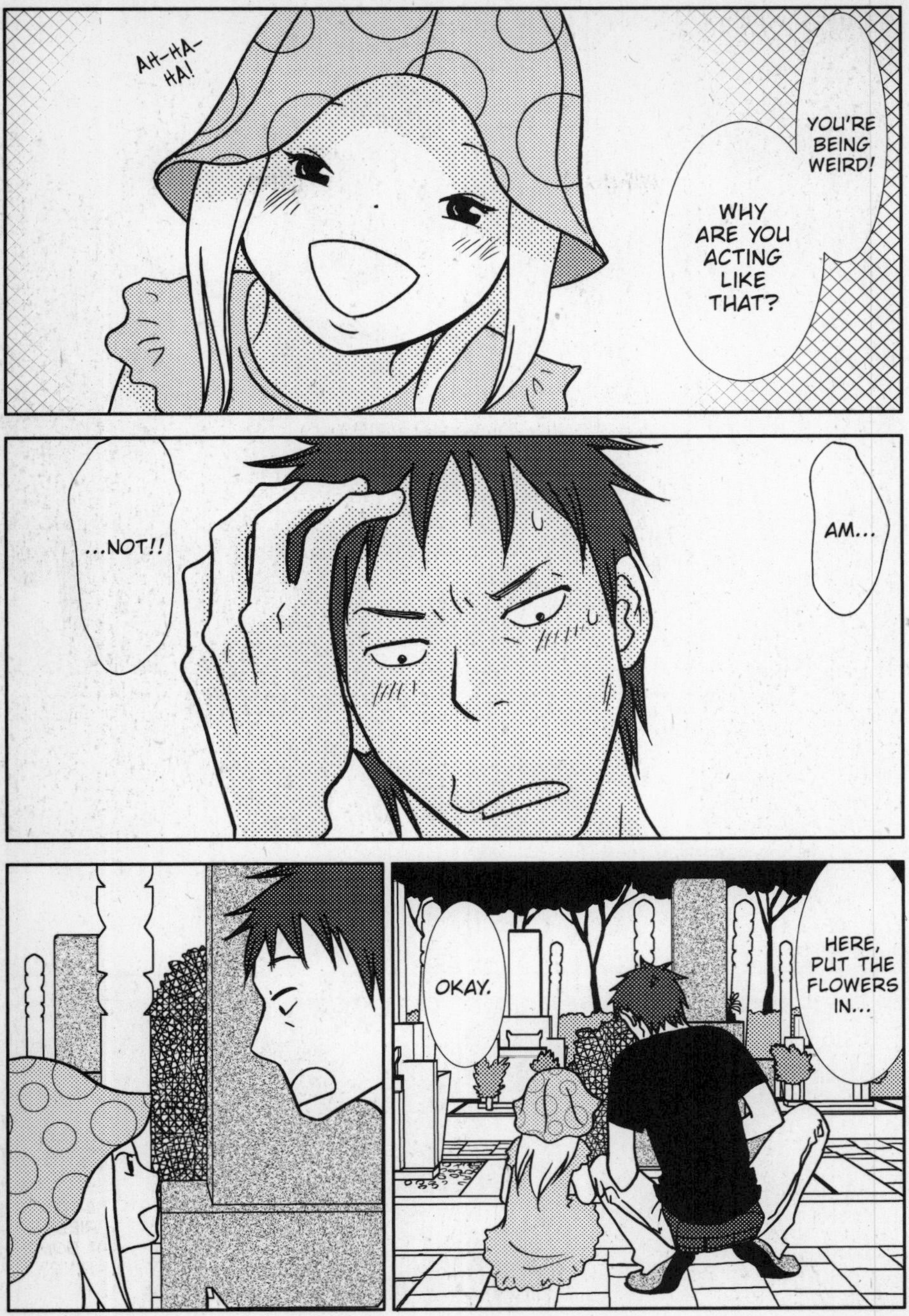
YOU'RE BEING WEIRD!
WHY ARE YOU ACTING LIKE THAT?
AH-HA-HA!
AM...
...NOT!!
HERE, PUT THE FLOWERS IN...
OKAY.

...NOT A BABY ANYMORE...

......

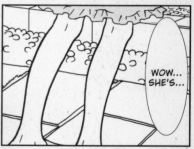

WOW... SHE'S...

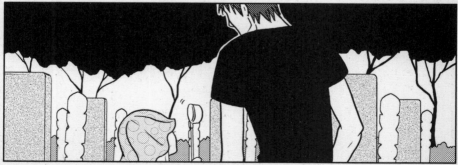

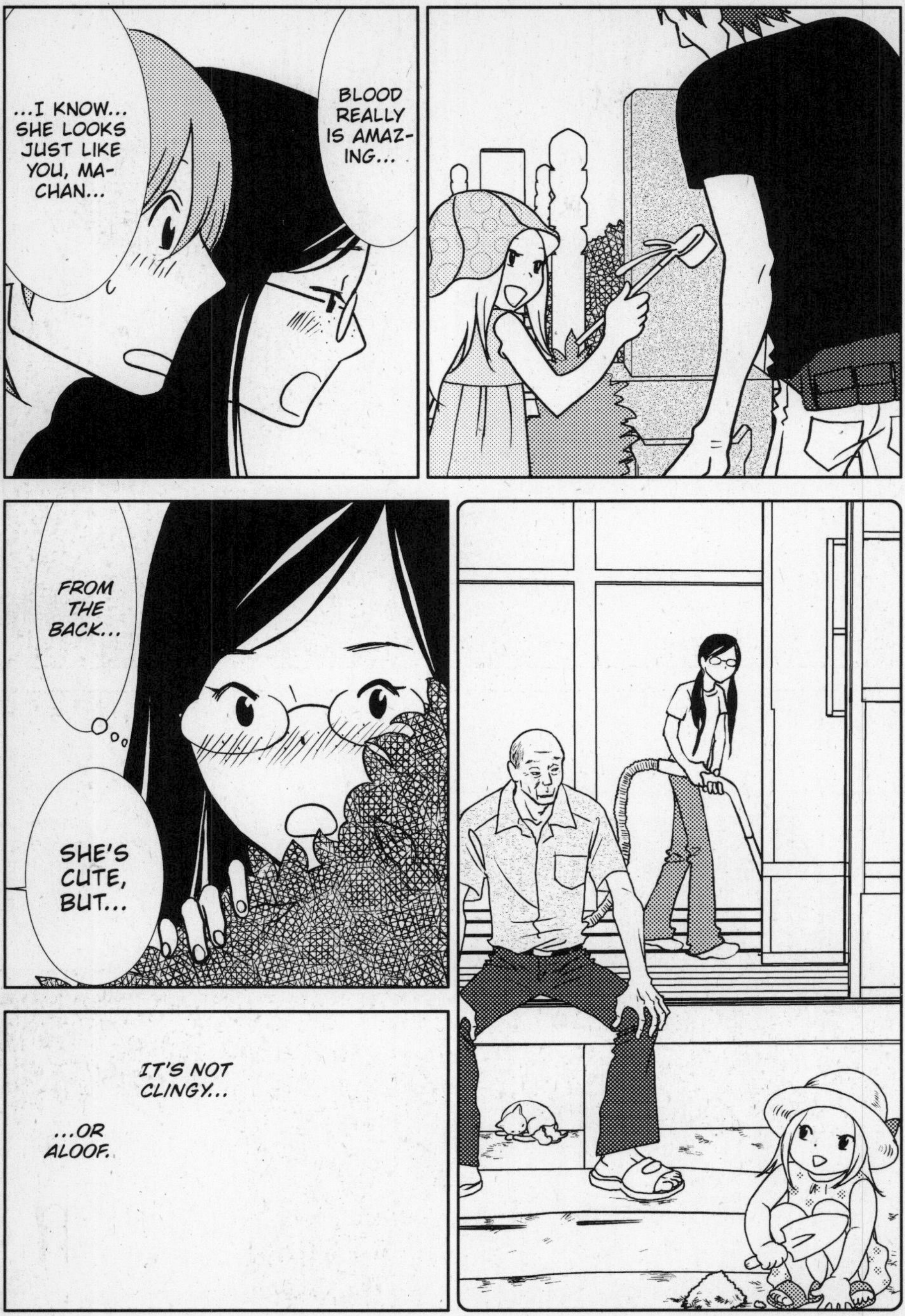
BLOOD REALLY IS AMAZING...
...I KNOW... SHE LOOKS JUST LIKE YOU, MA-CHAN...
FROM THE BACK...
SHE'S CUTE, BUT...
IT'S NOT CLINGY...
...OR ALOOF.

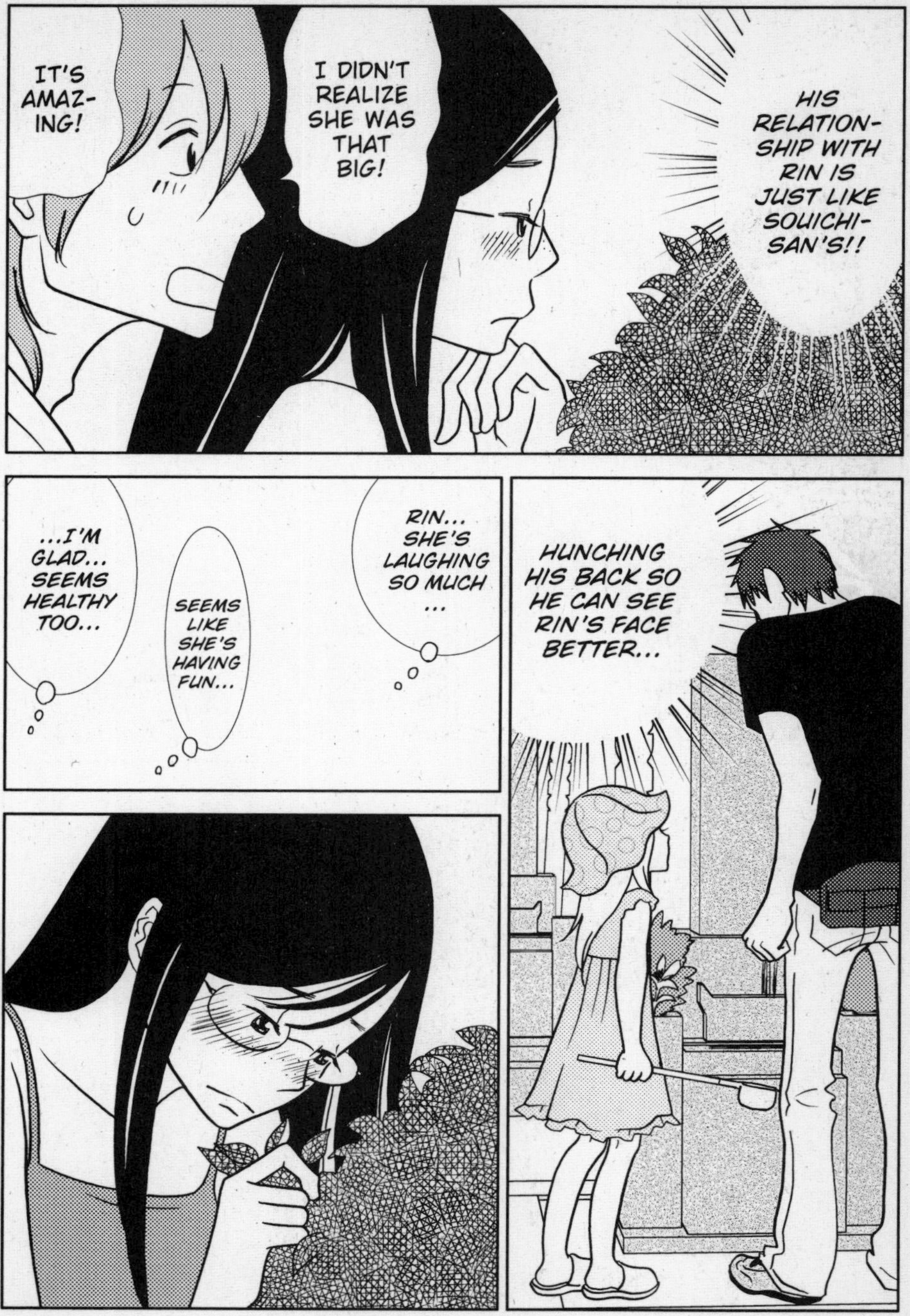
HIS RELATION-SHIP WITH RIN IS JUST LIKE SOUICHI-SAN'S!!
I DIDN'T REALIZE SHE WAS THAT BIG!
IT'S AMAZ-ING!
HUNCHING HIS BACK SO HE CAN SEE RIN'S FACE BETTER...
RIN... SHE'S LAUGHING SO MUCH ...
SEEMS LIKE SHE'S HAVING FUN...
...I'M GLAD... SEEMS HEALTHY TOO...

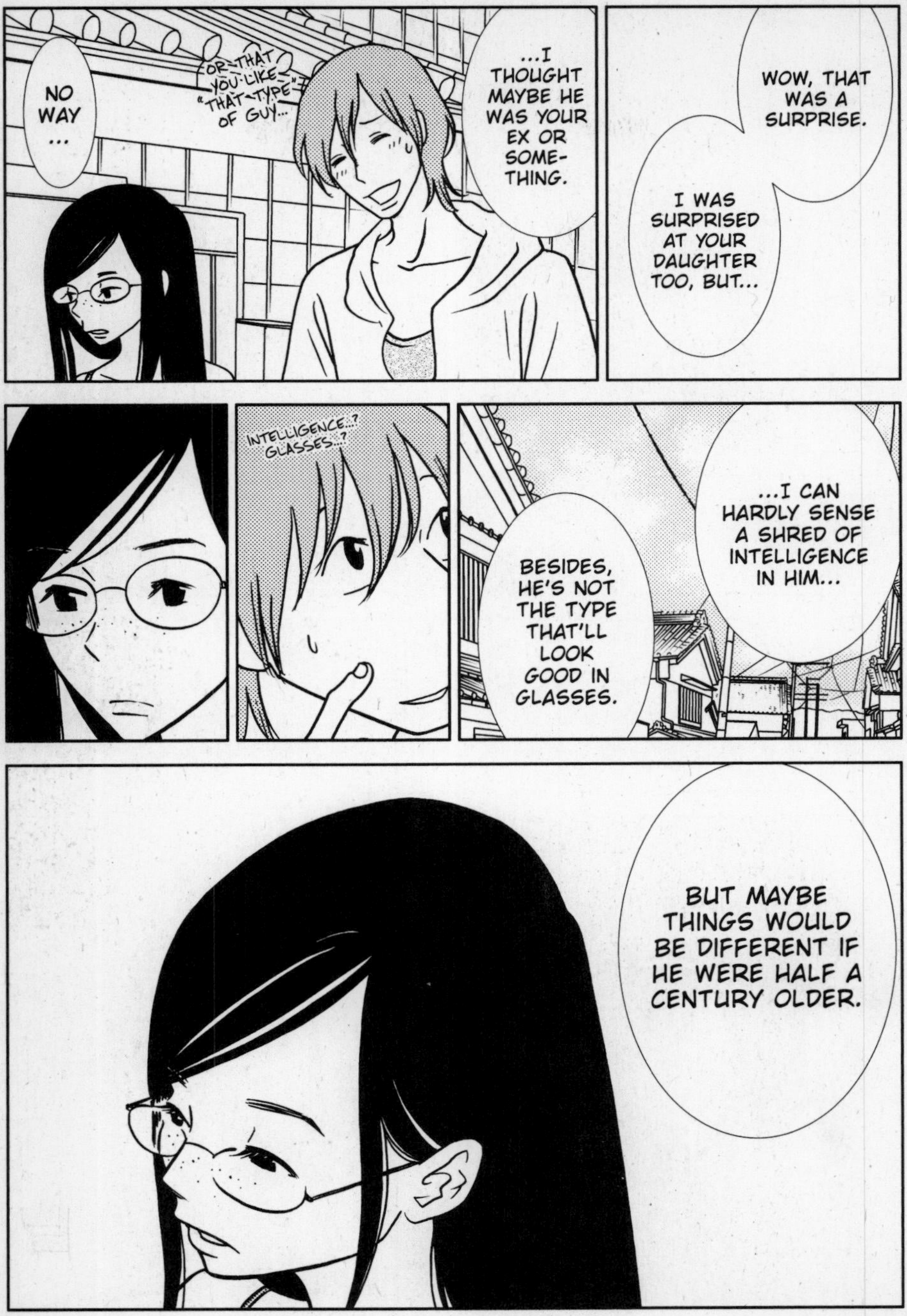
WOW, THAT WAS A SURPRISE.
I WAS SURPRISED AT YOUR DAUGHTER TOO, BUT...
...I THOUGHT MAYBE HE WAS YOUR EX OR SOME-THING.
OR THAT YOU LIKE "THAT TYPE" OF GUY...
NO WAY ...
...I CAN HARDLY SENSE A SHRED OF INTELLIGENCE IN HIM...
BESIDES, HE'S NOT THE TYPE THAT'LL LOOK GOOD IN GLASSES.
INTELLIGENCE..? GLASSES..?
BUT MAYBE THINGS WOULD BE DIFFERENT IF HE WERE HALF A CENTURY OLDER.

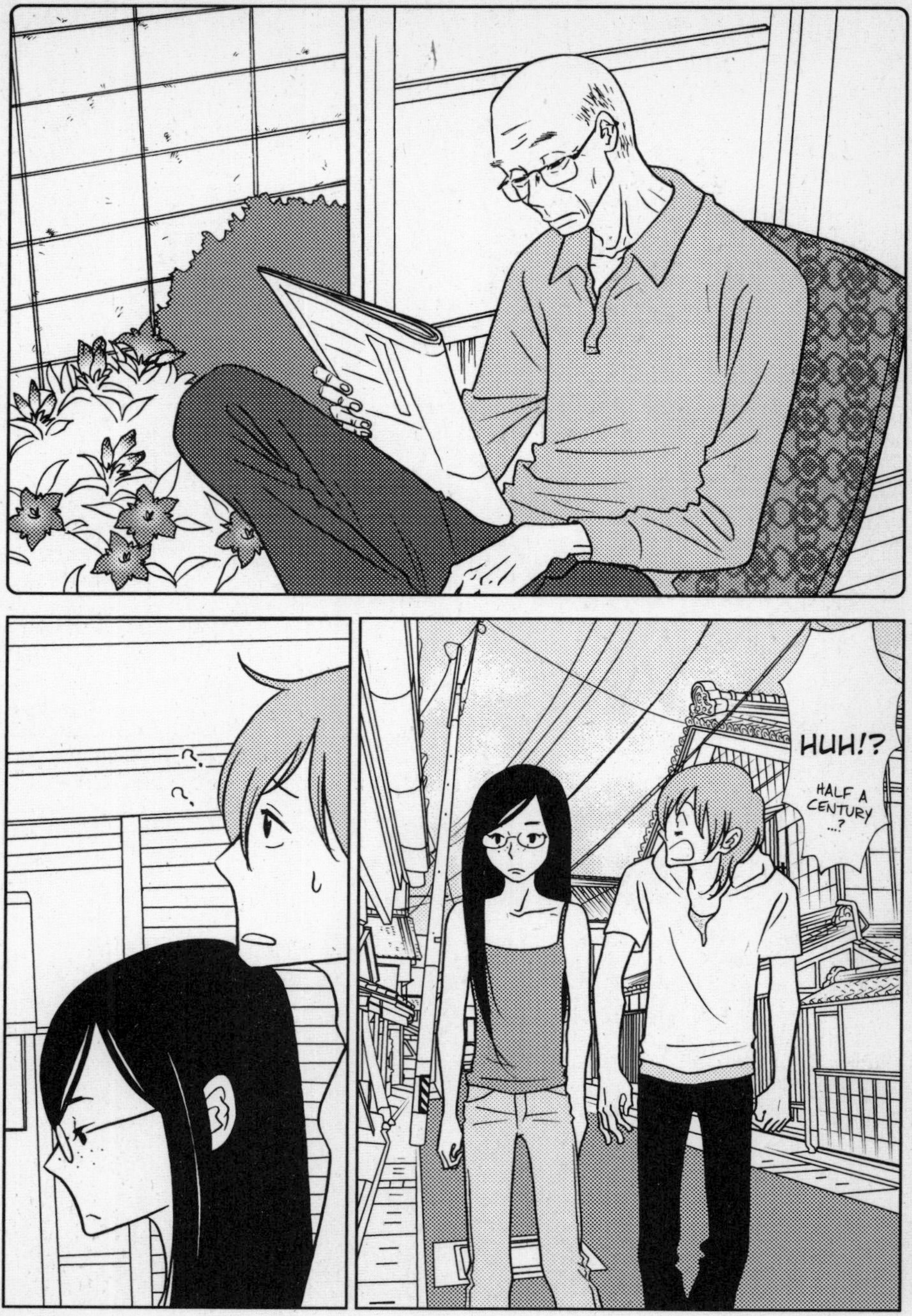
HUH!?
HALF A CENTURY ...?

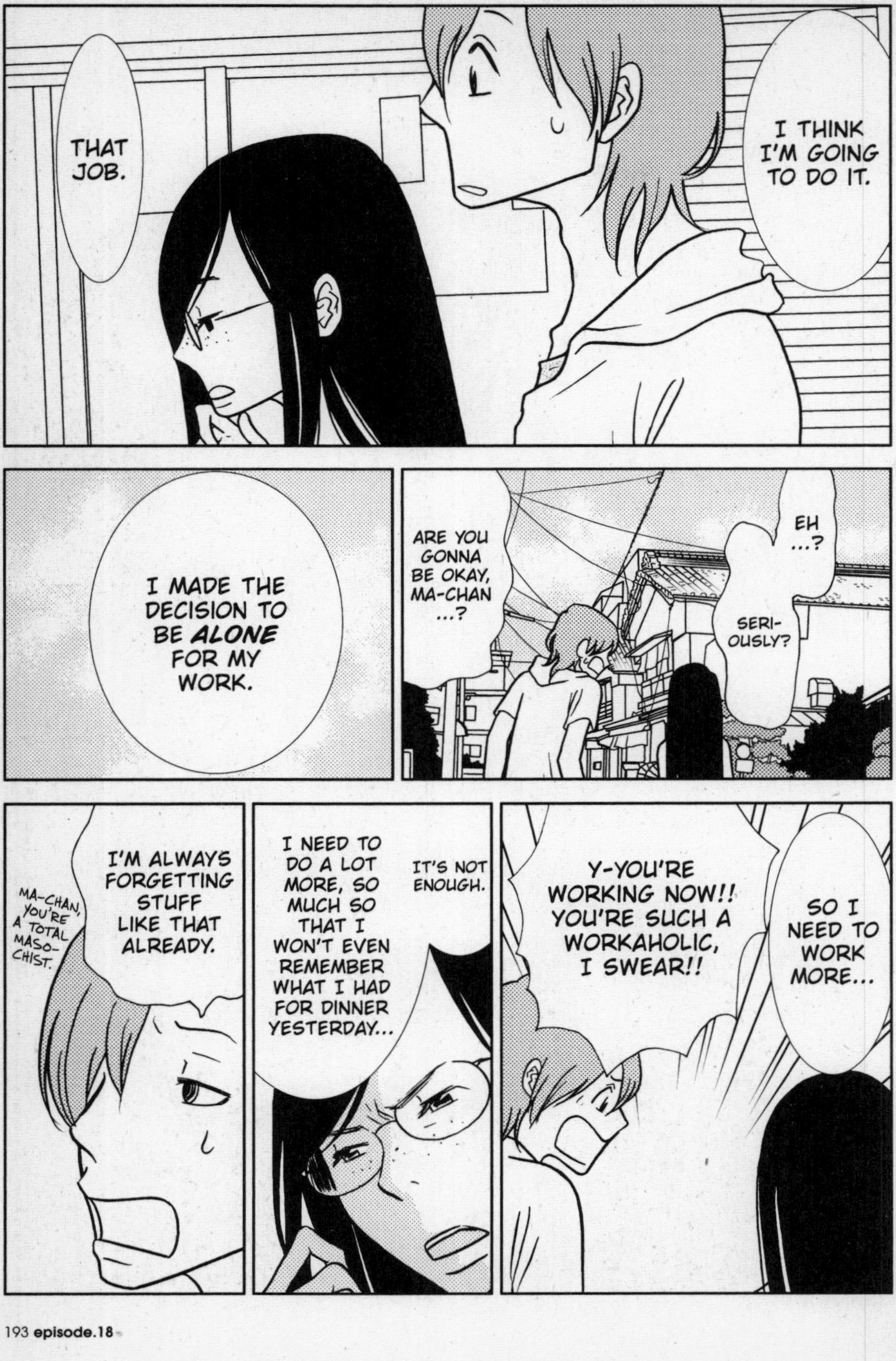
I THINK I'M GOING TO DO IT.
THAT JOB.
EH ...?
SERI-OUSLY?
ARE YOU GONNA BE OKAY, MA-CHAN ...?
I MADE THE DECISION TO BE *ALONE* FOR MY WORK.
SO I NEED TO WORK MORE...
Y-YOU'RE WORKING NOW!! YOU'RE SUCH A WORKAHOLIC, I SWEAR!!
IT'S NOT ENOUGH.
I NEED TO DO A LOT MORE, SO MUCH SO THAT I WON'T EVEN REMEMBER WHAT I HAD FOR DINNER YESTERDAY...
I'M ALWAYS FORGETTING STUFF LIKE THAT ALREADY.
MA-CHAN, YOU'RE A TOTAL MASO-CHIST.

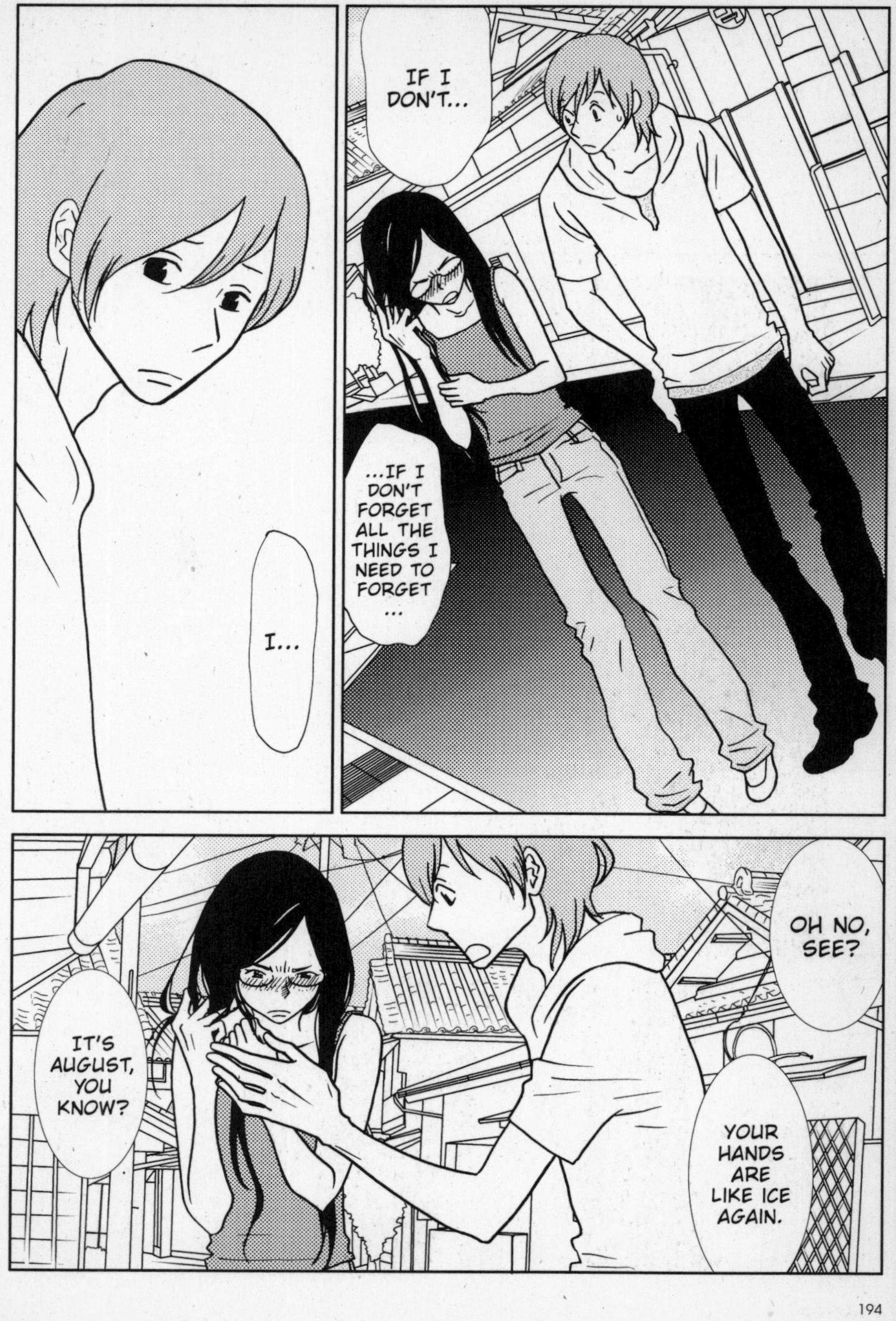
IF I DON'T...
...IF I DON'T FORGET ALL THE THINGS I NEED TO FORGET ...
I...
OH NO, SEE?
YOUR HANDS ARE LIKE ICE AGAIN.
IT'S AUGUST, YOU KNOW?

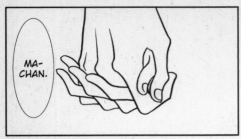

MA-CHAN.
LET'S GO SHOPPING!
GET OUR MINDS OFF THINGS.
CLOTHES, SHOES...
YEAH, SHOES!
MA-CHAN, YOU CAN WEAR SUPER HIGH HEELS NOW.

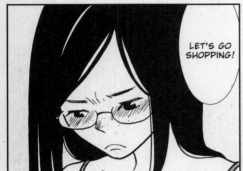

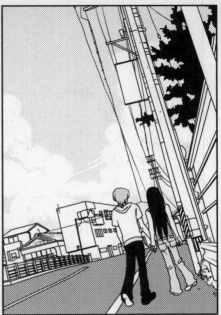

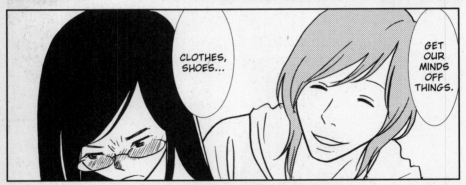

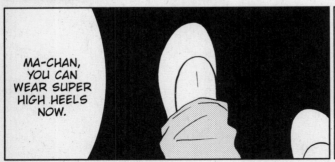

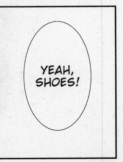

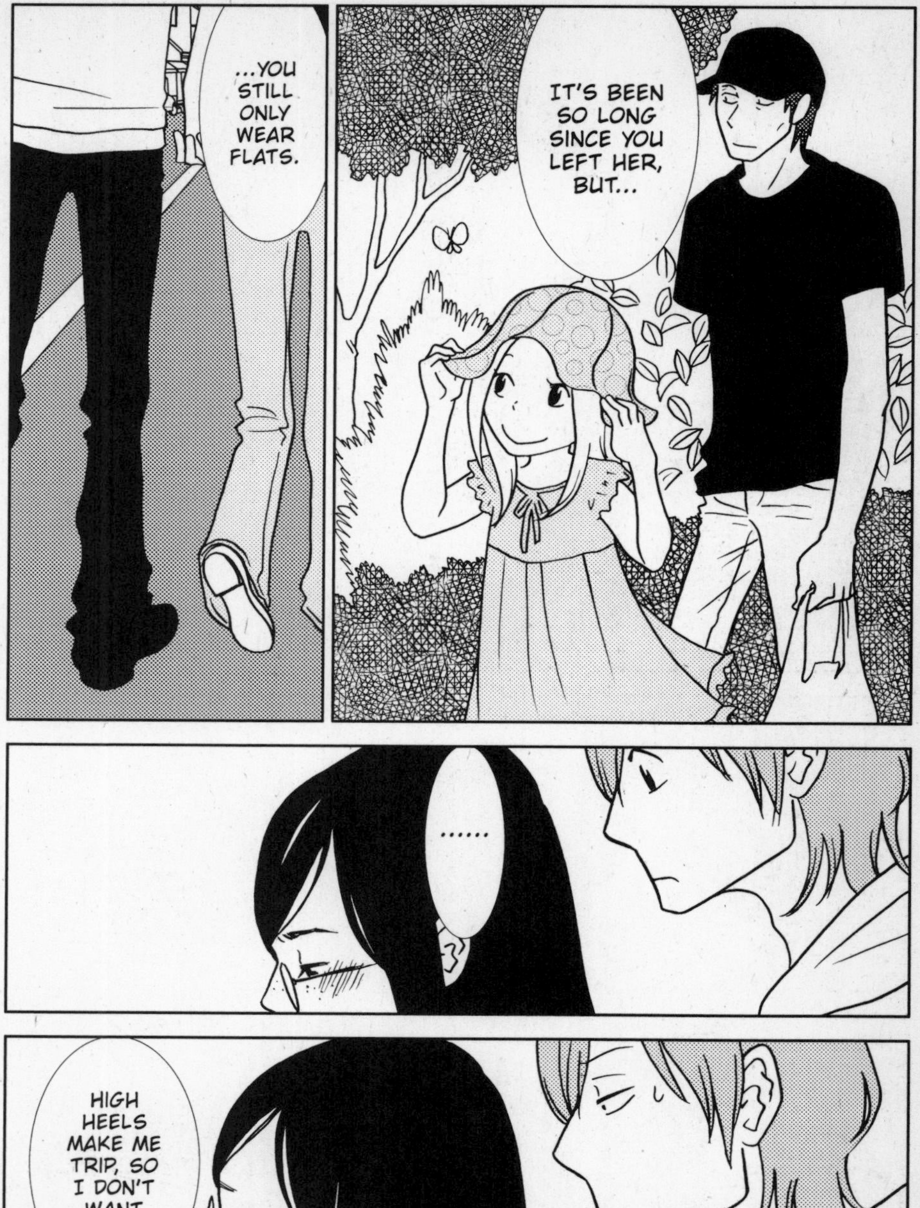
IT'S BEEN SO LONG SINCE YOU LEFT HER, BUT...
...YOU STILL ONLY WEAR FLATS.
......
HIGH HEELS MAKE ME TRIP, SO I DON'T WANT THEM...

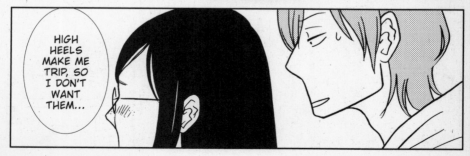

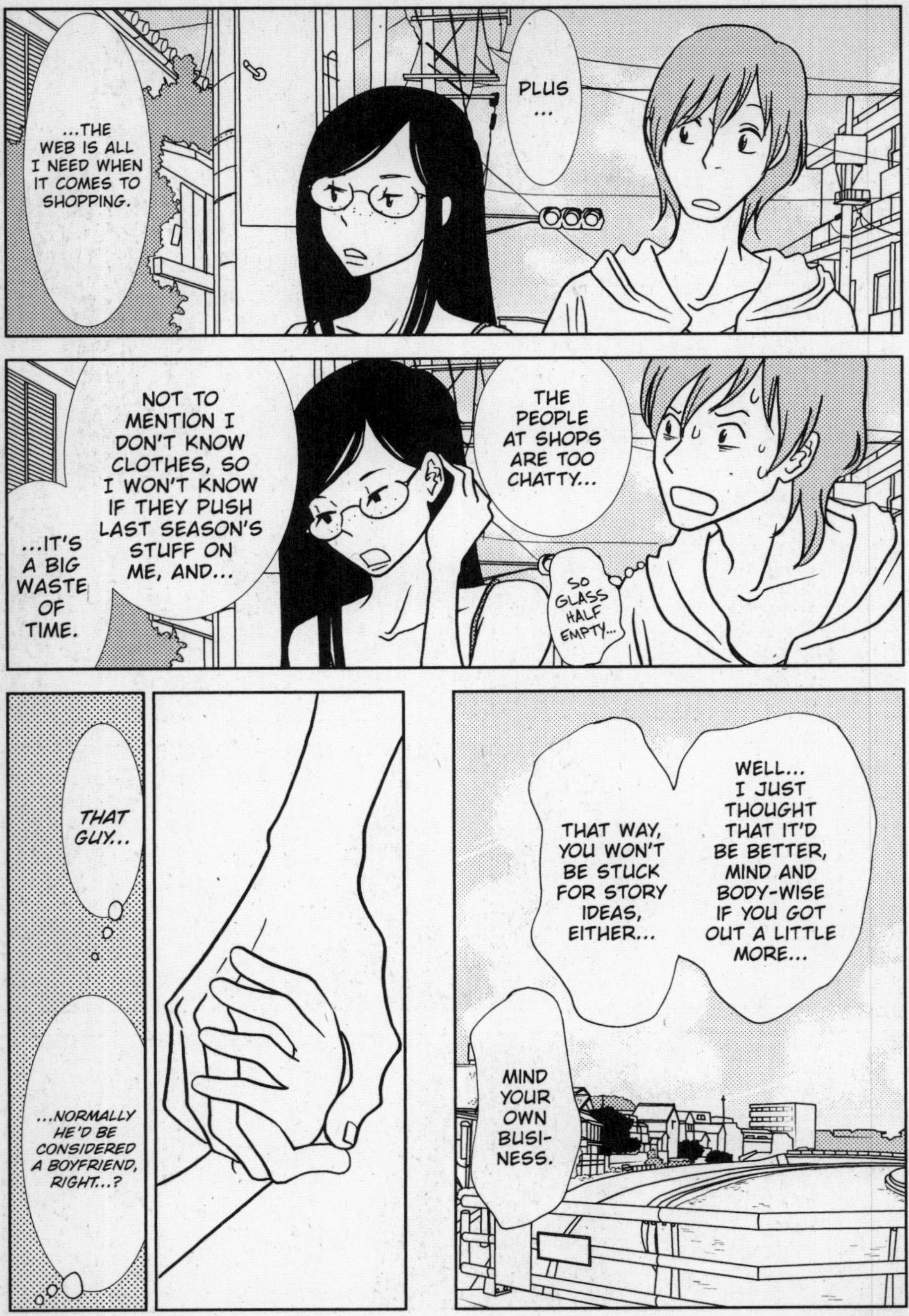
PLUS ...
...THE WEB IS ALL I NEED WHEN IT COMES TO SHOPPING.
THE PEOPLE AT SHOPS ARE TOO CHATTY...
NOT TO MENTION I DON'T KNOW CLOTHES, SO I WON'T KNOW IF THEY PUSH LAST SEASON'S STUFF ON ME, AND...
...IT'S A BIG WASTE OF TIME.
SO GLASS HALF EMPTY...
WELL... I JUST THOUGHT THAT IT'D BE BETTER, MIND AND BODY-WISE IF YOU GOT OUT A LITTLE MORE...
THAT WAY, YOU WON'T BE STUCK FOR STORY IDEAS, EITHER...
MIND YOUR OWN BUSI-NESS.
THAT GUY...
...NORMALLY HE'D BE CONSIDERED A BOYFRIEND, RIGHT...?

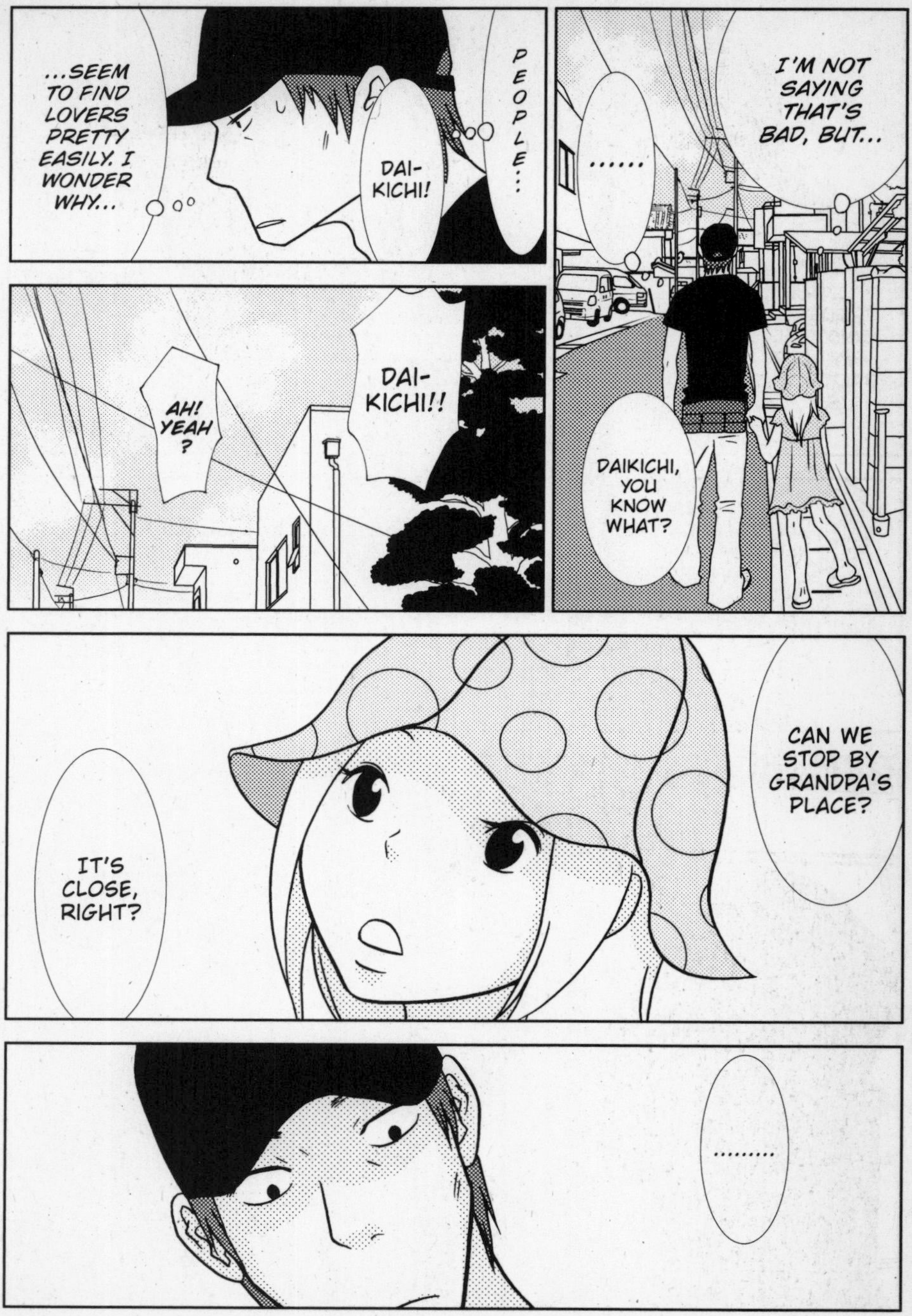
I'M NOT SAYING THAT'S BAD, BUT...
......
DAIKICHI, YOU KNOW WHAT?
PEOPLE...
DAI-KICHI!
...SEEM TO FIND LOVERS PRETTY EASILY. I WONDER WHY...
DAI-KICHI!!
AH! YEAH?
CAN WE STOP BY GRANDPA'S PLACE?
IT'S CLOSE, RIGHT?
....

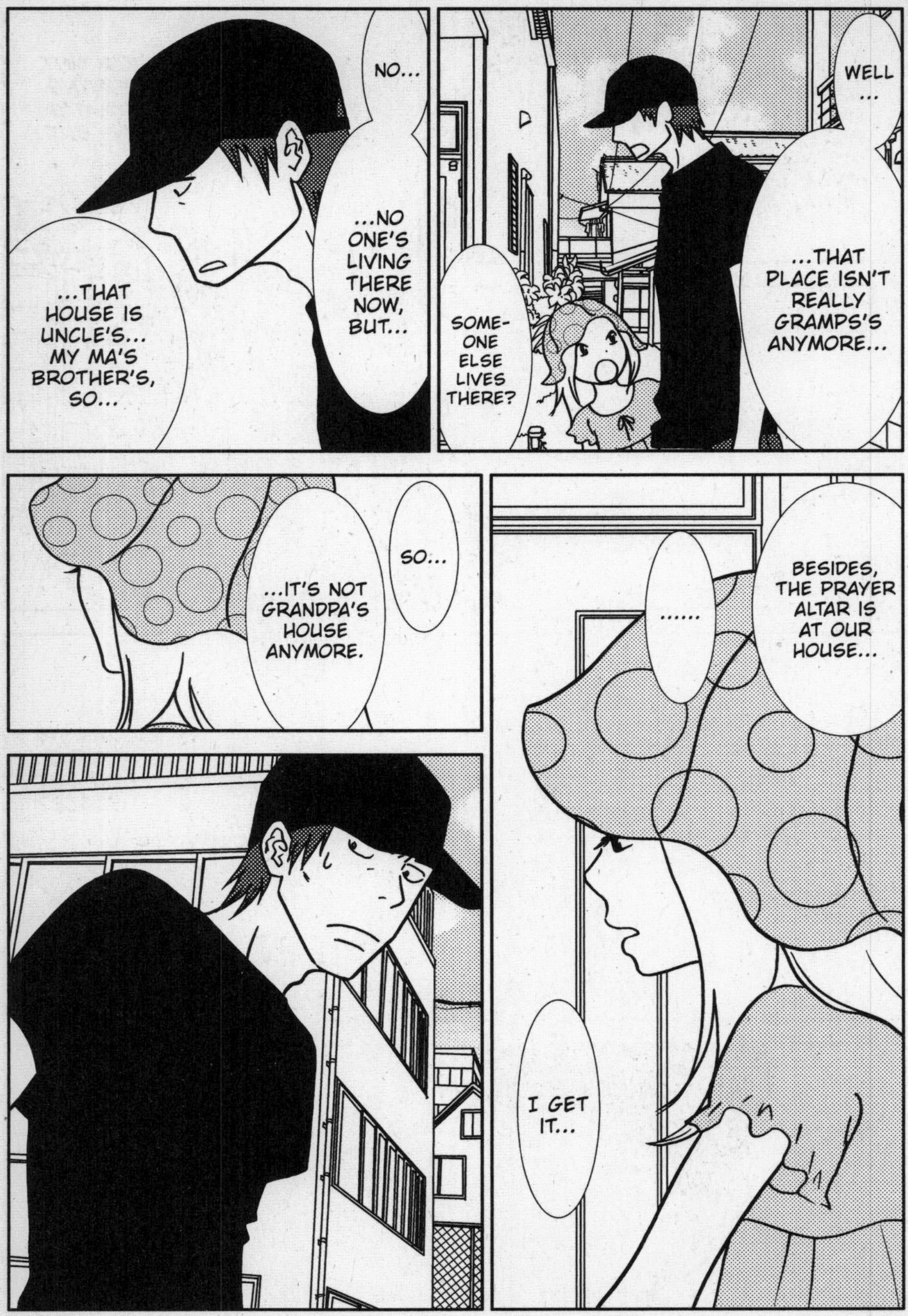
WELL ...
...THAT PLACE ISN'T REALLY GRAMPS'S ANYMORE...
SOME-ONE ELSE LIVES THERE?
NO...
...NO ONE'S LIVING THERE NOW, BUT...
...THAT HOUSE IS UNCLE'S... MY MA'S BROTHER'S, SO...
BESIDES, THE PRAYER ALTAR IS AT OUR HOUSE...
......
I GET IT...
SO...
...IT'S NOT GRANDPA'S HOUSE ANYMORE.

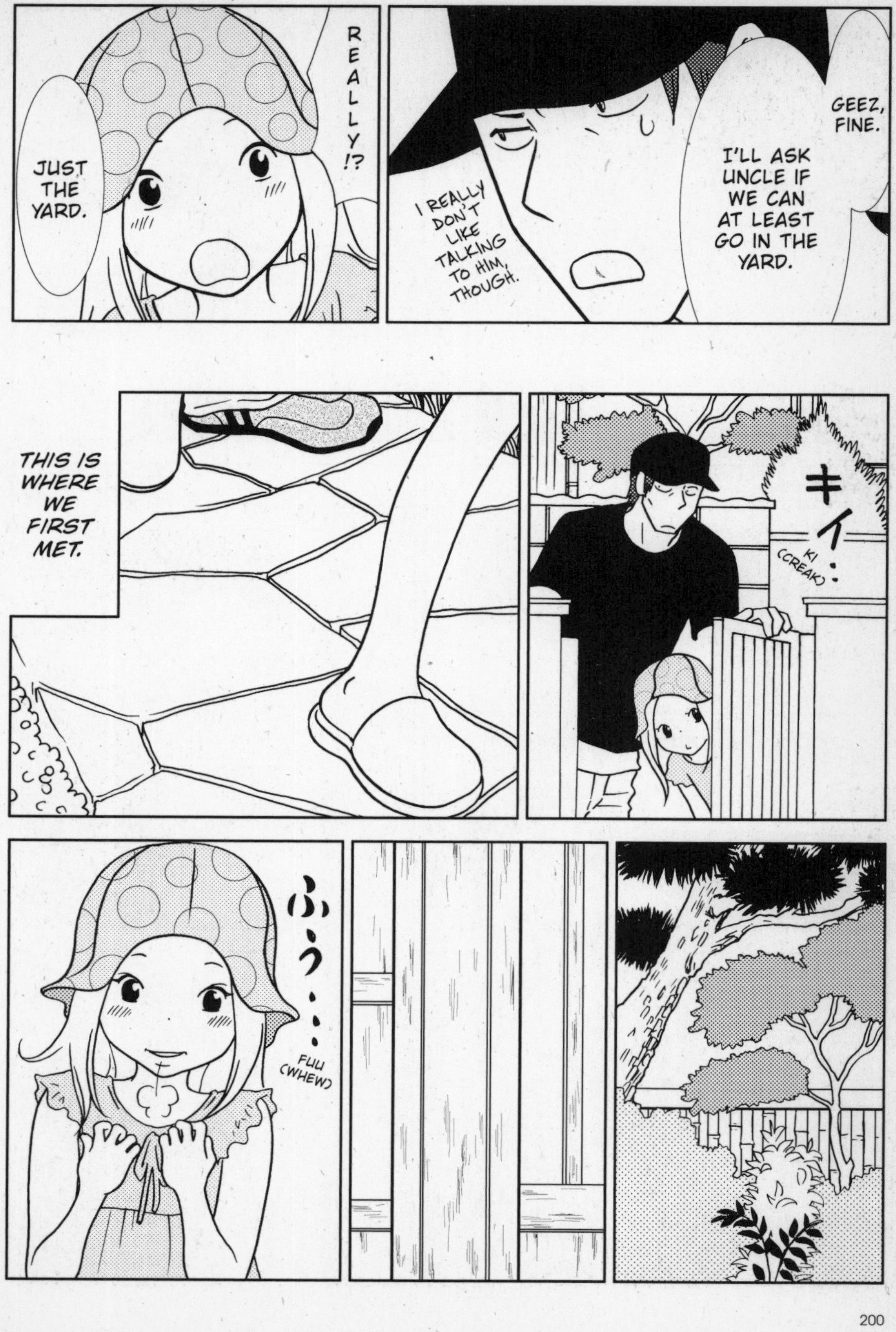
GEEZ, FINE.
I'LL ASK UNCLE IF WE CAN AT LEAST GO IN THE YARD.
I REALLY DON'T LIKE TALKING TO HIM, THOUGH.
REALLY!?
JUST THE YARD.
キイ・・・
KI (CREAK)
THIS IS WHERE WE FIRST MET.
ふう・・・
FUU (WHEW)

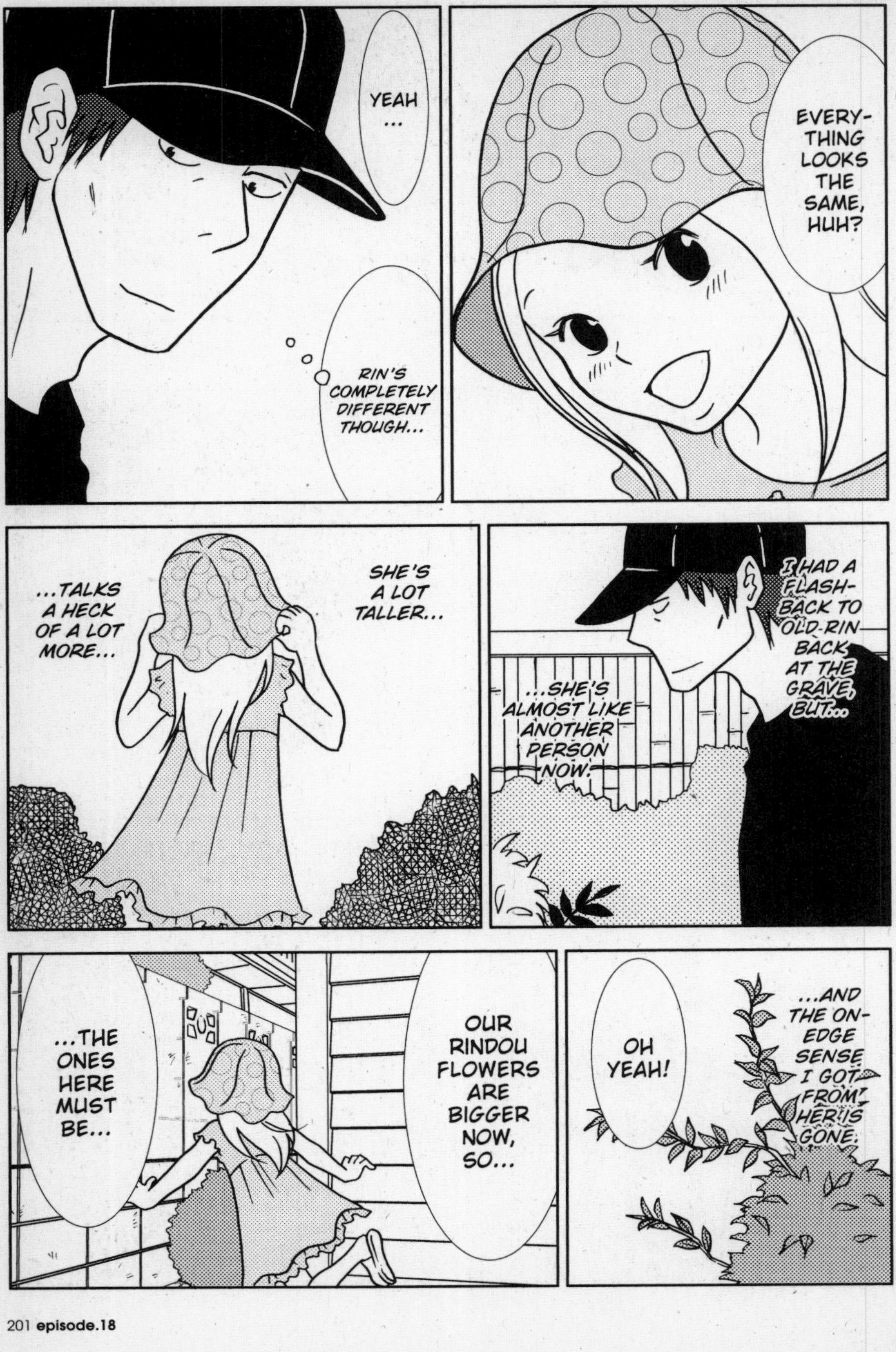
EVERY-THING LOOKS THE SAME, HUH?
YEAH ...
RIN'S COMPLETELY DIFFERENT THOUGH...
I HAD A FLASH-BACK TO OLD-RIN BACK AT THE GRAVE, BUT...
...SHE'S ALMOST LIKE ANOTHER PERSON NOW.
SHE'S A LOT TALLER...
...TALKS A HECK OF A LOT MORE...
...AND THE ON-EDGE SENSE I GOT FROM HER IS GONE.
OH YEAH!
OUR RINDOU FLOWERS ARE BIGGER NOW, SO...
...THE ONES HERE MUST BE...

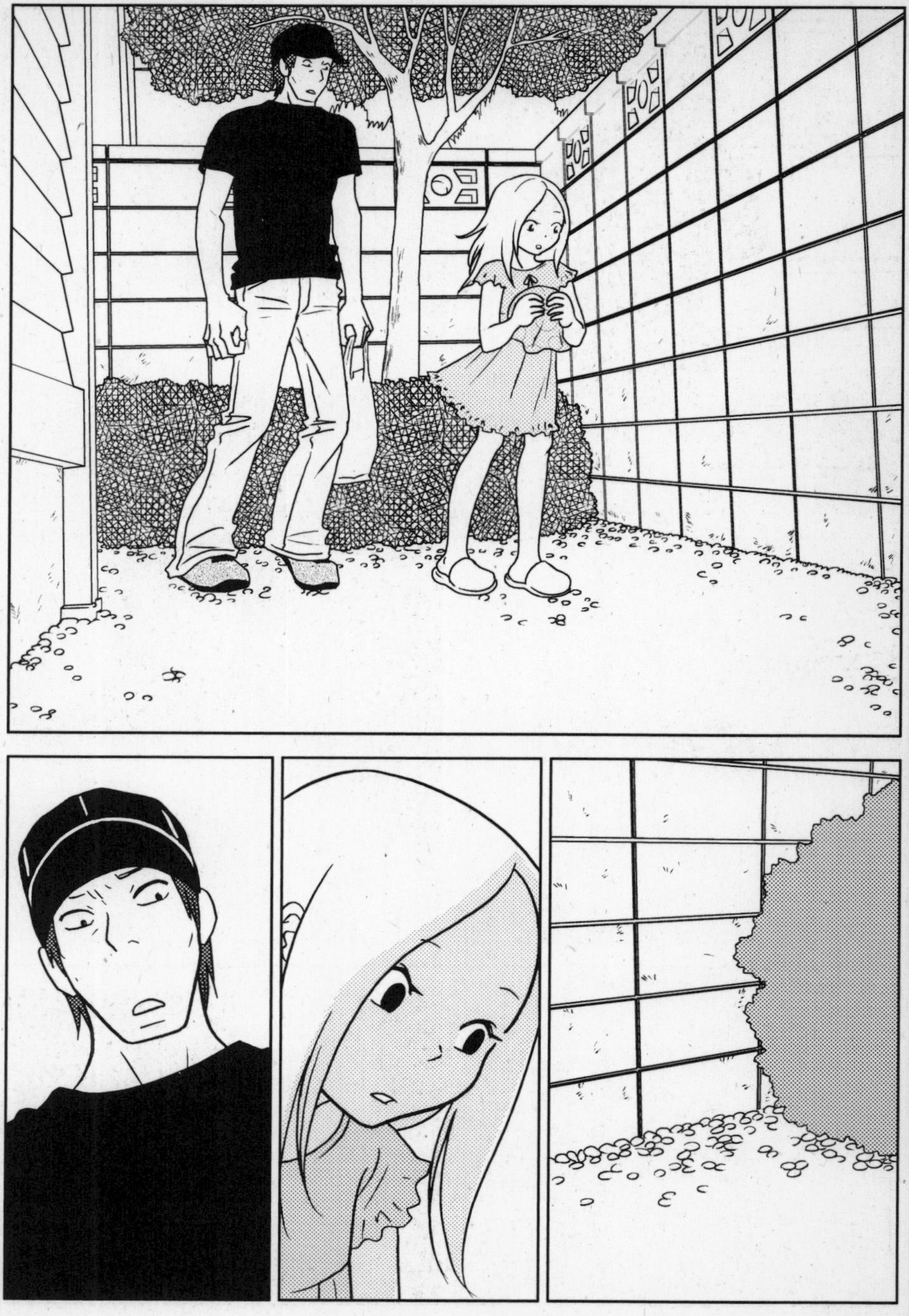

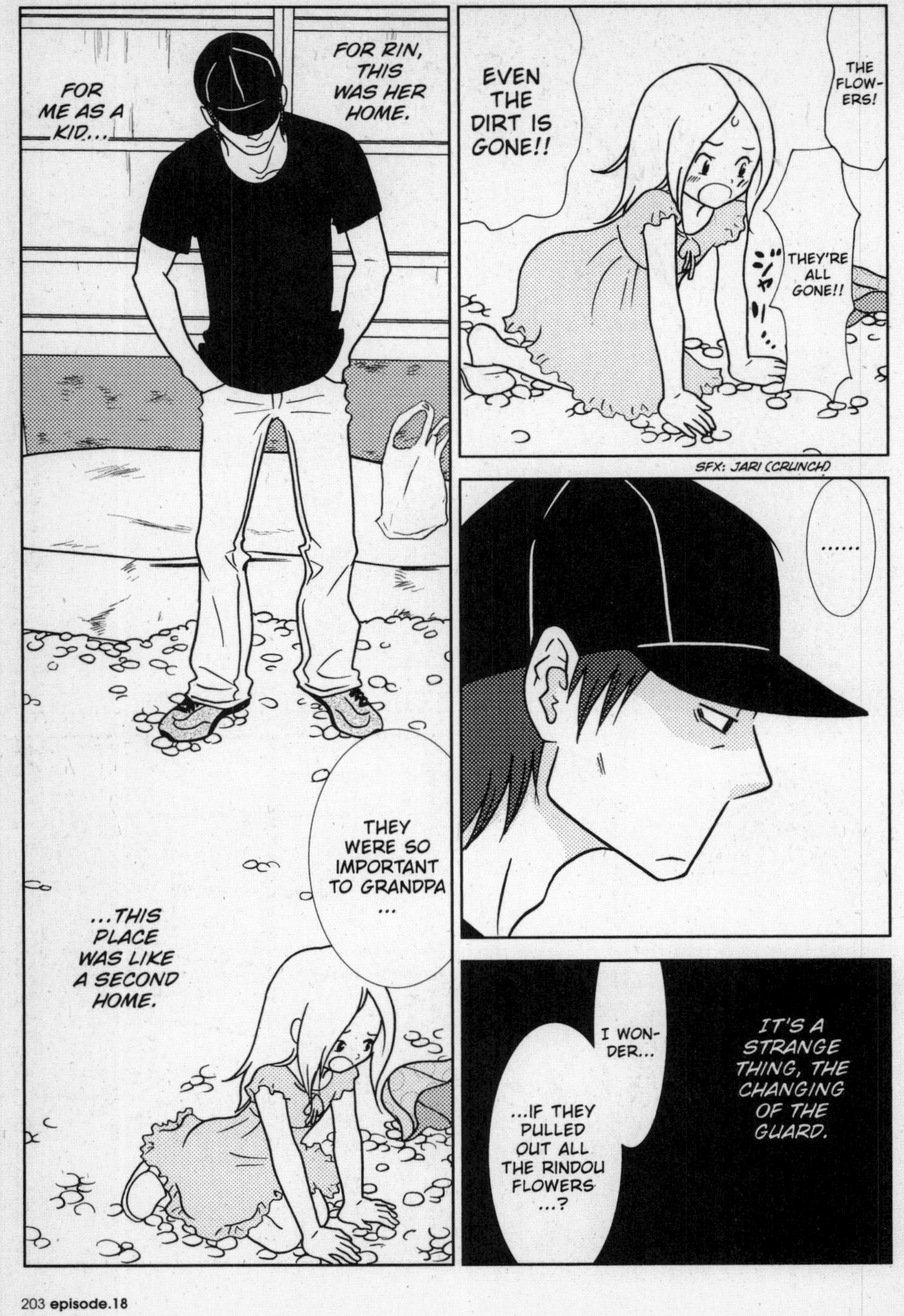
THE FLOWERS!
EVEN THE DIRT IS GONE!!
THEY'RE ALL GONE!!
SFX: JARI (CRUNCH)
......
IT'S A STRANGE THING, THE CHANGING OF THE GUARD.
I WONDER...
...IF THEY PULLED OUT ALL THE RINDOU FLOWERS ...?
FOR RIN, THIS WAS HER HOME.
FOR ME AS A KID...
THEY WERE SO IMPORTANT TO GRANDPA ...
...THIS PLACE WAS LIKE A SECOND HOME.

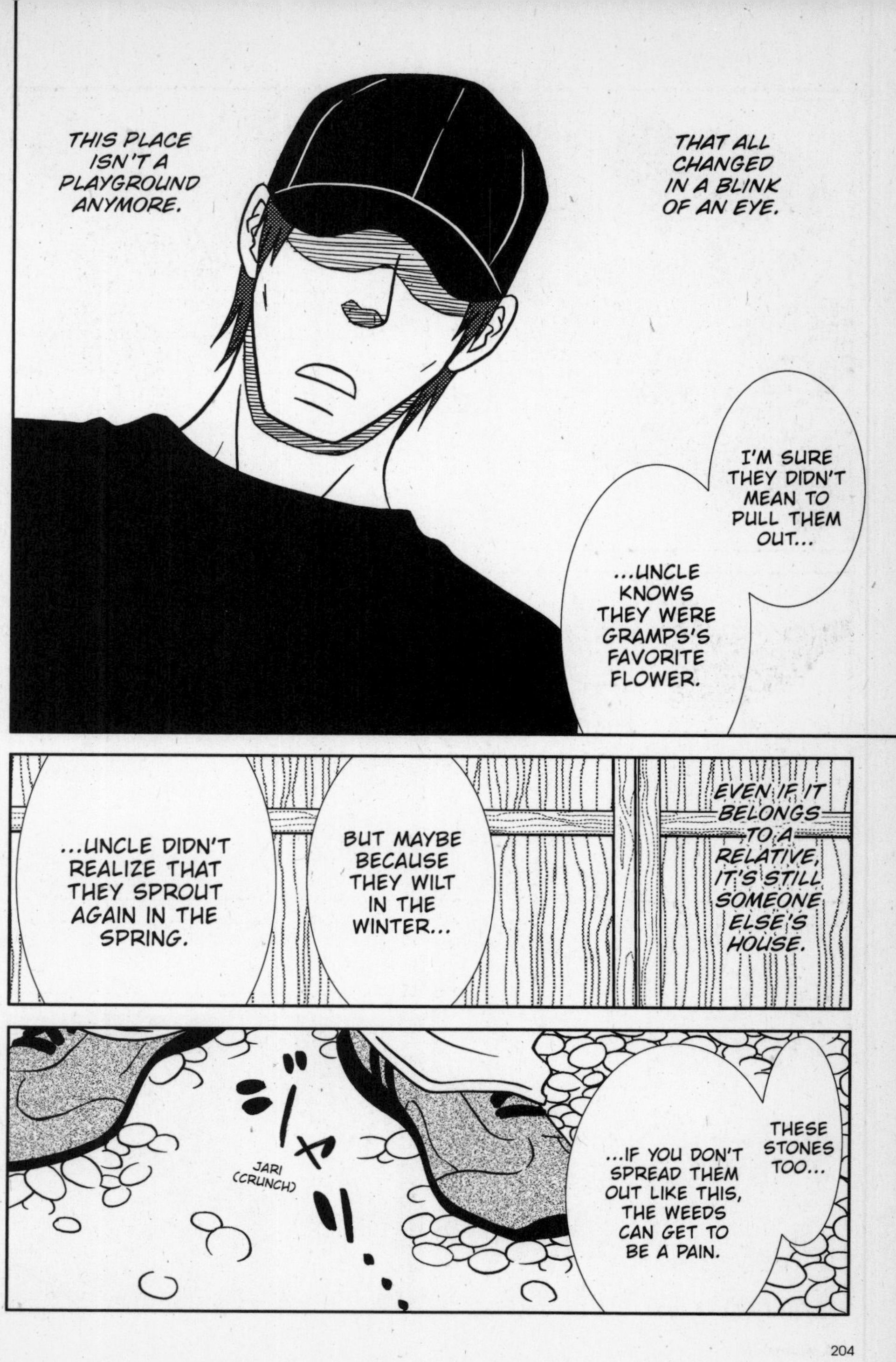
THAT ALL CHANGED IN A BLINK OF AN EYE.
THIS PLACE ISN'T A PLAYGROUND ANYMORE.
I'M SURE THEY DIDN'T MEAN TO PULL THEM OUT...
...UNCLE KNOWS THEY WERE GRAMPS'S FAVORITE FLOWER.
EVEN IF IT BELONGS TO A RELATIVE, IT'S STILL SOMEONE ELSE'S HOUSE.
BUT MAYBE BECAUSE THEY WILT IN THE WINTER...
...UNCLE DIDN'T REALIZE THAT THEY SPROUT AGAIN IN THE SPRING.
THESE STONES TOO...
...IF YOU DON'T SPREAD THEM OUT LIKE THIS, THE WEEDS CAN GET TO BE A PAIN.
JARI (CRUNCH)

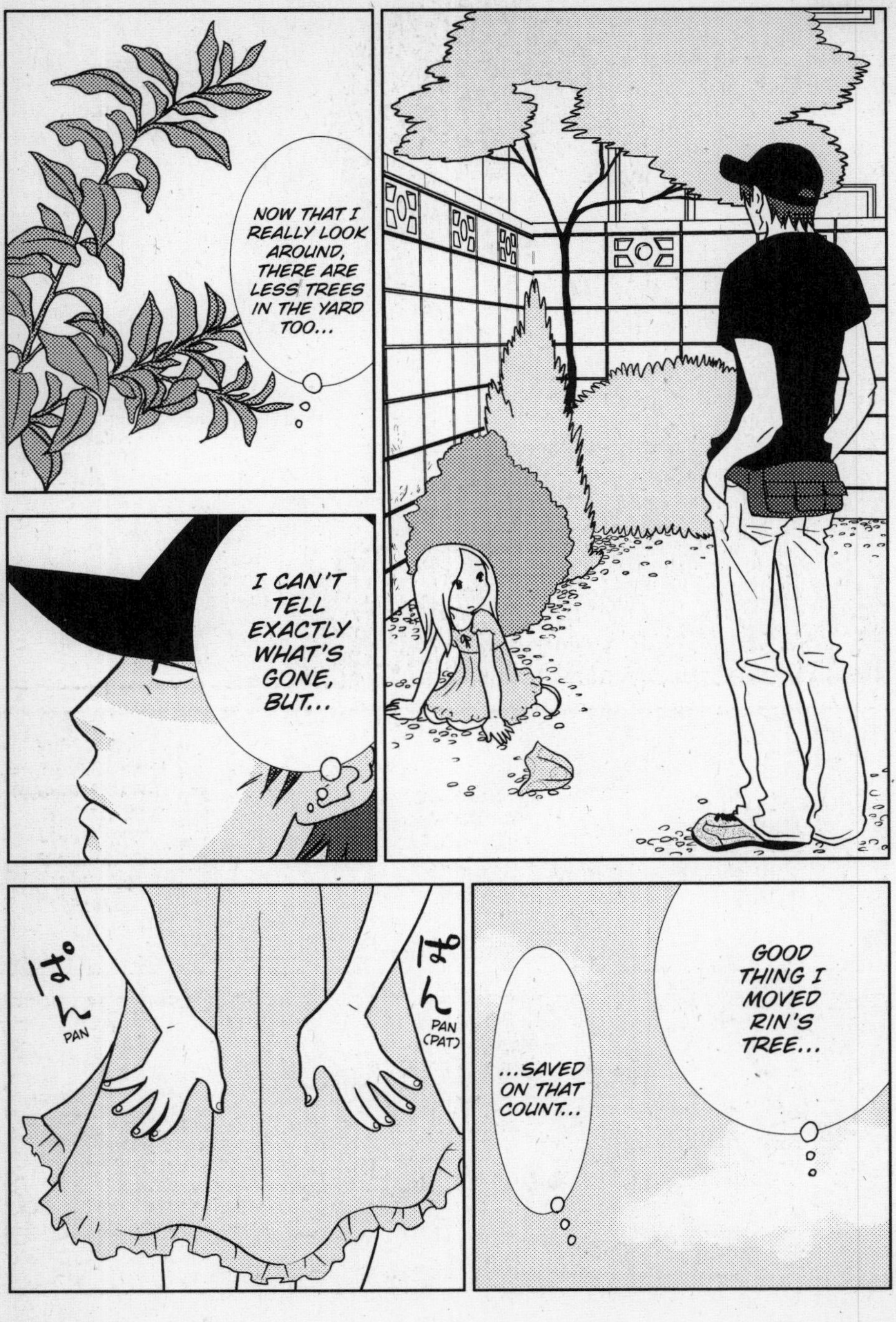
NOW THAT I REALLY LOOK AROUND, THERE ARE LESS TREES IN THE YARD TOO...
I CAN'T TELL EXACTLY WHAT'S GONE, BUT...
GOOD THING I MOVED RIN'S TREE...
...SAVED ON THAT COUNT...
ぱん
PAN (PAT)
ぱん
PAN

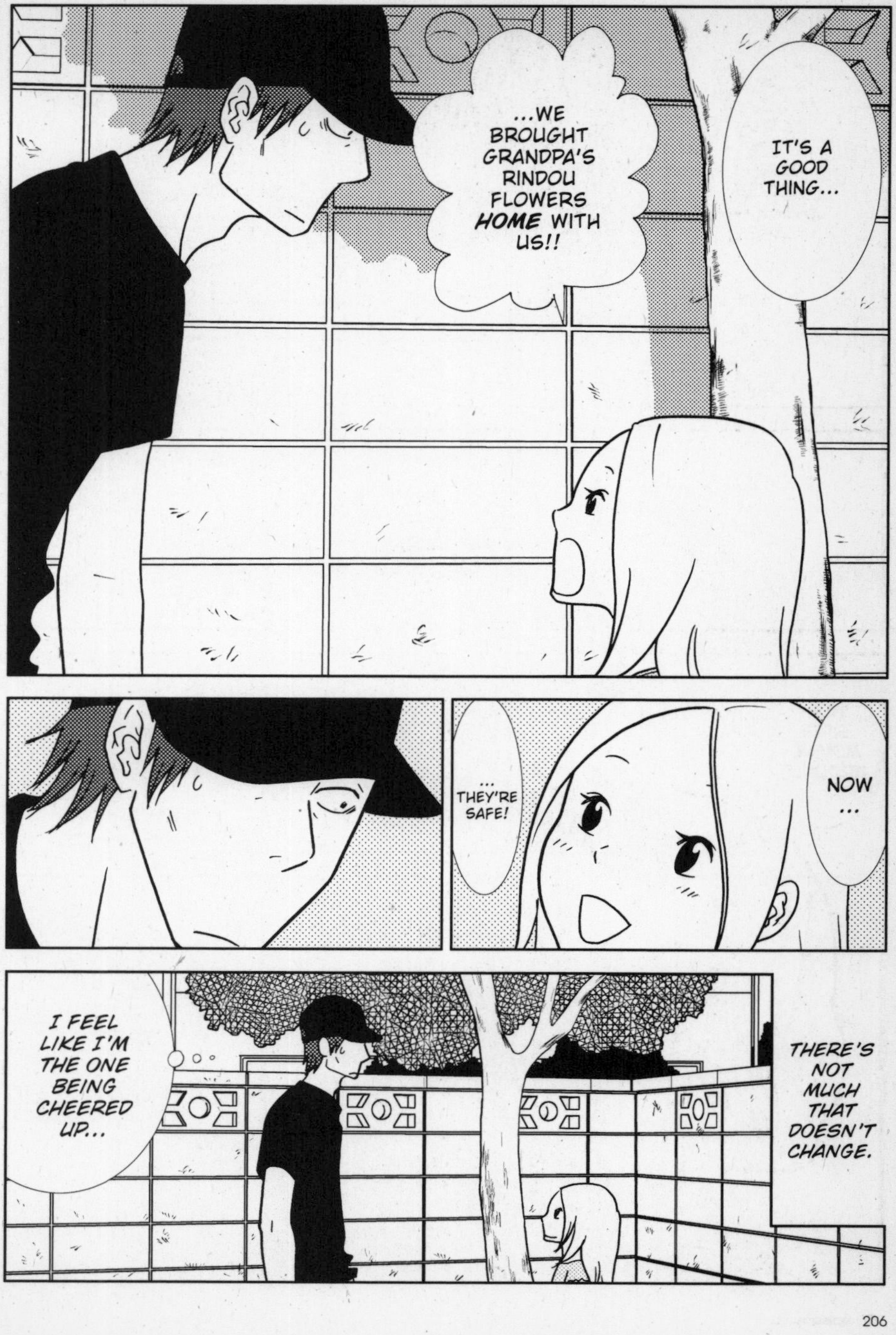
IT'S A GOOD THING...
...WE BROUGHT GRANDPA'S RINDOU FLOWERS **HOME** WITH US!!
NOW ...
... THEY'RE SAFE!
THERE'S NOT MUCH THAT DOESN'T CHANGE.
I FEEL LIKE I'M THE ONE BEING CHEERED UP...

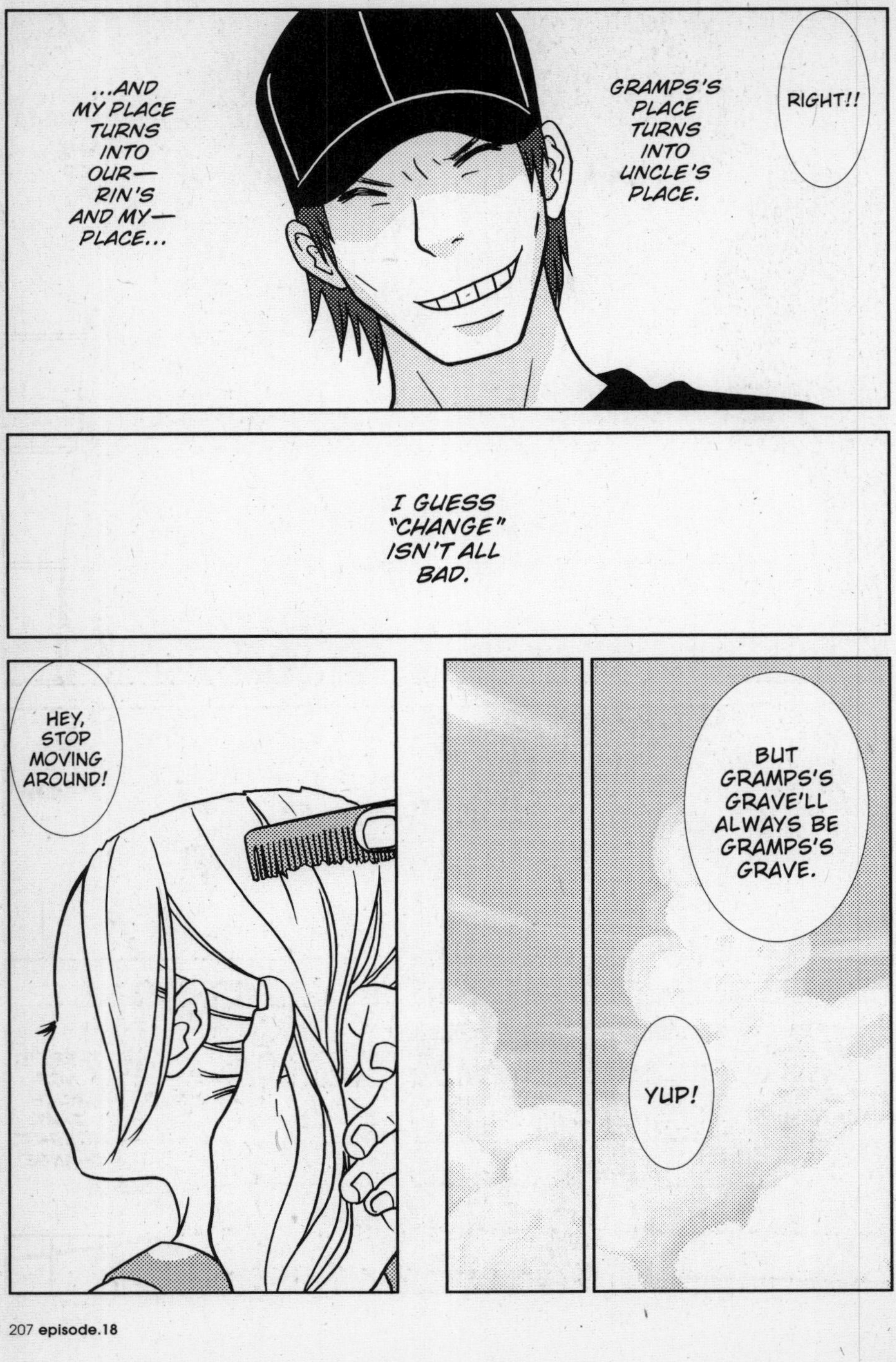
RIGHT!!
GRAMPS'S PLACE TURNS INTO UNCLE'S PLACE.
...AND MY PLACE TURNS INTO OUR— RIN'S AND MY— PLACE...
I GUESS "CHANGE" ISN'T ALL BAD.
BUT GRAMPS'S GRAVE'LL ALWAYS BE GRAMPS'S GRAVE.
YUP!
HEY, STOP MOVING AROUND!

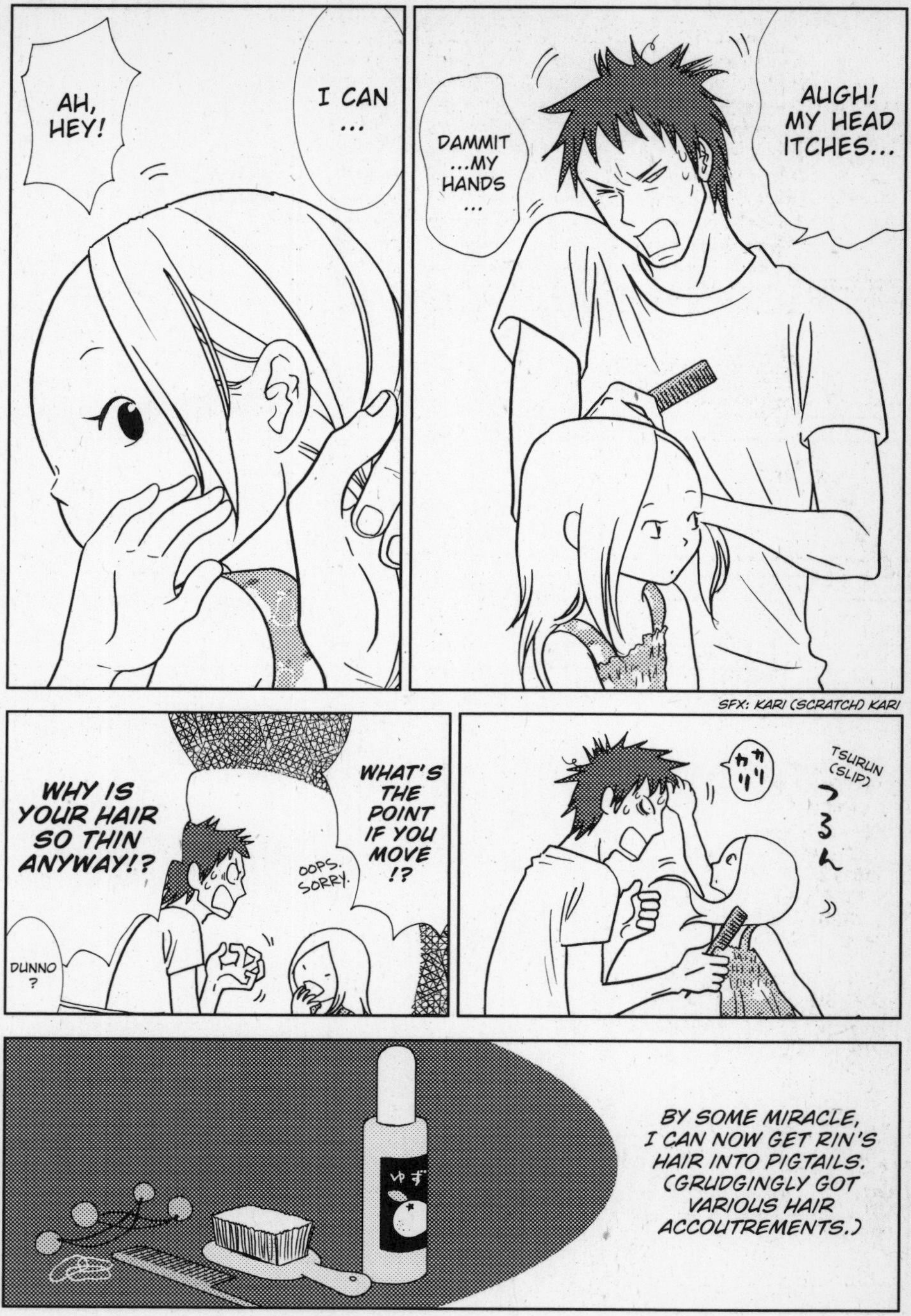
AUGH! MY HEAD ITCHES...
DAMMIT ...MY HANDS ...
I CAN ...
AH, HEY!
SFX: KARI (SCRATCH) KARI
カリカリ
TSURUN (SLIP)
つるん
WHAT'S THE POINT IF YOU MOVE !?
OOPS. SORRY.
WHY IS YOUR HAIR SO THIN ANYWAY!?
DUNNO ?
BY SOME MIRACLE, I CAN NOW GET RIN'S HAIR INTO PIGTAILS. (GRUDGINGLY GOT VARIOUS HAIR ACCOUTREMENTS.)
ゆず

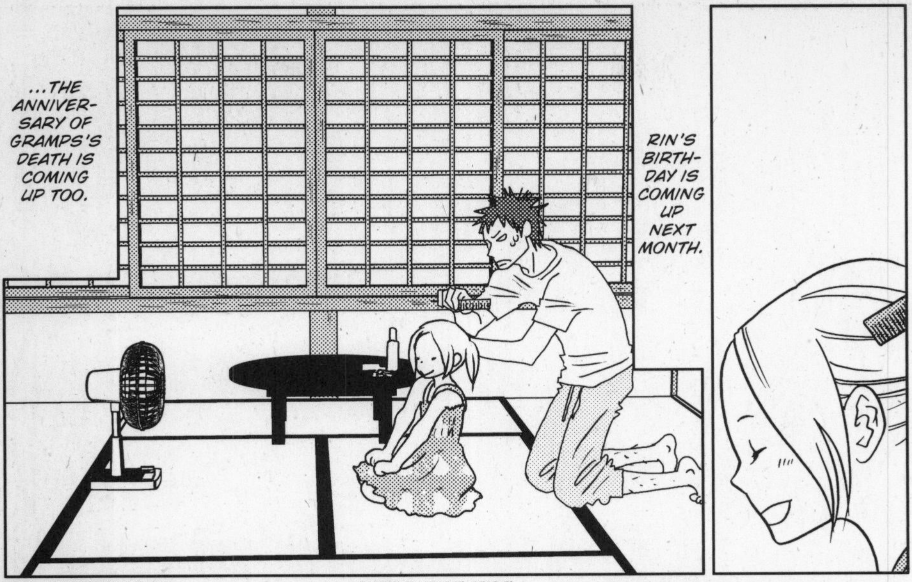
RIN'S BIRTHDAY IS COMING UP NEXT MONTH.
...THE ANNIVERSARY OF GRAMPS'S DEATH IS COMING UP TOO.

SFX: JYA (SKRITCH) JYA

BUBBLE: IDIOT! IDIOT!

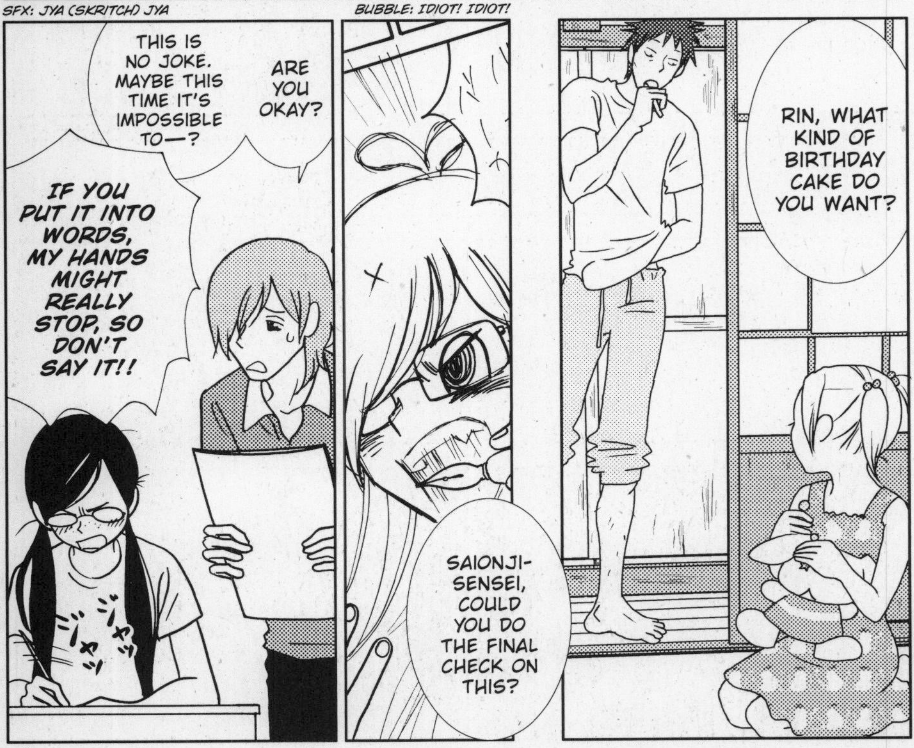
RIN, WHAT KIND OF BIRTHDAY CAKE DO YOU WANT?
SAIONJI-SENSEI, COULD YOU DO THE FINAL CHECK ON THIS?
ARE YOU OKAY?
THIS IS NO JOKE. MAYBE THIS TIME IT'S IMPOSSIBLE TO—?
IF YOU PUT IT INTO WORDS, MY HANDS MIGHT REALLY STOP, SO DON'T SAY IT!!

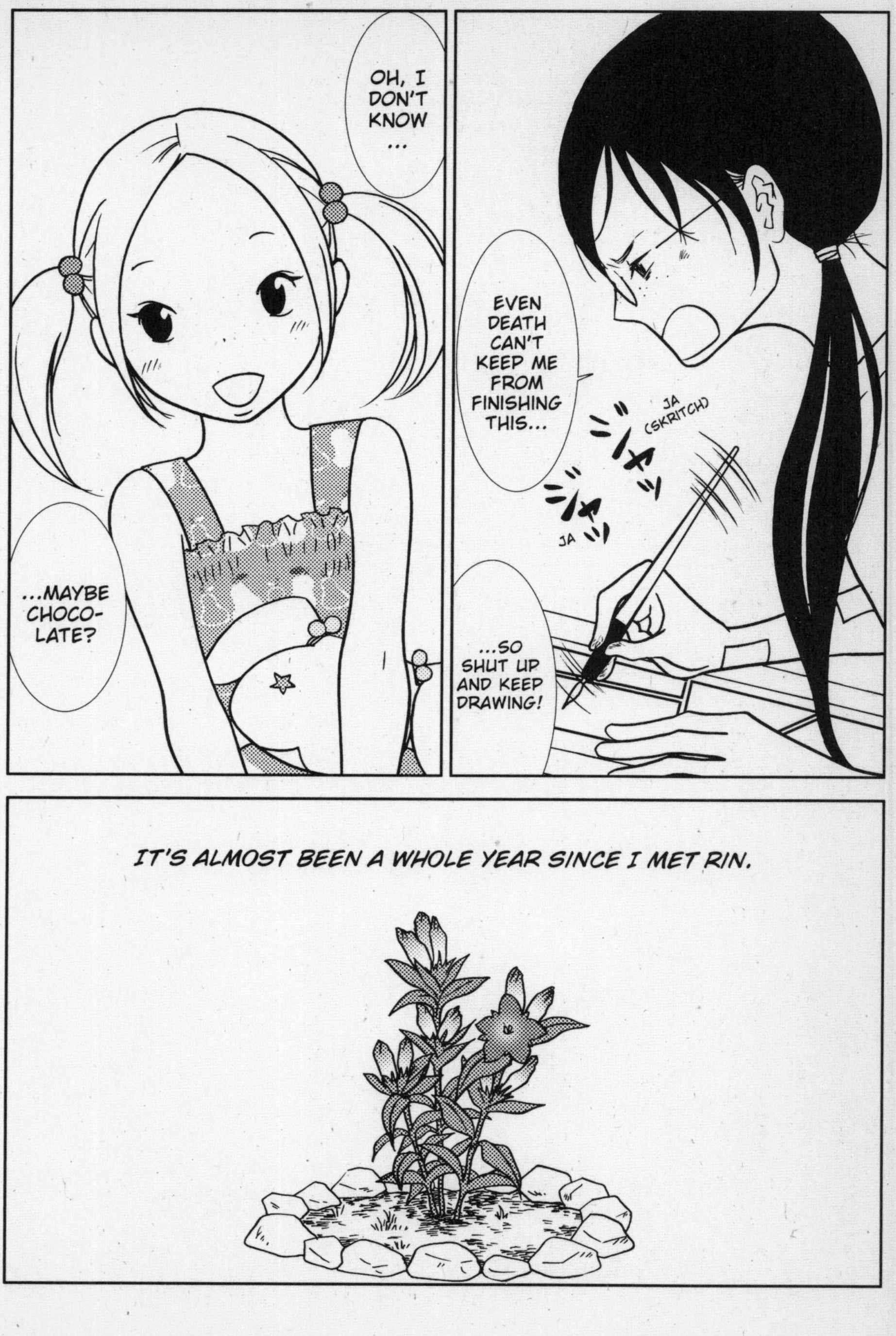
EVEN DEATH CAN'T KEEP ME FROM FINISHING THIS...
JA (SKRITCH)
JA
...SO SHUT UP AND KEEP DRAWING!
OH, I DON'T KNOW ...
...MAYBE CHOCO-LATE?
IT'S ALMOST BEEN A WHOLE YEAR SINCE I MET RIN.

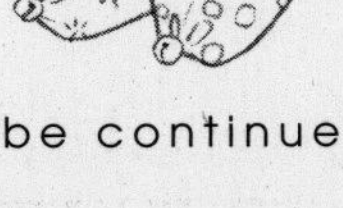

to be continued...

TRANSLATION NOTES

COMMON HONORIFICS

No honorific: Indicates familiarity or closeness; if used without permission or reason, addressing someone in this manner would constitute an insult.

-san: The Japanese equivalent of Mr./Mrs./Miss. If a situation calls for politeness, this is the fail-safe honorific.

-kun: Used most often when referring to boys (though it can be applied to girls as well), this indicates affection or familiarity. Occasionally used by older men among their peers, but it may also be used by anyone referring to a person of lower standing.

-chan: An affectionate honorific indicating familiarity used mostly in reference to girls; also used in reference to cute persons or animals of either gender.

Page 10
Golden osmanthus, silver osmanthus: Also known as the fragrant tea olive, these are two varieties of evergreen flowering shrubs that are native to Asia. The plants produce clusters of small, intensely fragrant flowers, as well as a purplish fruit. They are highly prized for this and are used in a variety of perfumes; in China, they are also used in teas, foods, and medicine. The plants can grow as much as forty feet in height.

Page 12
Loquat: An evergreen tree native to Asia, which is also known as the Japanese medlar and produces a juicy, oval, yellow-orange fruit, the taste of which resembles a mix of apricot, plum, and peach.

Page 13
Morning glories and sunflowers: Quickly developing flowers that students tend to plant at school or at home for science projects.

Page 13
Peaches and chestnuts three years: A part of a folk saying that means, "it takes time for one's actions to bear fruit." The full saying goes..."Peaches and chestnuts three years, and persimmons eight years."

Page 16
Kashiwade: Clapping one's hands twice in prayer, generally at chest height (at a shrine).

Page 27
"Bakabon": "Tensai Bakabon" ("Genius Bakabon"). A manga and anime series that originally ran in the '60s and has seen several reincarnations even to this day. It follows the adventures of Bakabon, a mischievious boy and his family. *Baka* is Japanese for "stupid."

"Bakabon" song: This is a reference to two lines in the Bakabon theme song, which go, "Mr. Sun / who rose from the west / sets to the east / 'Oh no!'"

Page 53
Itadakimasu: A phrase said before every meal. The phrase at the end of the meal is *gochisousama*, or "thank you for the delicious feast/meal."

Page 90
Psychogun: This is a reference to Cobra the Space Pirate, who had a psychogun on his left arm. "Cobra" was a manga that ran in the late '70s to early '80s and followed the exploits of a space pirate.

Page 111
The bullet train's got the runs: In the original, this is a pun on the word *unkou* ("to be in service/operation"). Kouki confuses this with the word for "poop," or *unko* (the difference between the two is a long *o* sound at the end of the word).

Page 119
Arare: Bite-sized rice crackers.

Page 126
Meat-and-potato stew: Called *nikujaga* in Japanese, this dish is a bit different from a Western dish that might have the same name. In Japan, it is a common comfort food dish of thinly sliced meat, potatoes, onions and other vegetables in a sweetened soy sauce-flavored broth.

Page 127
Class observation: When the parents and guardians of students visit a school while classes are in session to observe their children's school lives.

Teacher home visit: A home visit undertaken by a student's homeroom teacher. These generally take place at the beginning of the school year in April and last about ten to fifteen minutes per child. The teacher visits the homes of all their homeroom students in one day. The meeting is intended to assess the child's home environment.

Page 136
Counting in Japanese: The Japanese language uses counter words to quantify different nouns. For example, people are counted as *hitori* ("one person"), *futari* ("two people"), *san-nin* ("three people"); vehicles are counted as *ikki* ("one vehicle"), *nikki* ("two vehicles"); and animals are counted as *ippiki* ("one animal"), *nihiki* ("two animals"), *sanbiki* ("three animals"). Here, Kouki-kun is counting Mario as an animal or thing.

Page 143
Ka: Rin's class is learning to write *ka,* the sixth letter in the Japanese *hiragana* alphabet.

Page 166
Obon: A Buddhist custom honoring one's ancestors. This has evolved into a holiday where families visit family gravesites and attend celebrations.

Rindou: Japanese name for the bellflower, the bloom after which Rin is named.

Page 171
Getting water for the grave: Part of the Japanese ritual for tending graves, visitors usually pour water over the gravestone to clean it.

BUNNY**DROP**

Hello! This is YOTSUBA!

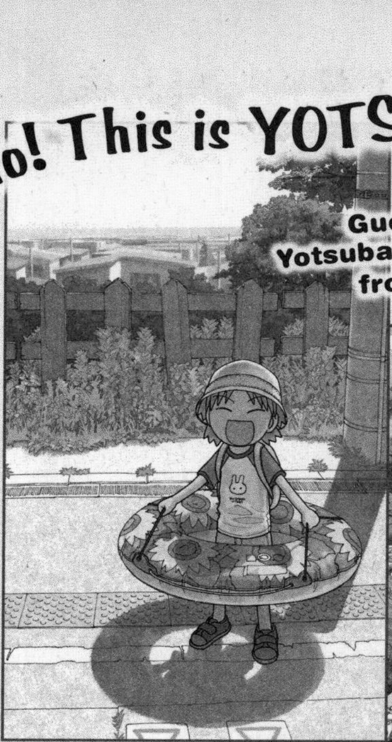

Guess what? Guess what?
Yotsuba and Daddy just moved here from waaaay over there!

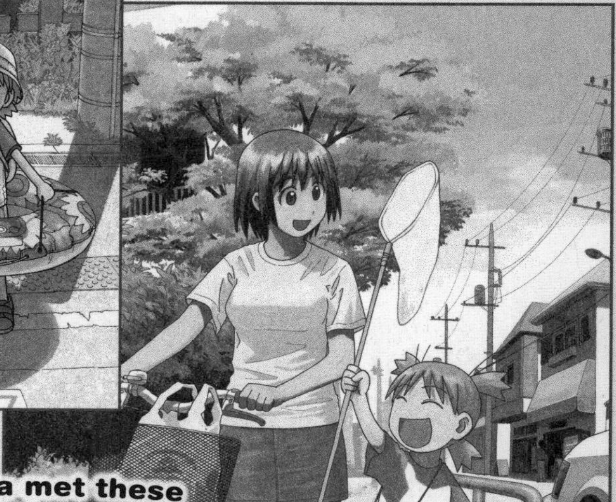

And Yotsuba met these nice people next door and made new friends to play with!

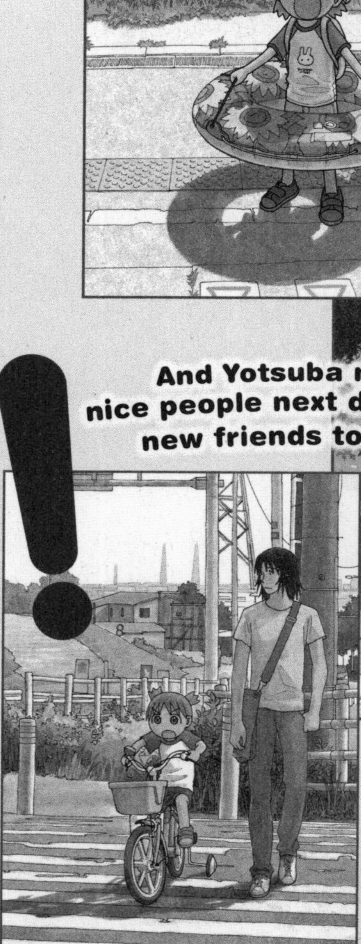

The pretty one took Yotsuba on a bike ride!
(Whoooa! There was a big hill!)

And Ena's a good drawer!
(Almost as good as Yotsuba!)

And their mom always gives Yotsuba ice cream!
(Yummy!)

And...
And...
OHHHH!

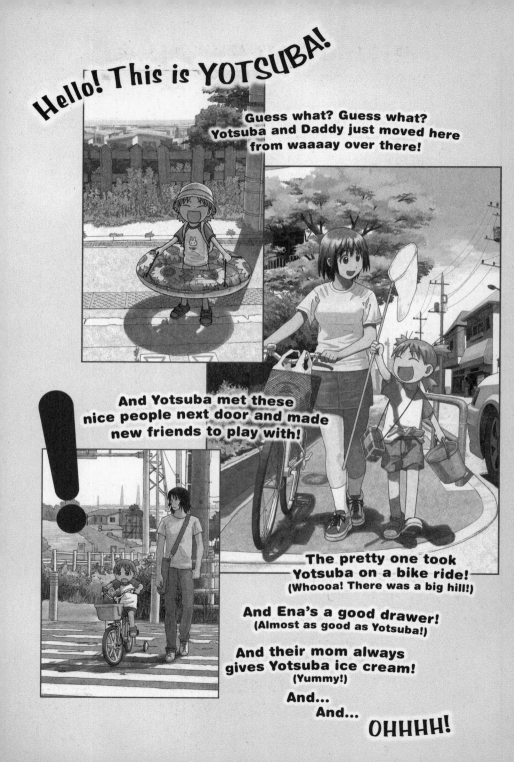

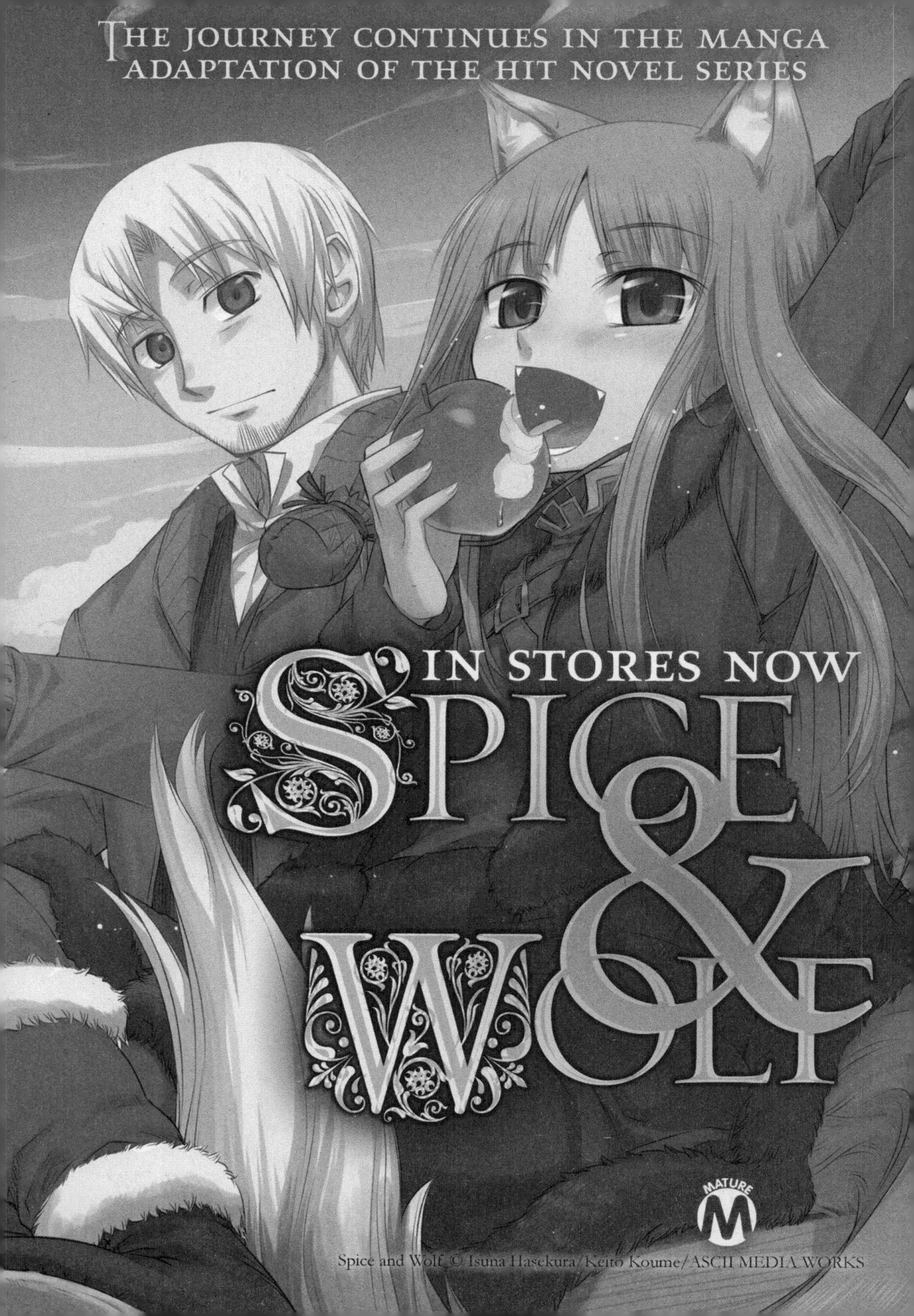
THE JOURNEY CONTINUES IN THE MANGA
ADAPTATION OF THE HIT NOVEL SERIES
IN STORES NOW
SPICE & WOLF
MATURE
M
Spice and Wolf © Isuna Hasekura/Keito Koume/ASCII MEDIA WORKS

IT'S AN ALL-OUT CAT FIGHT ON CAMPUS...

Cat-lovers flock to Matabi Academy, where each student is allowed to bring their pet cat to the dorms.

Unfortunately, the grounds aren't just crawling with cats...

...an ancient evil lurks on campus, and only the combined efforts of student and feline can hold them at bay...

IN STORES NOW!

1

C AT
PARADISE

YUJI IWAHARA

Becoming the princess... Isn't that every girl's dream?!

Monarchy rule ended long ago in Korea, but there are still other countries with kings, queens, princes and princesses. What if Korea had continued monarchism? What if all the beautiful palaces, which are now only historical relics, were actually filled with people? What if the glamorous royal family still maintained the palace customs? Welcome to a world where Korea still has the royal family living in their everyday lives! Only for this one high school girl, Chae-Kyung, is this a tragedy, since she has to marry the prince — who apparently is a total bastard!

THE ROYAL PALACE
Goong
vol.1 ~ 10

Park SoHee

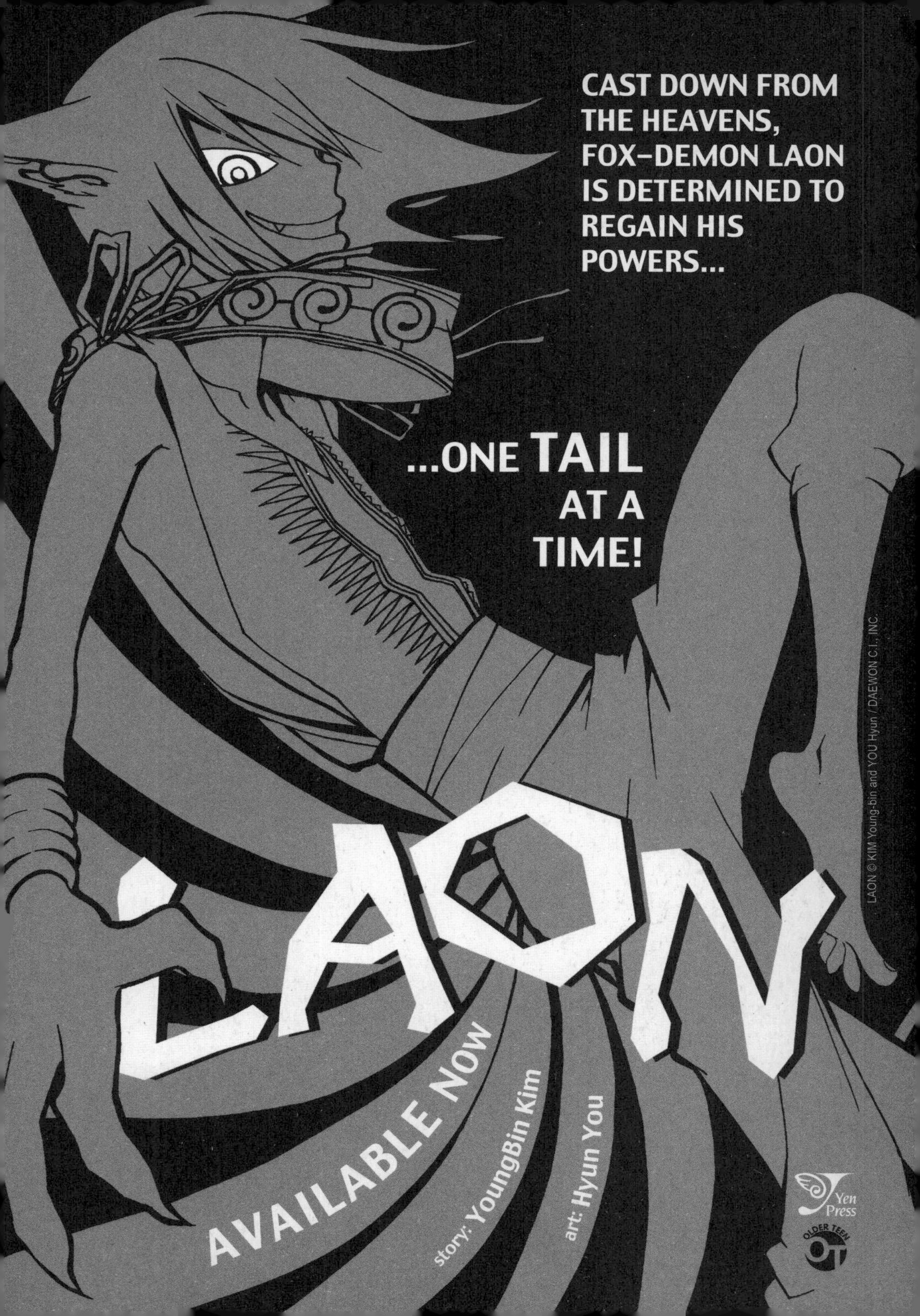
CAST DOWN FROM THE HEAVENS, FOX-DEMON LAON IS DETERMINED TO REGAIN HIS POWERS...
...ONE TAIL AT A TIME!
LAON
AVAILABLE NOW
story: YoungBin Kim
art: Hyun You
Yen Press
OLDER TEEN
OT
LAON © KIM Young-bin and YOU Hyun / DAEWON C.I., INC.

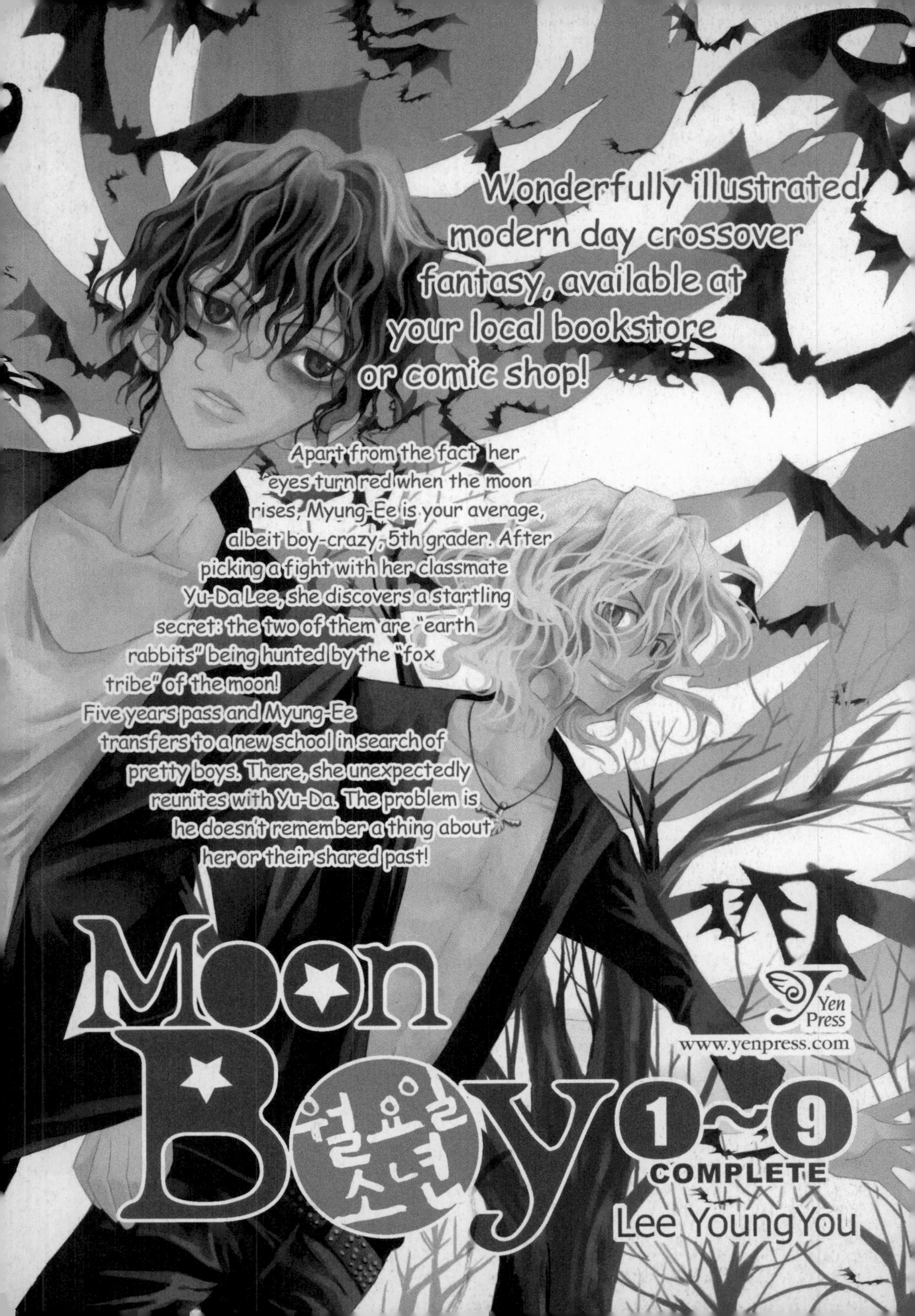
Wonderfully illustrated modern day crossover fantasy, available at your local bookstore or comic shop!
Apart from the fact her eyes turn red when the moon rises, Myung-Ee is your average, albeit boy-crazy, 5th grader. After picking a fight with her classmate Yu-Da Lee, she discovers a startling secret: the two of them are "earth rabbits" being hunted by the "fox tribe" of the moon!
Five years pass and Myung-Ee transfers to a new school in search of pretty boys. There, she unexpectedly reunites with Yu-Da. The problem is he doesn't remember a thing about her or their shared past!
Moon Boy
월요일 소년
1~9
COMPLETE
Lee YoungYou
Yen Press
www.yenpress.com

BUNNY DROP ❸

YUMI UNITA

Translation: Kaori Inoue   •   Lettering: Alexis Eckerman

BUNNY DROP Vol. 3 © 2007 by Yumi Unita. All rights reserved. First
published in Japan in 2007 by SHODENSHA PUBLISHING CO., LTD.,
Tokyo. English translation rights in USA, Canada, and UK arranged with
SHODENSHA PUBLISHING CO., LTD. and Hachette Book Group through
Tuttle-Mori Agency, Inc., Tokyo.

Translation © 2011 by Hachette Book Group, Inc.

Yen Press
Hachette Book Group
237 Park Avenue, New York, NY 10017

www.HachetteBookGroup.com
www.YenPress.com

Yen Press is an imprint of Hachette Book Group, Inc. The Yen Press name
and logo are trademarks of Hachette Book Group, Inc.

First Yen Press Edition: March 2011

ISBN: 978-0-7595-3120-8

10 9 8 7 6 5 4 3

BVG

Printed in the United States of America